Skip and Loafer 1

story & art by
Misaki Takamatsu

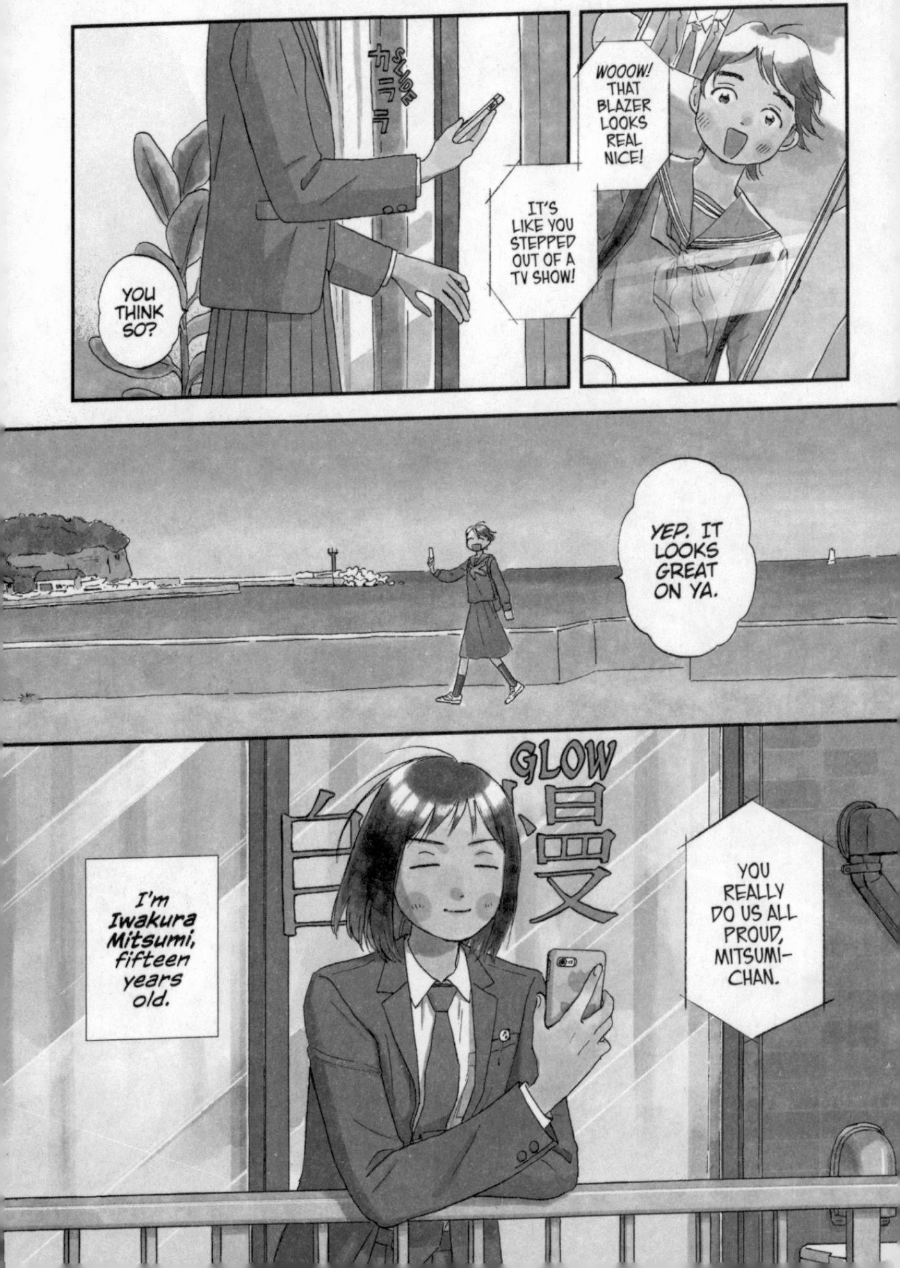
WOOOW! THAT BLAZER LOOKS REAL NICE!
IT'S LIKE YOU STEPPED OUT OF A TV SHOW!
カララ
SLIDE
YOU THINK SO?
YEP. IT LOOKS GREAT ON YA.
GLOW
YOU REALLY DO US ALL PROUD, MITSUMI-CHAN.
I'm Iwakura Mitsumi, fifteen years old.

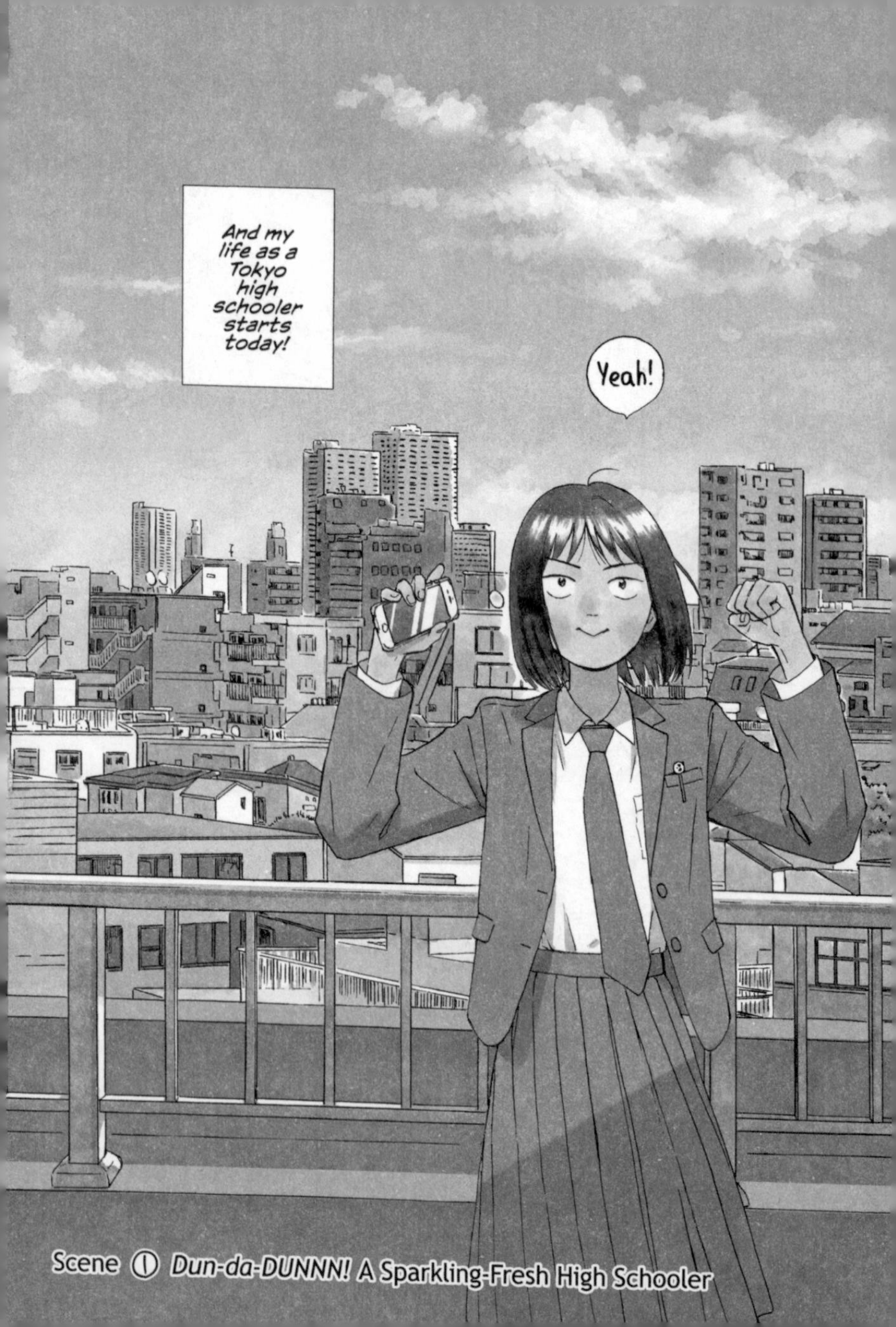
And my life as a Tokyo high schooler starts today!
Yeah!
Scene ① Dun-da-DUNNN! A Sparkling-Fresh High Schooler

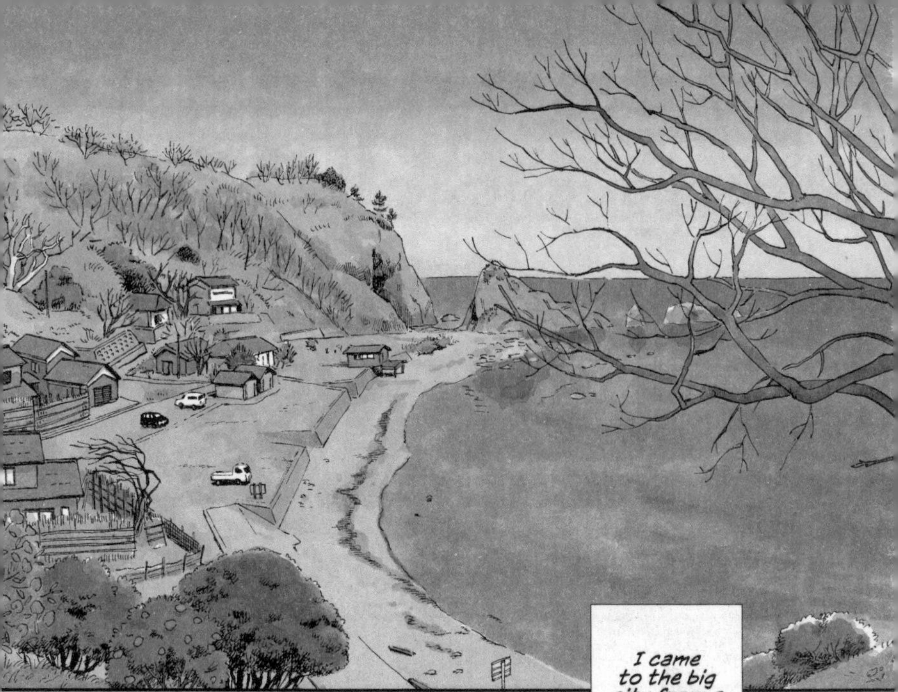
I came to the big city from a tiny town in Ishikawa Prefecture.
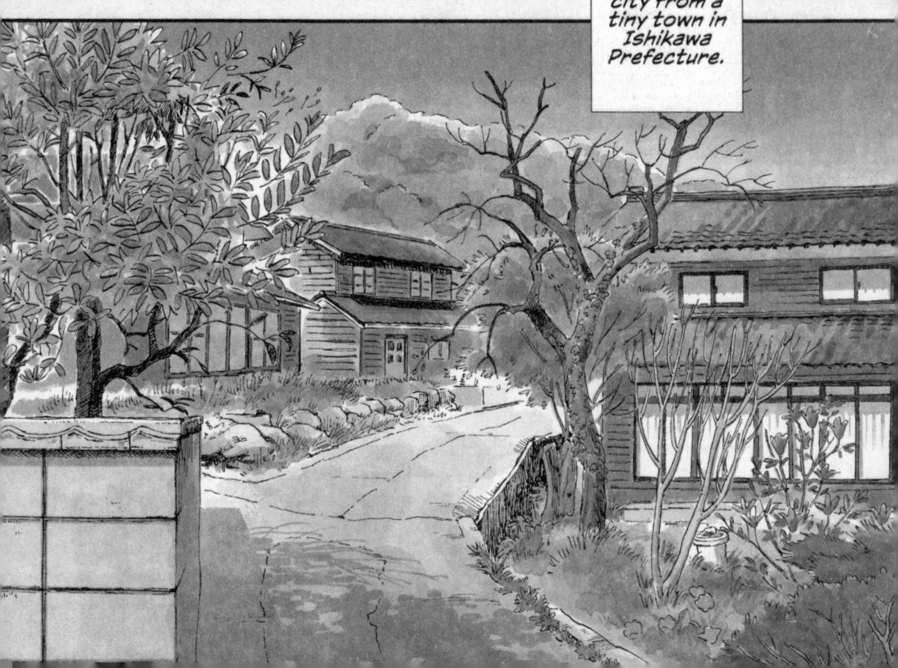

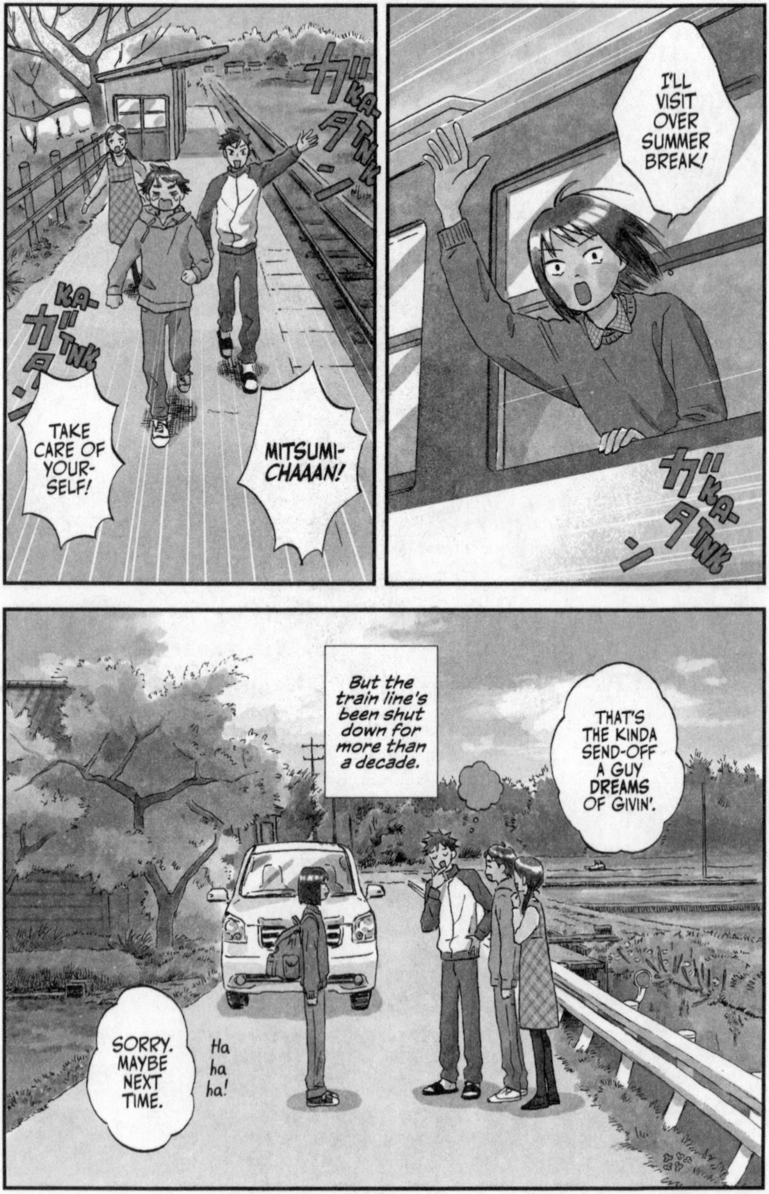
I'LL VISIT OVER SUMMER BREAK!
ガタン KA-TNK
ガタン KA-TNK
MITSUMI-CHAAAN!
ガタン KA-TNK
TAKE CARE OF YOURSELF!
THAT'S THE KINDA SEND-OFF A GUY DREAMS OF GIVIN'.
But the train line's been shut down for more than a decade.
Ha ha ha!
SORRY. MAYBE NEXT TIME.

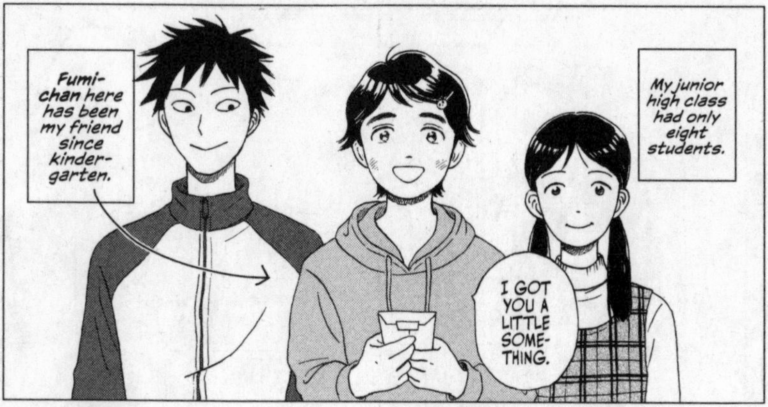
My junior high class had only eight students.
Fumi-chan here has been my friend since kinder-garten.
I GOT YOU A LITTLE SOME-THING.

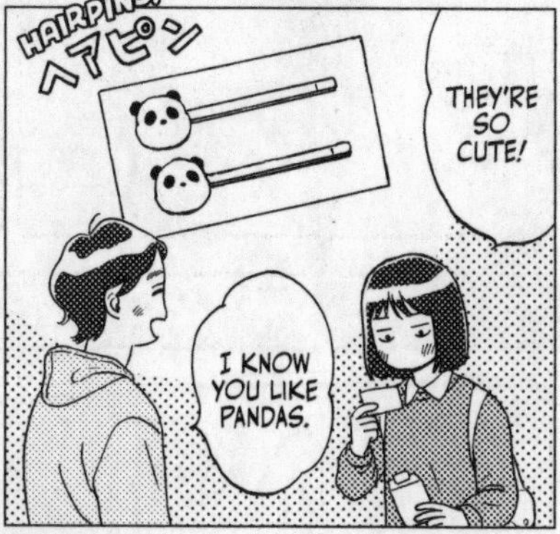
HAIRPINS, ヘアピン
THEY'RE SO CUTE!
I KNOW YOU LIKE PANDAS.

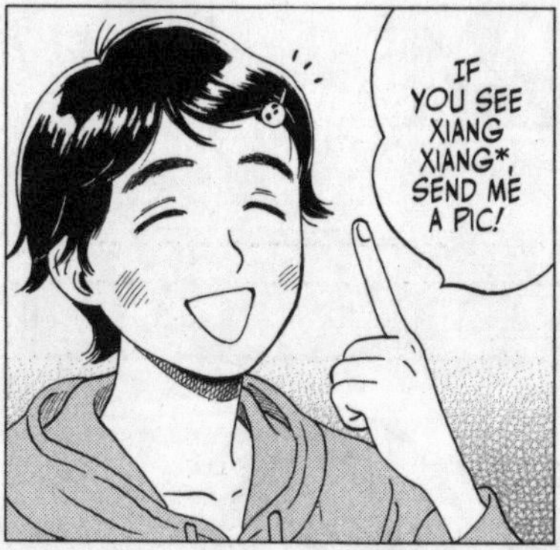
IF YOU SEE XIANG XIANG*, SEND ME A PIC!

*Xiang Xiang is the beloved adolescent panda of Tokyo's Ueno Zoo.

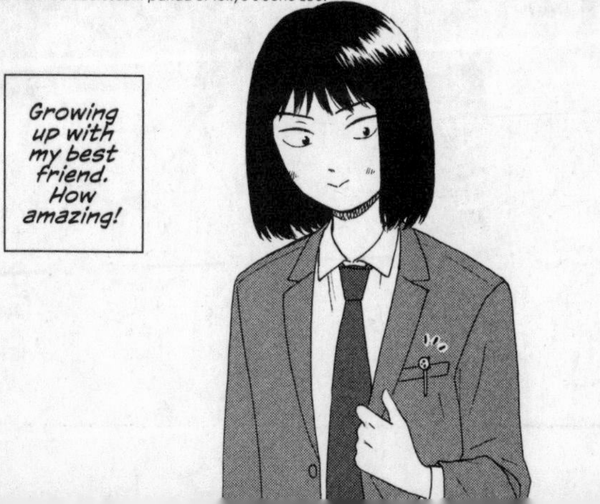
Growing up with my best friend. How amazing!

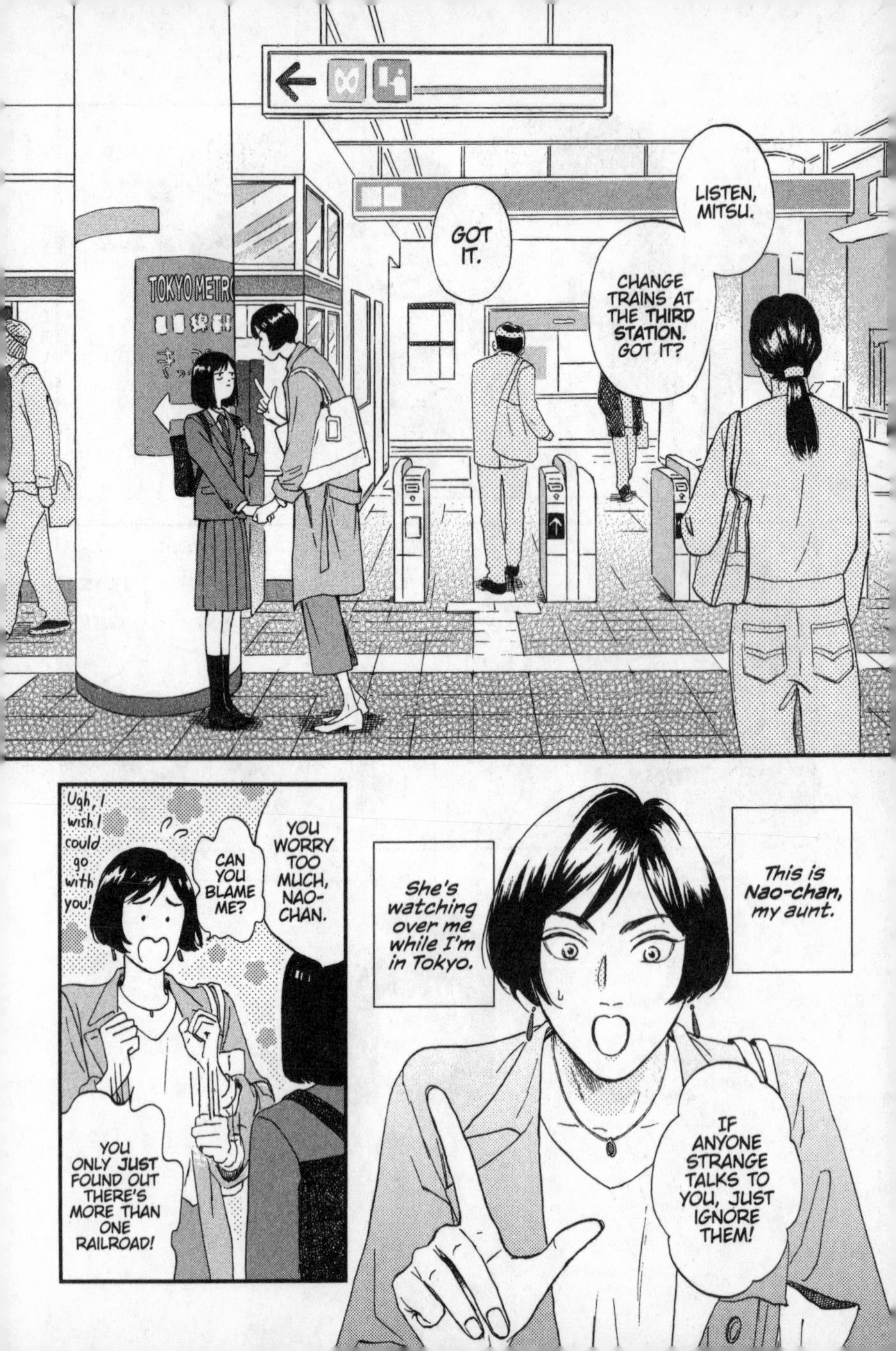
LISTEN, MITSU.
CHANGE TRAINS AT THE THIRD STATION. GOT IT?
GOT IT.
This is Nao-chan, my aunt.
She's watching over me while I'm in Tokyo.
IF ANYONE STRANGE TALKS TO YOU, JUST IGNORE THEM!
YOU WORRY TOO MUCH, NAO-CHAN.
CAN YOU BLAME ME?
Ugh, I wish I could go with you!
YOU ONLY JUST FOUND OUT THERE'S MORE THAN ONE RAILROAD!

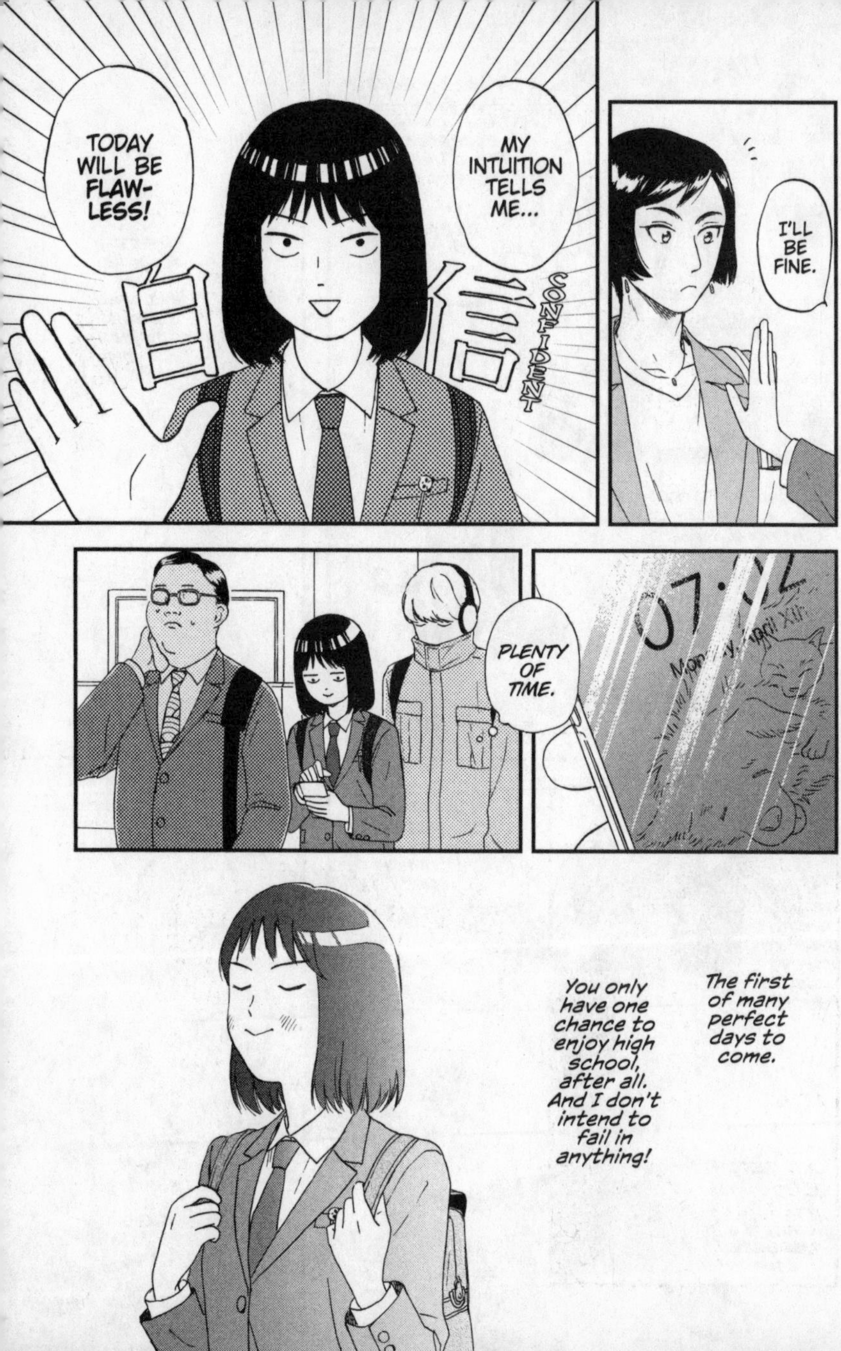
I'LL BE FINE.
MY INTUITION TELLS ME...
CONFIDENT
自信
TODAY WILL BE FLAWLESS!
PLENTY OF TIME.
The first of many perfect days to come.
You only have one chance to enjoy high school, after all. And I don't intend to fail in anything!

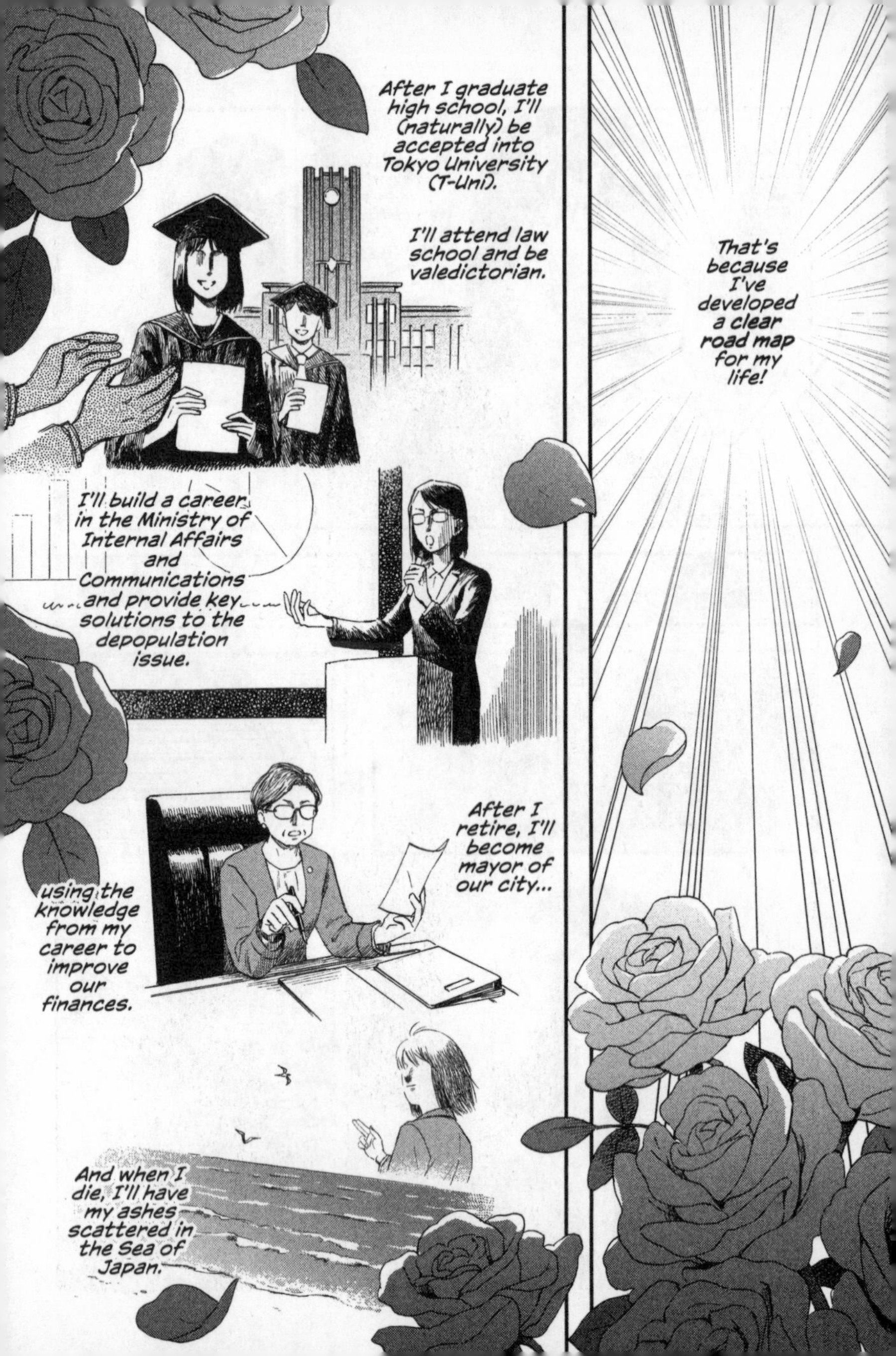
That's because I've developed a clear road map for my life!
After I graduate high school, I'll (naturally) be accepted into Tokyo University (T-Uni).
I'll attend law school and be valedictorian.
I'll build a career in the Ministry of Internal Affairs and Communications and provide key solutions to the depopulation issue.
After I retire, I'll become mayor of our city...
using the knowledge from my career to improve our finances.
And when I die, I'll have my ashes scattered in the Sea of Japan.

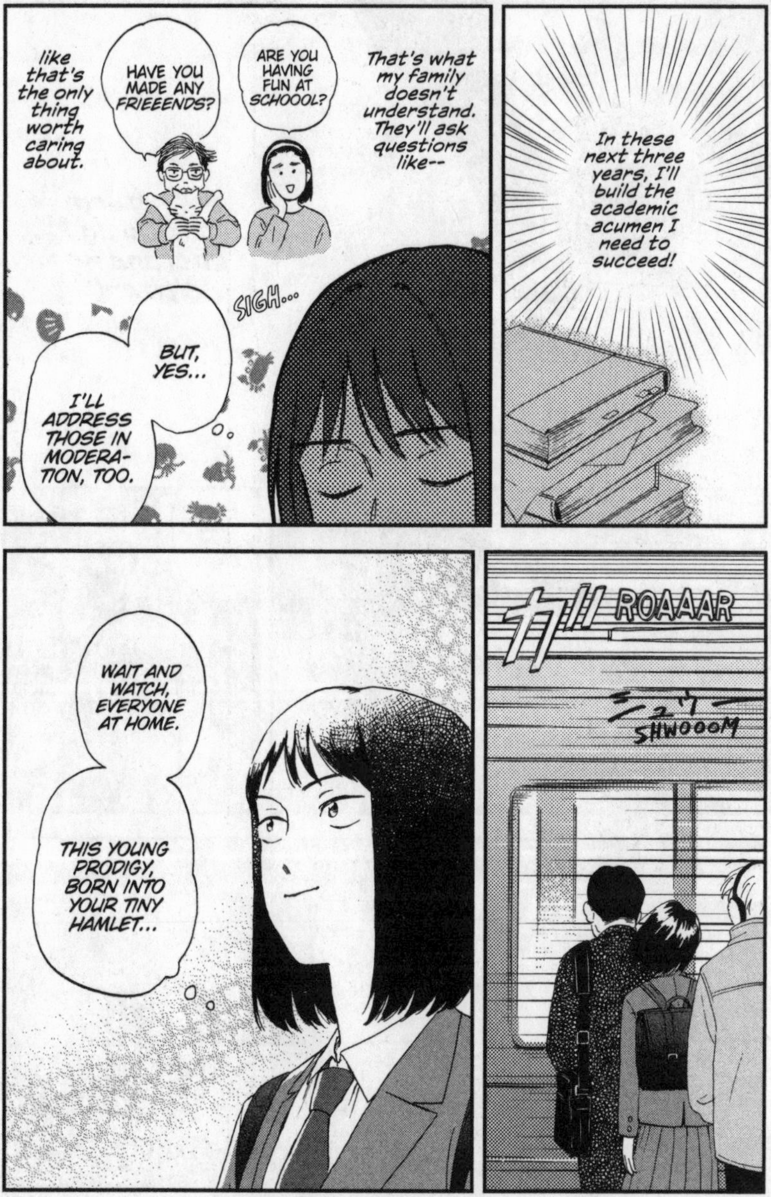
In these next three years, I'll build the academic acumen I need to succeed!
That's what my family doesn't understand. They'll ask questions like--
ARE YOU HAVING FUN AT SCHOOOL?
HAVE YOU MADE ANY FRIEEENDS?
like that's the only thing worth caring about.
SIGH...
BUT, YES...
I'LL ADDRESS THOSE IN MODERATION, TOO.
カ!! ROAAAR
シュウー SHWOOOM
WAIT AND WATCH, EVERYONE AT HOME.
THIS YOUNG PRODIGY, BORN INTO YOUR TINY HAMLET...

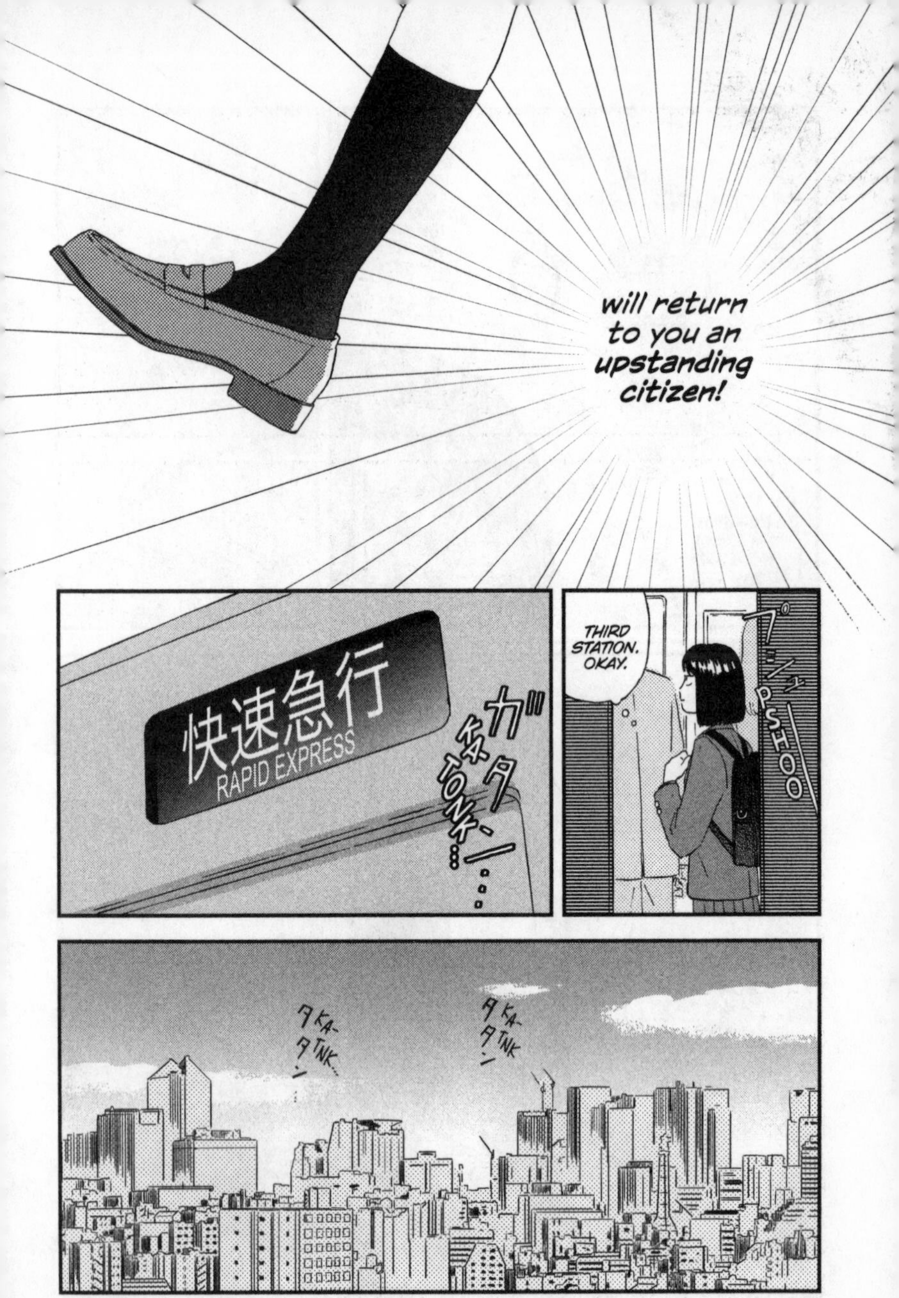

will return to you an upstanding citizen!
THIRD STATION. OKAY.
PSHOO
快速急行
RAPID EXPRESS
KA-TONK...
KA-TNK
KA-TNK...

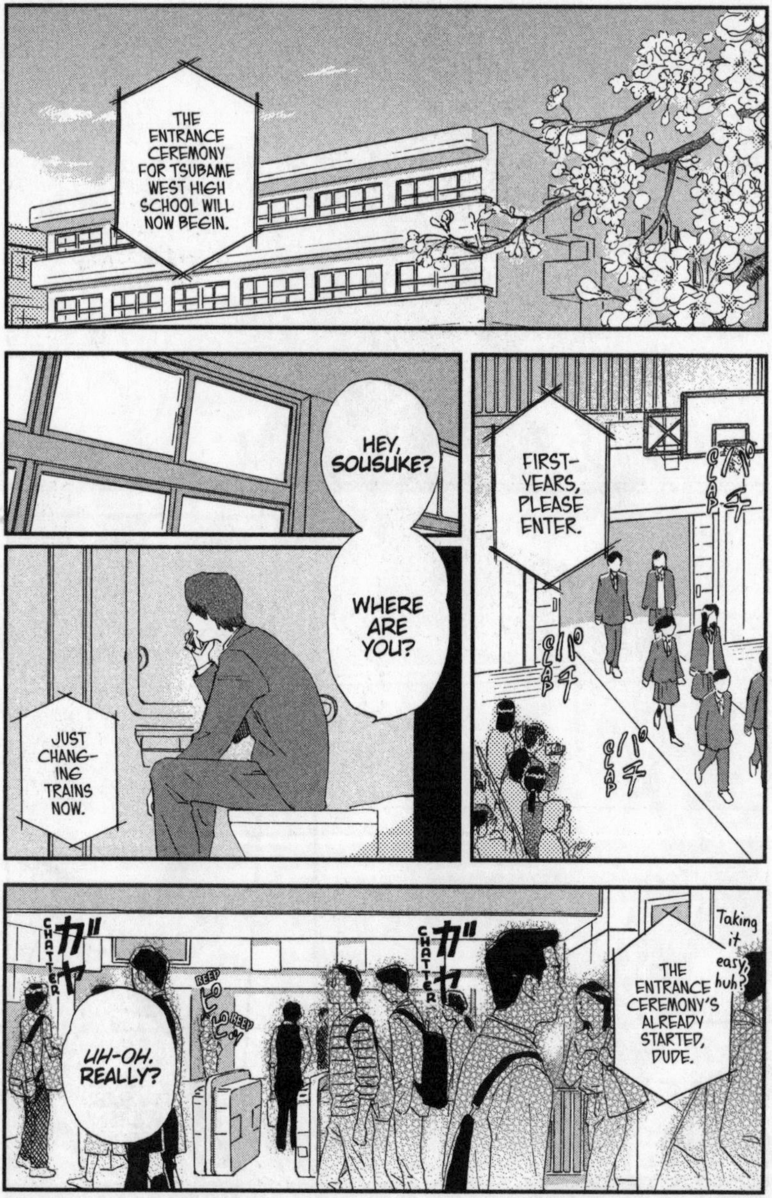
THE ENTRANCE CEREMONY FOR TSUBAME WEST HIGH SCHOOL WILL NOW BEGIN.
FIRST-YEARS, PLEASE ENTER.
パチ CLAP
パチ CLAP
パチ CLAP
HEY, SOUSUKE?
WHERE ARE YOU?
JUST CHANGING TRAINS NOW.
Taking it easy, huh?
THE ENTRANCE CEREMONY'S ALREADY STARTED, DUDE.
ガヤ CHATTER
BEEP
BEEP
UH-OH. REALLY?
ガヤ CHATTER

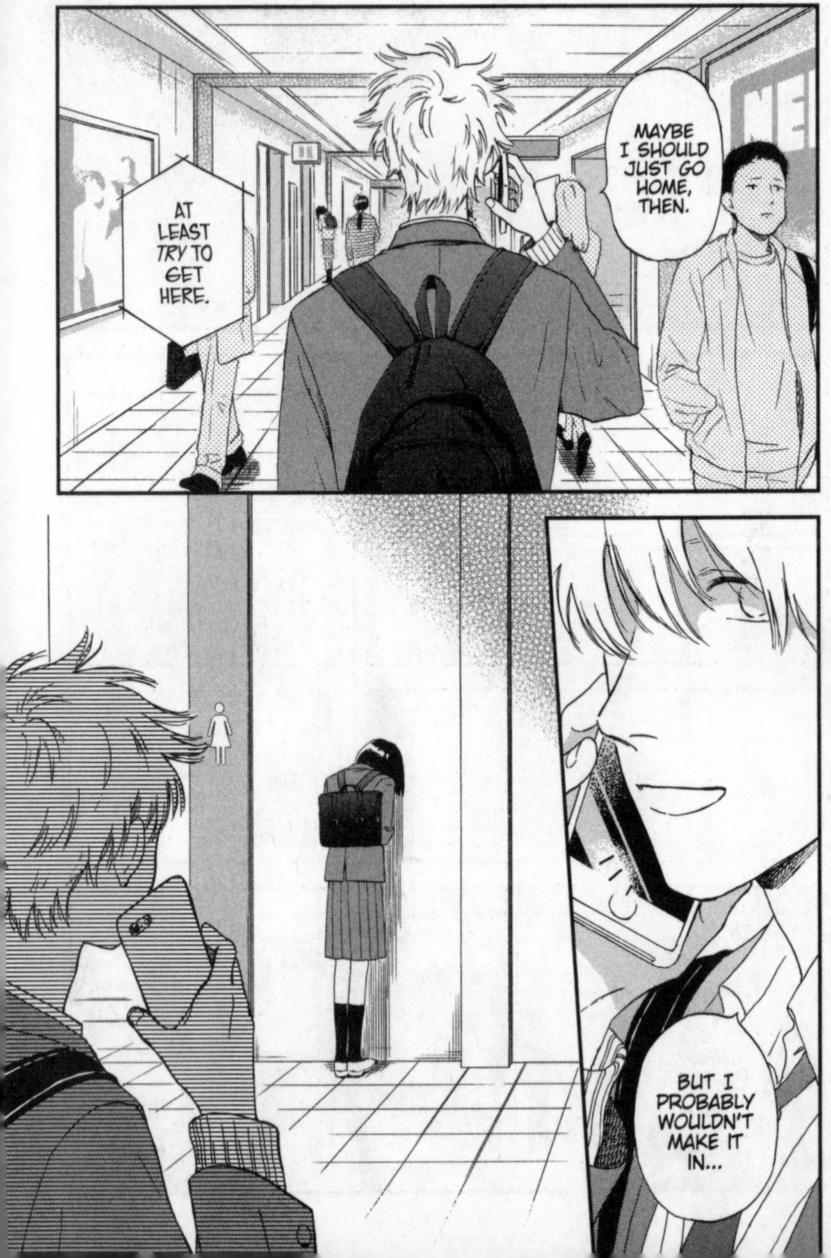
MAYBE I SHOULD JUST GO HOME, THEN.
AT LEAST *TRY* TO GET HERE.
BUT I PROBABLY WOULDN'T MAKE IT IN...

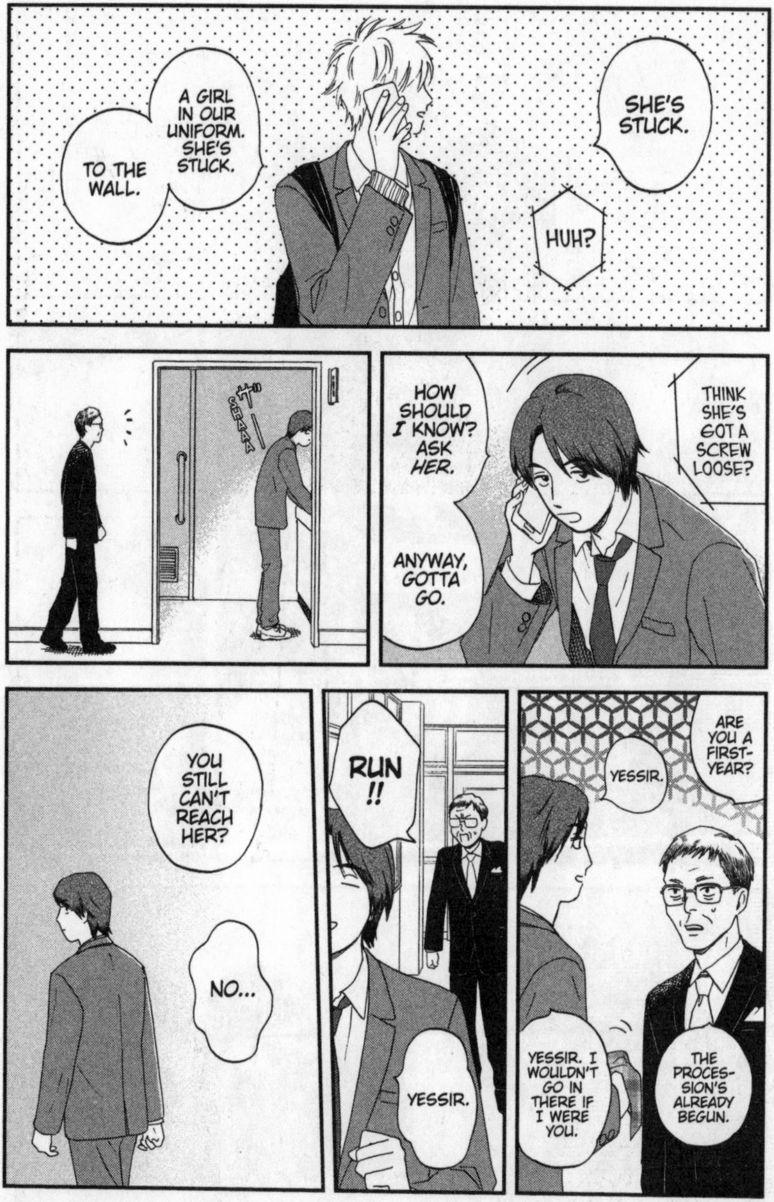
SHE'S STUCK.
HUH?
A GIRL IN OUR UNIFORM. SHE'S STUCK.
TO THE WALL.
THINK SHE'S GOT A SCREW LOOSE?
HOW SHOULD I KNOW? ASK HER.
ANYWAY, GOTTA GO.
SHAAA
ARE YOU A FIRST-YEAR?
YESSIR.
THE PROCES-SION'S ALREADY BEGUN.
YESSIR. I WOULDN'T GO IN THERE IF I WERE YOU.
RUN!!
YESSIR.
YOU STILL CAN'T REACH HER?
NO...

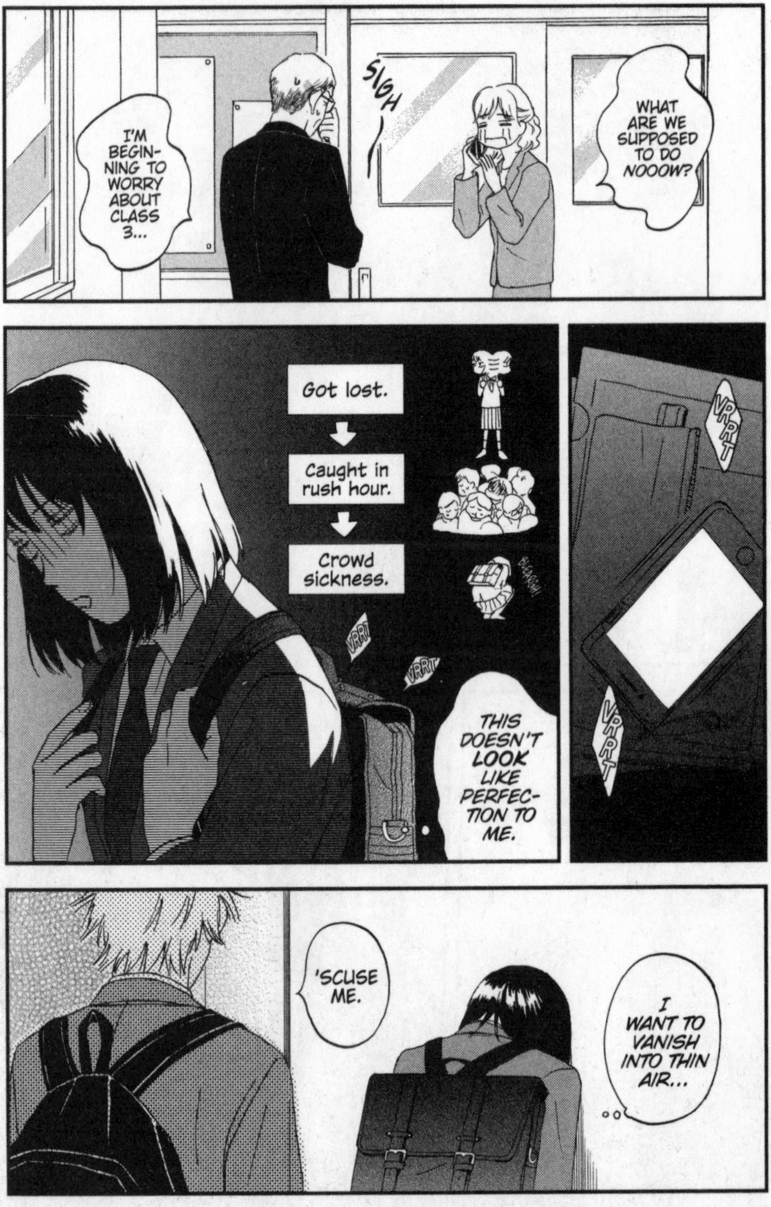
WHAT ARE WE SUPPOSED TO DO NOOOW?
SIGH
I'M BEGIN-NING TO WORRY ABOUT CLASS 3...
VRRT
VRRT
Got lost.
Caught in rush hour.
Crowd sickness.
VRRT
VRRT
THIS DOESN'T LOOK LIKE PERFEC-TION TO ME.
I WANT TO VANISH INTO THIN AIR...
'SCUSE ME.

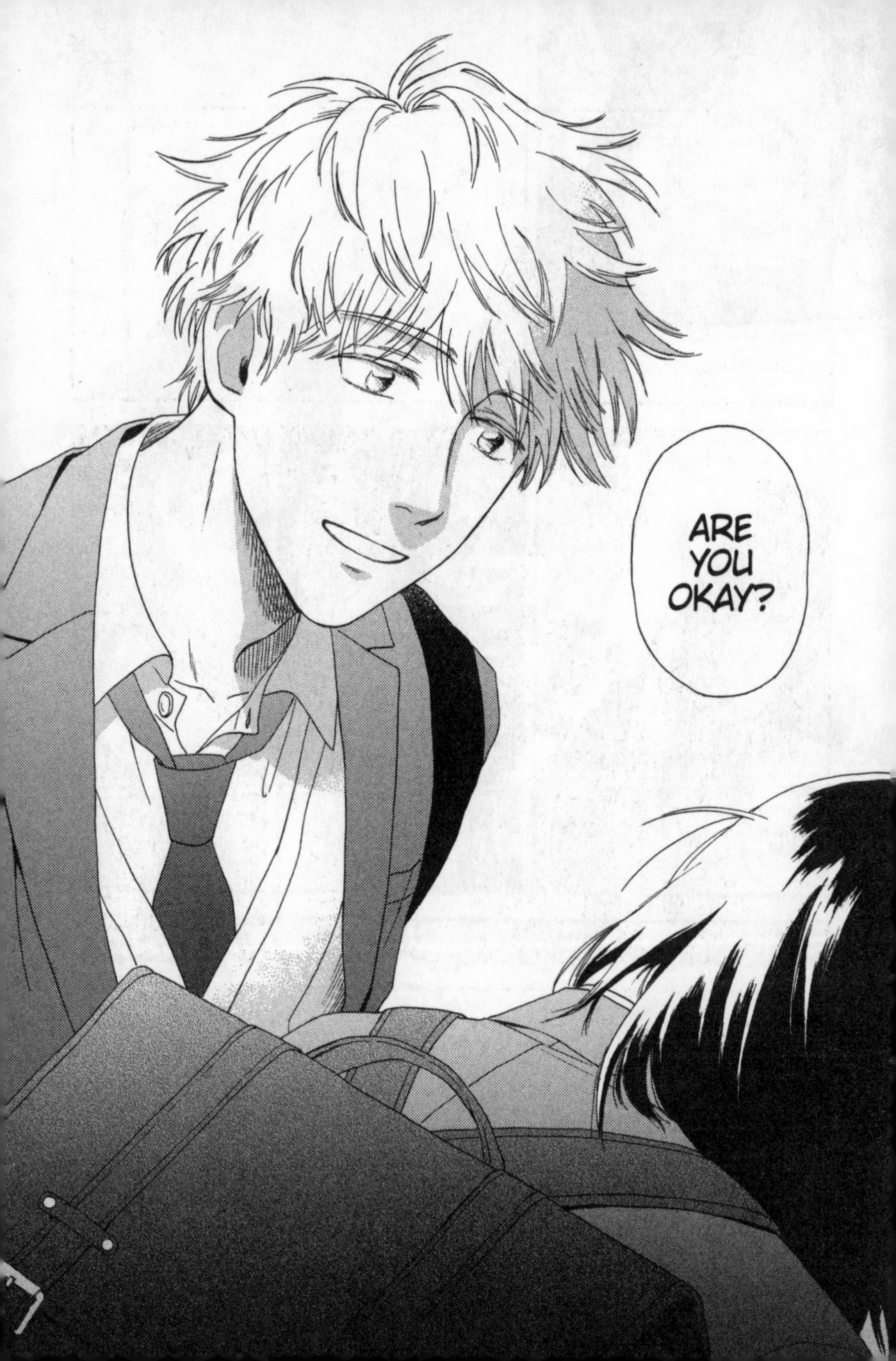
ARE YOU OKAY?

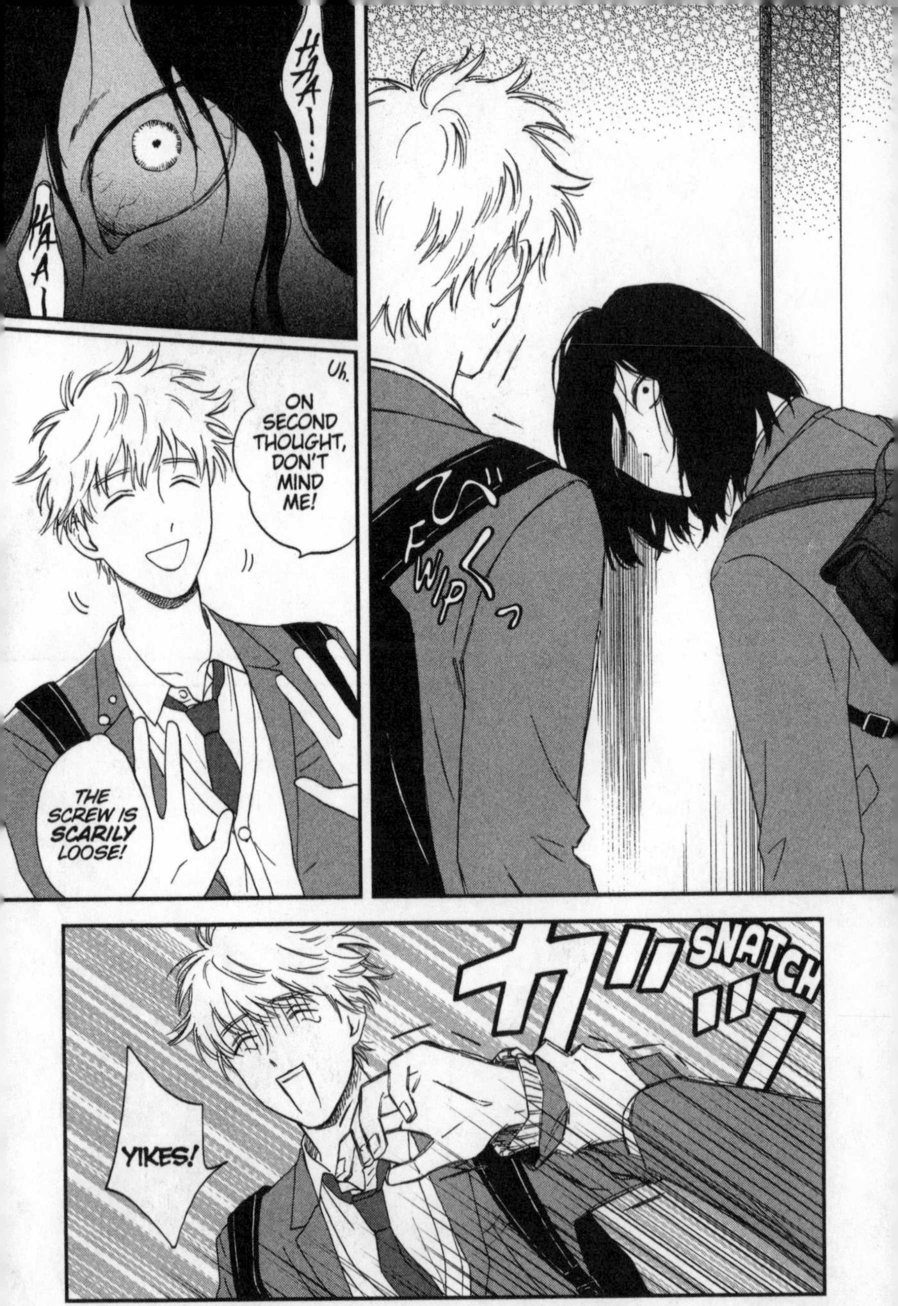
FWIP
HAAI...
HAAI
Uh.
ON SECOND THOUGHT, DON'T MIND ME!
THE SCREW IS SCARILY LOOSE!
SNATCH
YIKES!

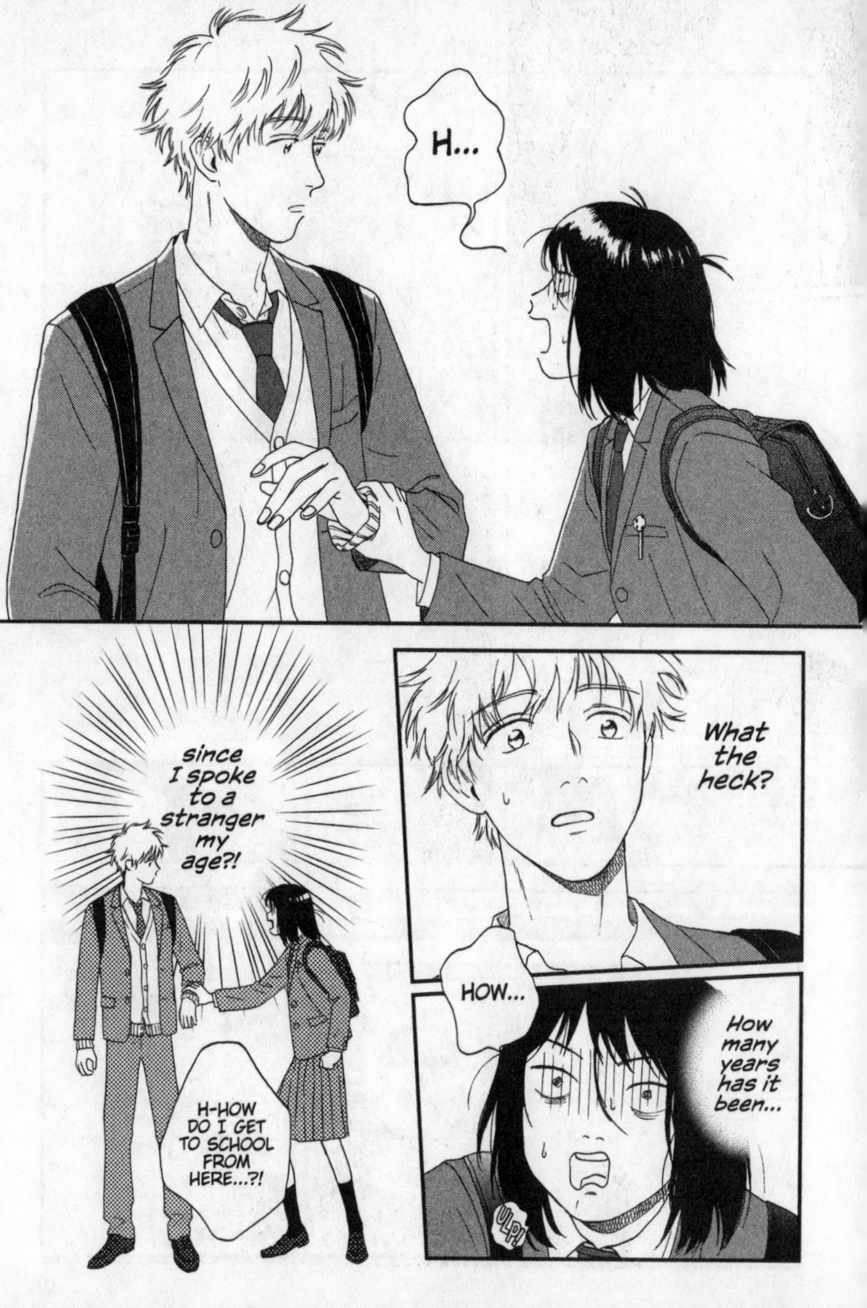
H...
What the heck?
HOW...
How many years has it been...
ULP!
since I spoke to a stranger my age?!
H-HOW DO I GET TO SCHOOL FROM HERE...?!

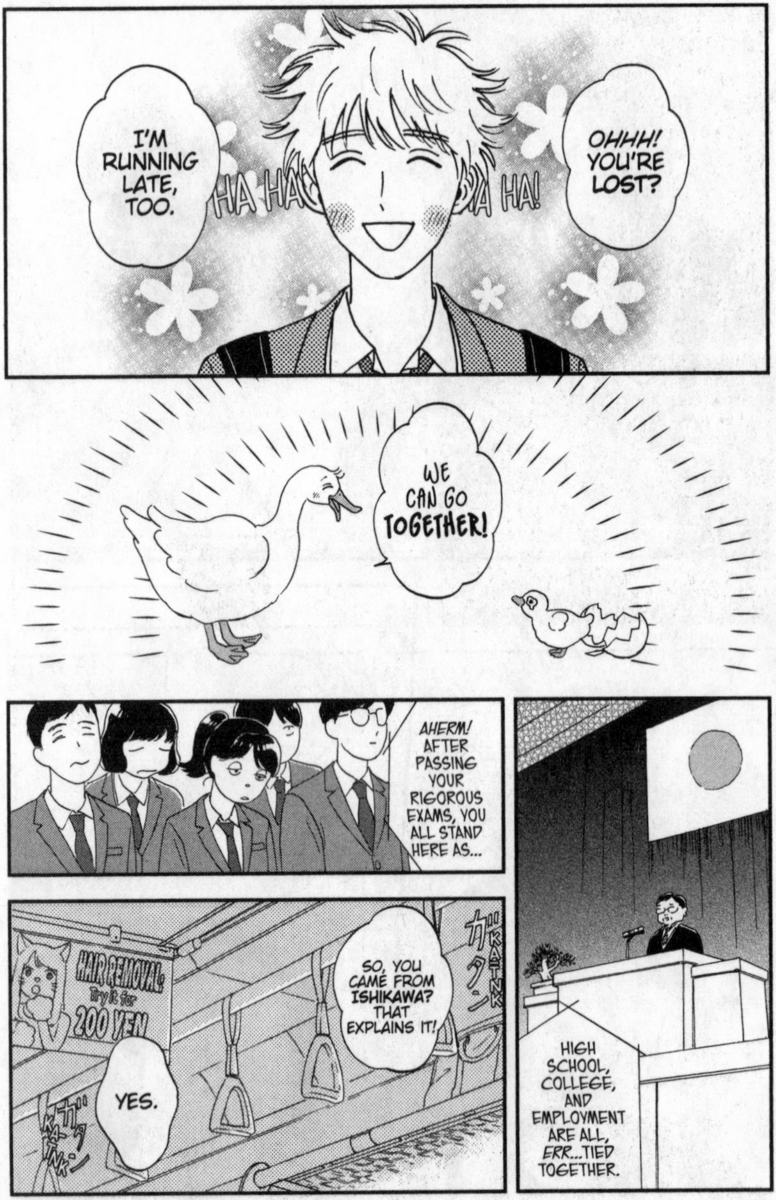
OHHH! YOU'RE LOST?
A HA!
HA HA
I'M RUNNING LATE, TOO.
WE CAN GO TOGETHER!
HIGH SCHOOL, COLLEGE, AND EMPLOYMENT ARE ALL, ERR...TIED TOGETHER.
AHERM! AFTER PASSING YOUR RIGOROUS EXAMS, YOU ALL STAND HERE AS...
KA-TNK
SO, YOU CAME FROM ISHIKAWA? THAT EXPLAINS IT!
HAIR REMOVAL Try it for 200 YEN
YES.
KA-TNK

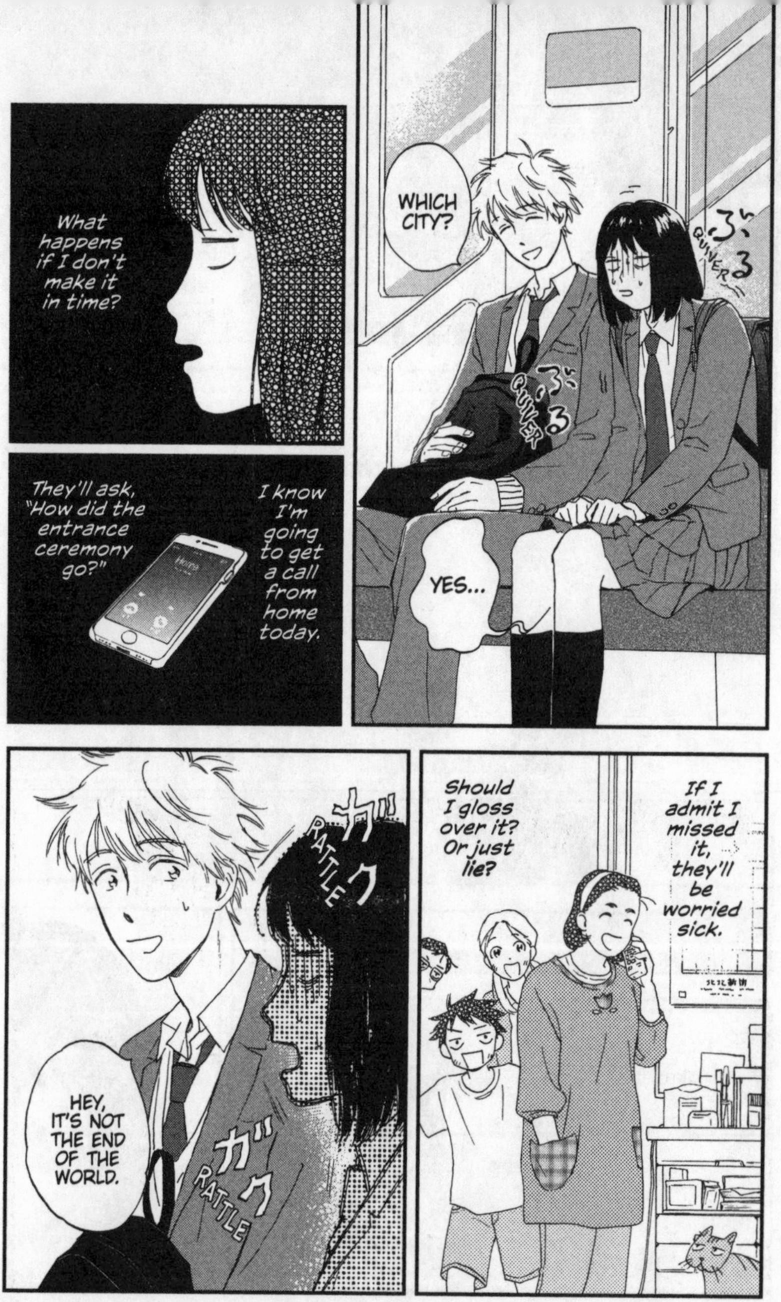
WHICH CITY?
QUIVER
QUIVER
YES...
What happens if I don't make it in time?
I know I'm going to get a call from home today.
They'll ask, "How did the entrance ceremony go?"
If I admit I missed it, they'll be worried sick.
Should I gloss over it? Or just lie?
ガク
RATTLE
ガク
RATTLE
HEY, IT'S NOT THE END OF THE WORLD.

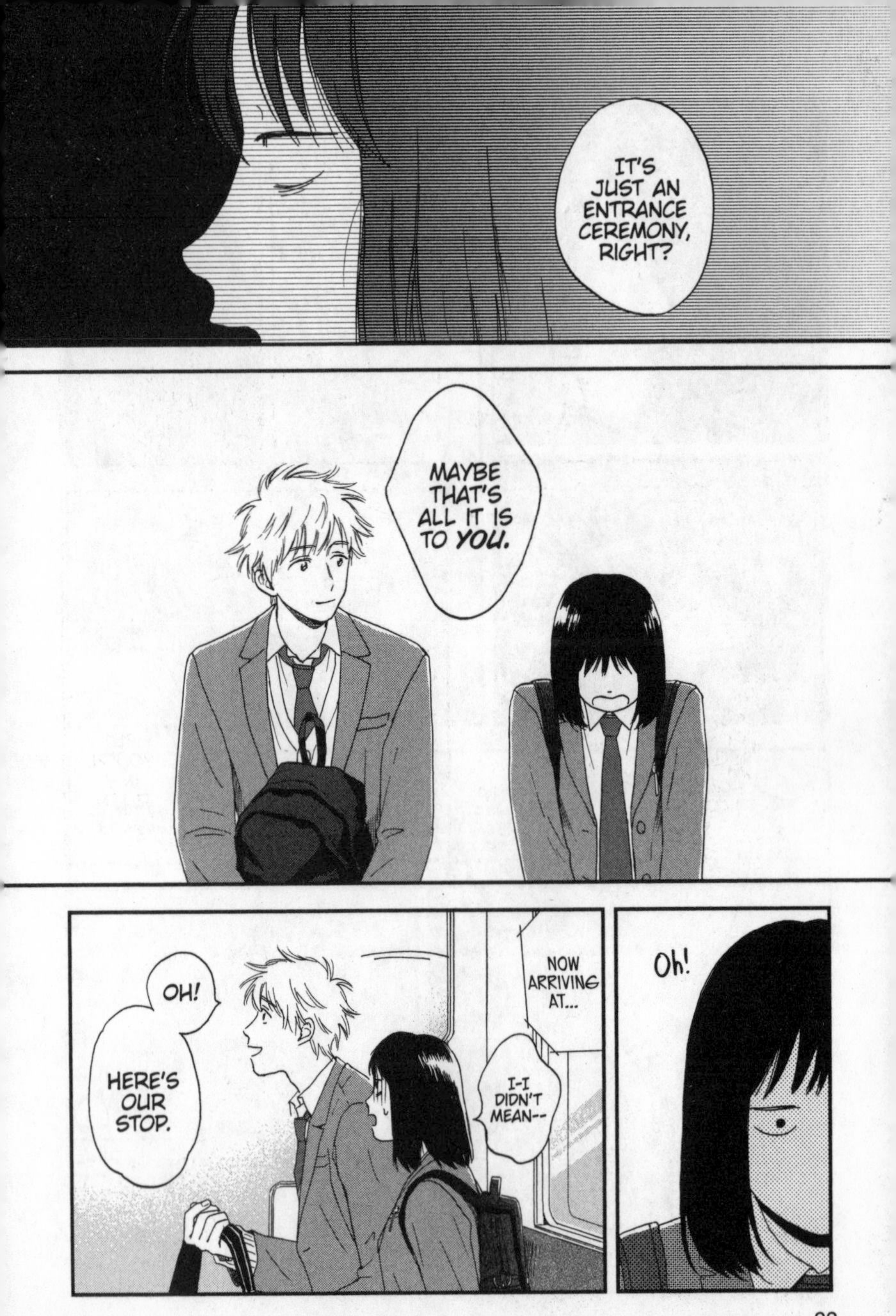
IT'S JUST AN ENTRANCE CEREMONY, RIGHT?
MAYBE THAT'S ALL IT IS TO *YOU.*
Oh!
NOW ARRIVING AT...
OH!
HERE'S OUR STOP.
I-I DIDN'T MEAN--

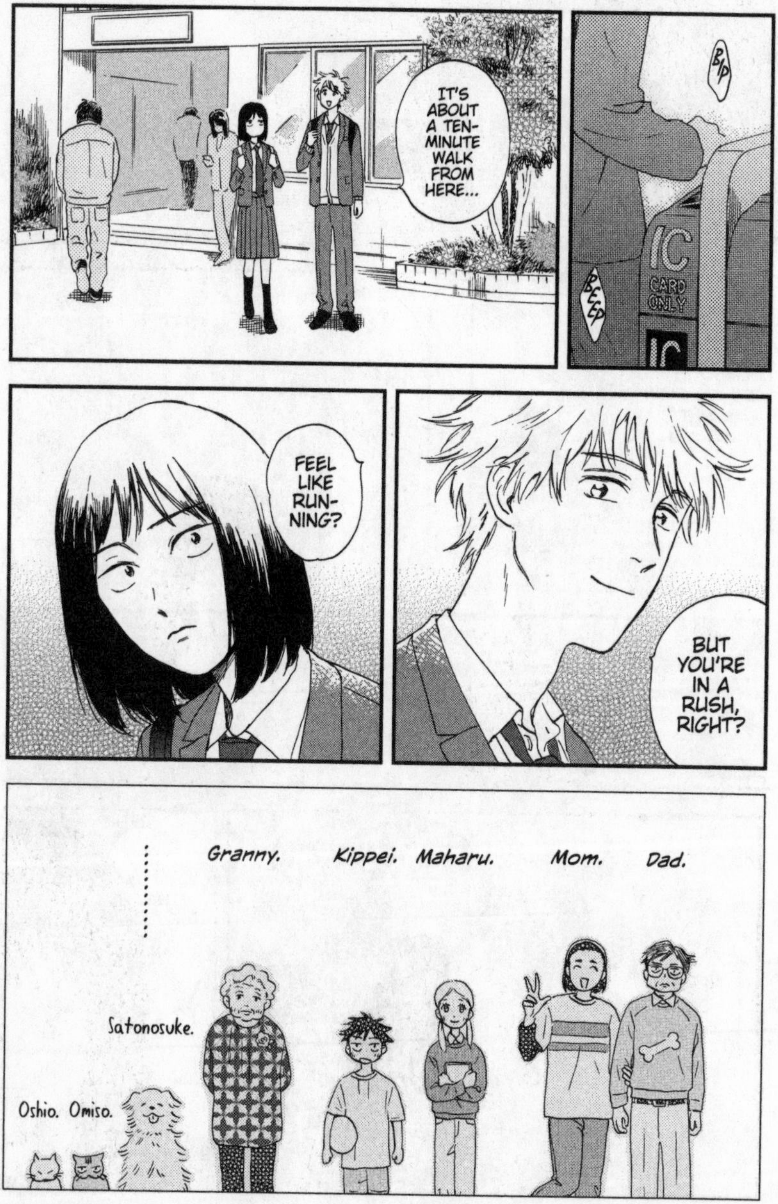
BIP
IC
BEEP
CARD ONLY
IC
IT'S ABOUT A TEN-MINUTE WALK FROM HERE...
BUT YOU'RE IN A RUSH, RIGHT?
FEEL LIKE RUNNING?
Dad.
Mom.
Maharu.
Kippei.
Granny.
......
Satonosuke.
Omiso.
Oshio.

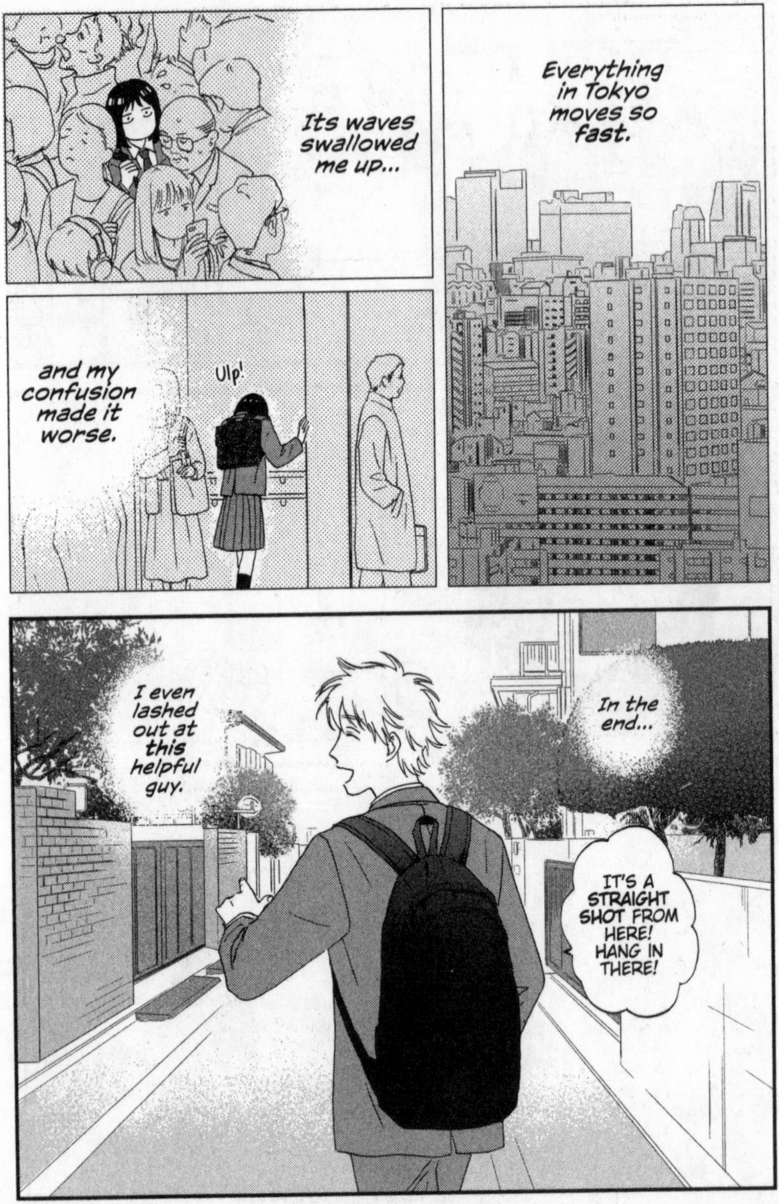
Everything in Tokyo moves so fast.
Its waves swallowed me up...
Ulp!
and my confusion made it worse.
In the end...
I even lashed out at this helpful guy.
IT'S A STRAIGHT SHOT FROM HERE! HANG IN THERE!

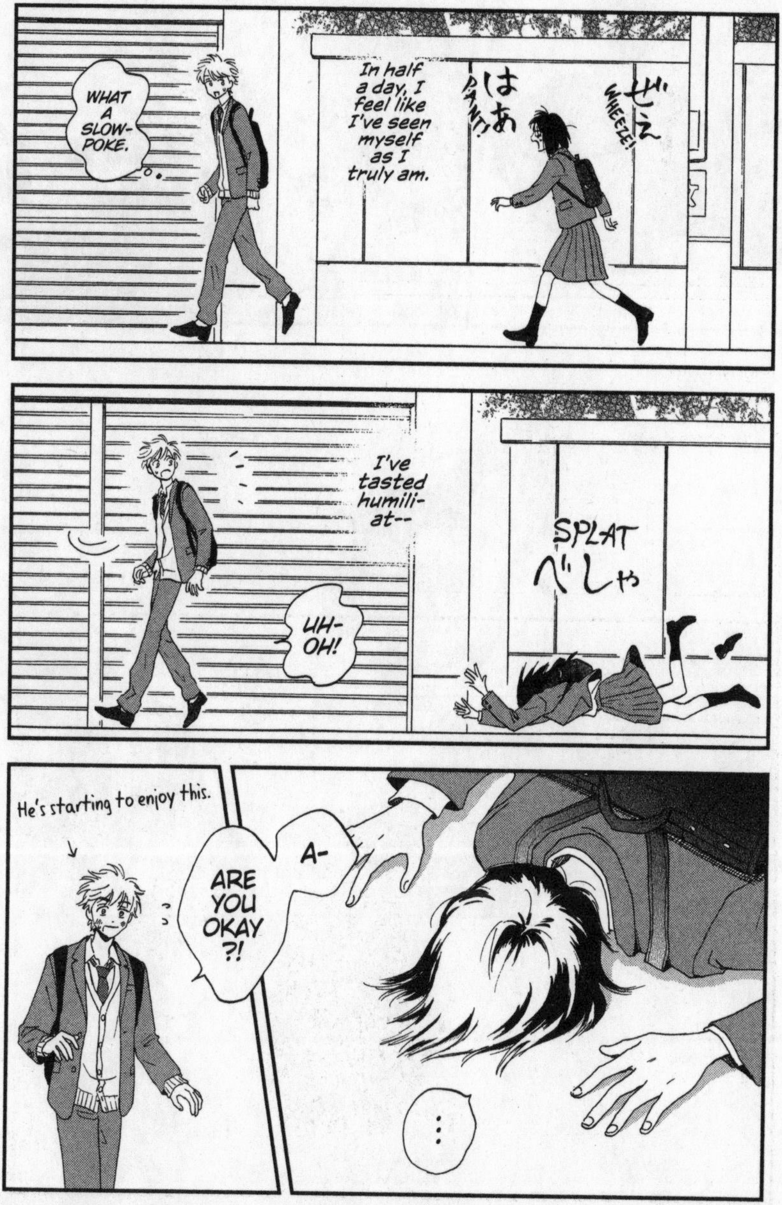
ぜぇ
WHEEZE!
はぁ
PANT!
In half a day, I feel like I've seen myself as I truly am.
WHAT A SLOWPOKE.
SPLAT
べしゃ
I've tasted humili-at--
UH-OH!
A-
ARE YOU OKAY?!
...
He's starting to enjoy this.

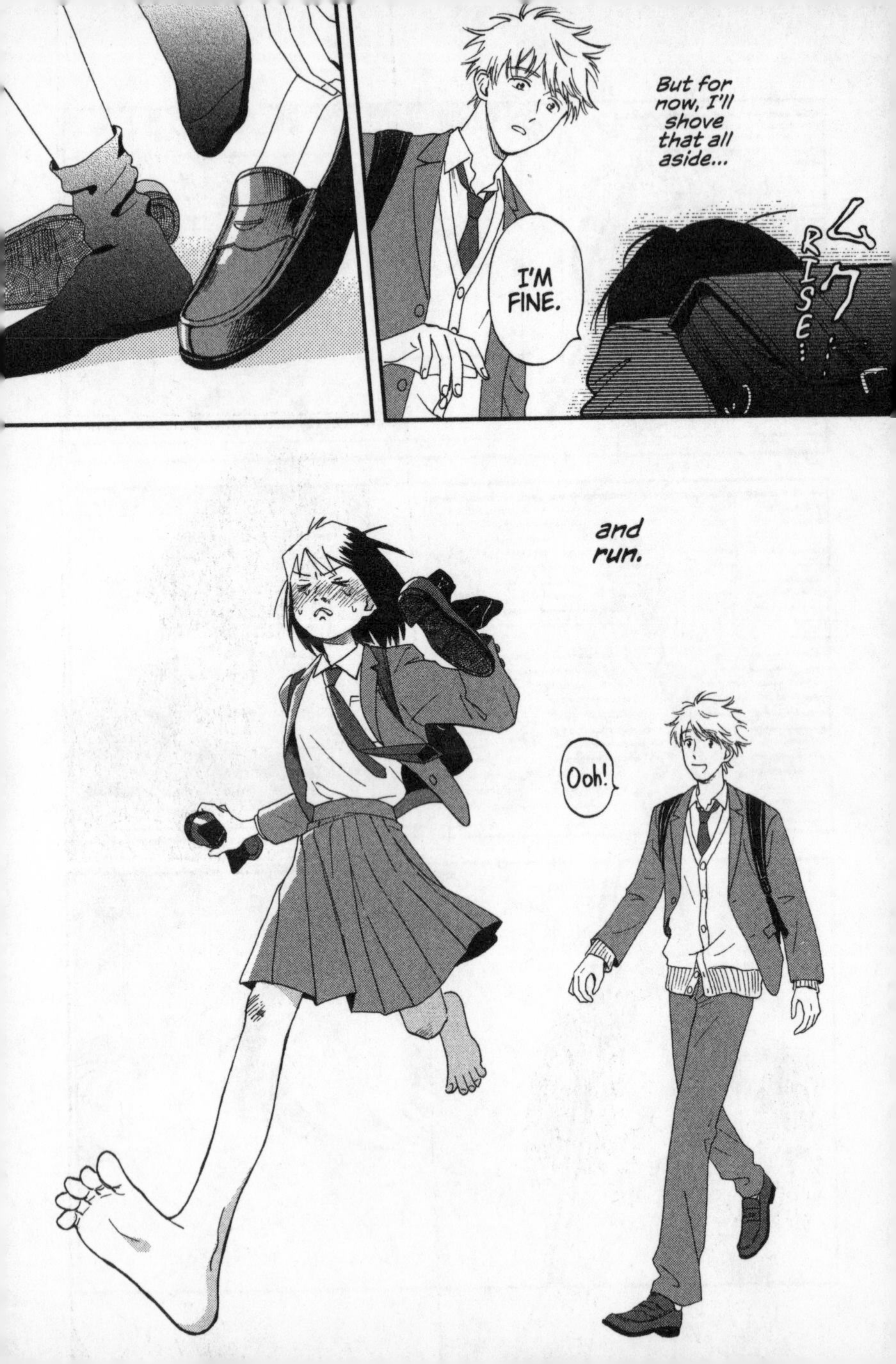

But for now, I'll shove that all aside...
ムク
RISE...
I'M FINE.
and run.
Ooh!

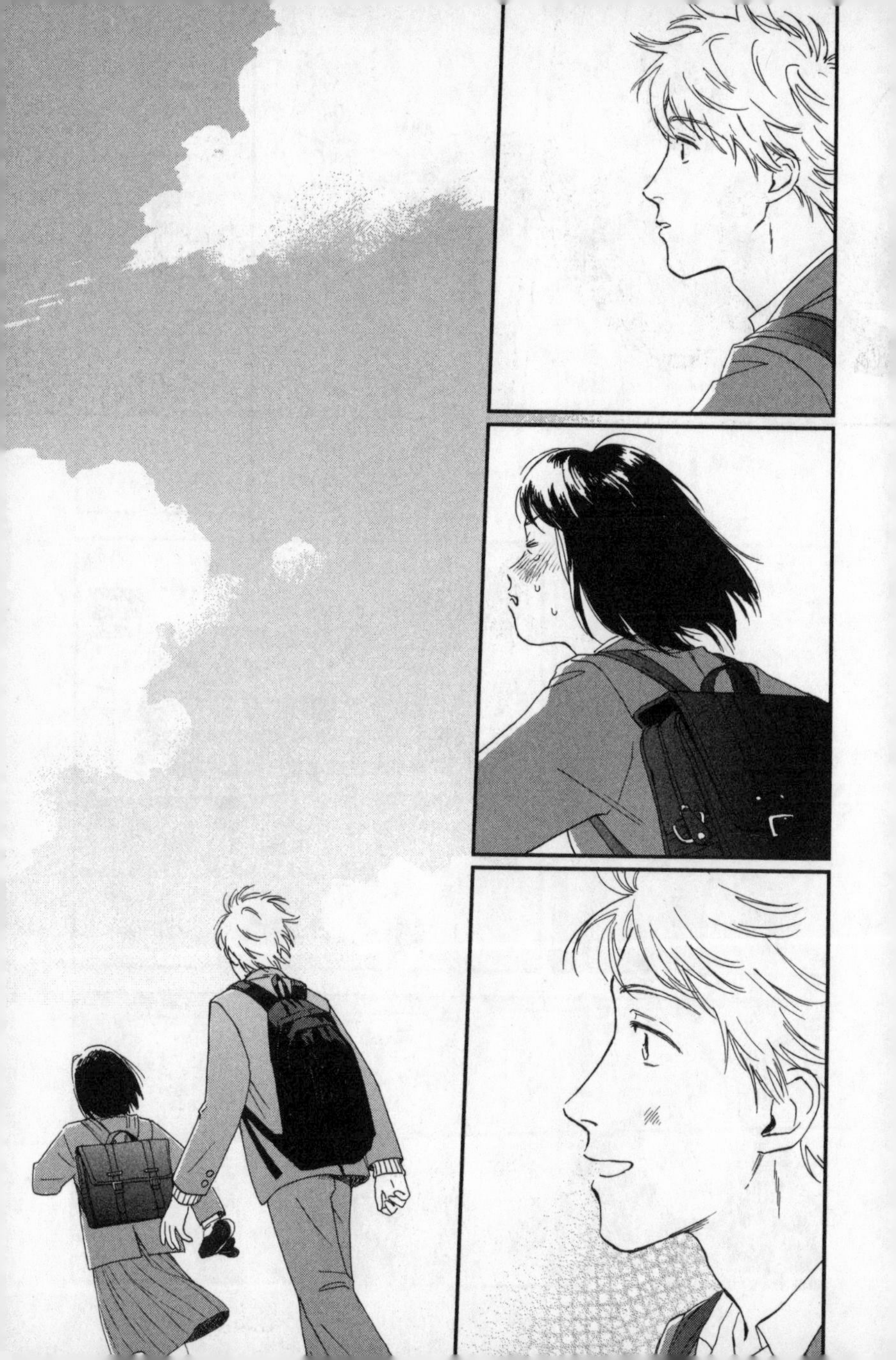

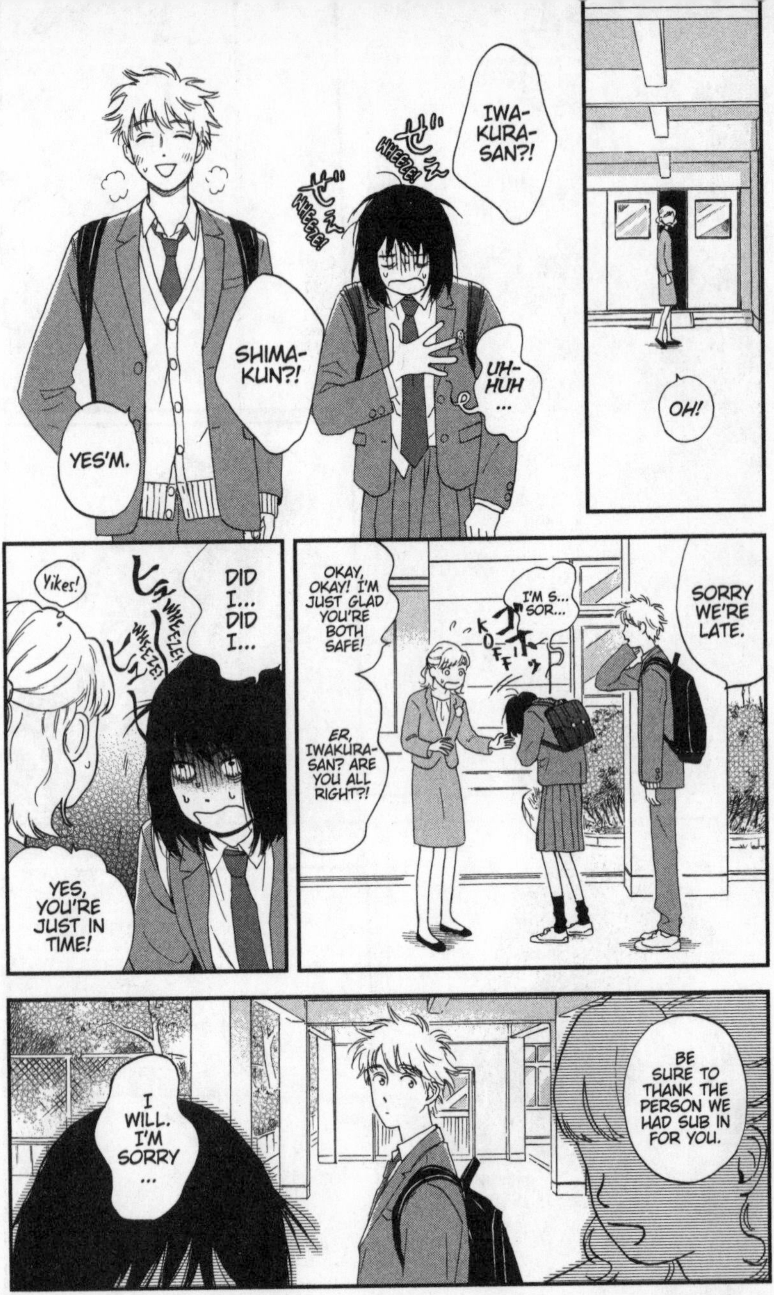
OH!
IWAKURA-SAN?!
ぜぇ WHEEZE!
ぜぇ WHEEZE!
UH-HUH...
SHIMA-KUN?!
YES'M.
SORRY WE'RE LATE.
I'M S... SOR...
KOFF
OKAY, OKAY! I'M JUST GLAD YOU'RE BOTH SAFE!
ER, IWAKURA-SAN? ARE YOU ALL RIGHT?!
DID I... DID I...
WHEEZE!
WHEEZE!
Yikes!
YES, YOU'RE JUST IN TIME!
BE SURE TO THANK THE PERSON WE HAD SUB IN FOR YOU.
I WILL. I'M SORRY...

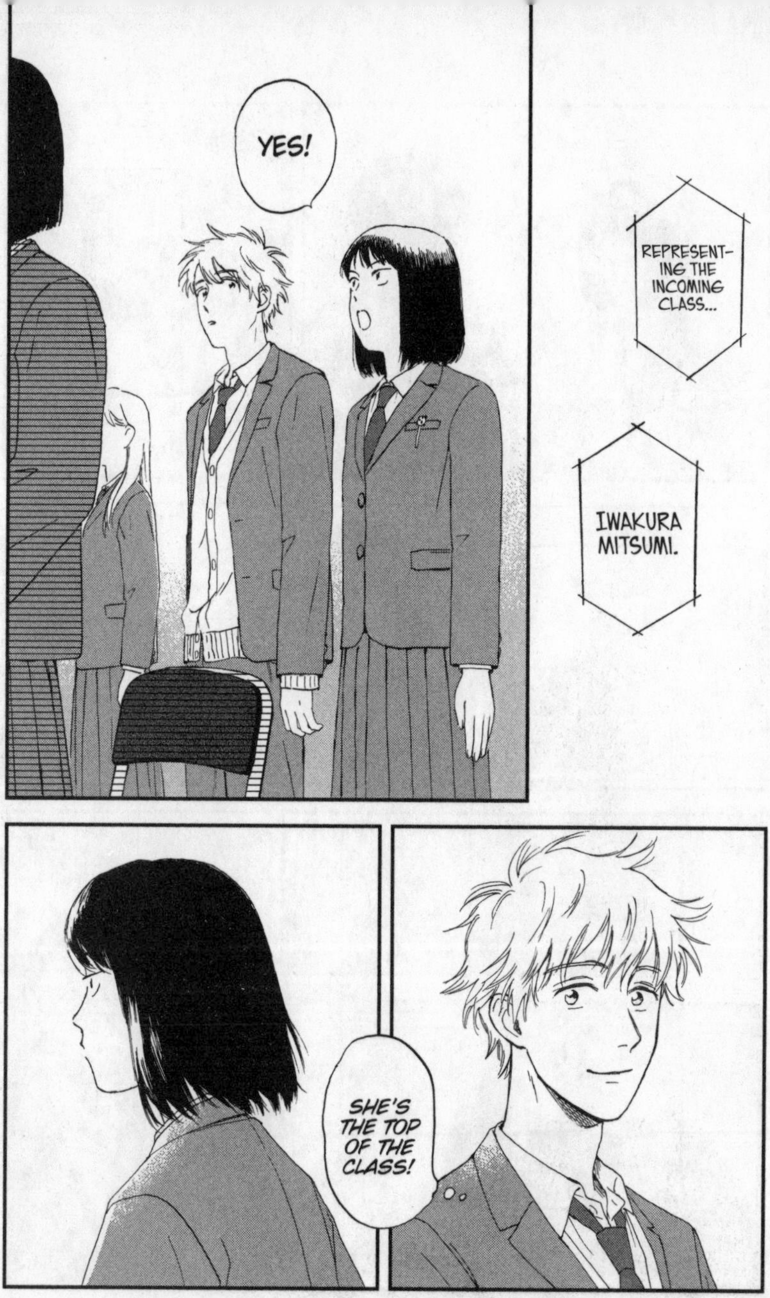
REPRESENTING THE INCOMING CLASS...
IWAKURA MITSUMI.
YES!
SHE'S THE TOP OF THE CLASS!

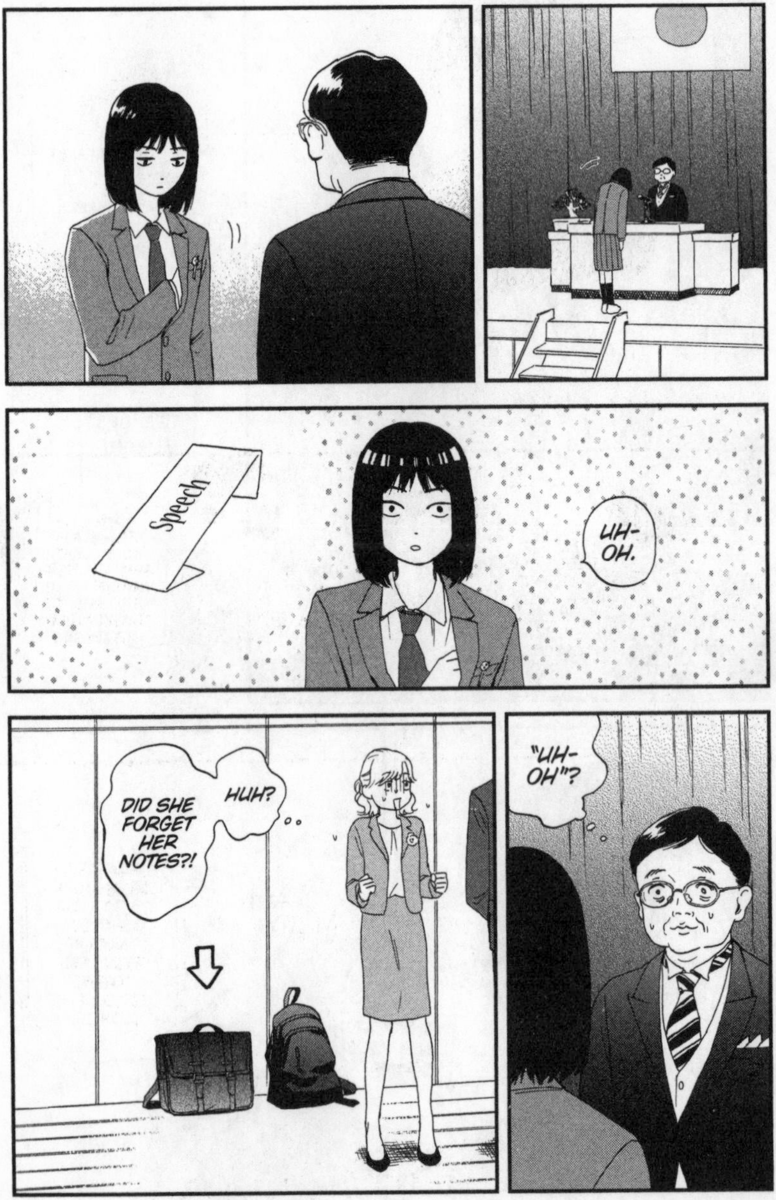
UH-OH.
Speech
"UH-OH"?
HUH?
DID SHE FORGET HER NOTES?!

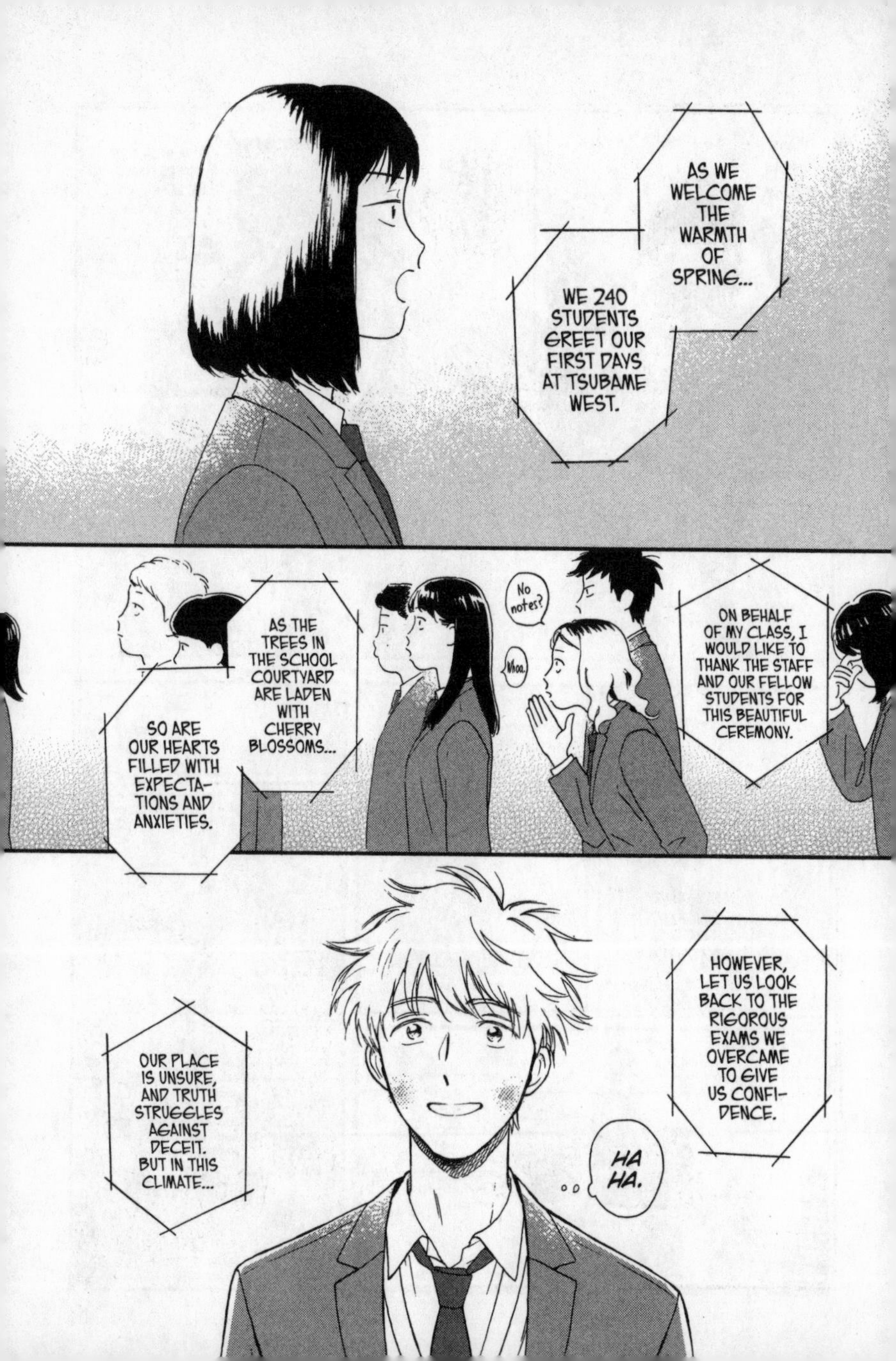
AS WE WELCOME THE WARMTH OF SPRING...
WE 240 STUDENTS GREET OUR FIRST DAYS AT TSUBAME WEST.
ON BEHALF OF MY CLASS, I WOULD LIKE TO THANK THE STAFF AND OUR FELLOW STUDENTS FOR THIS BEAUTIFUL CEREMONY.
No notes?
Whoa.
AS THE TREES IN THE SCHOOL COURTYARD ARE LADEN WITH CHERRY BLOSSOMS...
SO ARE OUR HEARTS FILLED WITH EXPECTA-TIONS AND ANXIETIES.
HOWEVER, LET US LOOK BACK TO THE RIGOROUS EXAMS WE OVERCAME TO GIVE US CONFI-DENCE.
HA HA.
OUR PLACE IS UNSURE, AND TRUTH STRUGGLES AGAINST DECEIT. BUT IN THIS CLIMATE...

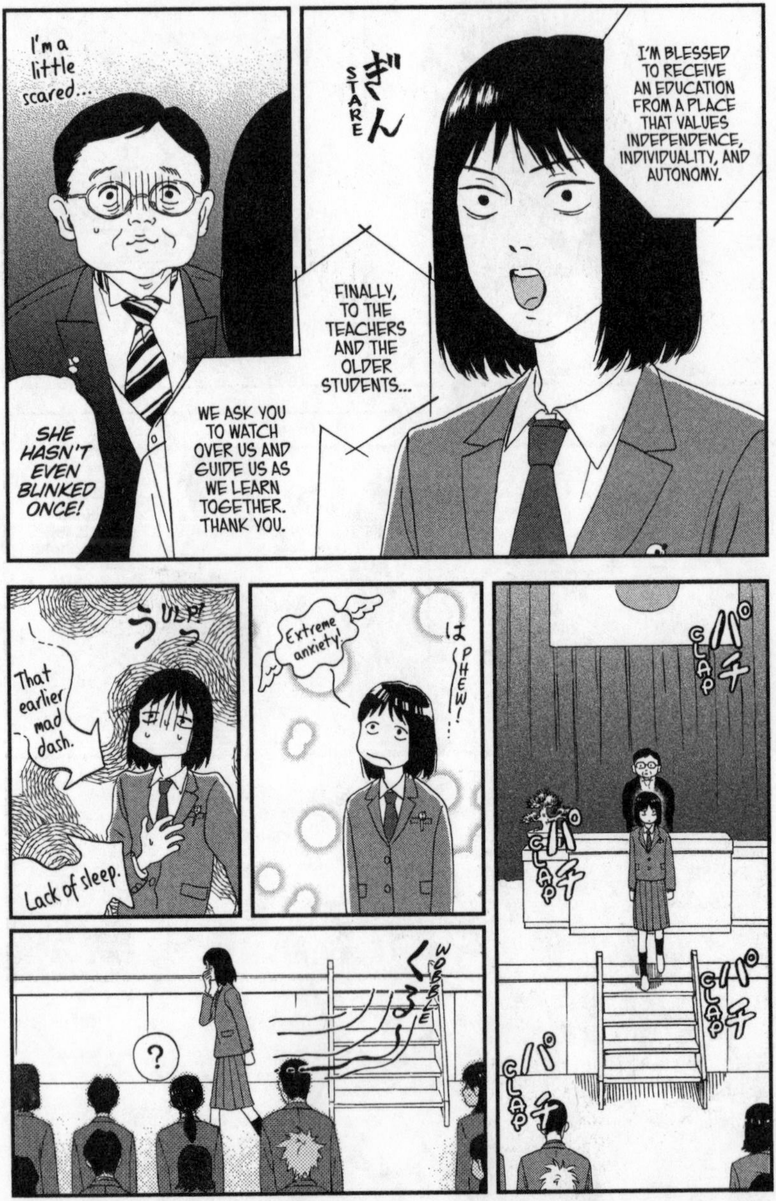
ぎん
STARE
I'M BLESSED TO RECEIVE AN EDUCATION FROM A PLACE THAT VALUES INDEPENDENCE, INDIVIDUALITY, AND AUTONOMY.
FINALLY, TO THE TEACHERS AND THE OLDER STUDENTS...
WE ASK YOU TO WATCH OVER US AND GUIDE US AS WE LEARN TOGETHER. THANK YOU.
I'm a little scared...
SHE HASN'T EVEN BLINKED ONCE!
パチ
CLAP
パチ
CLAP
パチ
CLAP
パチ
CLAP
Extreme anxiety!
は
PHEW!...
う
ULP!
That earlier mad dash.
Lack of sleep.
くる
WOBBLE
?

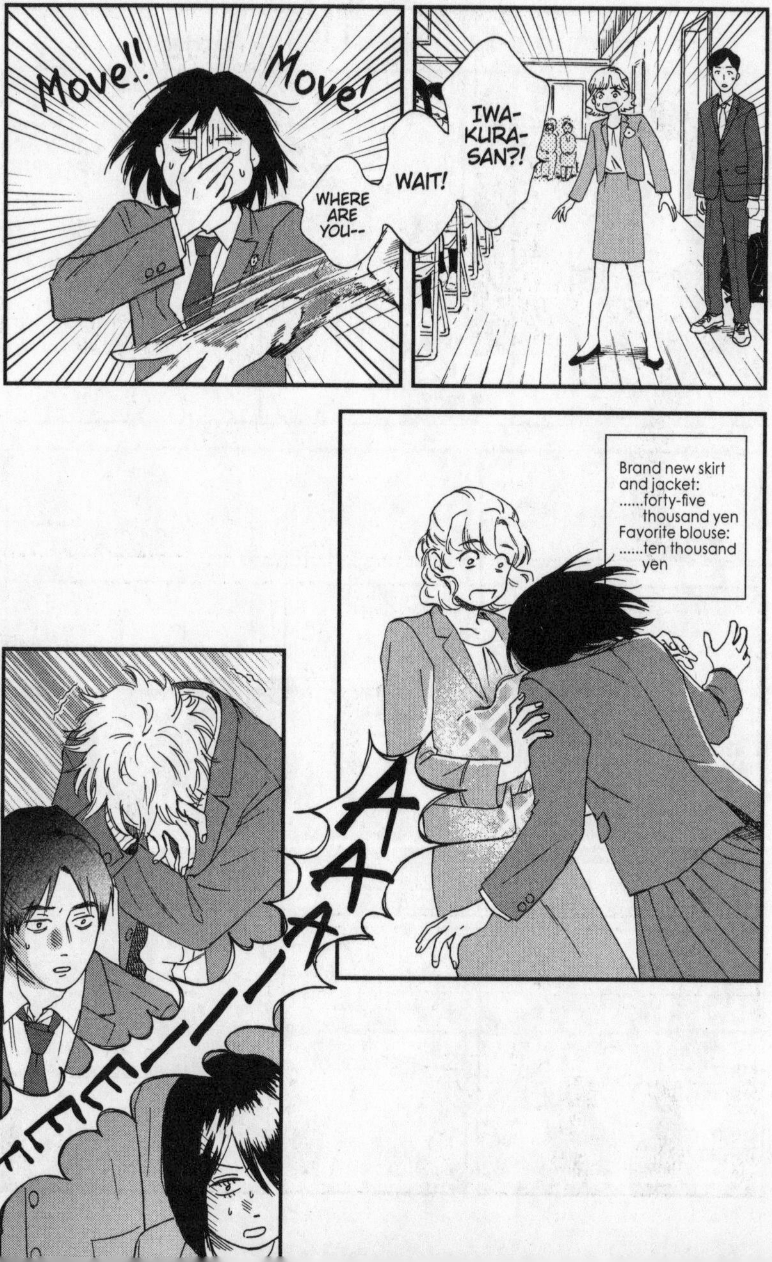
IWA-KURA-SAN?!
WAIT!
WHERE ARE YOU--
Move!
Move!!
Brand new skirt and jacket: ......forty-five thousand yen
Favorite blouse: ......ten thousand yen
AAA——EEE!!

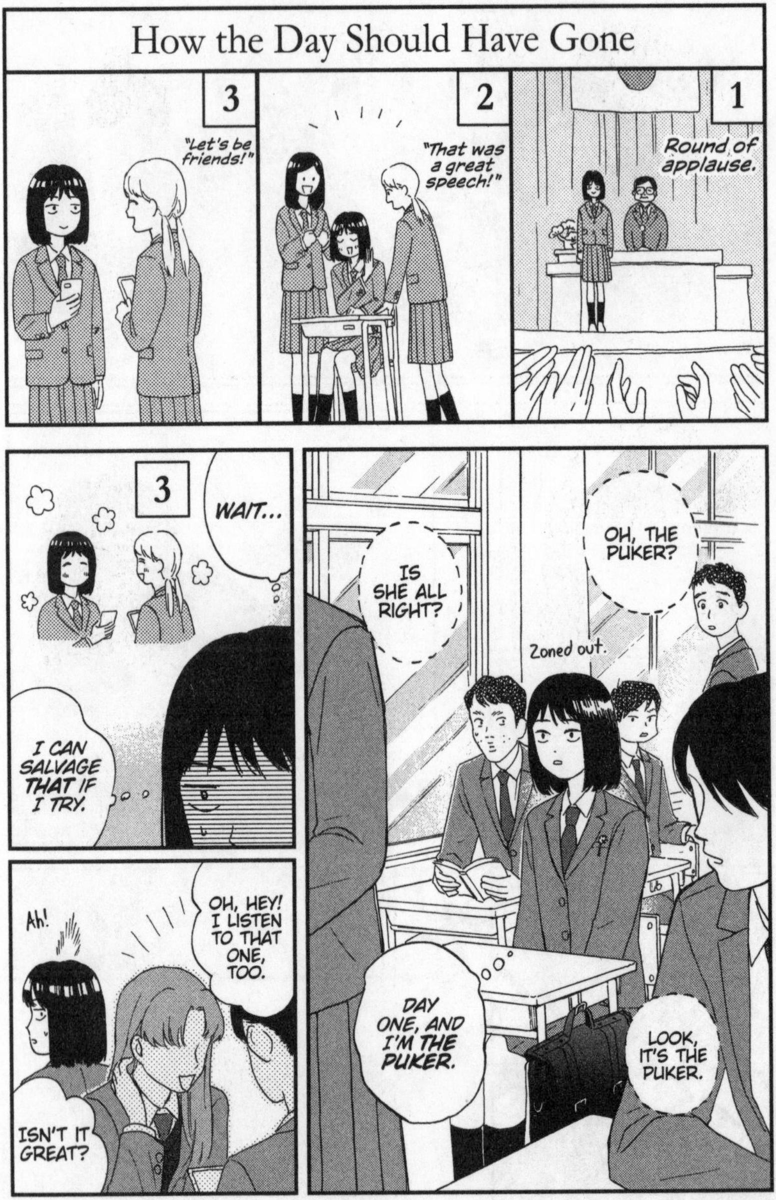
How the Day Should Have Gone
1
Round of applause.
2
"That was a great speech!"
3
"Let's be friends!"
OH, THE PUKER?
IS SHE ALL RIGHT?
Zoned out.
LOOK, IT'S THE PUKER.
DAY ONE, AND I'M THE PUKER.
3
WAIT...
I CAN SALVAGE THAT IF I TRY.
OH, HEY! I LISTEN TO THAT ONE, TOO.
Ah!
ISN'T IT GREAT?

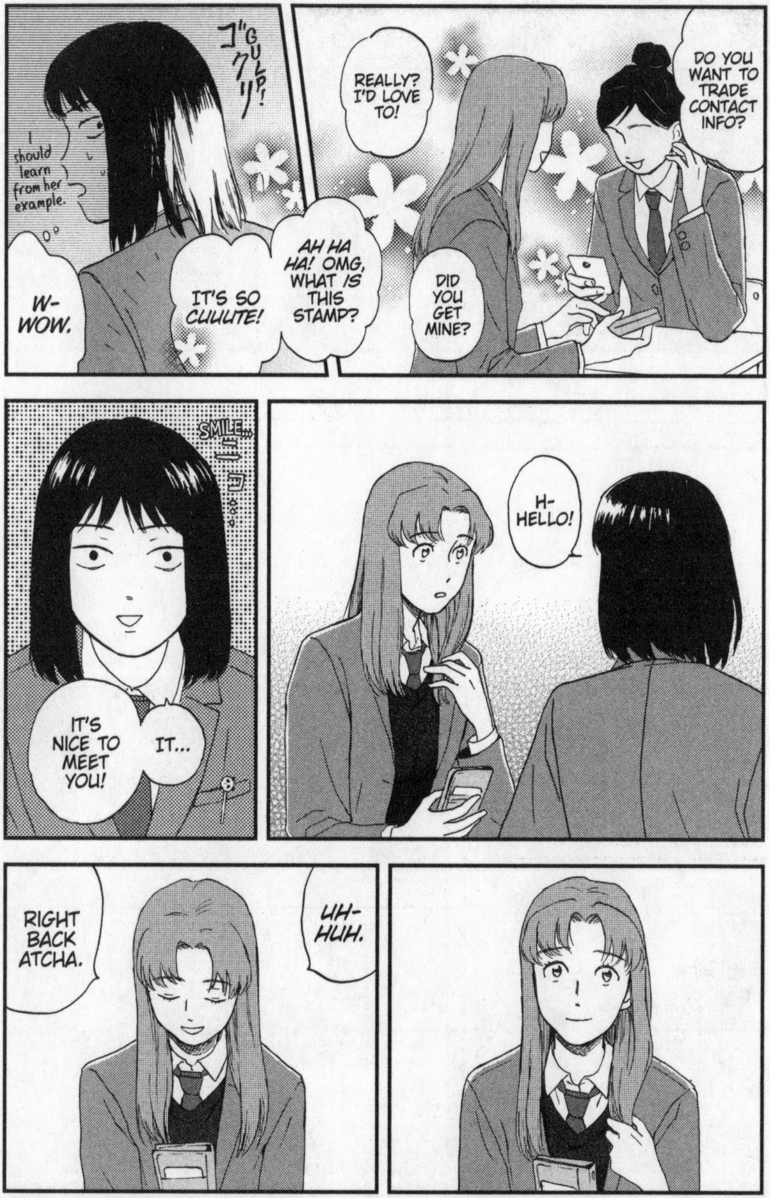
DO YOU WANT TO TRADE CONTACT INFO?
REALLY? I'D LOVE TO!
DID YOU GET MINE?
AH HA HA! OMG, WHAT IS THIS STAMP?
IT'S SO CUUUTE!
GULP!
I should learn from her example.
W-WOW.
H-HELLO!
SMILE...
IT...
IT'S NICE TO MEET YOU!
UH-HUH.
RIGHT BACK ATCHA.

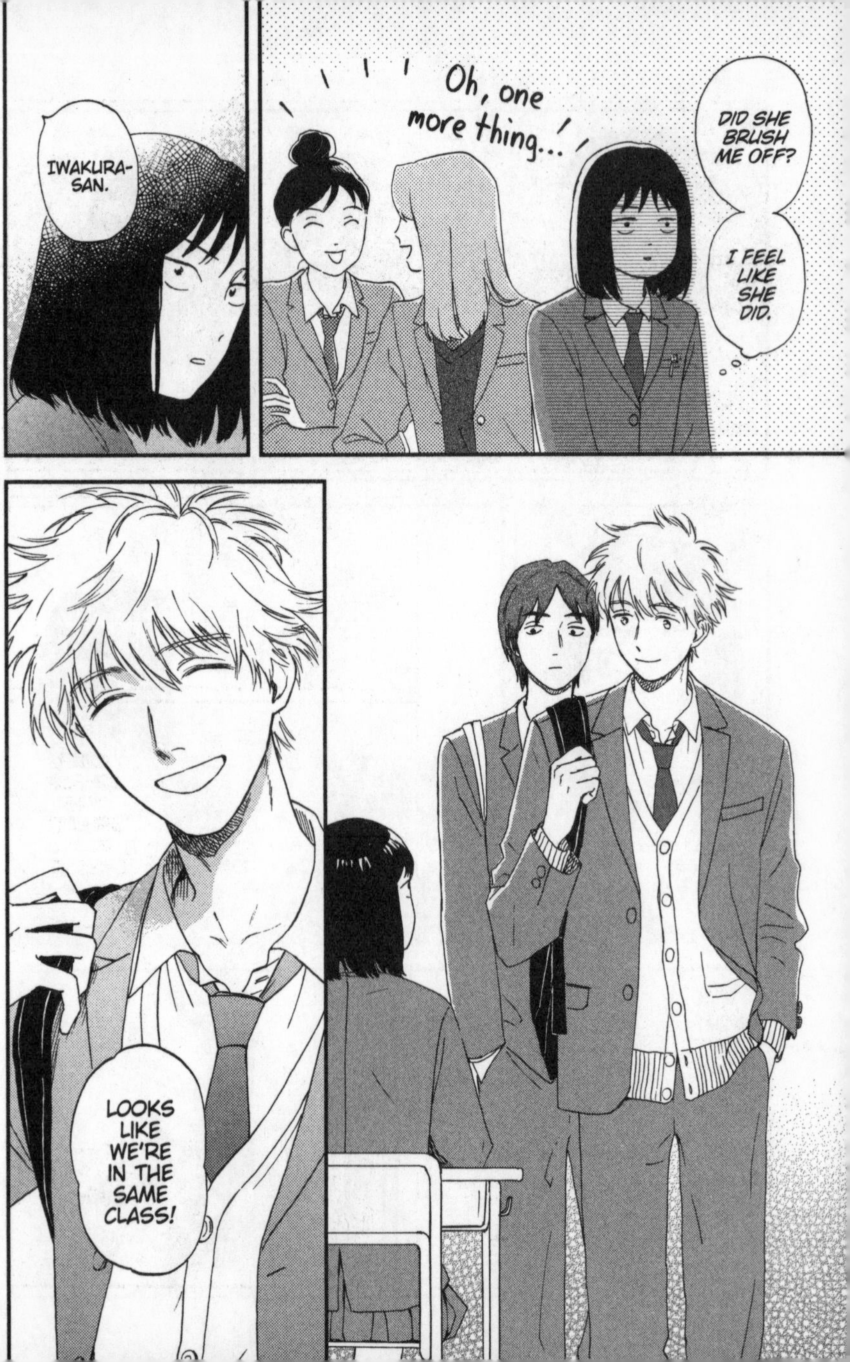
DID SHE BRUSH ME OFF?
I FEEL LIKE SHE DID.
Oh, one more thing...
IWAKURA-SAN.
LOOKS LIKE WE'RE IN THE SAME CLASS!

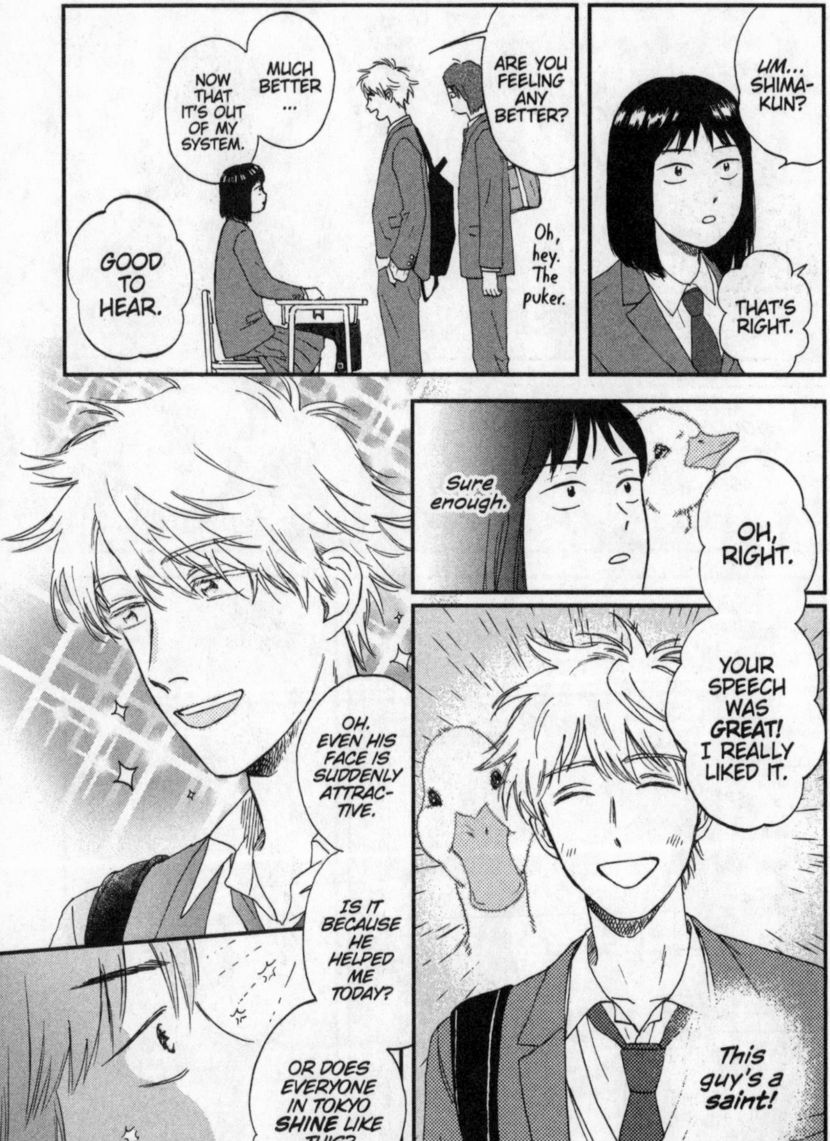

UM... SHIMA-KUN?
THAT'S RIGHT.
ARE YOU FEELING ANY BETTER?
MUCH BETTER ...
NOW THAT IT'S OUT OF MY SYSTEM.
Oh, hey. The puker.
GOOD TO HEAR.
OH, RIGHT.
Sure enough.
YOUR SPEECH WAS GREAT! I REALLY LIKED IT.
This guy's a saint!
OH. EVEN HIS FACE IS SUDDENLY ATTRAC-TIVE.
IS IT BECAUSE HE HELPED ME TODAY?
OR DOES EVERYONE IN TOKYO SHINE LIKE THIS?

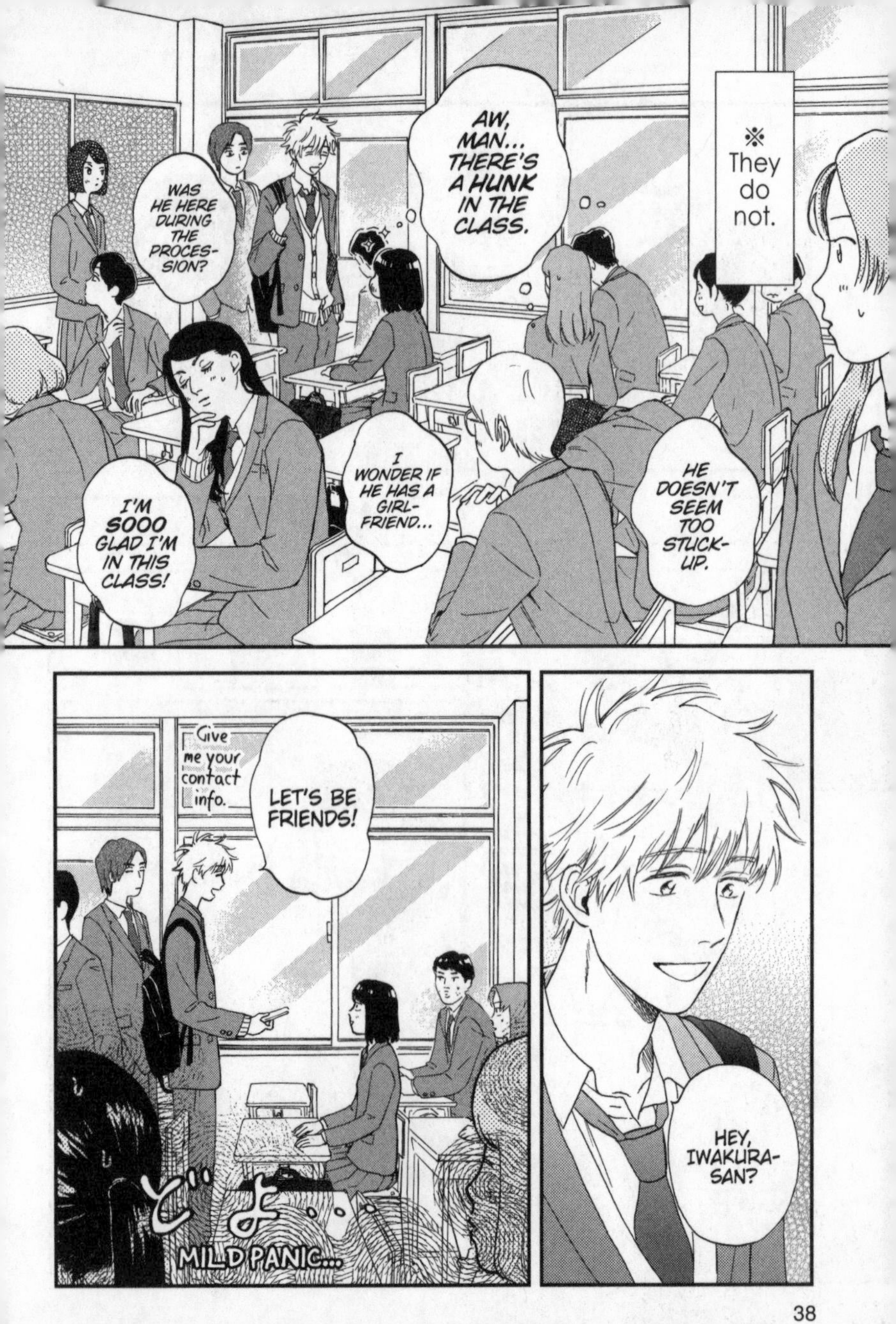
※ They do not.
AW, MAN... THERE'S A HUNK IN THE CLASS.
WAS HE HERE DURING THE PROCES-SION?
HE DOESN'T SEEM TOO STUCK-UP.
I WONDER IF HE HAS A GIRL-FRIEND...
I'M SOOO GLAD I'M IN THIS CLASS!
HEY, IWAKURA-SAN?
LET'S BE FRIENDS!
Give me your contact info.
どよ…
MILD PANIC...

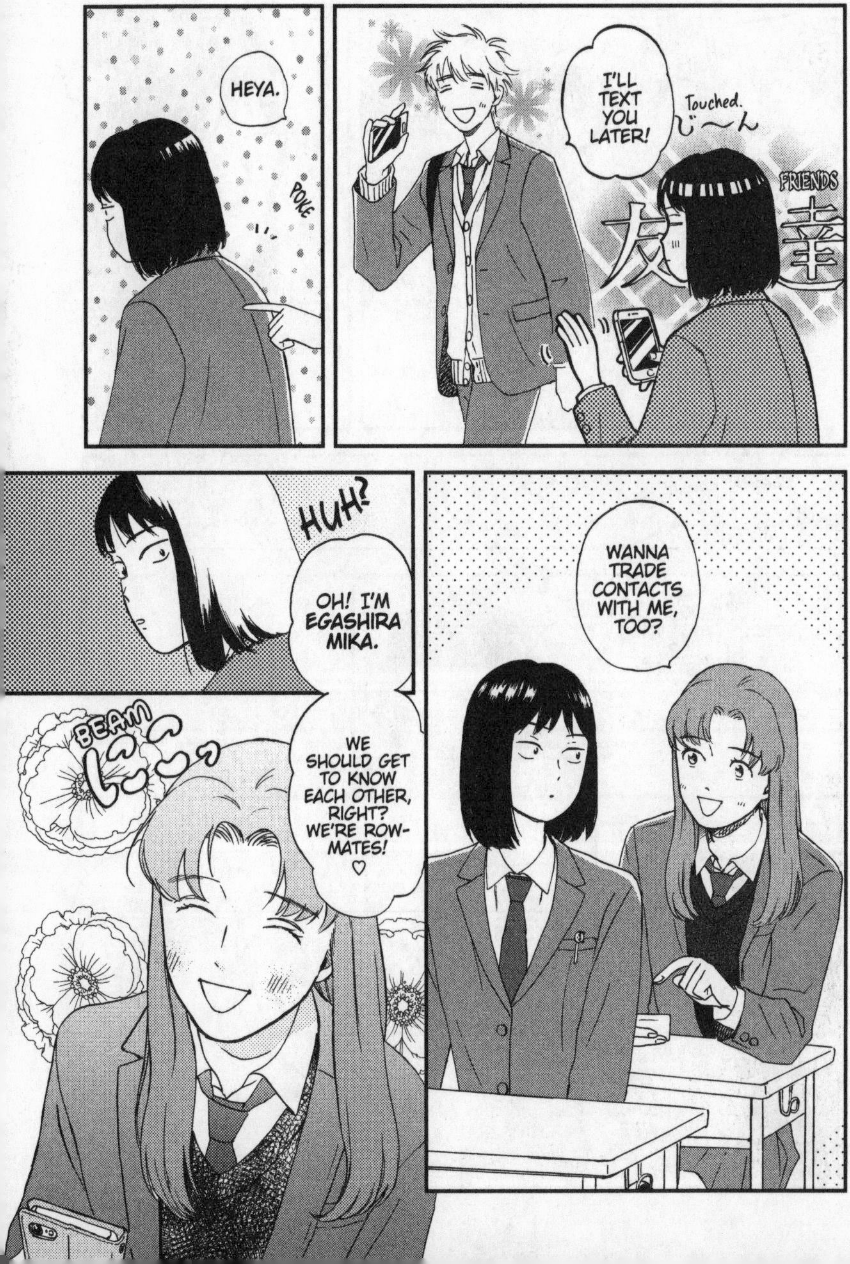
I'LL TEXT YOU LATER!
Touched.
じ〜ん
FRIENDS
友達
HEYA.
POKE
WANNA TRADE CONTACTS WITH ME, TOO?
HUH?
OH! I'M EGASHIRA MIKA.
BEAM
WE SHOULD GET TO KNOW EACH OTHER, RIGHT? WE'RE ROW-MATES! ♡

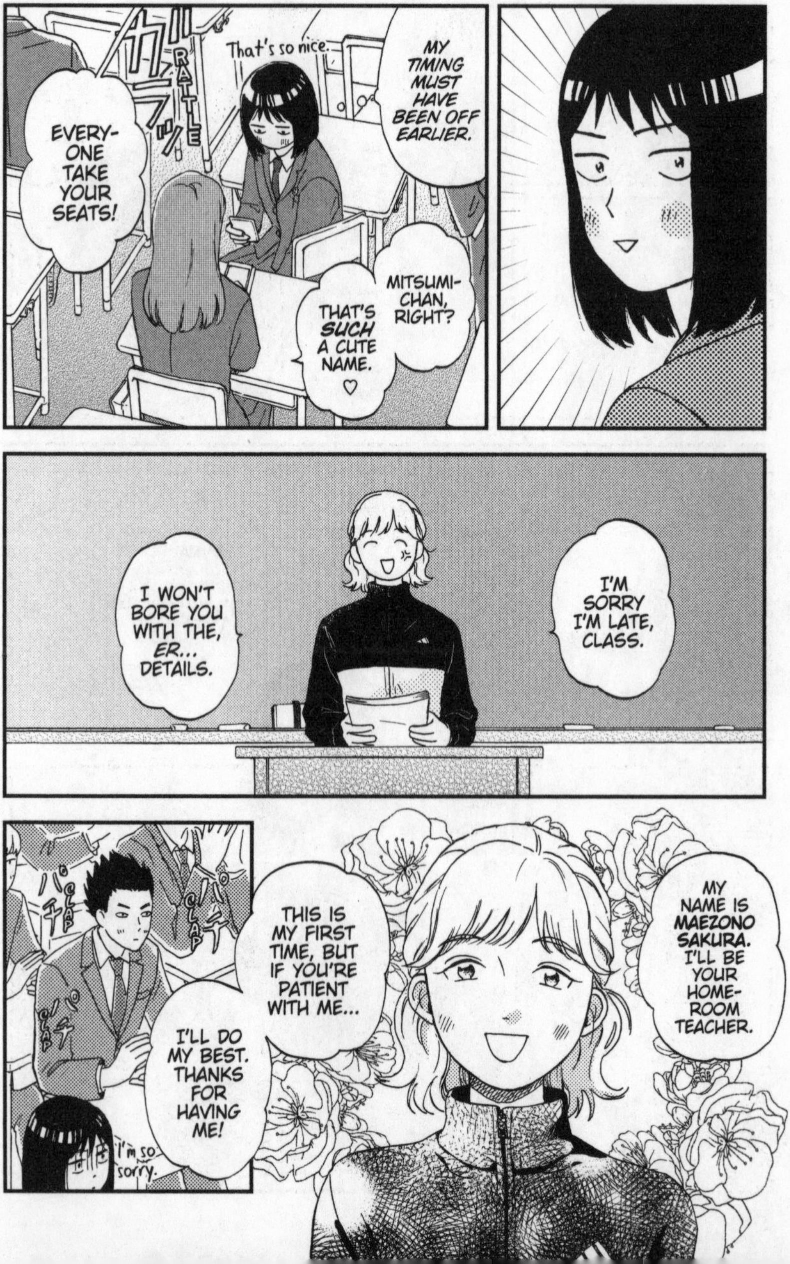
MY TIMING MUST HAVE BEEN OFF EARLIER.
That's so nice.
RATTLE
EVERYONE TAKE YOUR SEATS!
MITSUMI-CHAN, RIGHT?
THAT'S *SUCH* A CUTE NAME. ♡
I'M SORRY I'M LATE, CLASS.
I WON'T BORE YOU WITH THE, *ER*... DETAILS.
MY NAME IS MAEZONO SAKURA. I'LL BE YOUR HOMEROOM TEACHER.
THIS IS MY FIRST TIME, BUT IF YOU'RE PATIENT WITH ME...
I'LL DO MY BEST. THANKS FOR HAVING ME!
CLAP CLAP
CLAP
CLAP
I'm so sorry.

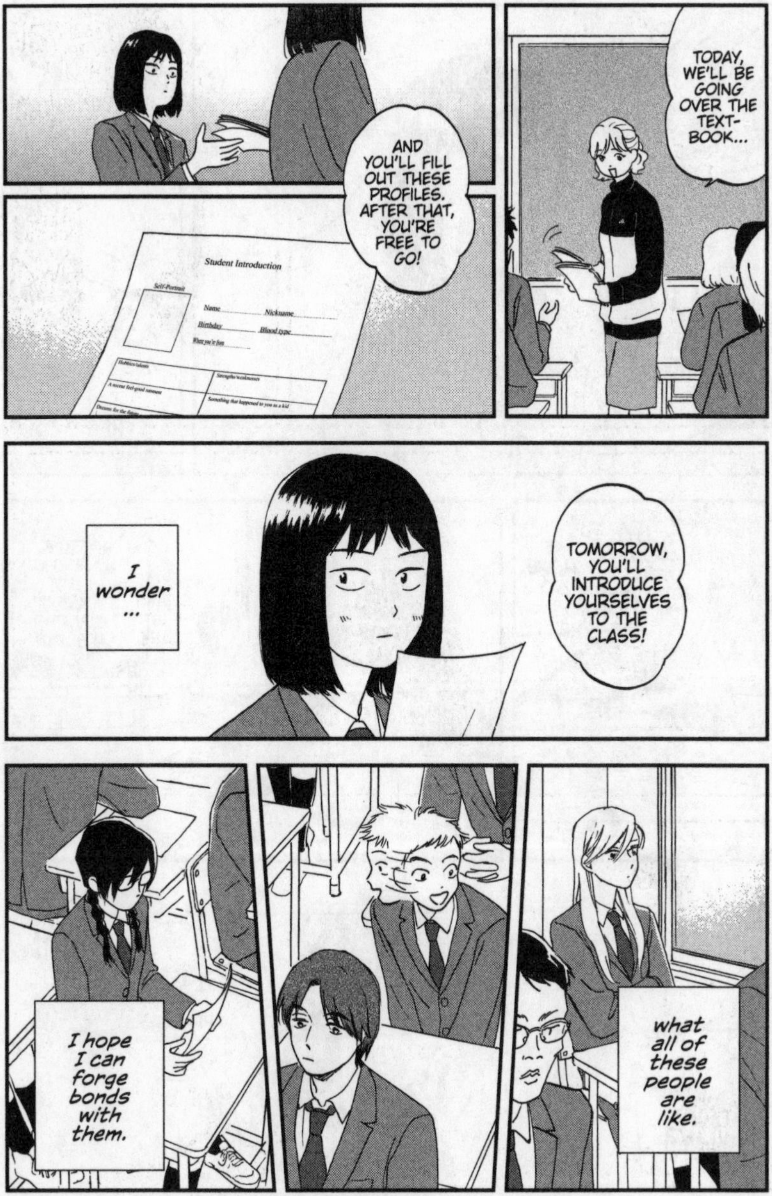
TODAY, WE'LL BE GOING OVER THE TEXT-BOOK...
AND YOU'LL FILL OUT THESE PROFILES. AFTER THAT, YOU'RE FREE TO GO!
Student Introduction
Self-Portrait
Name
Nickname
Birthday
Blood type
TOMORROW, YOU'LL INTRODUCE YOURSELVES TO THE CLASS!
I wonder ...
what all of these people are like.
I hope I can forge bonds with them.

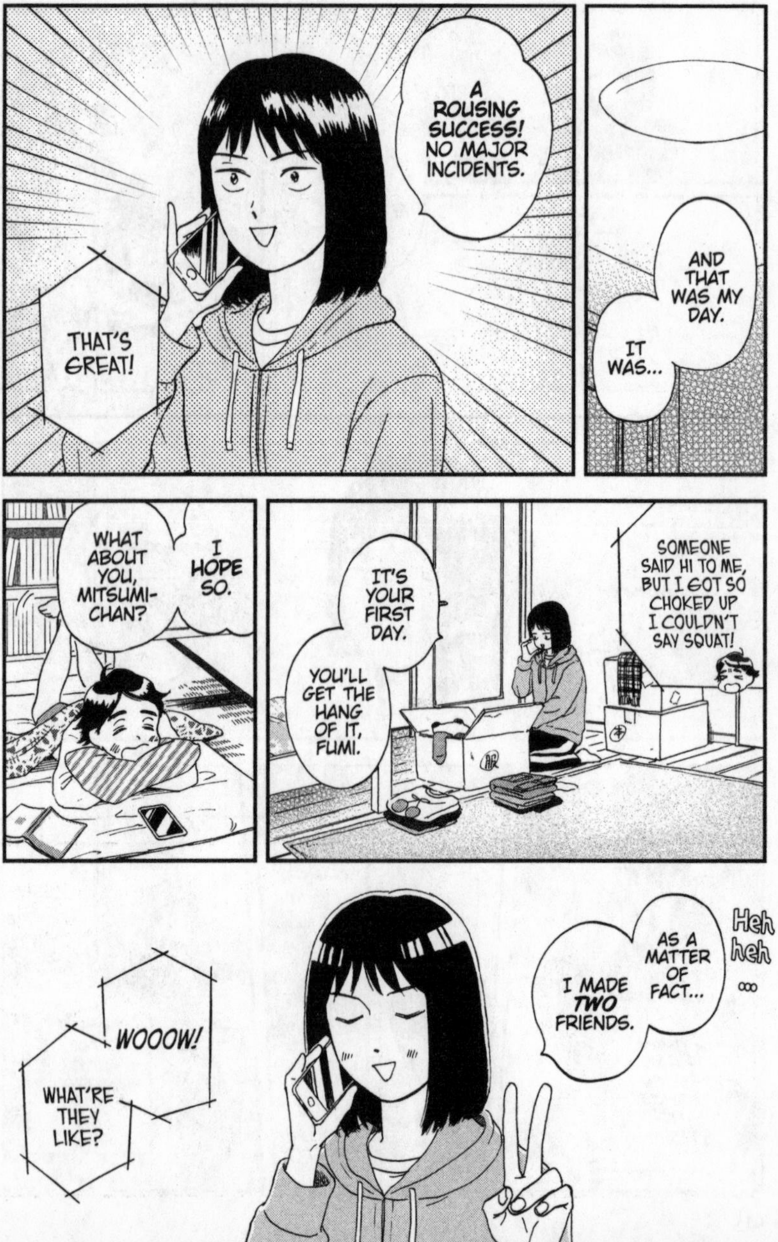
AND THAT WAS MY DAY.
IT WAS...
A ROUSING SUCCESS! NO MAJOR INCIDENTS.
THAT'S GREAT!
SOMEONE SAID HI TO ME, BUT I GOT SO CHOKED UP I COULDN'T SAY SQUAT!
IT'S YOUR FIRST DAY.
YOU'LL GET THE HANG OF IT, FUMI.
I HOPE SO.
WHAT ABOUT YOU, MITSUMI-CHAN?
Heh heh ...
AS A MATTER OF FACT...
I MADE *TWO* FRIENDS.
WOOOW!
WHAT'RE THEY LIKE?

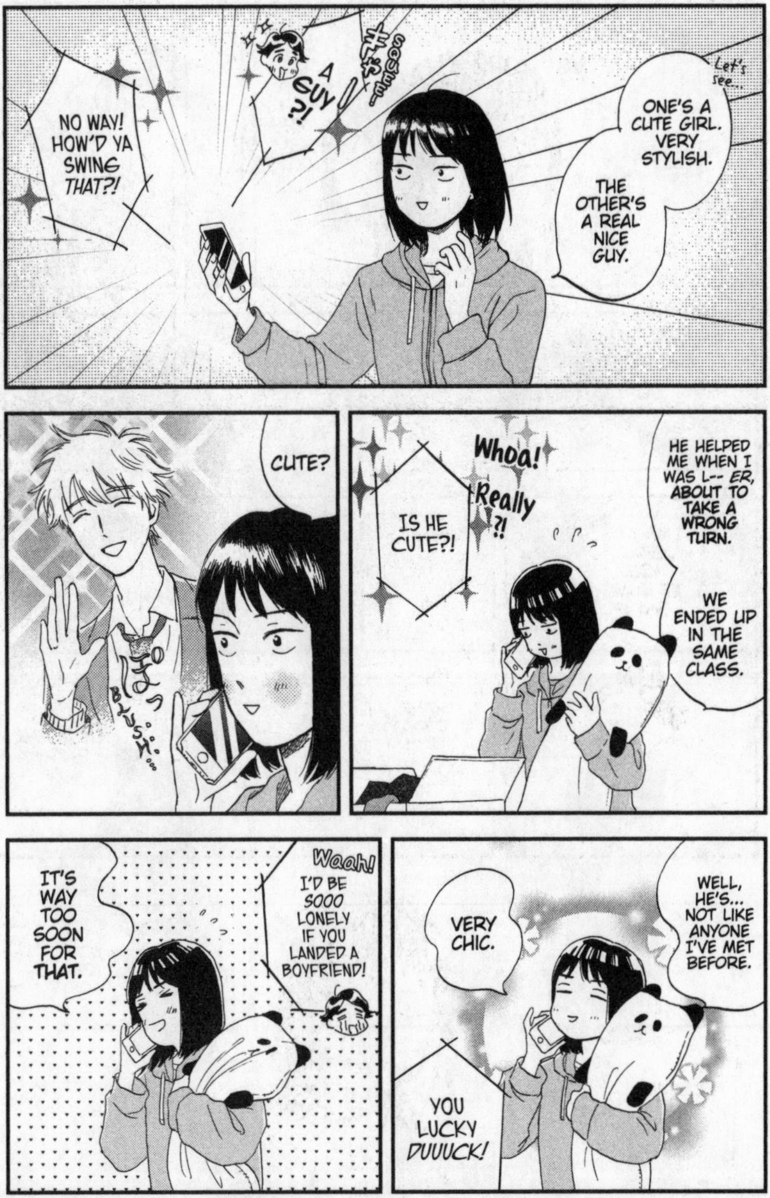
Let's see...
ONE'S A CUTE GIRL. VERY STYLISH.
THE OTHER'S A REAL NICE GUY.
キャー
SQUEE-
A GUY?!
NO WAY! HOW'D YA SWING *THAT*?!
HE HELPED ME WHEN I WAS L-- *ER*, ABOUT TO TAKE A WRONG TURN.
WE ENDED UP IN THE SAME CLASS.
Whoa!
Really?!
IS HE CUTE?!
CUTE?
ぽっ
BLUSH...
WELL, HE'S... NOT LIKE ANYONE I'VE MET BEFORE.
VERY CHIC.
YOU LUCKY *DUUUCK!*
Waah!
I'D BE SOOO LONELY IF YOU LANDED A BOYFRIEND!
IT'S WAY TOO SOON FOR THAT.

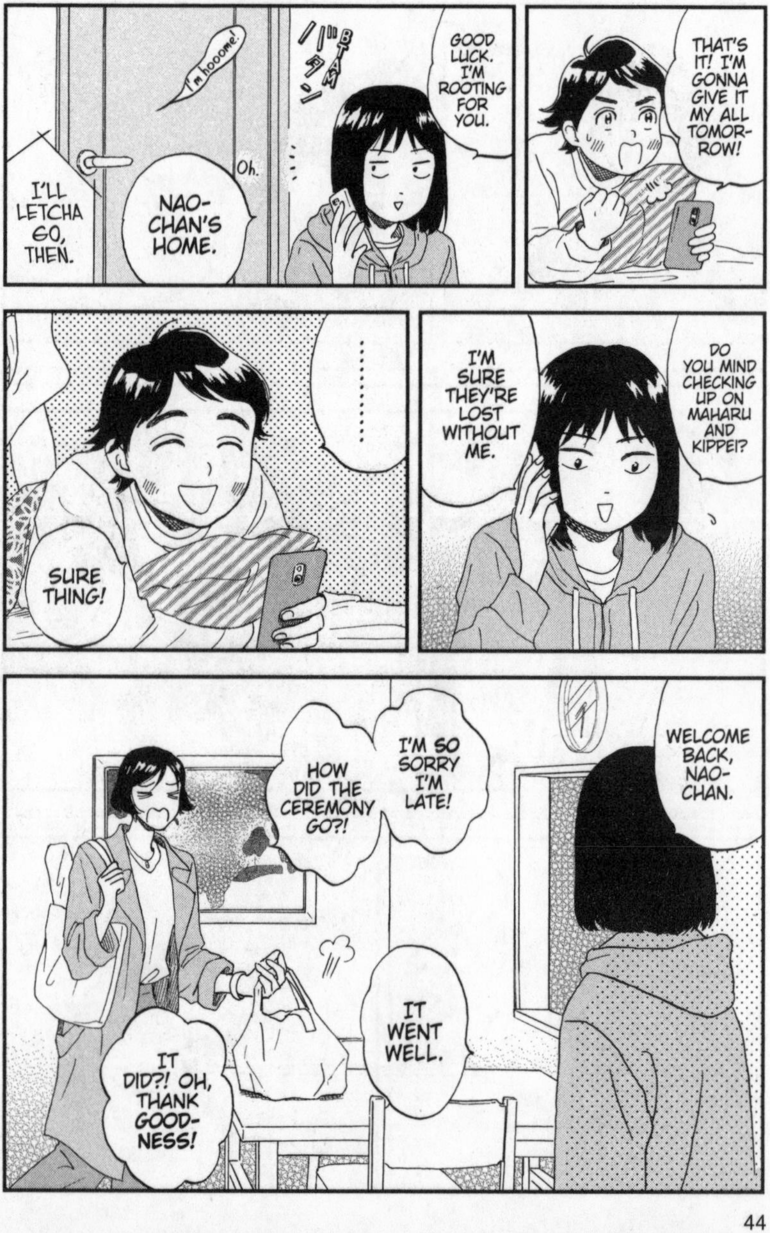

THAT'S IT! I'M GONNA GIVE IT MY ALL TOMORROW!
GOOD LUCK. I'M ROOTING FOR YOU.
BLAM
I'm hooome!
Oh.
NAO-CHAN'S HOME.
I'LL LETCHA GO, THEN.
DO YOU MIND CHECKING UP ON MAHARU AND KIPPEI?
I'M SURE THEY'RE LOST WITHOUT ME.
......
SURE THING!
WELCOME BACK, NAO-CHAN.
I'M SO SORRY I'M LATE!
HOW DID THE CEREMONY GO?!
IT WENT WELL.
IT DID?! OH, THANK GOODNESS!

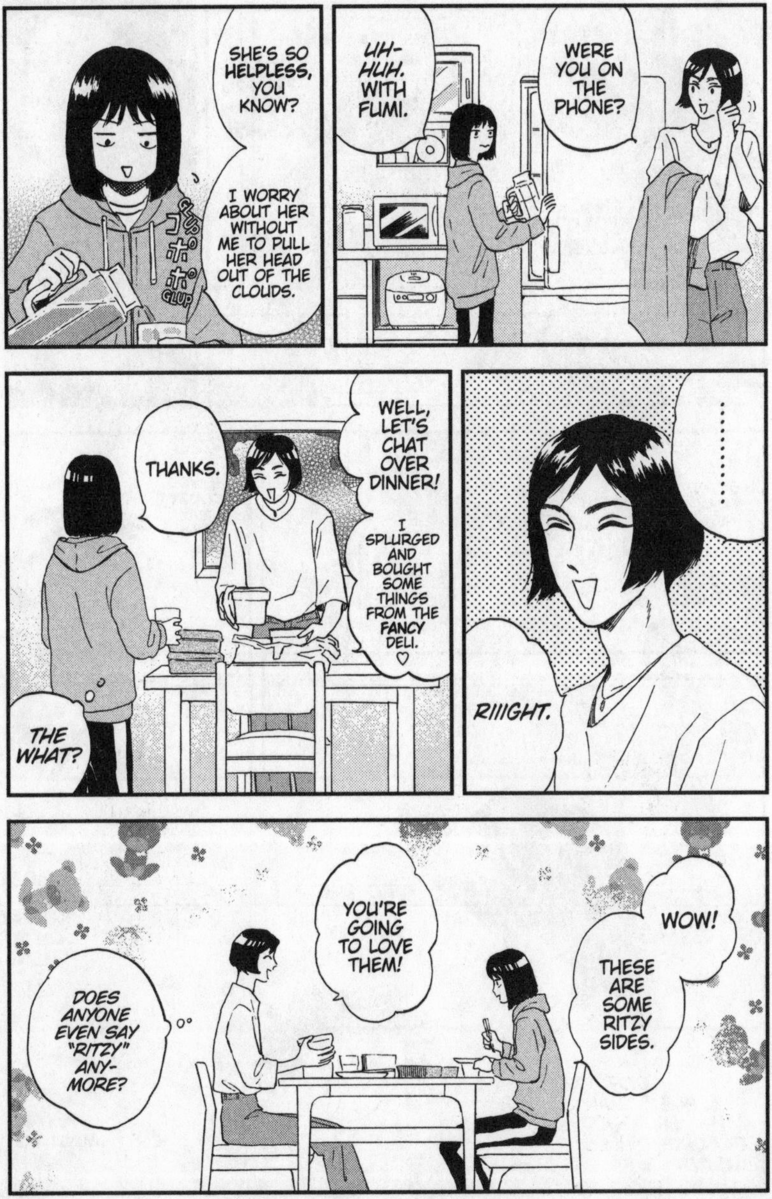
WERE YOU ON THE PHONE?
UH-HUH. WITH FUMI.
SHE'S SO HELPLESS, YOU KNOW?
I WORRY ABOUT HER WITHOUT ME TO PULL HER HEAD OUT OF THE CLOUDS.
GLUP ゴポポ GLUP
......
RIIIGHT.
WELL, LET'S CHAT OVER DINNER!
I SPLURGED AND BOUGHT SOME THINGS FROM THE FANCY DELI. ♡
THANKS.
THE WHAT?
WOW!
THESE ARE SOME RITZY SIDES.
YOU'RE GOING TO LOVE THEM!
DOES ANYONE EVEN SAY "RITZY" ANY-MORE?

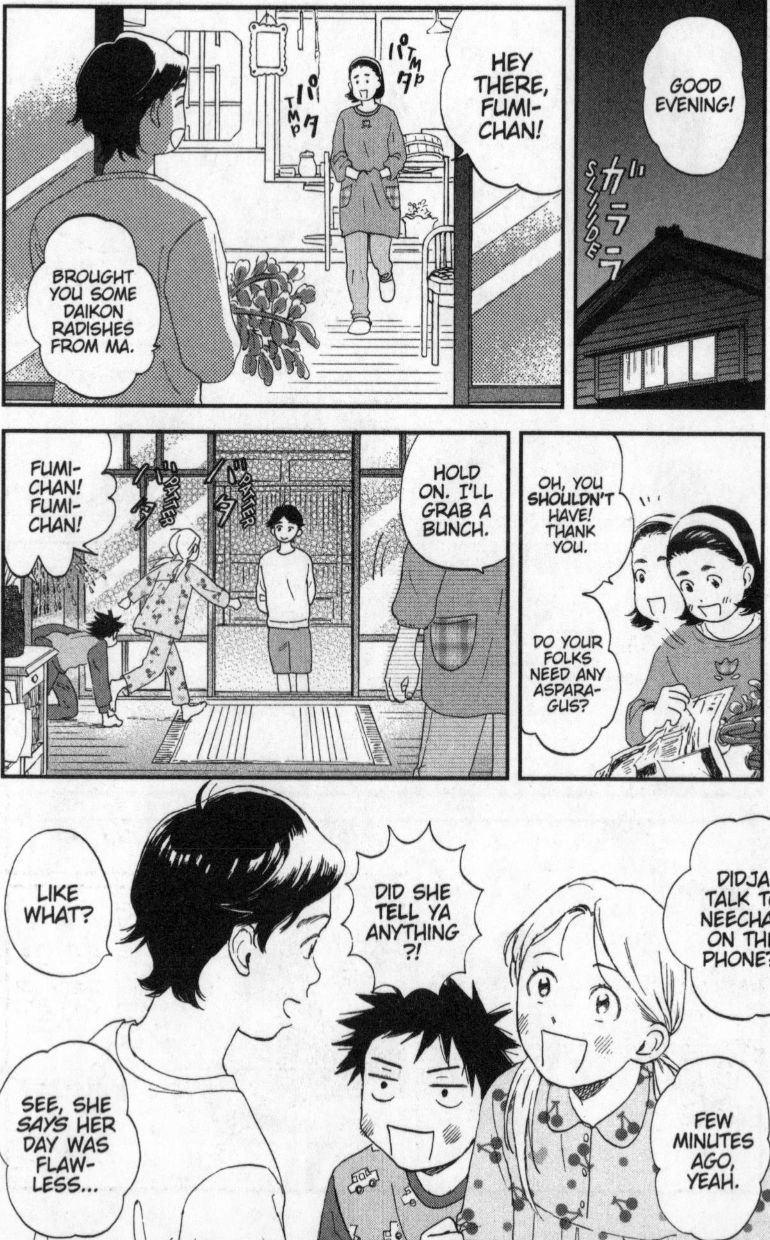
GOOD EVENING!
SLIDE
HEY THERE, FUMI-CHAN!
TMP
TMP
BROUGHT YOU SOME DAIKON RADISHES FROM MA.
OH, YOU SHOULDN'T HAVE! THANK YOU.
DO YOUR FOLKS NEED ANY ASPARAGUS?
HOLD ON. I'LL GRAB A BUNCH.
PATTER
PATTER
FUMI-CHAN! FUMI-CHAN!
DIDJA TALK TO NEECHAN ON THE PHONE?!
DID SHE TELL YA ANYTHING?!
LIKE WHAT?
FEW MINUTES AGO, YEAH.
SEE, SHE SAYS HER DAY WAS FLAWLESS...

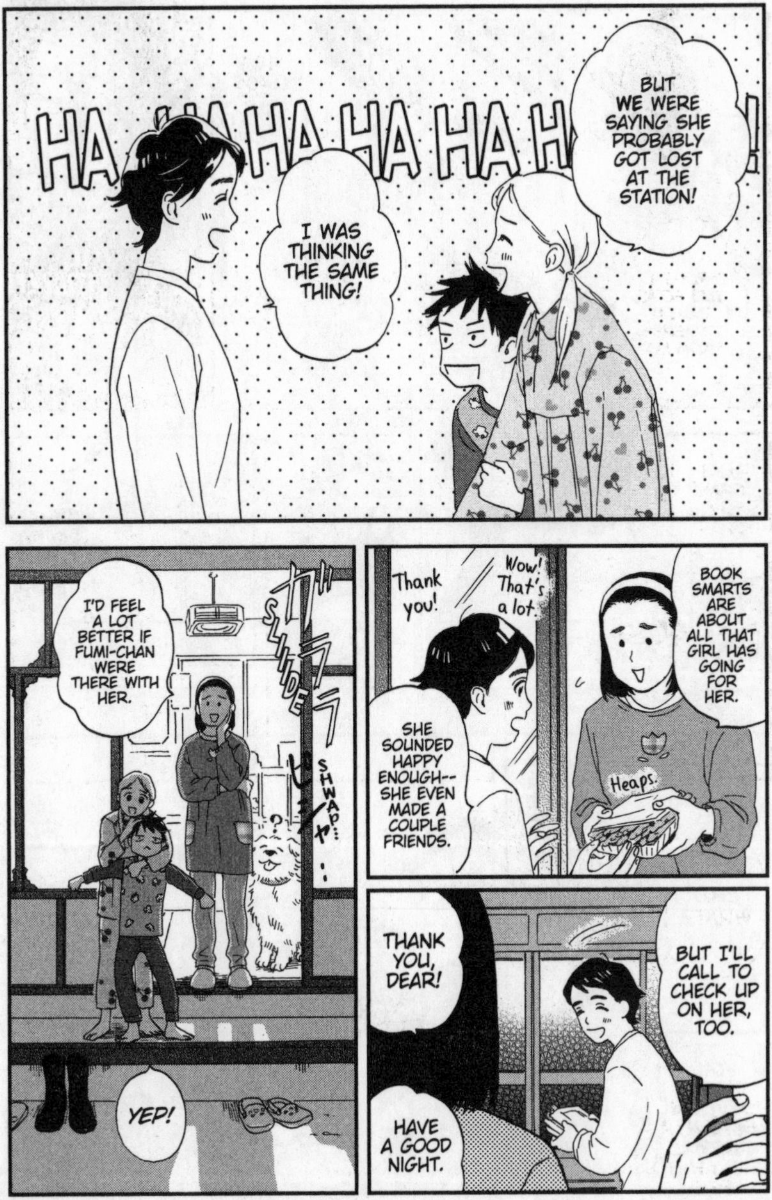
BUT WE WERE SAYING SHE PROBABLY GOT LOST AT THE STATION!
HA HA HA HA HA HA!
I WAS THINKING THE SAME THING!
BOOK SMARTS ARE ABOUT ALL THAT GIRL HAS GOING FOR HER.
SHE SOUNDED HAPPY ENOUGH-- SHE EVEN MADE A COUPLE FRIENDS.
Heaps.
Wow! That's a lot.
Thank you!
BUT I'LL CALL TO CHECK UP ON HER, TOO.
THANK YOU, DEAR!
HAVE A GOOD NIGHT.
I'D FEEL A LOT BETTER IF FUMI-CHAN WERE THERE WITH HER.
SLIDE
SHWAP...
?
YEP!

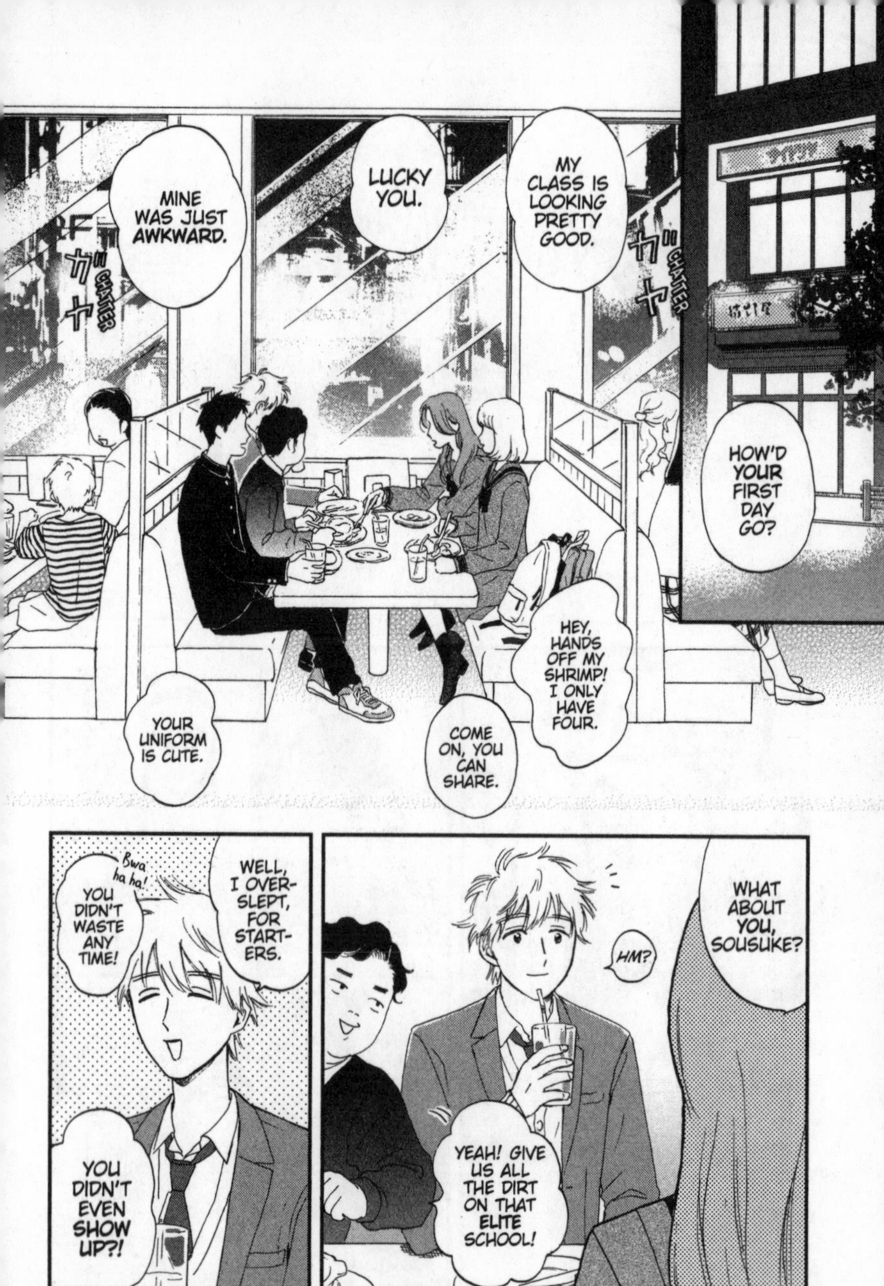
HOW'D YOUR FIRST DAY GO?
MY CLASS IS LOOKING PRETTY GOOD.
ガヤ CHATTER
LUCKY YOU.
MINE WAS JUST AWKWARD.
ガヤ CHATTER
HEY, HANDS OFF MY SHRIMP! I ONLY HAVE FOUR.
COME ON, YOU CAN SHARE.
YOUR UNIFORM IS CUTE.
WHAT ABOUT YOU, SOUSUKE?
HM?
YEAH! GIVE US ALL THE DIRT ON THAT ELITE SCHOOL!
WELL, I OVERSLEPT, FOR STARTERS.
Bwa ha ha!
YOU DIDN'T WASTE ANY TIME!
YOU DIDN'T EVEN SHOW UP?!

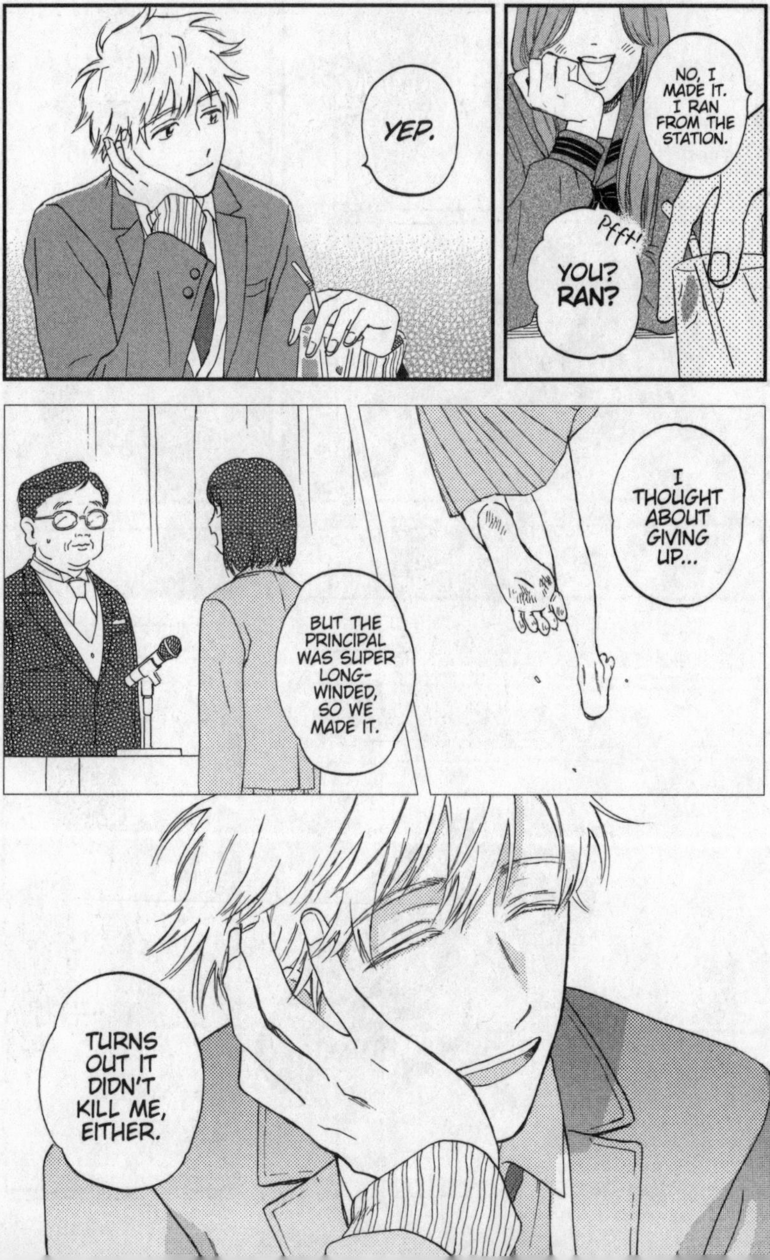
NO, I MADE IT. I RAN FROM THE STATION.
Pfft!
YOU? RAN?
YEP.
I THOUGHT ABOUT GIVING UP...
BUT THE PRINCIPAL WAS SUPER LONG-WINDED, SO WE MADE IT.
TURNS OUT IT DIDN'T KILL ME, EITHER.

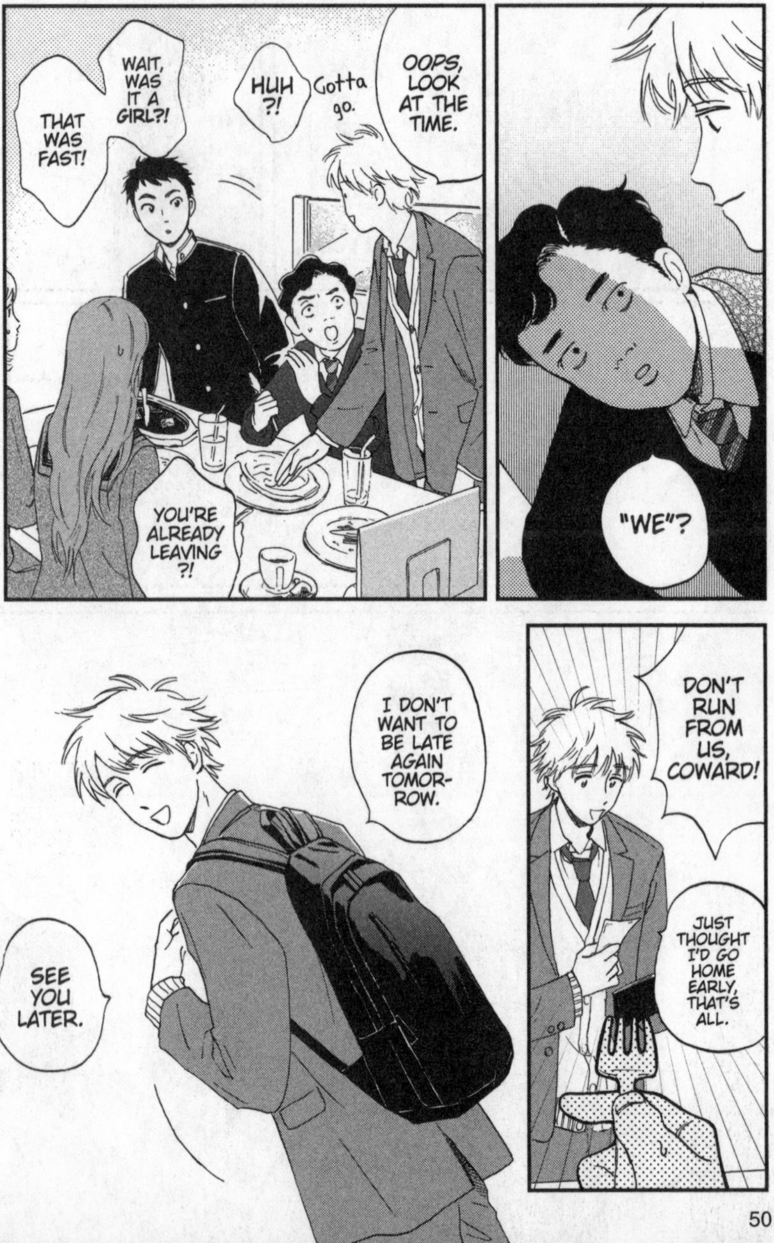
"WE"?
OOPS, LOOK AT THE TIME.
Gotta go.
HUH?!
WAIT, WAS IT A GIRL?!
THAT WAS FAST!
YOU'RE ALREADY LEAVING?!
DON'T RUN FROM US, COWARD!
JUST THOUGHT I'D GO HOME EARLY, THAT'S ALL.
I DON'T WANT TO BE LATE AGAIN TOMORROW.
SEE YOU LATER.

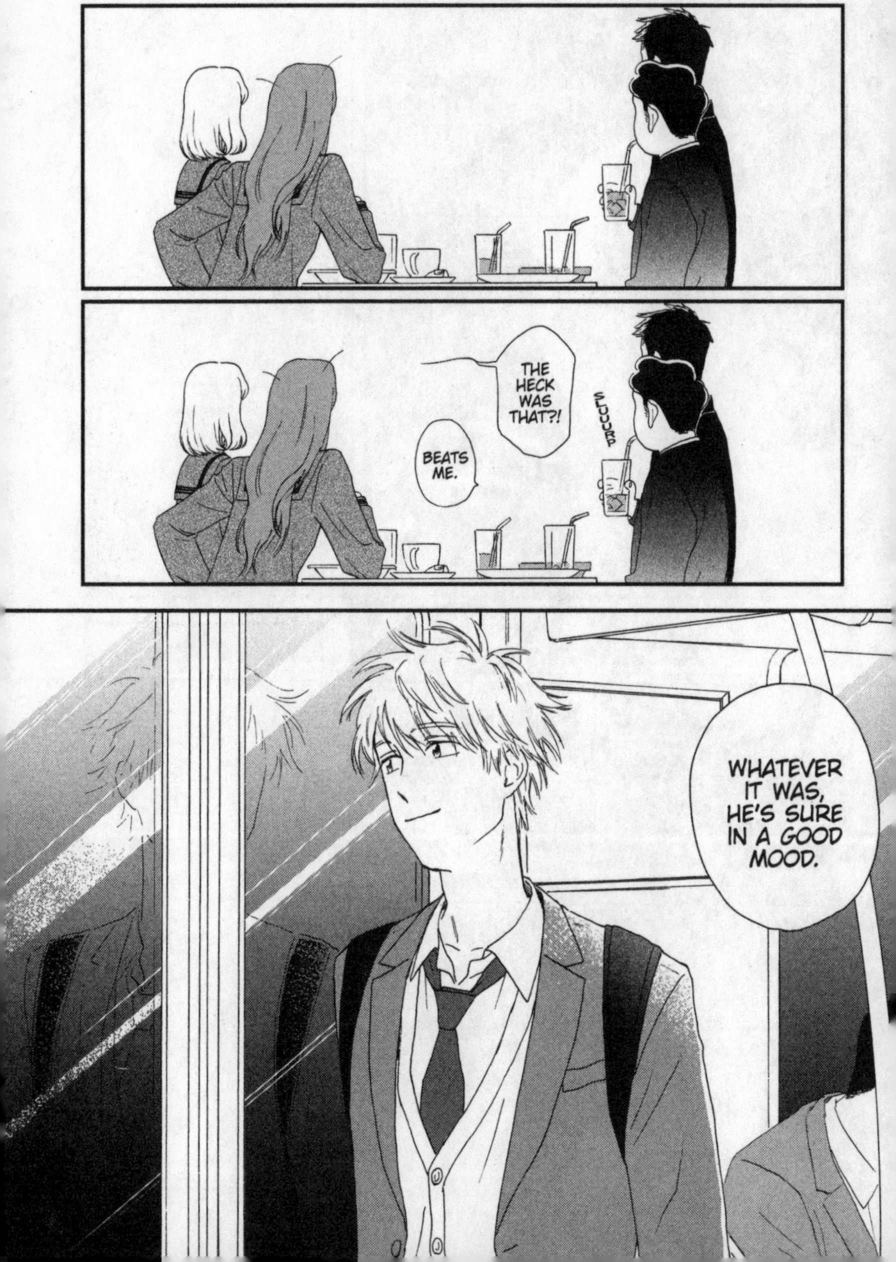
THE HECK WAS THAT?!
SLUUURP
BEATS ME.
WHATEVER IT WAS, HE'S SURE IN A GOOD MOOD.

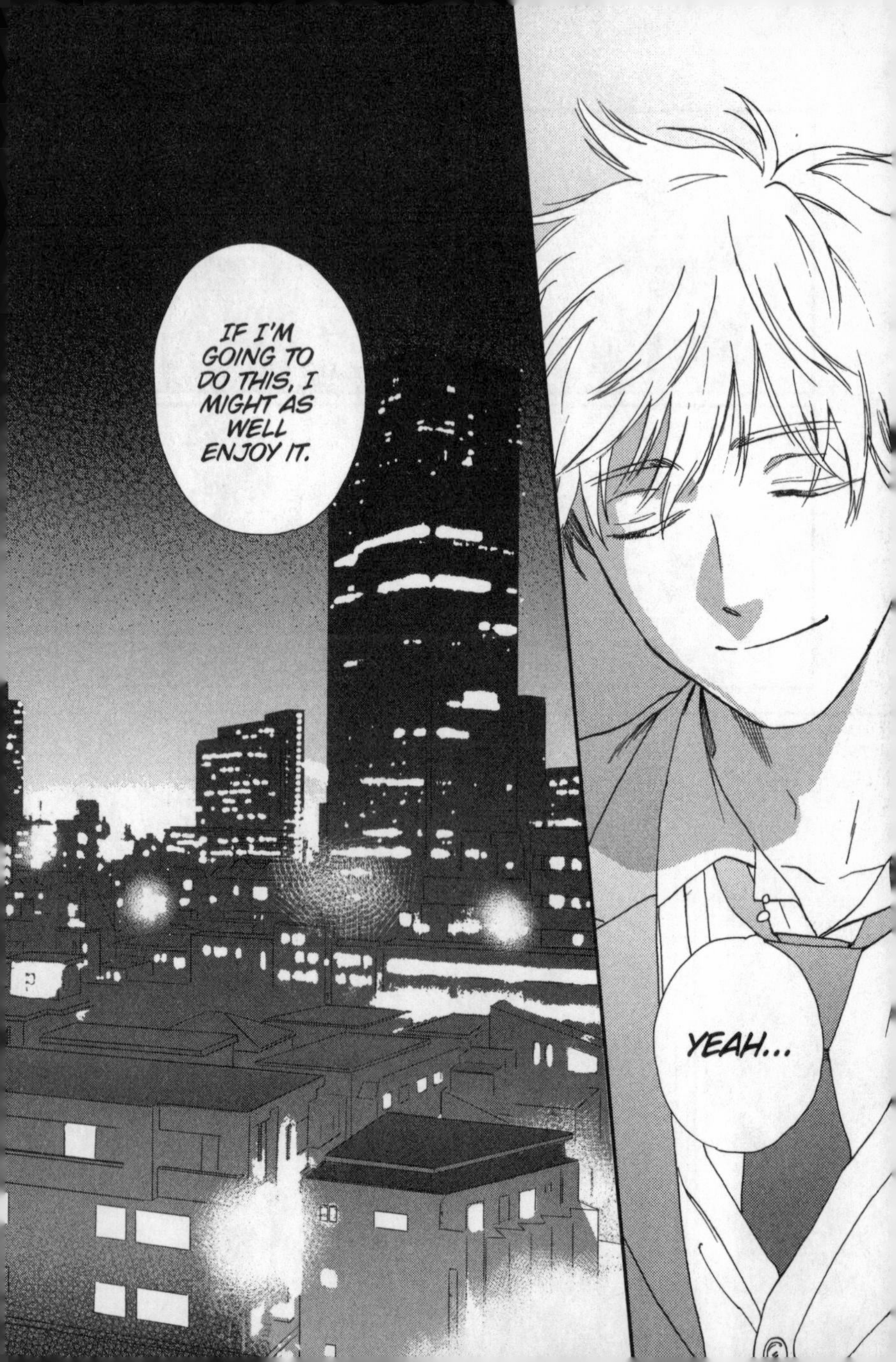
YEAH...
IF I'M GOING TO DO THIS, I MIGHT AS WELL ENJOY IT.

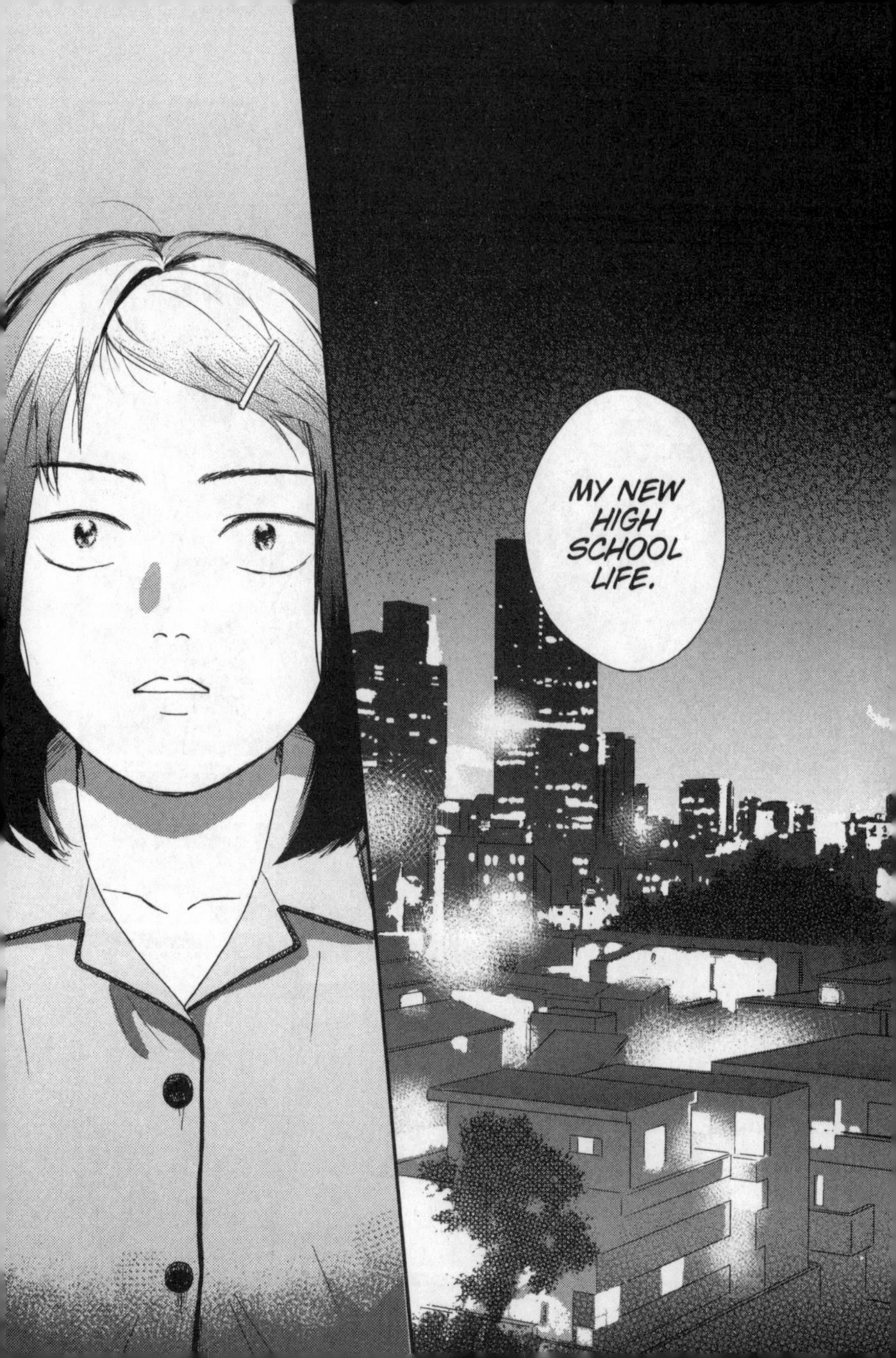
MY NEW HIGH SCHOOL LIFE.

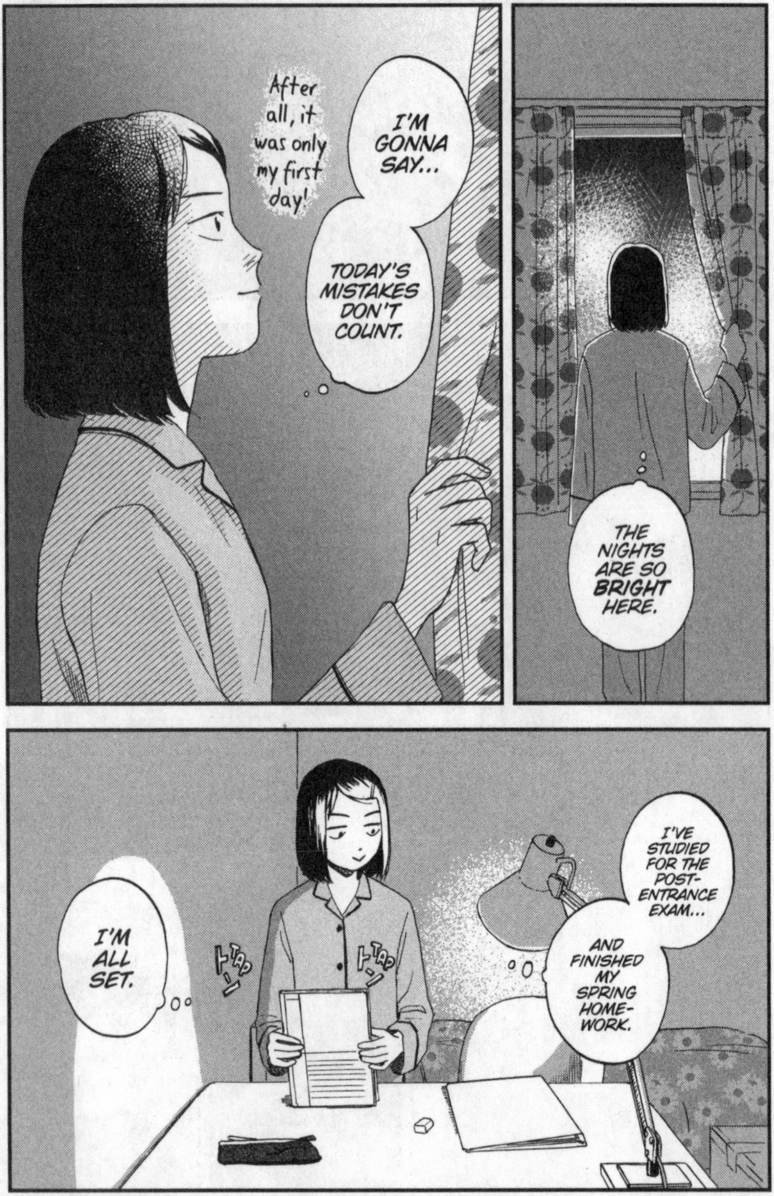
THE NIGHTS ARE SO BRIGHT HERE.
I'M GONNA SAY...
TODAY'S MISTAKES DON'T COUNT.
After all, it was only my first day!
I'VE STUDIED FOR THE POST-ENTRANCE EXAM...
AND FINISHED MY SPRING HOME-WORK.
TAP
TAP
I'M ALL SET.

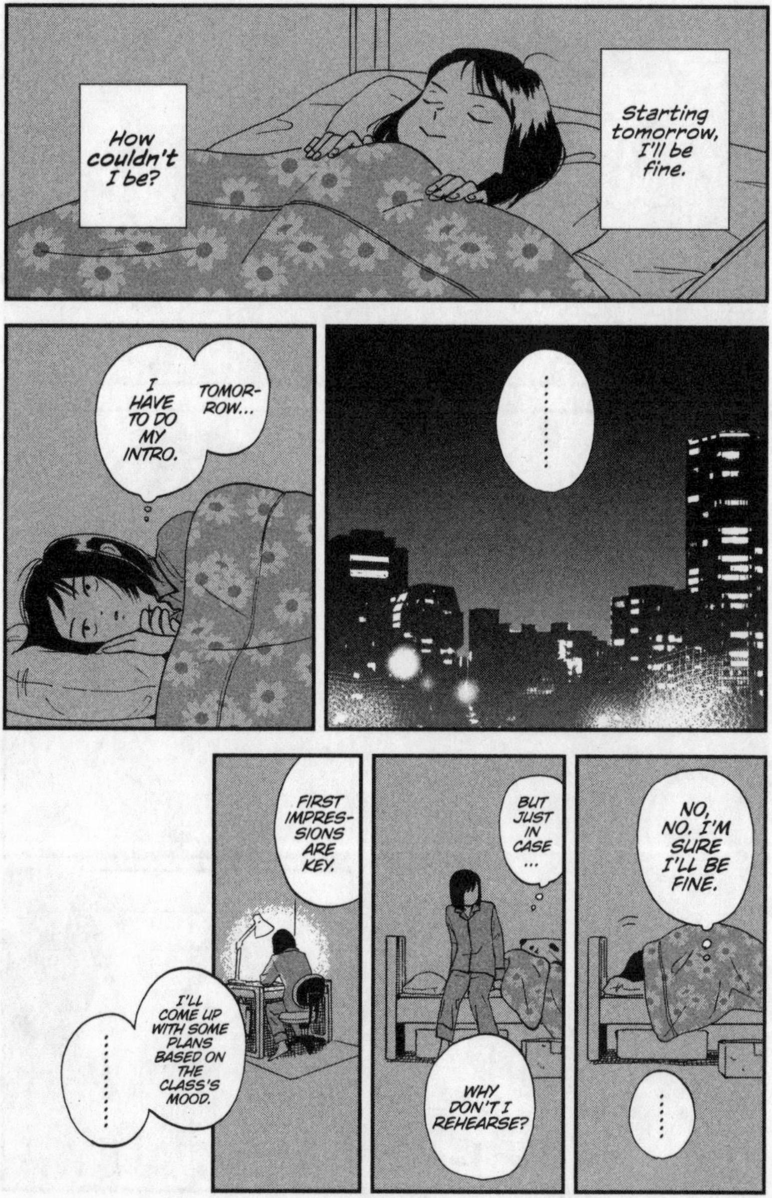
Starting tomorrow, I'll be fine.
How couldn't I be?
......
TOMORROW...
I HAVE TO DO MY INTRO.
NO, NO. I'M SURE I'LL BE FINE.
......
BUT JUST IN CASE...
WHY DON'T I REHEARSE?
FIRST IMPRESSIONS ARE KEY.
I'LL COME UP WITH SOME PLANS BASED ON THE CLASS'S MOOD.
......

OH!

GOOD MORNING, MI--

CLICK

First impressions are key.

YIKES.

Scene ① END

Skip and Loafer

Skip
and
Loafer

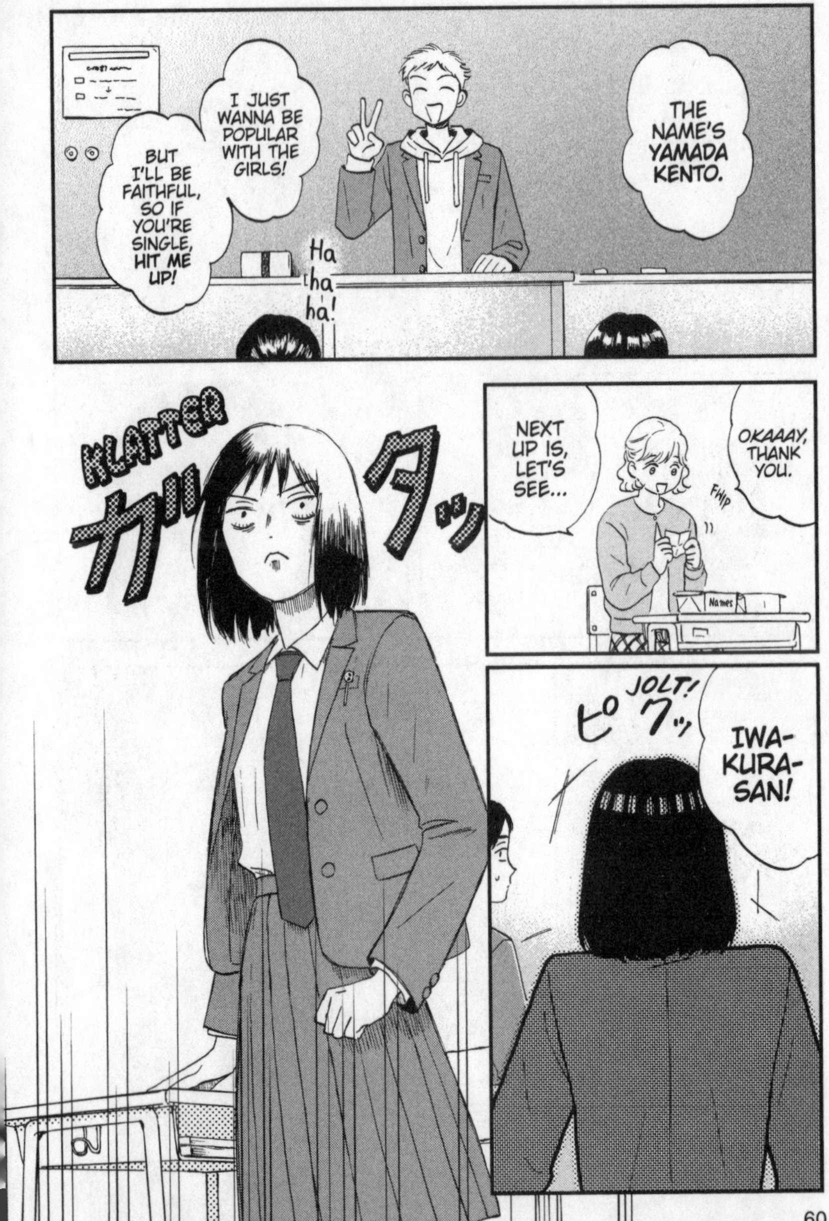
THE NAME'S YAMADA KENTO.
I JUST WANNA BE POPULAR WITH THE GIRLS!
BUT I'LL BE FAITHFUL, SO IF YOU'RE SINGLE, HIT ME UP!
Ha ha ha!
OKAAAY, THANK YOU.
FLIP
NEXT UP IS, LET'S SEE...
Names
IWAKURA-SAN!
JOLT!
ピクッ
KLATTER
ガタッ

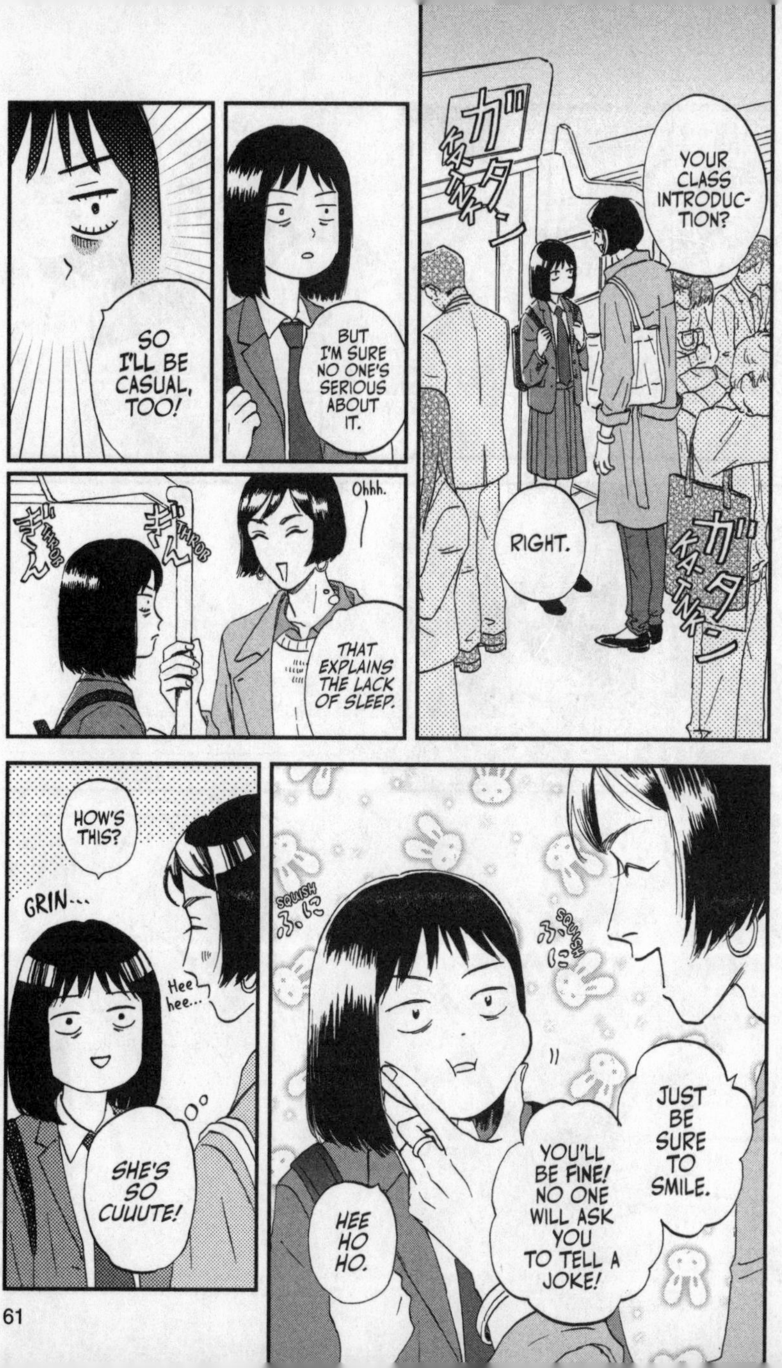
KA-TNK
YOUR CLASS INTRODUCTION?
RIGHT.
KA-TNK
BUT I'M SURE NO ONE'S SERIOUS ABOUT IT.
SO I'LL BE CASUAL, TOO!
THROB
THROB
Ohhh.
THAT EXPLAINS THE LACK OF SLEEP.
JUST BE SURE TO SMILE.
SQUISH
SQUISH
YOU'LL BE FINE! NO ONE WILL ASK YOU TO TELL A JOKE!
HEE HO HO.
HOW'S THIS?
GRIN...
Hee hee...
SHE'S SO CUUUTE!

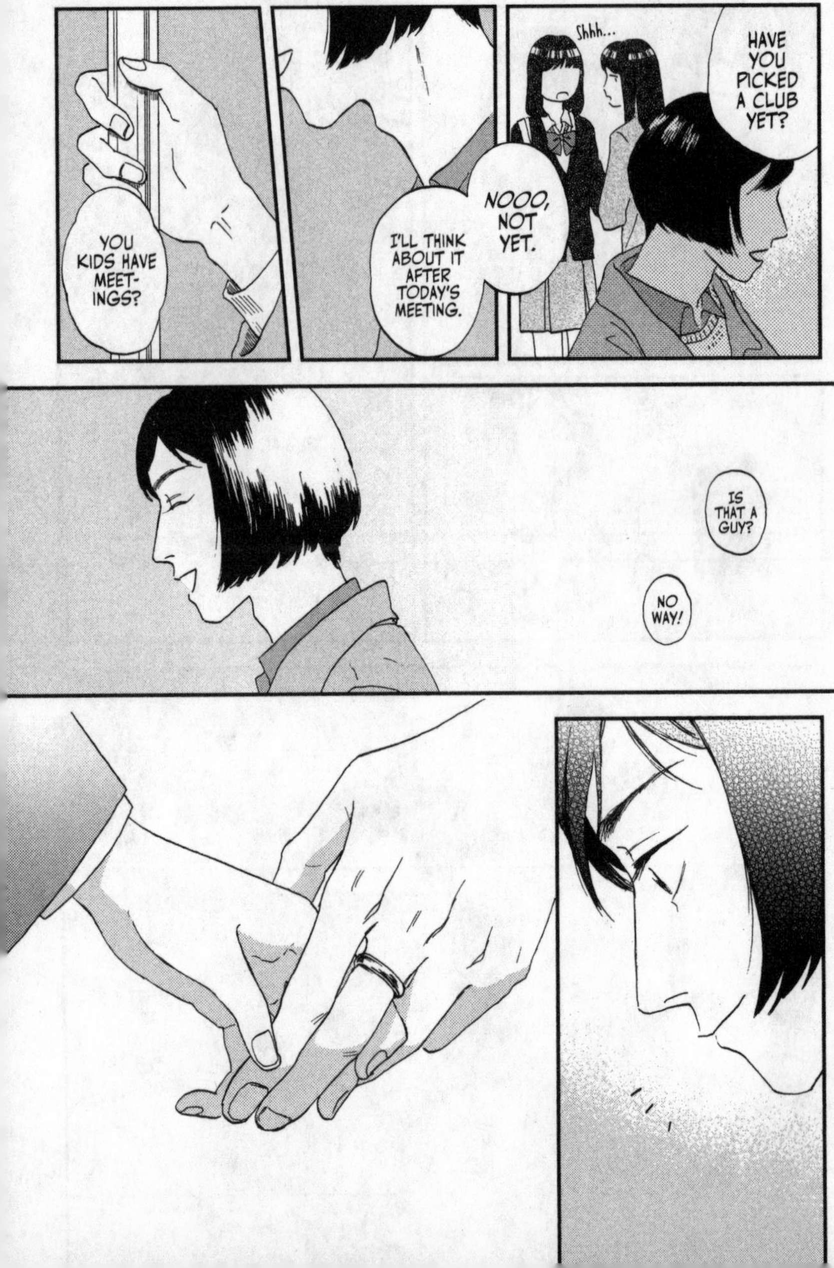
HAVE YOU PICKED A CLUB YET?
Shhh...
NOOO, NOT YET.
I'LL THINK ABOUT IT AFTER TODAY'S MEETING.
YOU KIDS HAVE MEET-INGS?
IS THAT A GUY?
NO WAY!

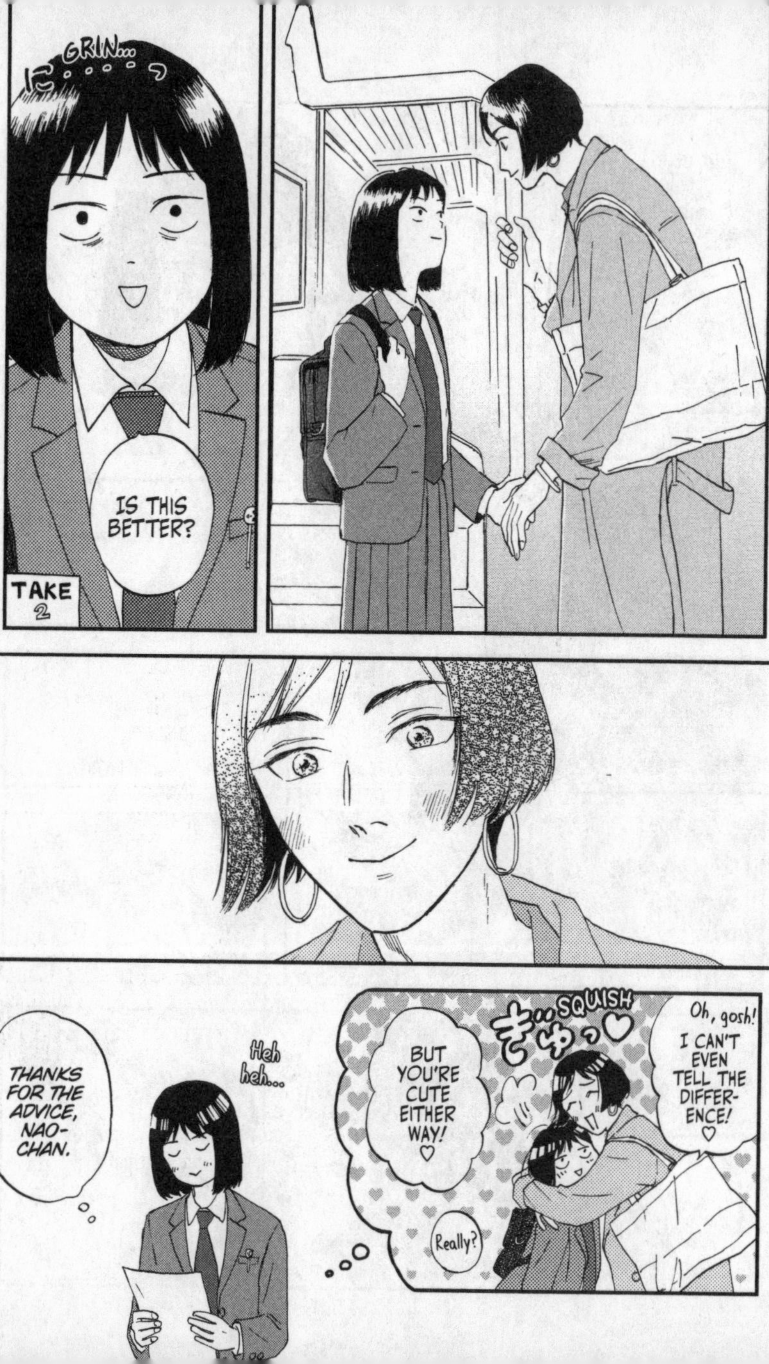
GRIN...
IS THIS BETTER?
TAKE 2
Oh, gosh! I CAN'T EVEN TELL THE DIFFER-ENCE! ♡
ぎゅっ♡ SQUISH
BUT YOU'RE CUTE EITHER WAY! ♡
Really?
Heh heh...
THANKS FOR THE ADVICE, NAO-CHAN.

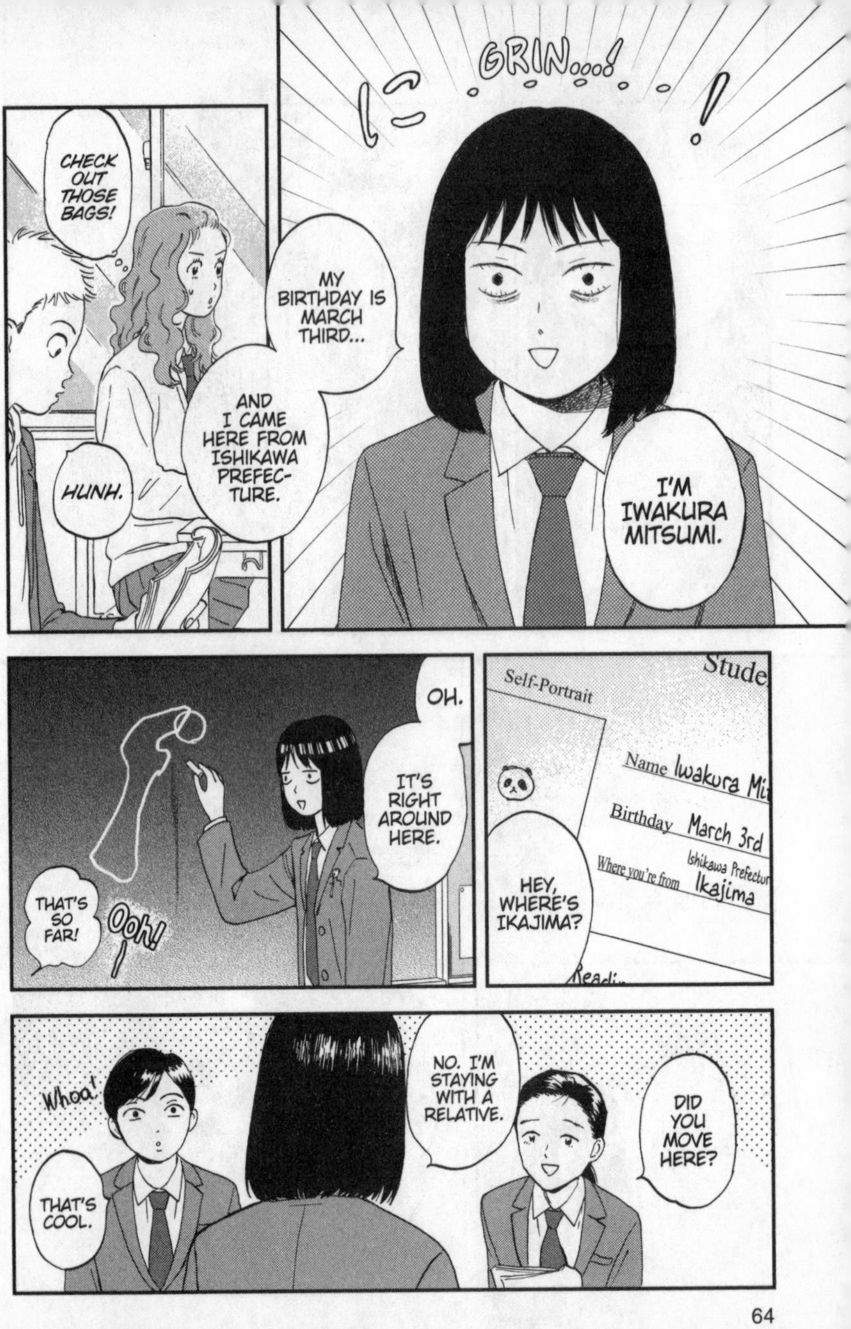
GRIN...!
I'M IWAKURA MITSUMI.
MY BIRTHDAY IS MARCH THIRD...
AND I CAME HERE FROM ISHIKAWA PREFEC- TURE.
CHECK OUT THOSE BAGS!
HUNH.
Stude
Self-Portrait
Name Iwakura Mi
Birthday March 3rd
Where you're from Ishikawa Prefectur Ikajima
Readi
HEY, WHERE'S IKAJIMA?
OH.
IT'S RIGHT AROUND HERE.
Ooh!
THAT'S SO FAR!
DID YOU MOVE HERE?
NO. I'M STAYING WITH A RELATIVE.
Whoa!
THAT'S COOL.

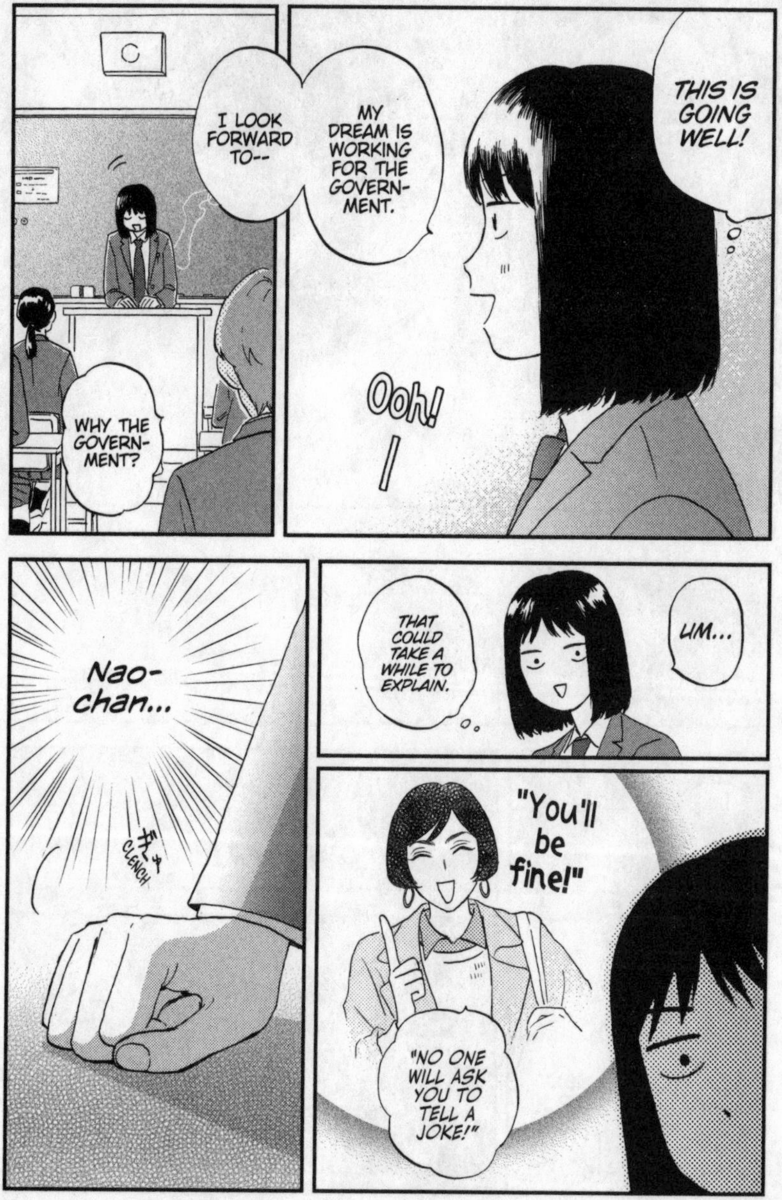
THIS IS GOING WELL!
MY DREAM IS WORKING FOR THE GOVERN-MENT.
I LOOK FORWARD TO--
Ooh!
WHY THE GOVERN-MENT?
UM...
THAT COULD TAKE A WHILE TO EXPLAIN.
"You'll be fine!"
"NO ONE WILL ASK YOU TO TELL A JOKE!"
Nao-chan...
CLENCH

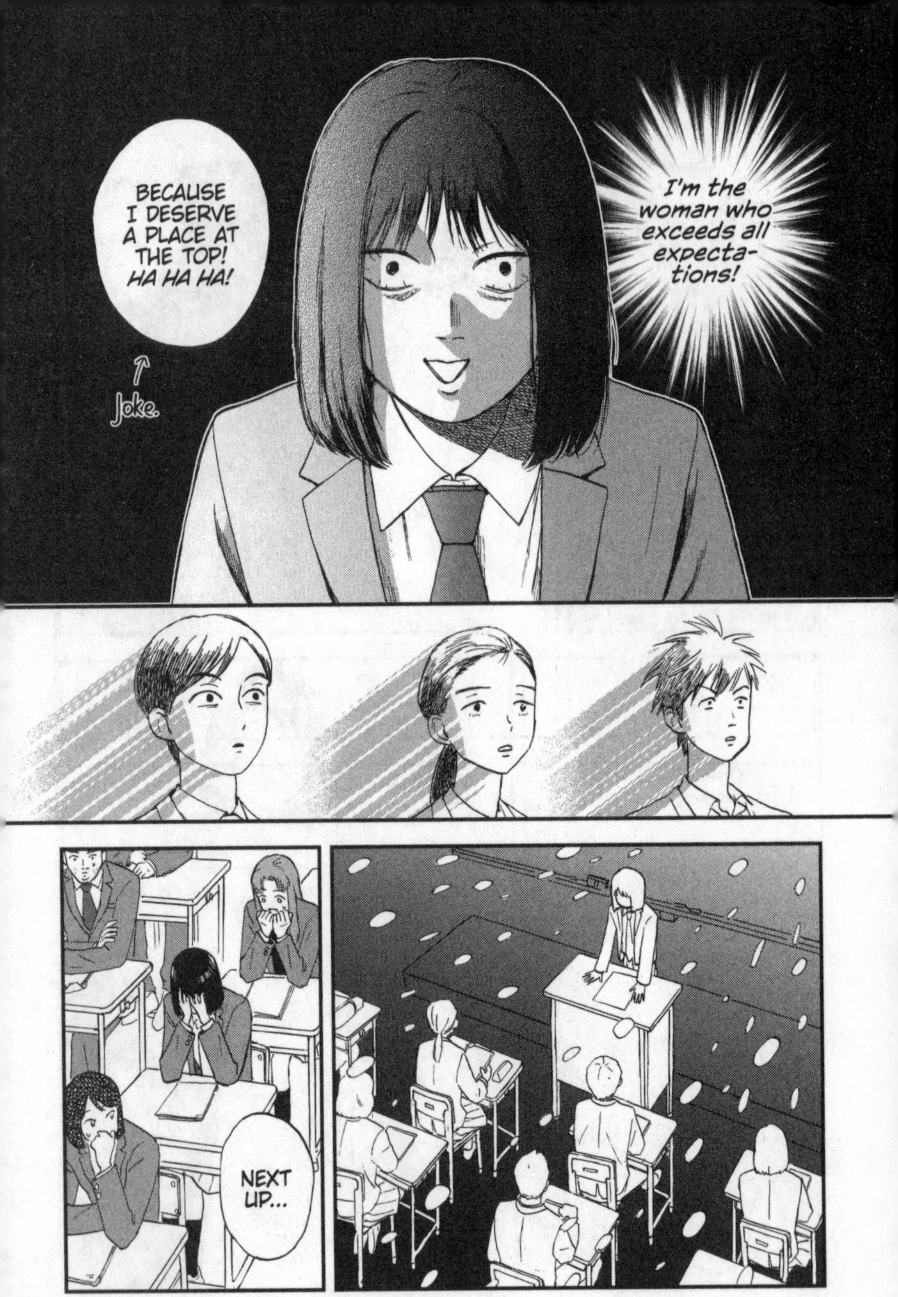
I'm the woman who exceeds all expectations!
BECAUSE I DESERVE A PLACE AT THE TOP! HA HA HA!
Joke.
NEXT UP...

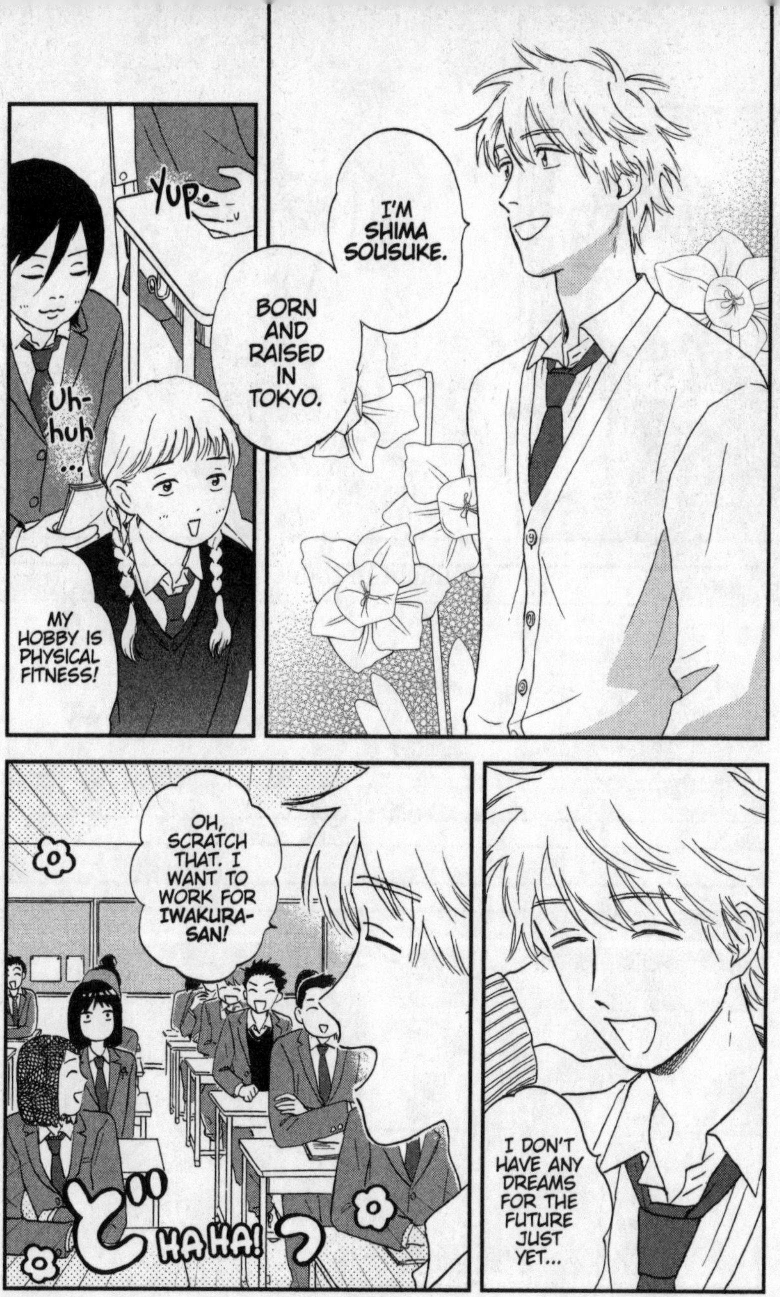
I'M SHIMA SOUSUKE.
BORN AND RAISED IN TOKYO.
Yup.
Uh-huh...
MY HOBBY IS PHYSICAL FITNESS!
I DON'T HAVE ANY DREAMS FOR THE FUTURE JUST YET...
OH, SCRATCH THAT. I WANT TO WORK FOR IWAKURA-SAN!
ど HAHA! っ

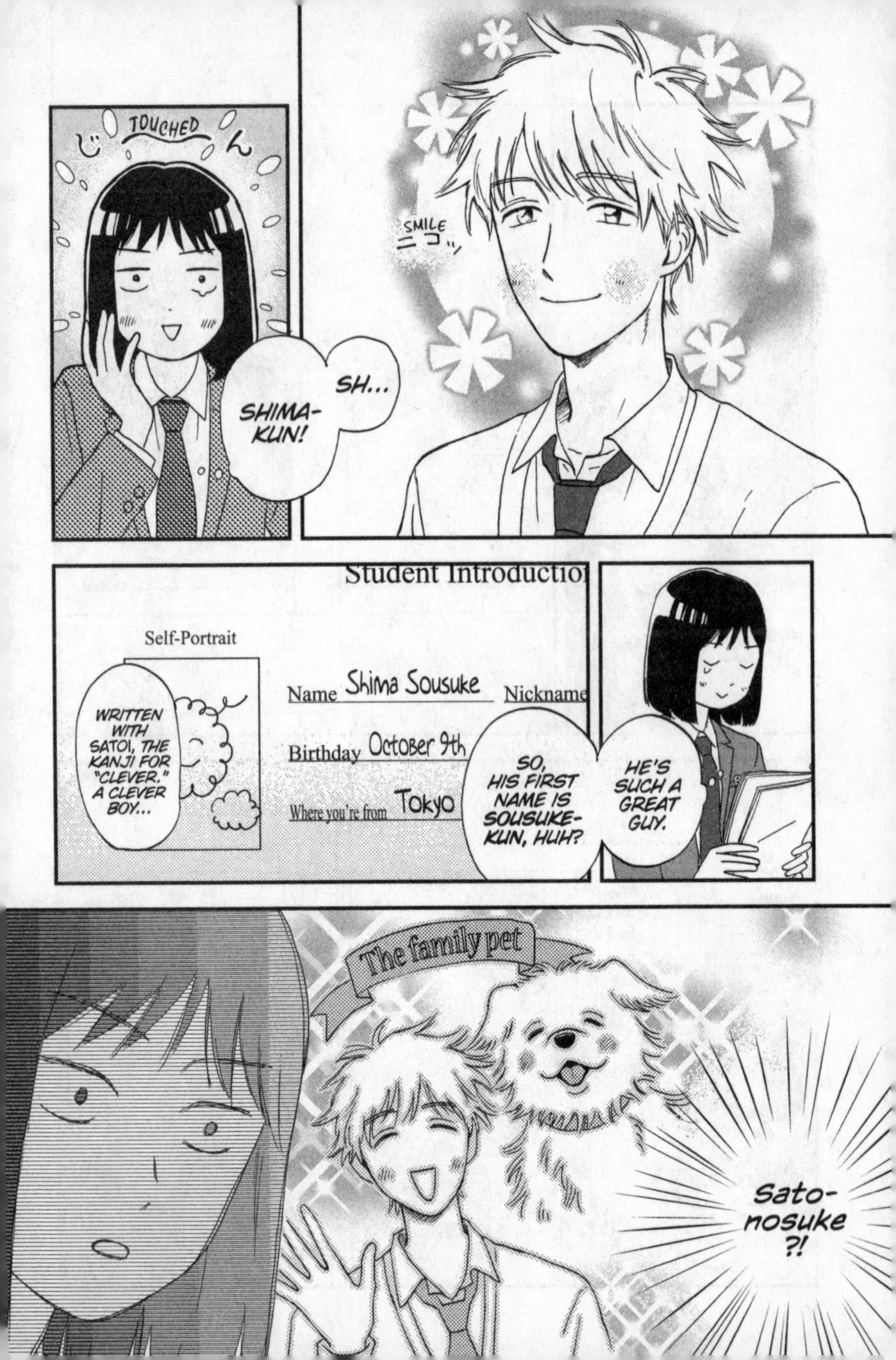
SMILE
ニコッ
TOUCHED
じ
ん
SH... SHIMA-KUN!
HE'S SUCH A GREAT GUY.
SO, HIS FIRST NAME IS SOUSUKE-KUN, HUH?
Student Introductio
Self-Portrait
Name Shima Sousuke
Nickname
Birthday October 9th
Where you're from Tokyo
WRITTEN WITH SATOI, THE KANJI FOR "CLEVER." A CLEVER BOY...
The family pet
Sato-nosuke ?!

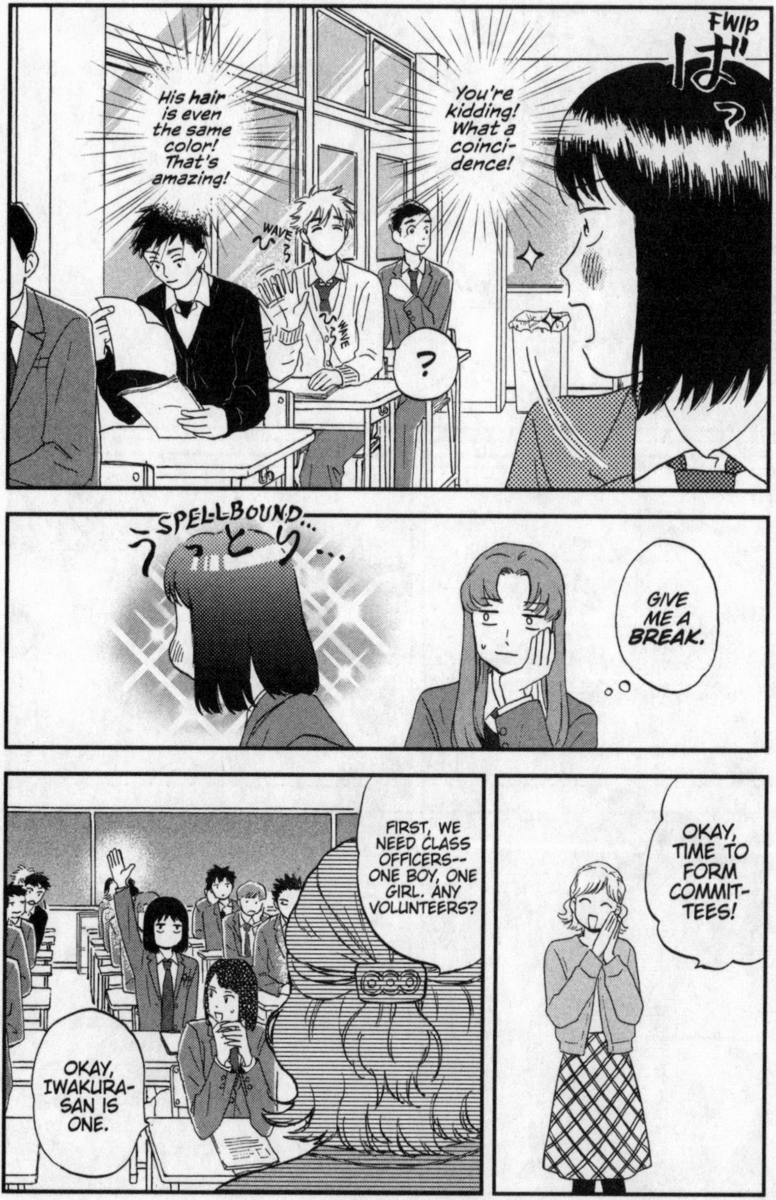
FWIP
ばっ
You're kidding! What a coincidence!
His hair is even the same color! That's amazing!
WAVE
WAVE
?
GIVE ME A BREAK.
SPELLBOUND...
うっとり…
OKAY, TIME TO FORM COMMITTEES!
FIRST, WE NEED CLASS OFFICERS-- ONE BOY, ONE GIRL. ANY VOLUNTEERS?
OKAY, IWAKURA-SAN IS ONE.

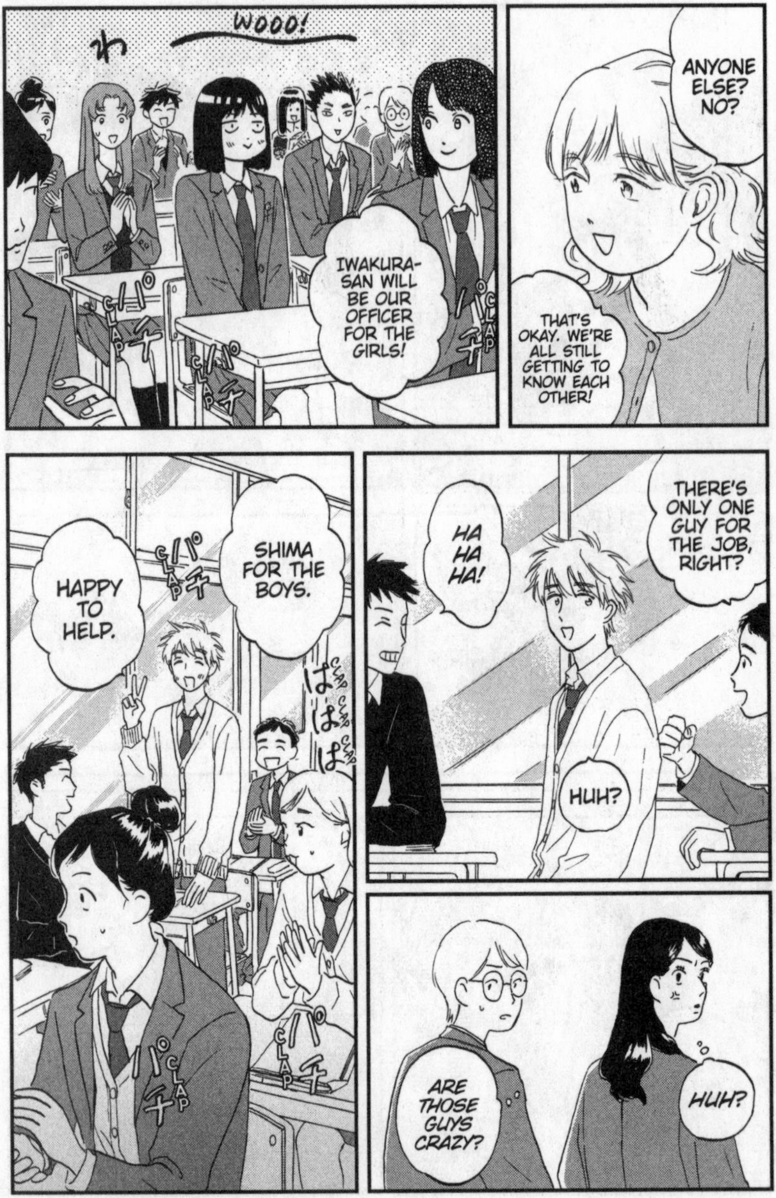
ANYONE ELSE? NO?
THAT'S OKAY. WE'RE ALL STILL GETTING TO KNOW EACH OTHER!
WOOO!
わ
IWAKURA-SAN WILL BE OUR OFFICER FOR THE GIRLS!
パチ CLAP
パチ CLAP
パチ CLAP
THERE'S ONLY ONE GUY FOR THE JOB, RIGHT?
HA HA HA!
HUH?
HUH?
ARE THOSE GUYS CRAZY?
SHIMA FOR THE BOYS.
パチ CLAP
HAPPY TO HELP.
ぱちぱち CLAP CLAP CLAP
パチ CLAP
パチ CLAP

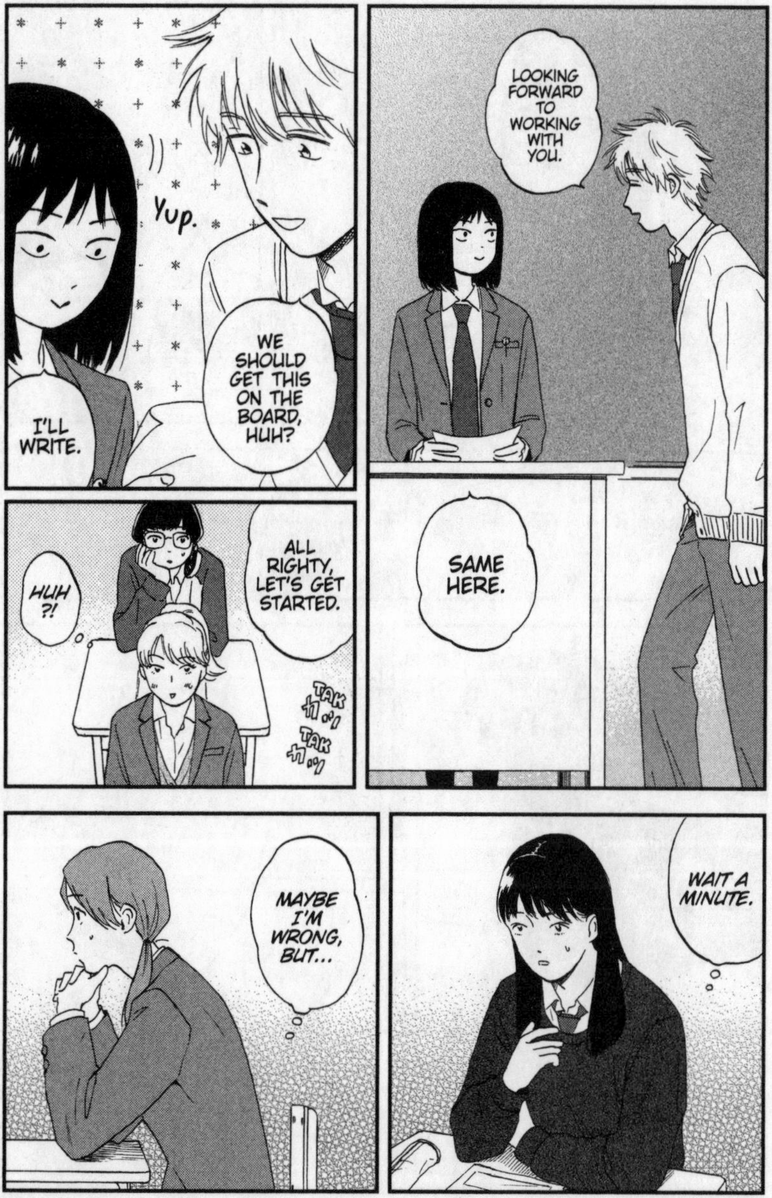

LOOKING FORWARD TO WORKING WITH YOU.
SAME HERE.
WE SHOULD GET THIS ON THE BOARD, HUH?
Yup.
I'LL WRITE.
ALL RIGHTY, LET'S GET STARTED.
HUH?!
TAK
TAK
WAIT A MINUTE.
MAYBE I'M WRONG, BUT...

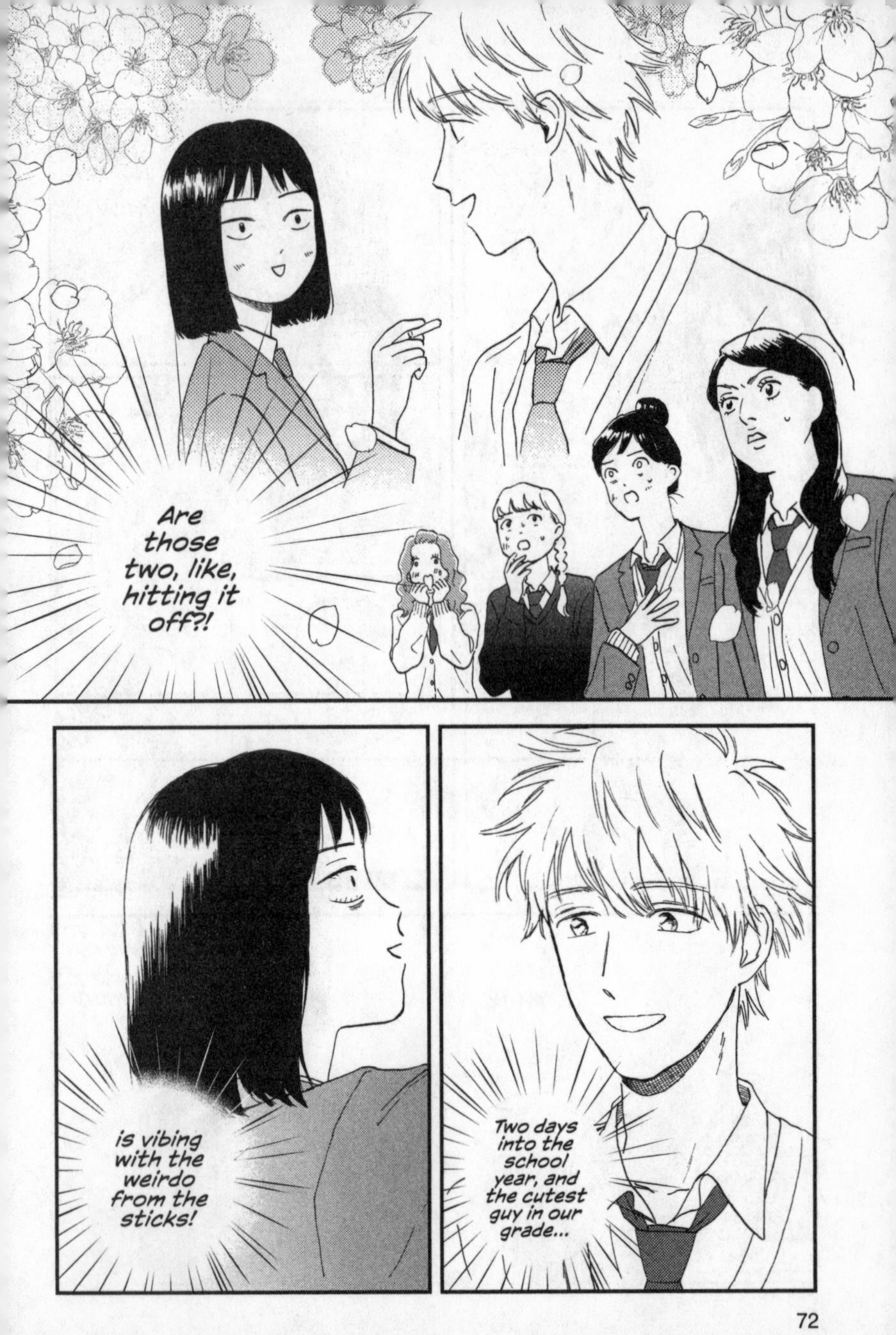
Are those two, like, hitting it off?!
Two days into the school year, and the cutest guy in our grade...
is vibing with the weirdo from the sticks!

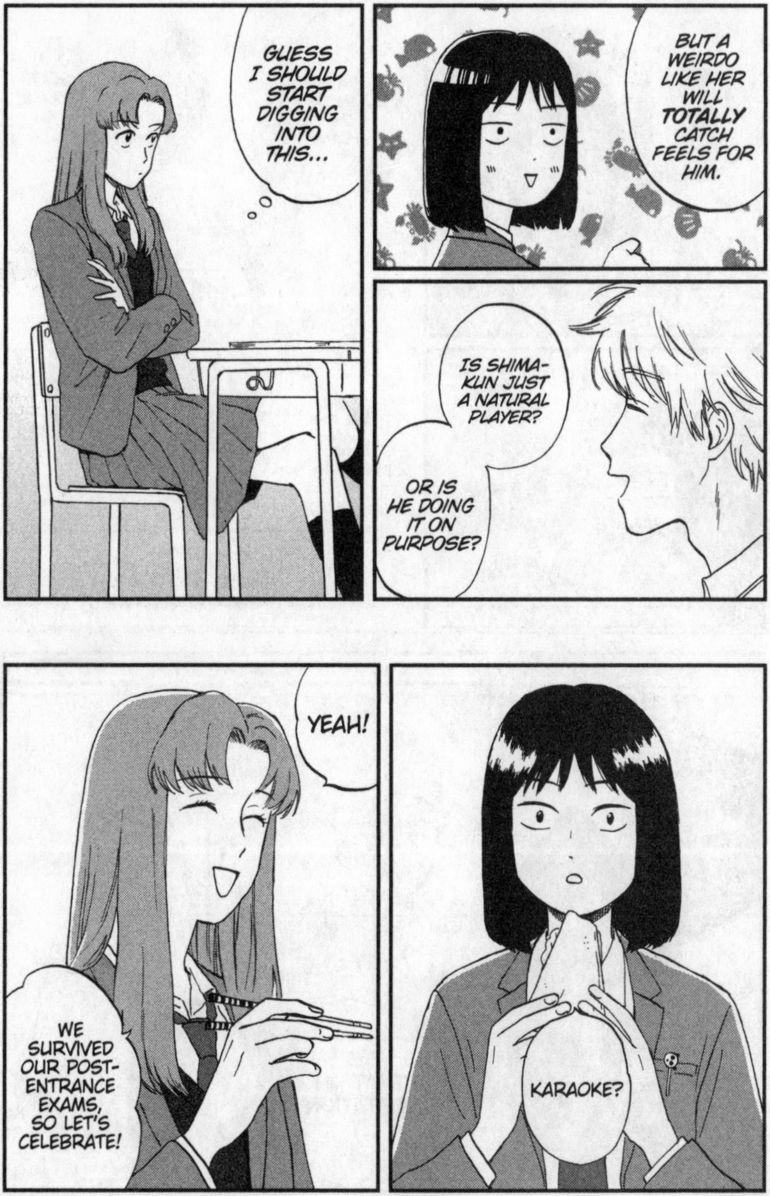
BUT A WEIRDO LIKE HER WILL TOTALLY CATCH FEELS FOR HIM.
IS SHIMA-KUN JUST A NATURAL PLAYER?
OR IS HE DOING IT ON PURPOSE?
GUESS I SHOULD START DIGGING INTO THIS...
KARAOKE?
YEAH!
WE SURVIVED OUR POST-ENTRANCE EXAMS, SO LET'S CELEBRATE!

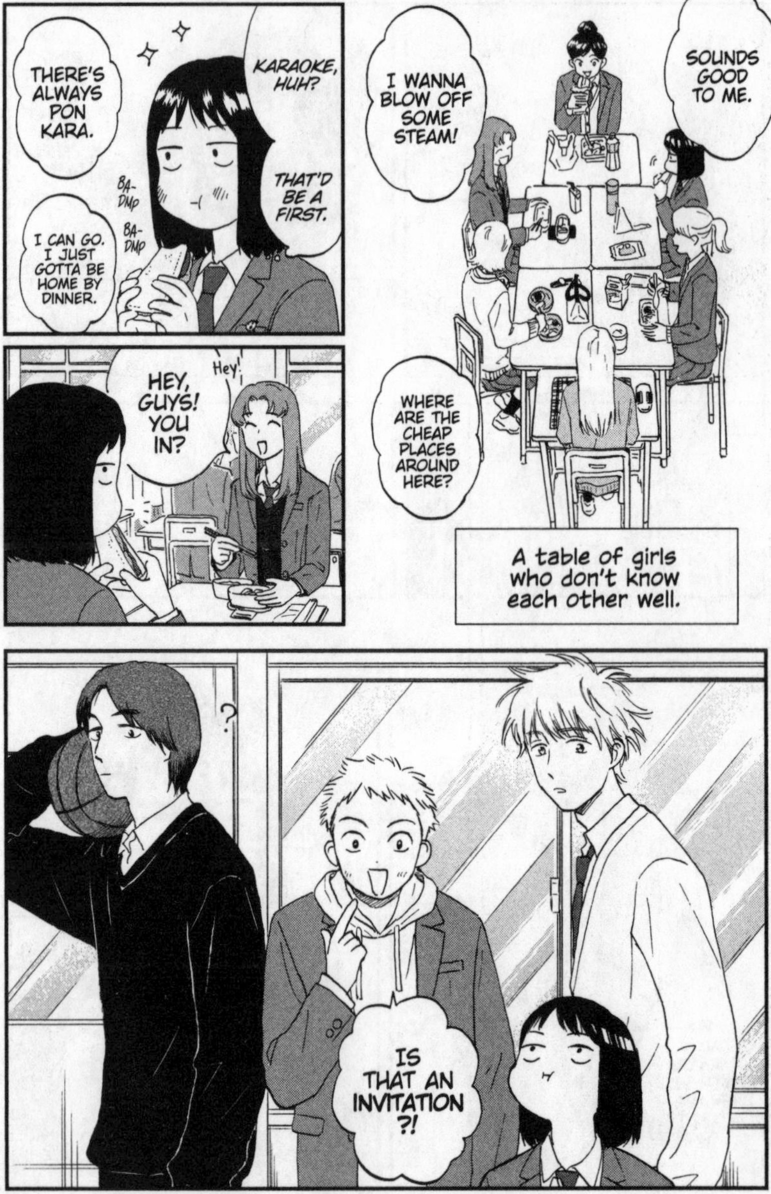
SOUNDS GOOD TO ME.
I WANNA BLOW OFF SOME STEAM!
WHERE ARE THE CHEAP PLACES AROUND HERE?
A table of girls who don't know each other well.
KARAOKE, HUH?
THAT'D BE A FIRST.
THERE'S ALWAYS PON KARA.
BA-DMP
BA-DMP
I CAN GO. I JUST GOTTA BE HOME BY DINNER.
Hey!
HEY, GUYS! YOU IN?
?
IS THAT AN INVITATION ?!

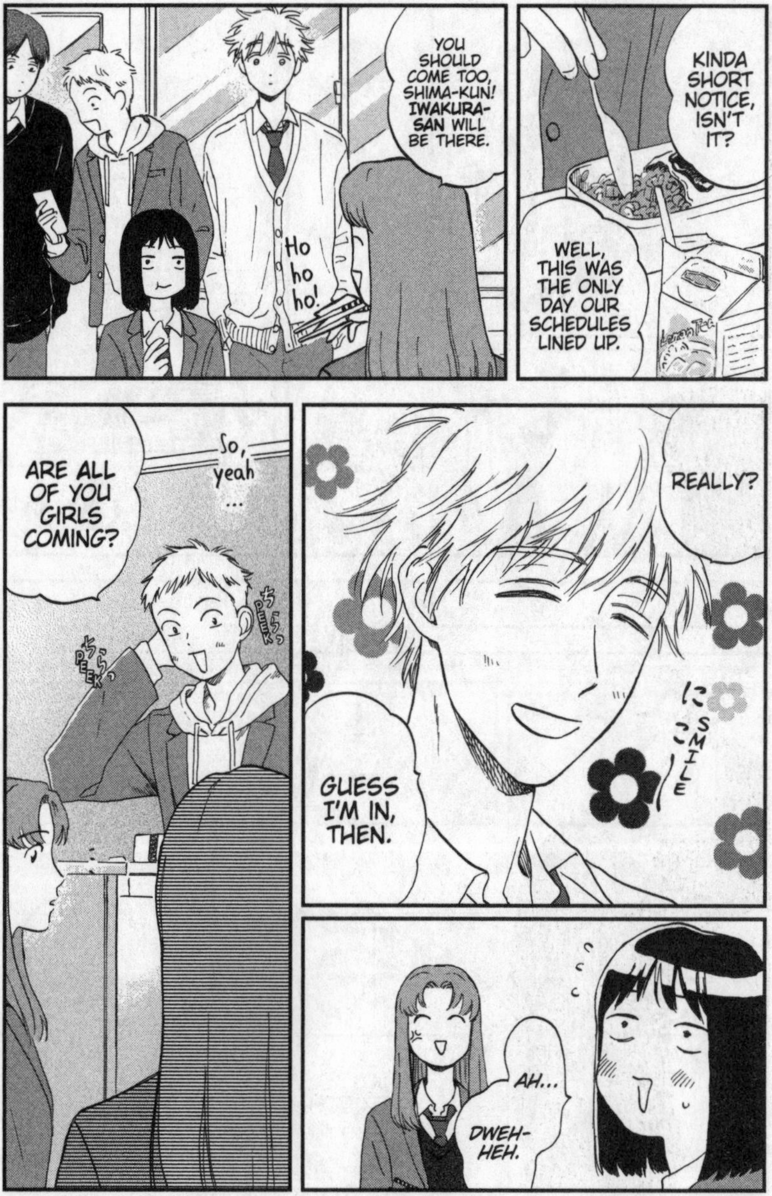
KINDA SHORT NOTICE, ISN'T IT?
WELL, THIS WAS THE ONLY DAY OUR SCHEDULES LINED UP.
YOU SHOULD COME TOO, SHIMA-KUN! IWAKURA-SAN WILL BE THERE.
Ho ho ho!
REALLY?
にこっ SMILE
GUESS I'M IN, THEN.
AH...
DWEH-HEH.
ARE ALL OF YOU GIRLS COMING?
So, yeah...
ちらっ PEEK
ちらっ PEEK

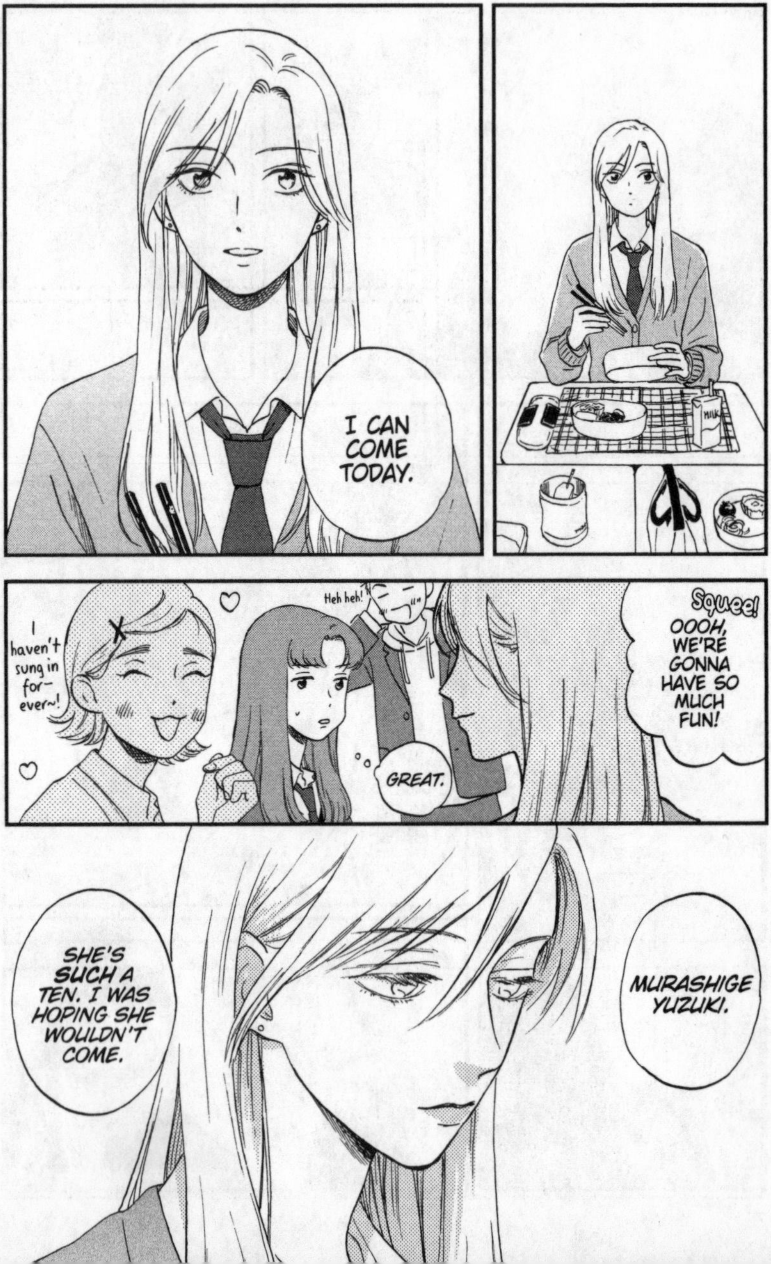
I CAN COME TODAY.
Squee!
OOOH, WE'RE GONNA HAVE SO MUCH FUN!
Heh heh!
GREAT.
I haven't sung in for-ever~!
MURASHIGE YUZUKI.
SHE'S SUCH A TEN. I WAS HOPING SHE WOULDN'T COME.

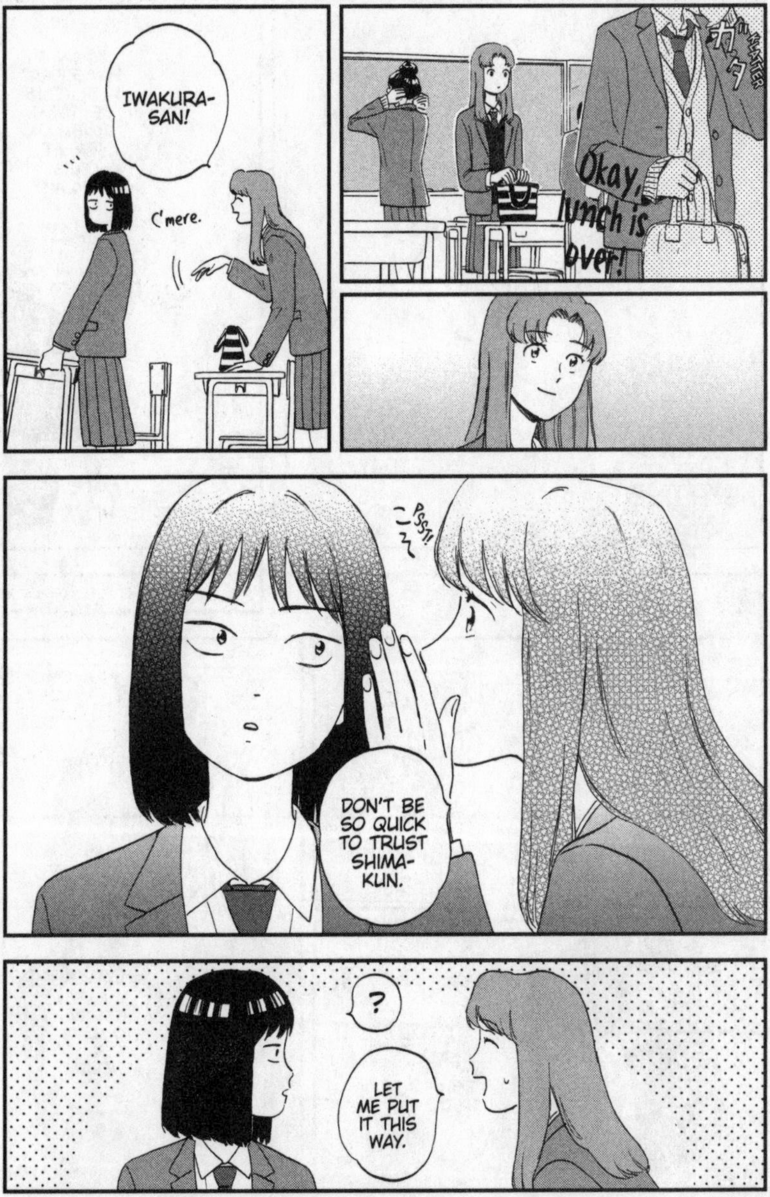
ガタ
CLATTER
Okay, lunch is over!
IWAKURA-SAN!
...
C'mere.
PSST!!
DON'T BE SO QUICK TO TRUST SHIMA-KUN.
?
LET ME PUT IT THIS WAY.

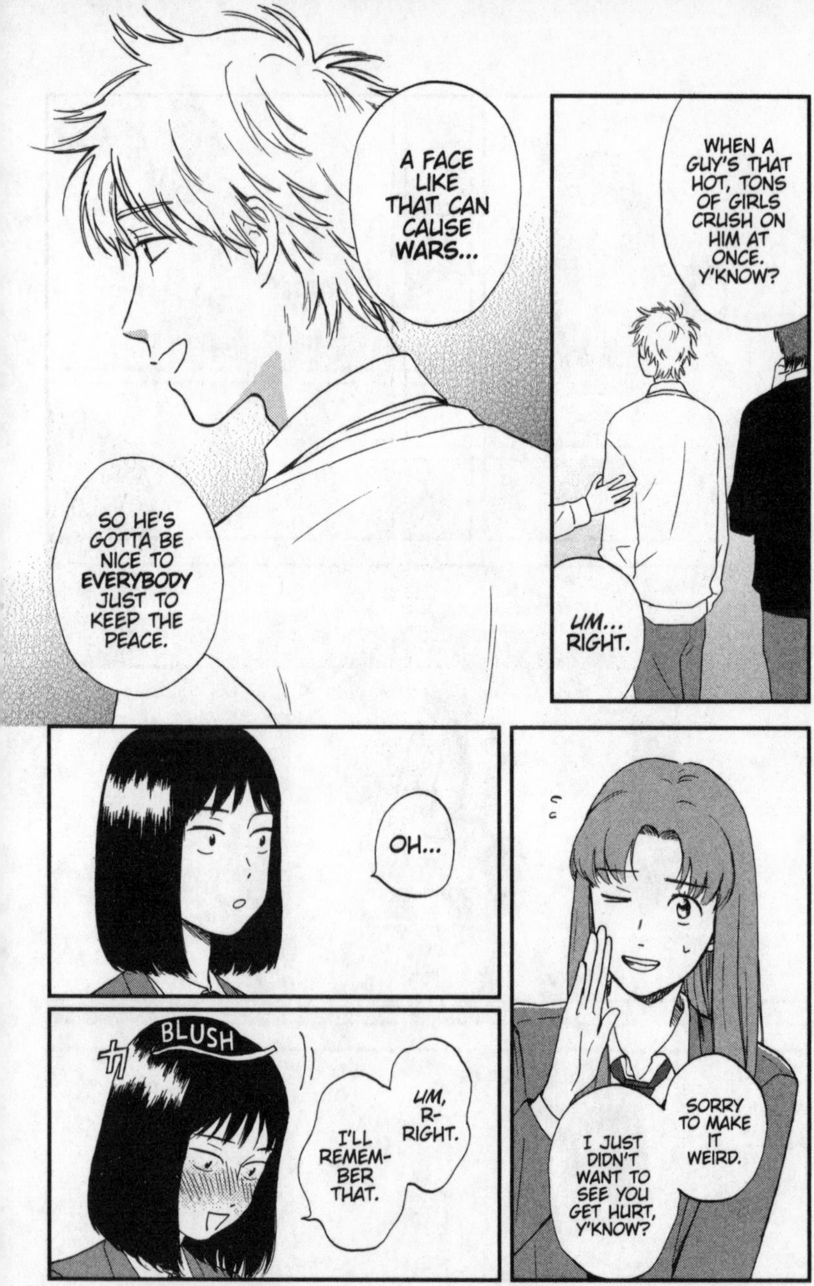
WHEN A GUY'S THAT HOT, TONS OF GIRLS CRUSH ON HIM AT ONCE. Y'KNOW?
UM... RIGHT.
A FACE LIKE THAT CAN CAUSE WARS...
SO HE'S GOTTA BE NICE TO EVERYBODY JUST TO KEEP THE PEACE.
SORRY TO MAKE IT WEIRD.
I JUST DIDN'T WANT TO SEE YOU GET HURT, Y'KNOW?
OH...
BLUSH
UM, R-RIGHT.
I'LL REMEM-BER THAT.

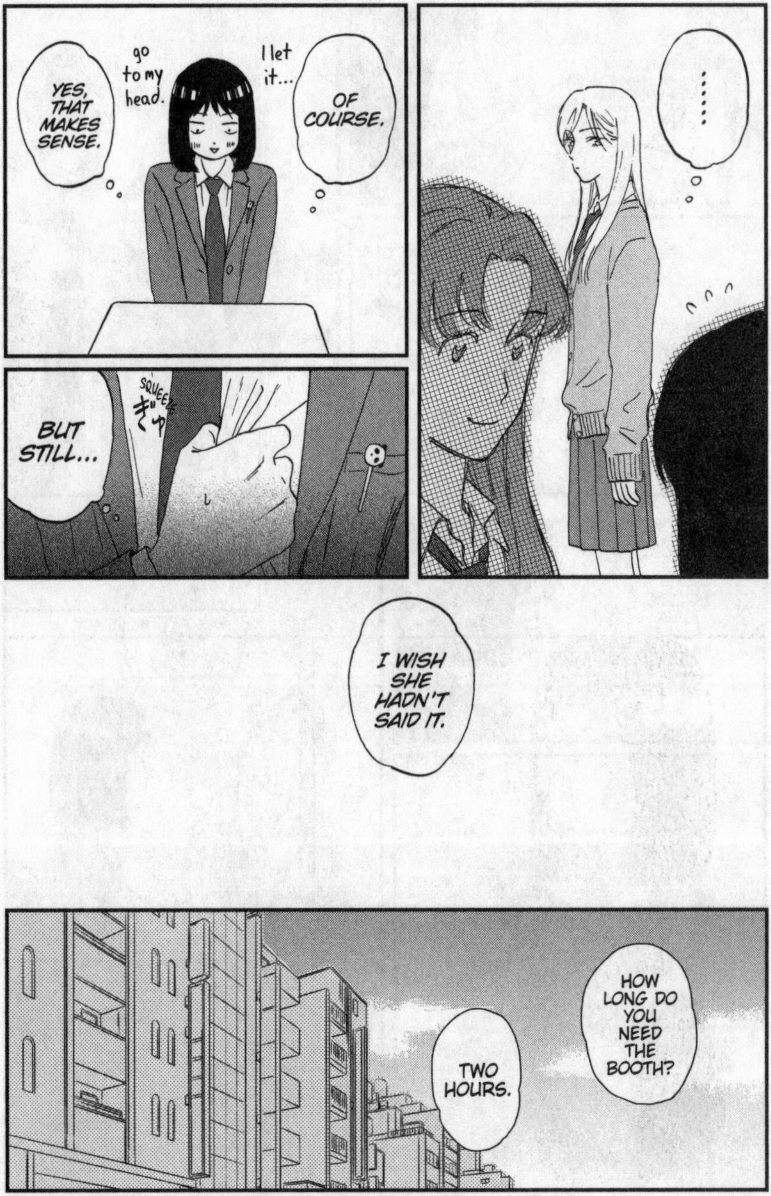
......
OF COURSE.
I let it...
go to my head.
YES, THAT MAKES SENSE.
ぎゅ SQUEEZE
BUT STILL...
I WISH SHE HADN'T SAID IT.
HOW LONG DO YOU NEED THE BOOTH?
TWO HOURS.

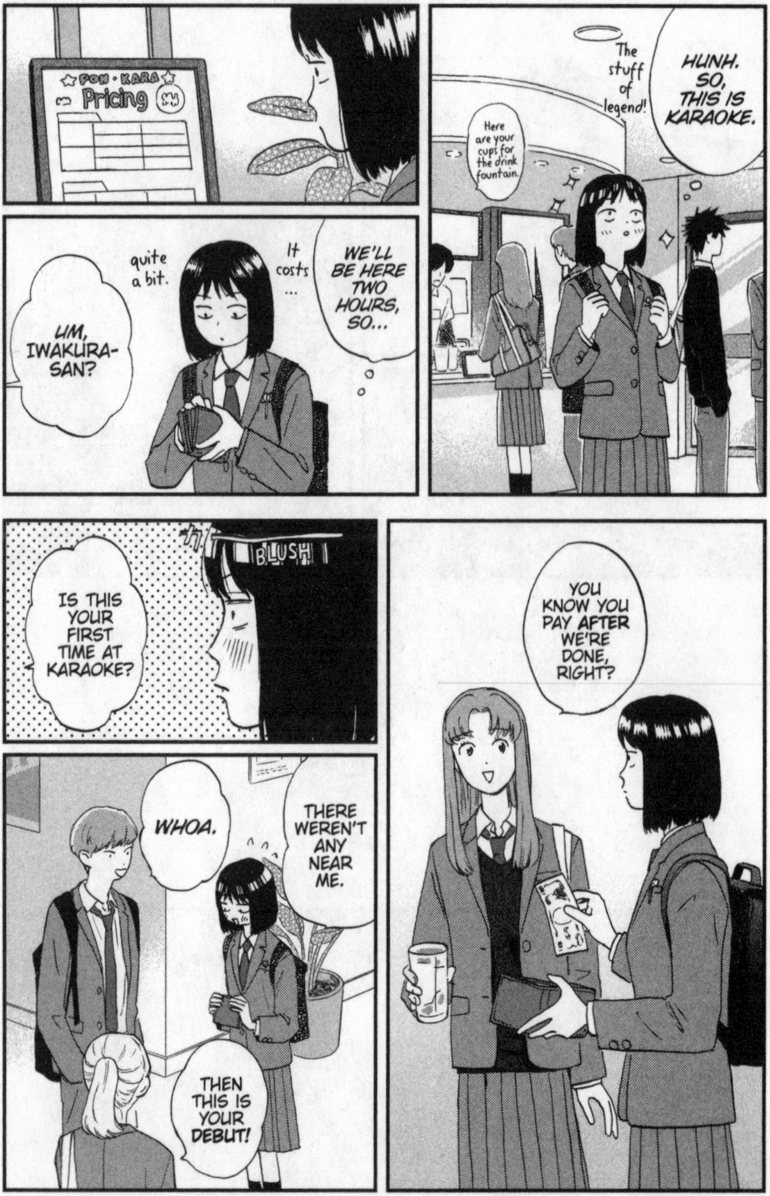
HUNH. SO, THIS IS KARAOKE.
The stuff of legend!
Here are your cups for the drink fountain.
PON・KARA
Pricing
WE'LL BE HERE TWO HOURS, SO...
It costs ...
quite a bit.
UM, IWAKURA-SAN?
YOU KNOW YOU PAY AFTER WE'RE DONE, RIGHT?
BLUSH
IS THIS YOUR FIRST TIME AT KARAOKE?
THERE WEREN'T ANY NEAR ME.
WHOA.
THEN THIS IS YOUR DEBUT!

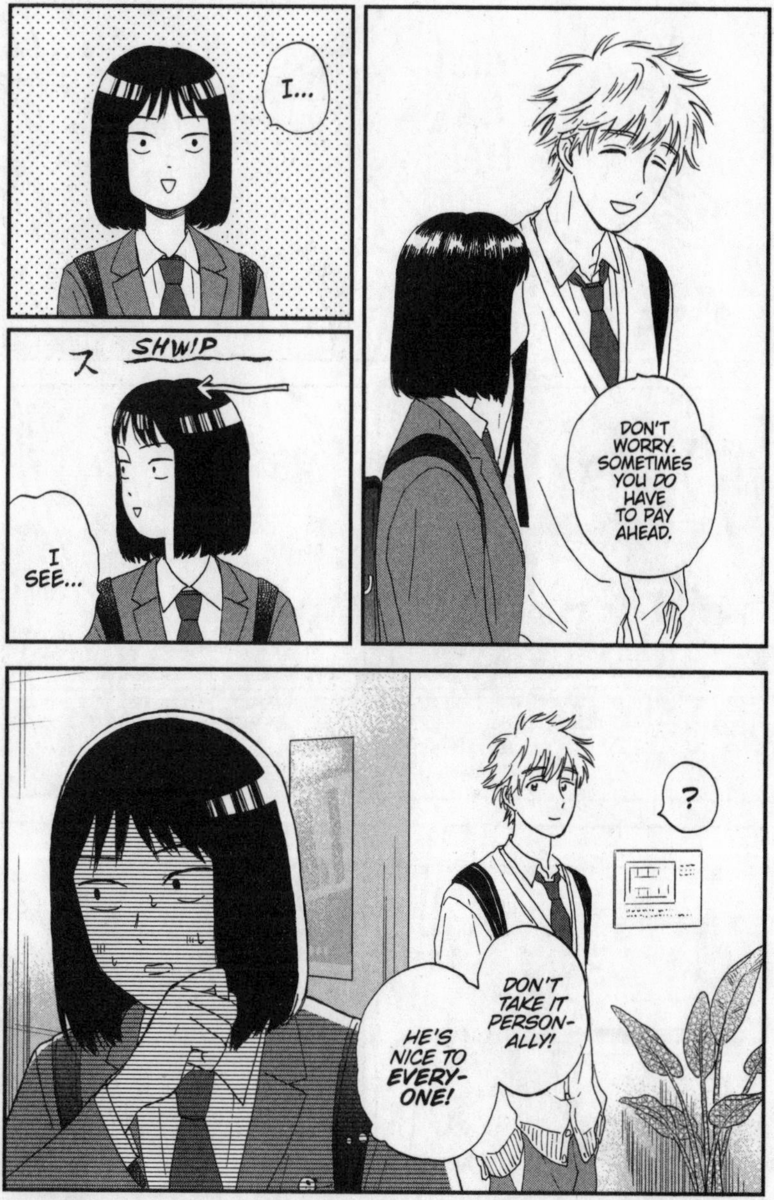
DON'T WORRY. SOMETIMES YOU DO HAVE TO PAY AHEAD.
I...
ス
SHWIP
I SEE...
?
DON'T TAKE IT PERSON-ALLY!
HE'S NICE TO EVERY-ONE!

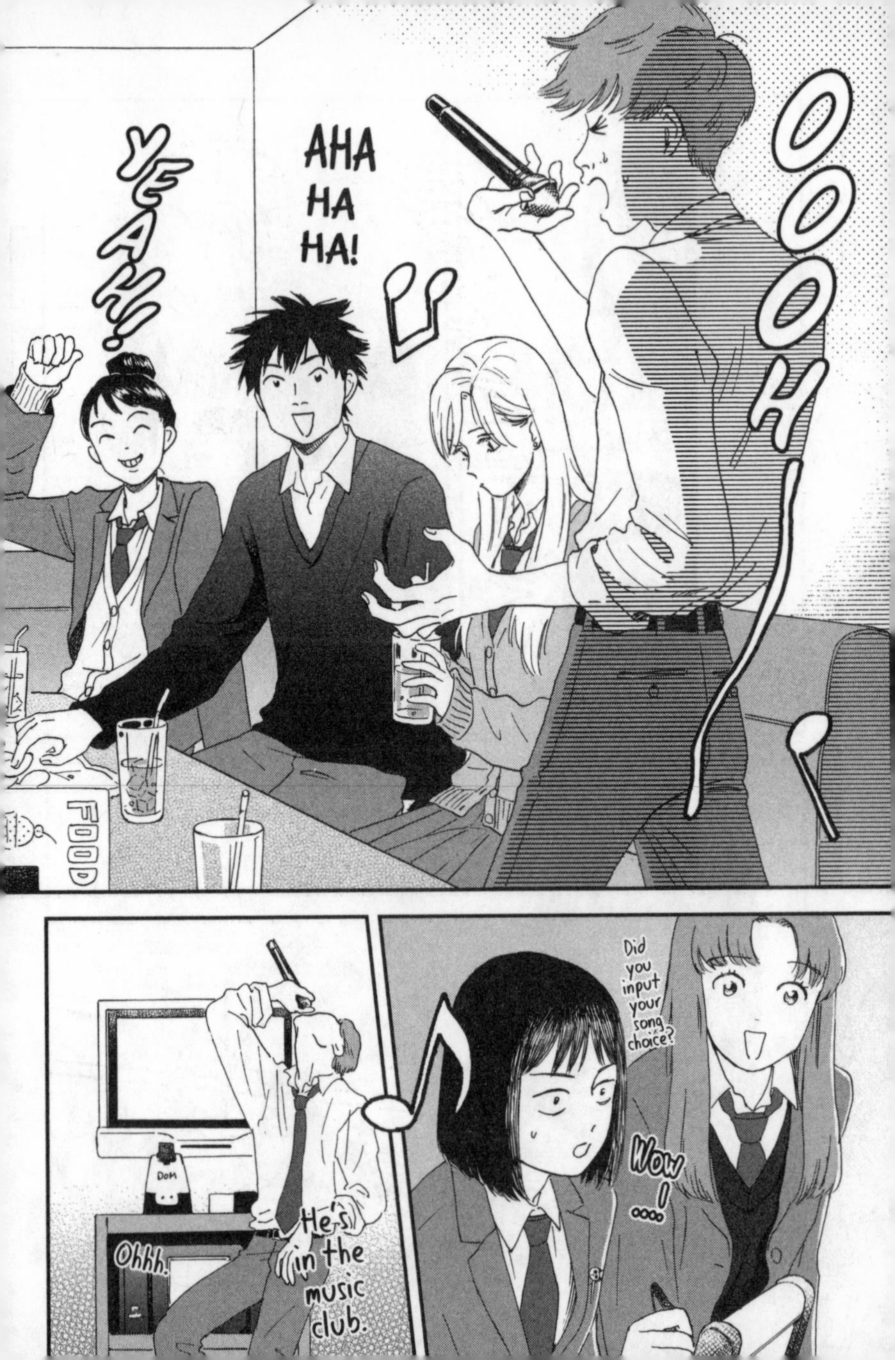
OOOOH!
AHA HA HA!
YEAH!!
FOOD
Did you input your song choice?
Wow!...
DOM
He's in the music club.
Ohhh.

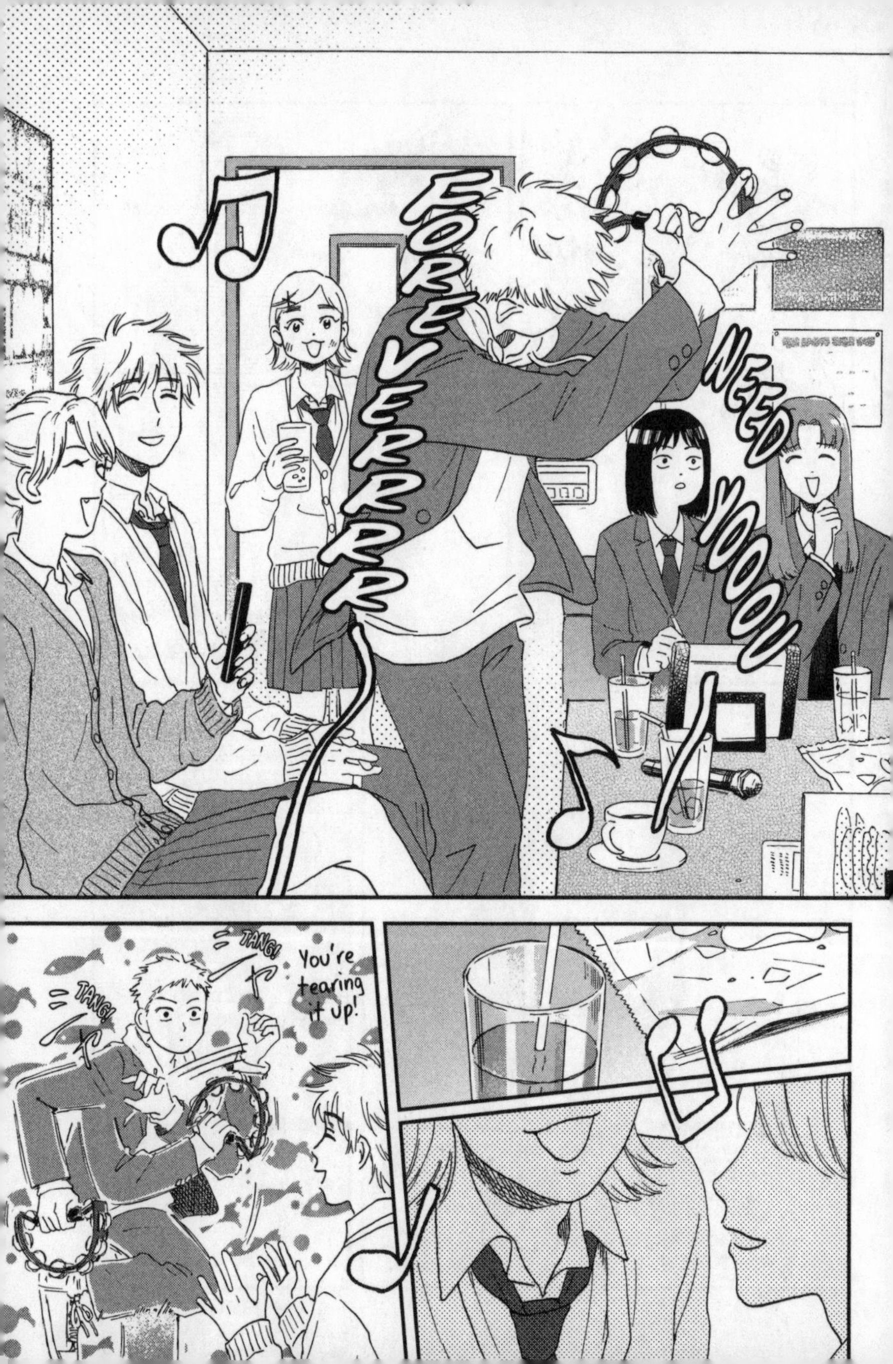
NEED YOOOOU
FOREVERRRR
TANG!
You're tearing it up!
TANG!

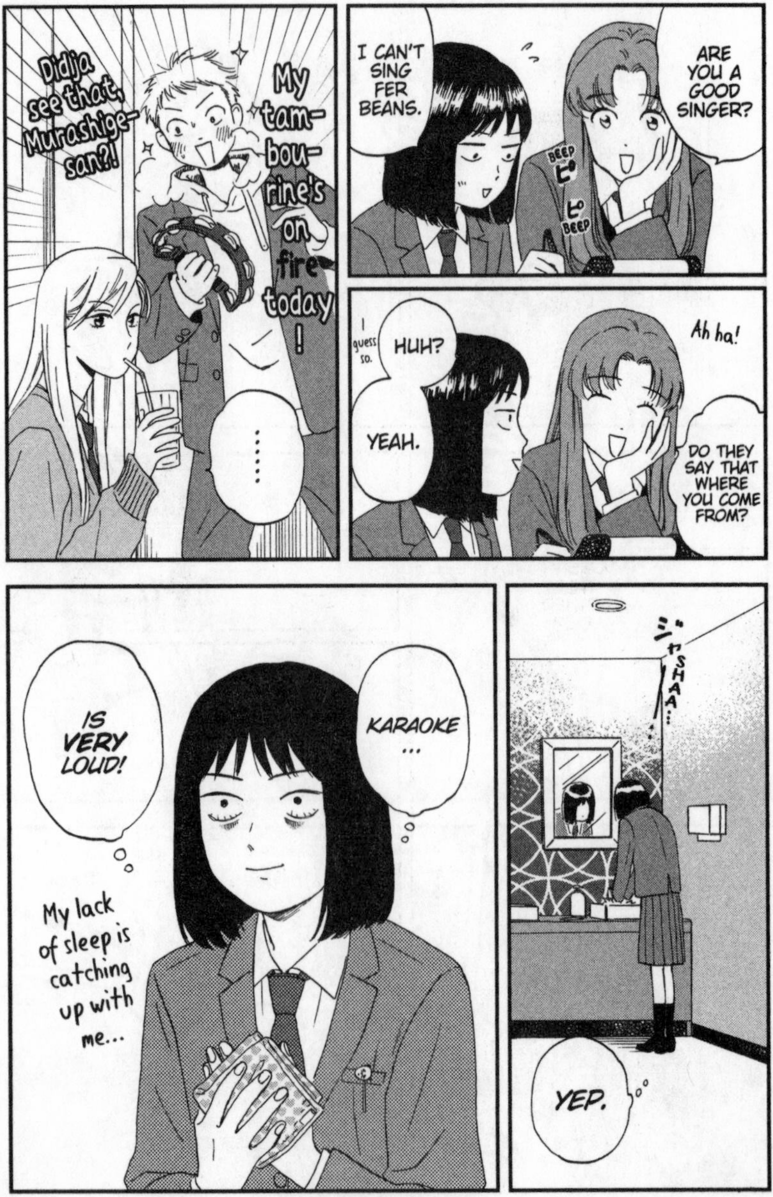
ARE YOU A GOOD SINGER?
BEEP ピ
ピ BEEP
I CAN'T SING FER BEANS.
Ah ha!
DO THEY SAY THAT WHERE YOU COME FROM?
HUH?
I guess so.
YEAH.
My tam-bou-rine's on fire today!
Didja see that, Murashige-san?!
......
ジャ SHAA...
YEP.
KARAOKE ...
IS VERY LOUD!
My lack of sleep is catching up with me...

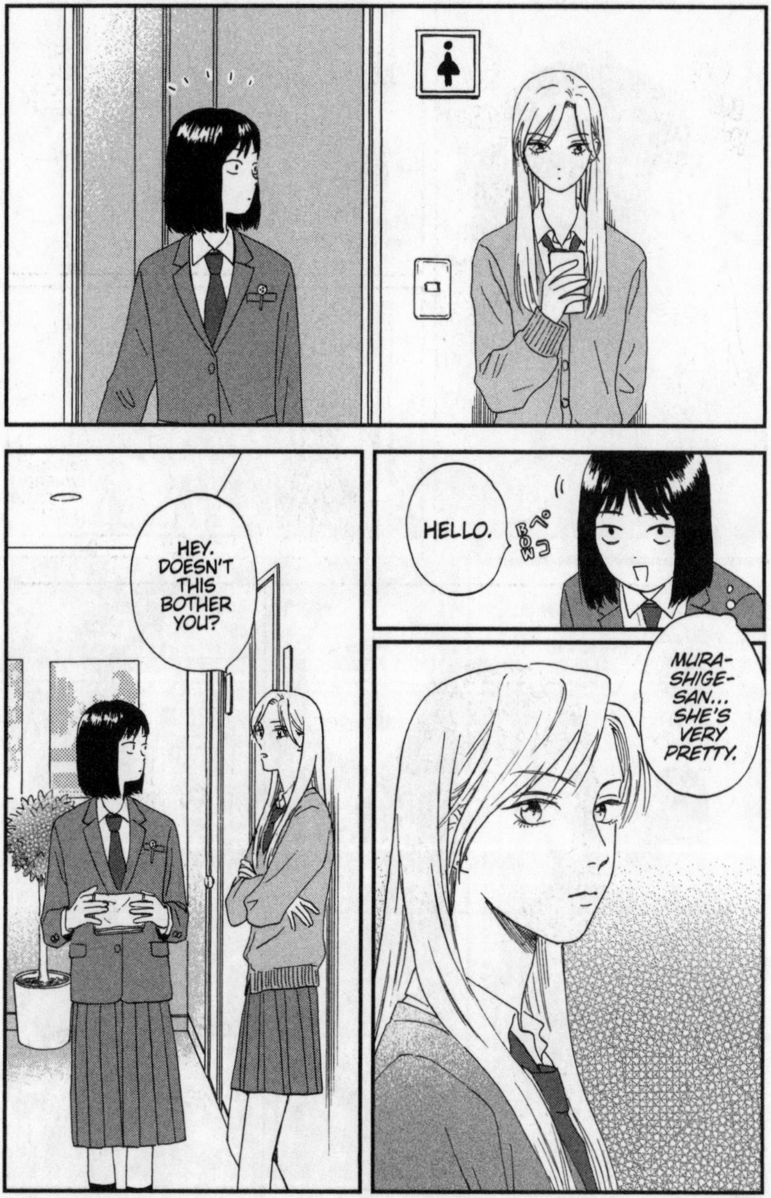
HELLO.
ペコ BOW
MURA-SHIGE-SAN... SHE'S VERY PRETTY.
HEY. DOESN'T THIS BOTHER YOU?

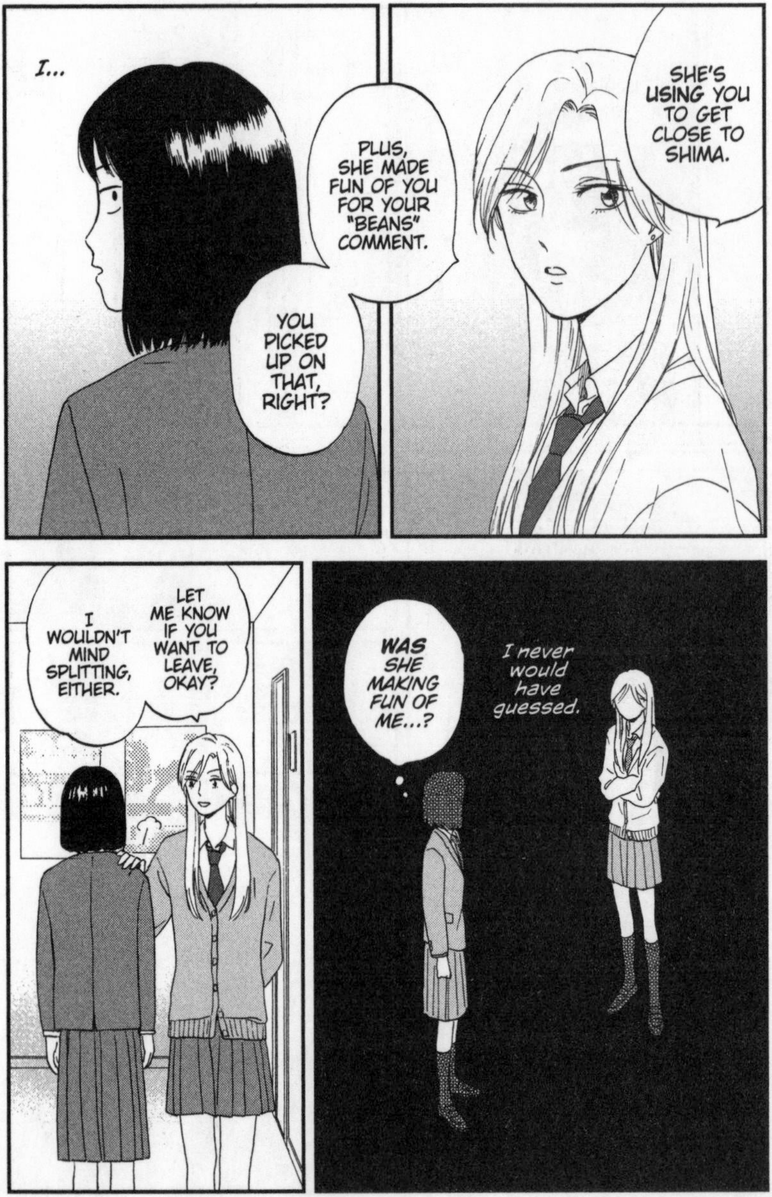
SHE'S USING YOU TO GET CLOSE TO SHIMA.
PLUS, SHE MADE FUN OF YOU FOR YOUR "BEANS" COMMENT.
YOU PICKED UP ON THAT, RIGHT?
I...
I never would have guessed.
WAS SHE MAKING FUN OF ME...?
LET ME KNOW IF YOU WANT TO LEAVE, OKAY?
I WOULDN'T MIND SPLITTING, EITHER.

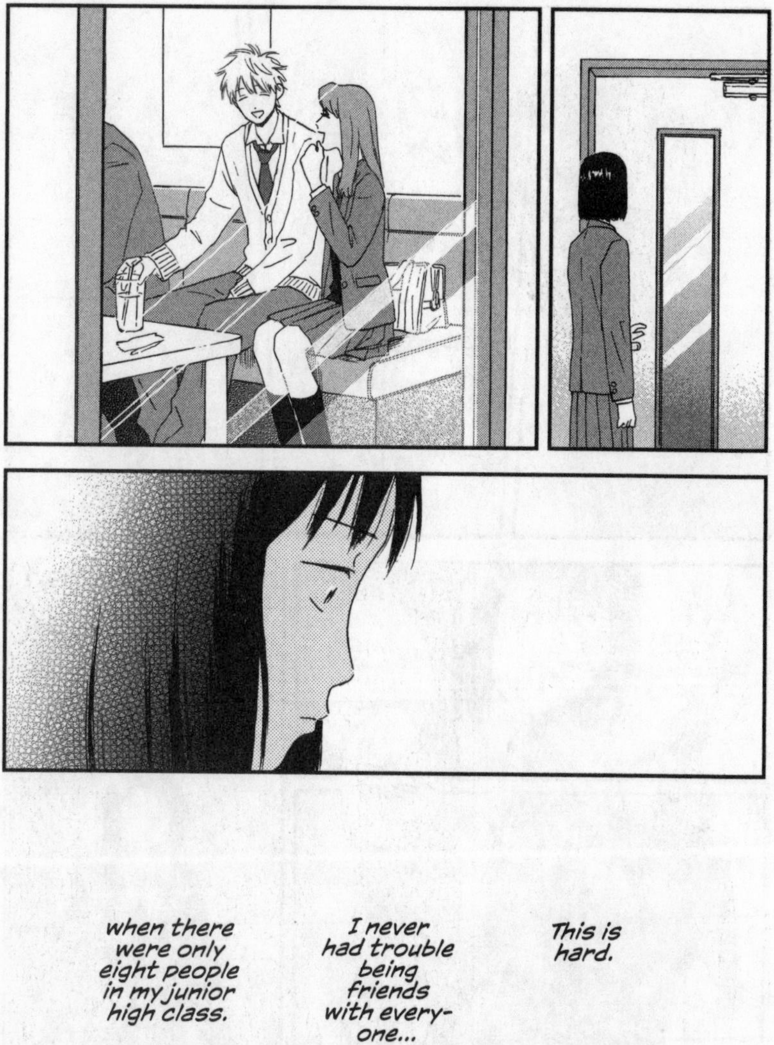
This is hard.
I never had trouble being friends with every-one...
when there were only eight people in my junior high class.

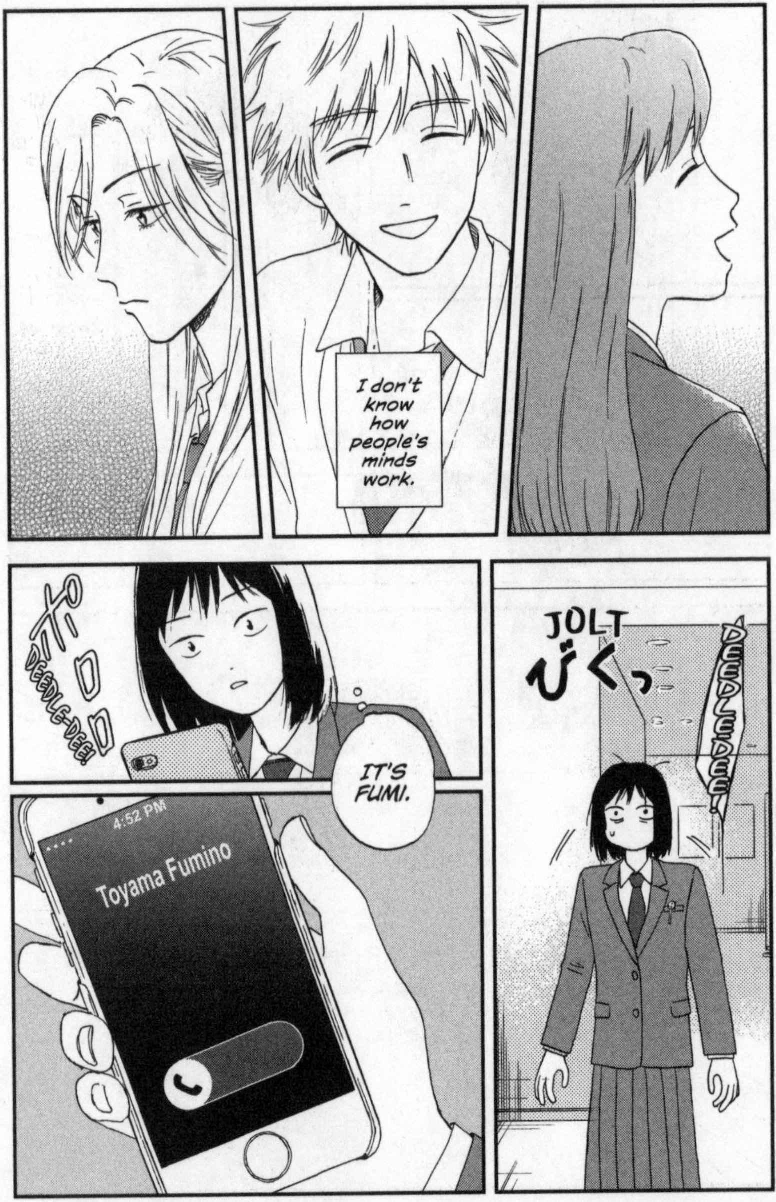
I don't know how people's minds work.
JOLT
びくっ
DEEDLEDEE
DEEDLE-DEE!
IT'S FUMI.
4:52 PM
Toyama Fumino

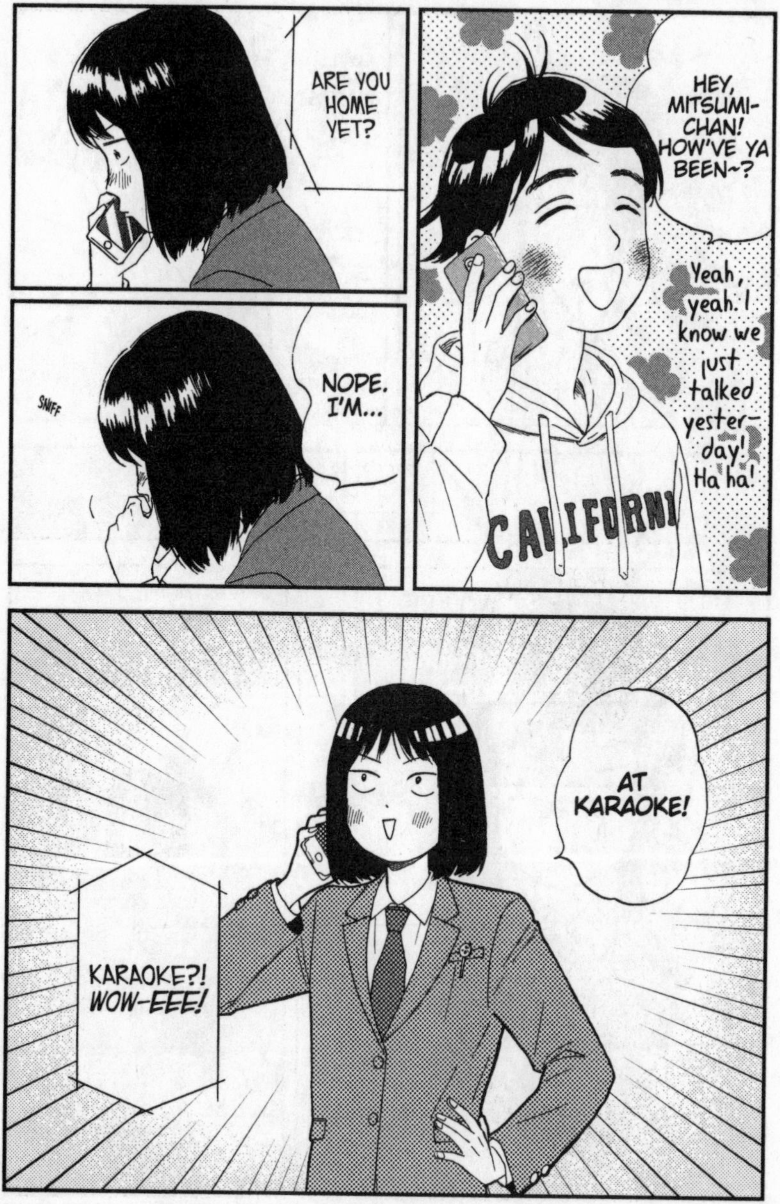
HEY, MITSUMI-CHAN! HOW'VE YA BEEN~?
Yeah, yeah. I know we just talked yester-day! Ha ha!
CALIFORNI
ARE YOU HOME YET?
SNIFF
NOPE. I'M...
AT KARAOKE!
KARAOKE?! WOW-EEE!

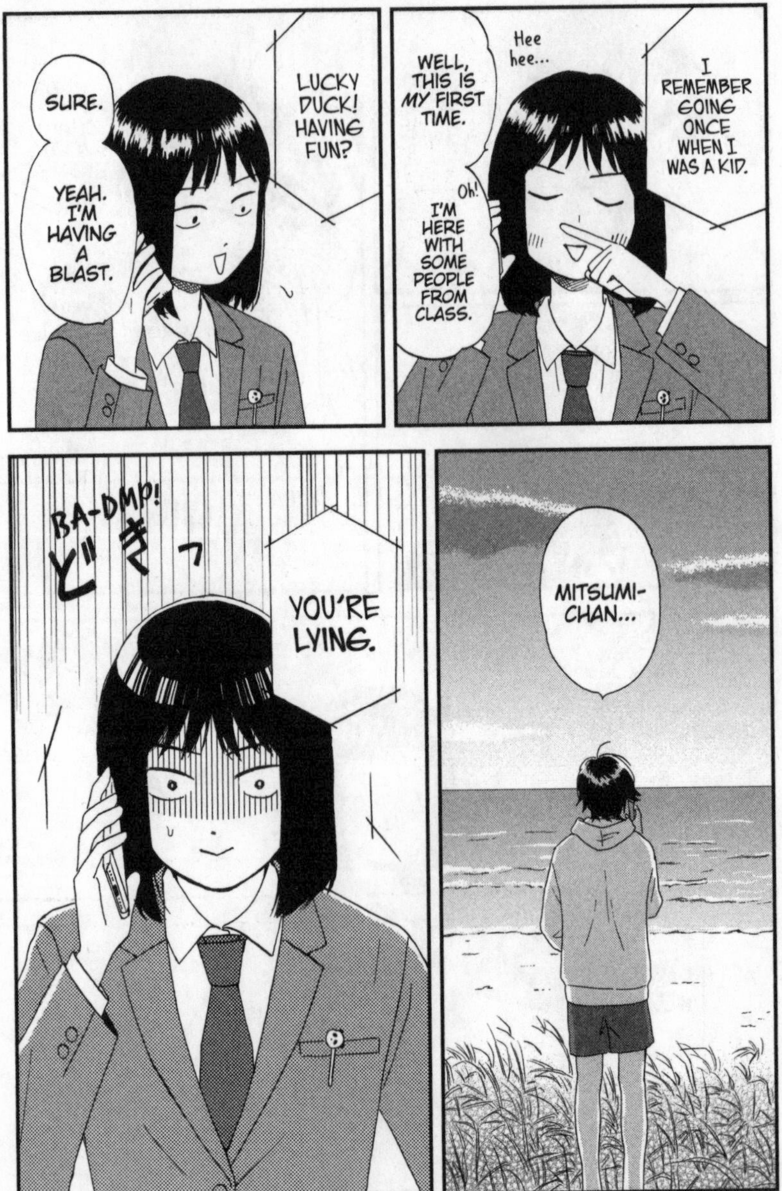
I REMEMBER GOING ONCE WHEN I WAS A KID.
Hee hee...
WELL, THIS IS MY FIRST TIME.
Oh! I'M HERE WITH SOME PEOPLE FROM CLASS.
LUCKY DUCK! HAVING FUN?
SURE.
YEAH. I'M HAVING A BLAST.
MITSUMI-CHAN...
YOU'RE LYING.
BA-DMP!
どきっ

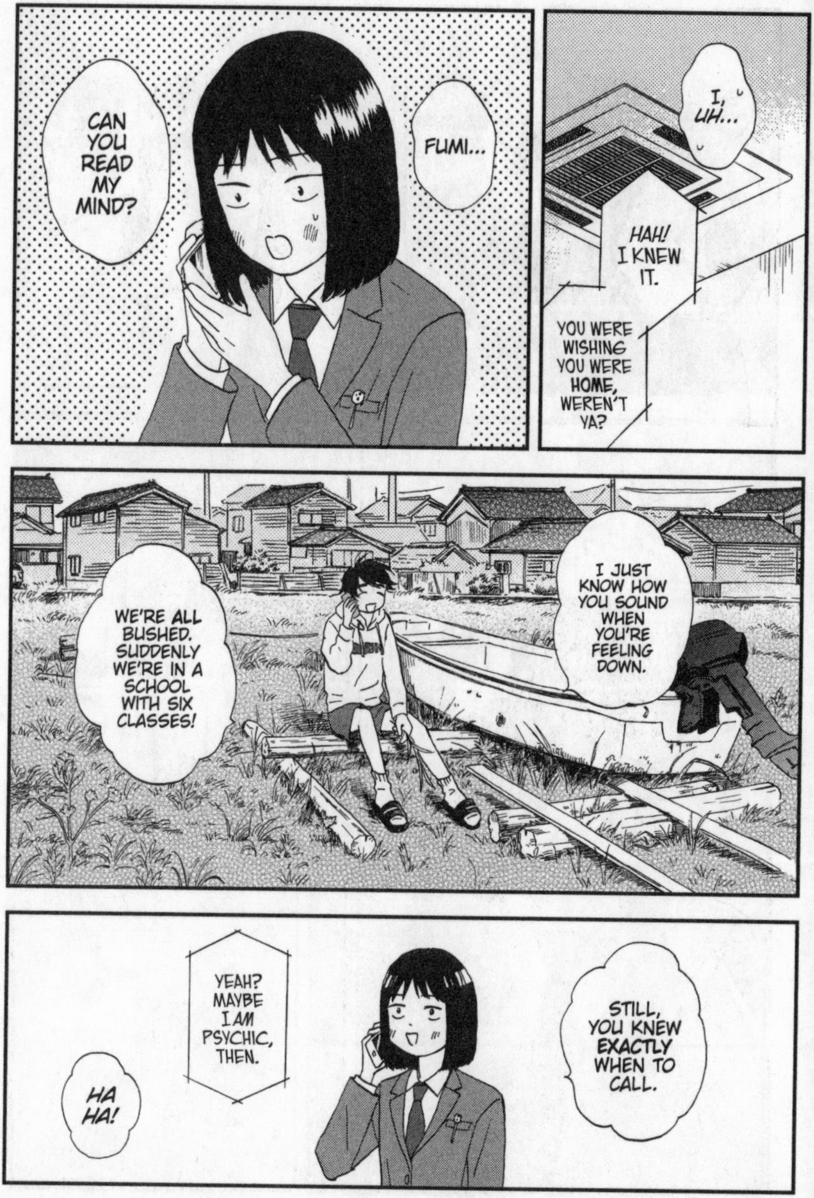

I, UH...
HAH! I KNEW IT.
YOU WERE WISHING YOU WERE HOME, WEREN'T YA?
FUMI...
CAN YOU READ MY MIND?
I JUST KNOW HOW YOU SOUND WHEN YOU'RE FEELING DOWN.
WE'RE ALL BUSHED. SUDDENLY WE'RE IN A SCHOOL WITH SIX CLASSES!
STILL, YOU KNEW EXACTLY WHEN TO CALL.
YEAH? MAYBE I AM PSYCHIC, THEN.
HA HA!

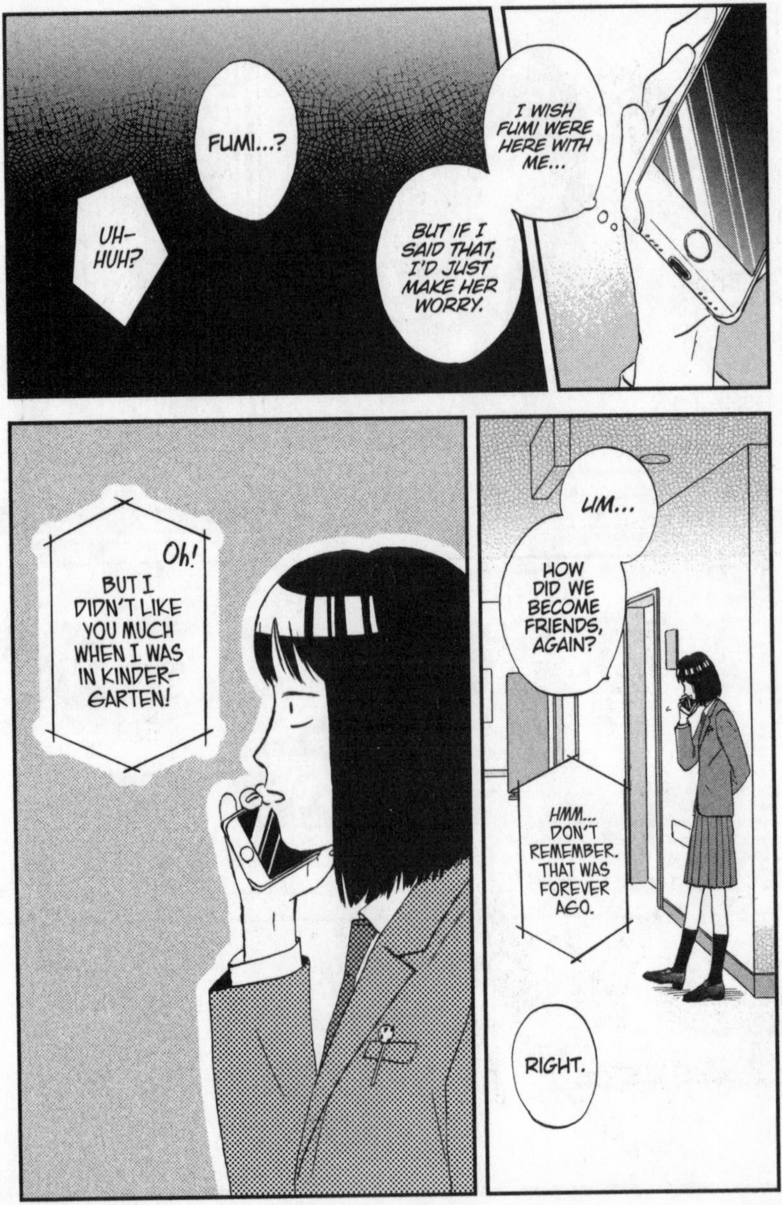
I WISH FUMI WERE HERE WITH ME...
BUT IF I SAID THAT, I'D JUST MAKE HER WORRY.
FUMI...?
UH-HUH?
UM...
HOW DID WE BECOME FRIENDS, AGAIN?
HMM... DON'T REMEMBER. THAT WAS FOREVER AGO.
RIGHT.
Oh!
BUT I DIDN'T LIKE YOU MUCH WHEN I WAS IN KINDER-GARTEN!

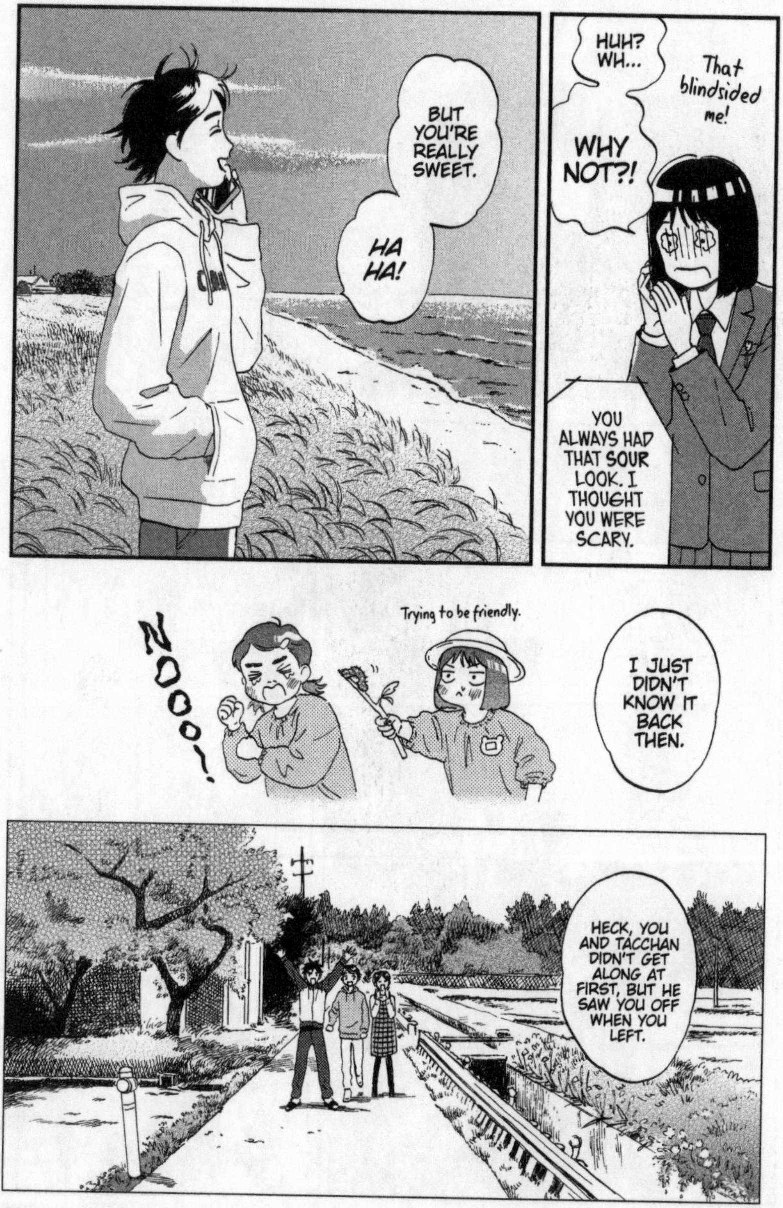
HUH? WH...
WHY NOT?!
That blindsided me!
YOU ALWAYS HAD THAT SOUR LOOK. I THOUGHT YOU WERE SCARY.
BUT YOU'RE REALLY SWEET.
HA HA!
I JUST DIDN'T KNOW IT BACK THEN.
Trying to be friendly.
NOOO!
HECK, YOU AND TACCHAN DIDN'T GET ALONG AT FIRST, BUT HE SAW YOU OFF WHEN YOU LEFT.

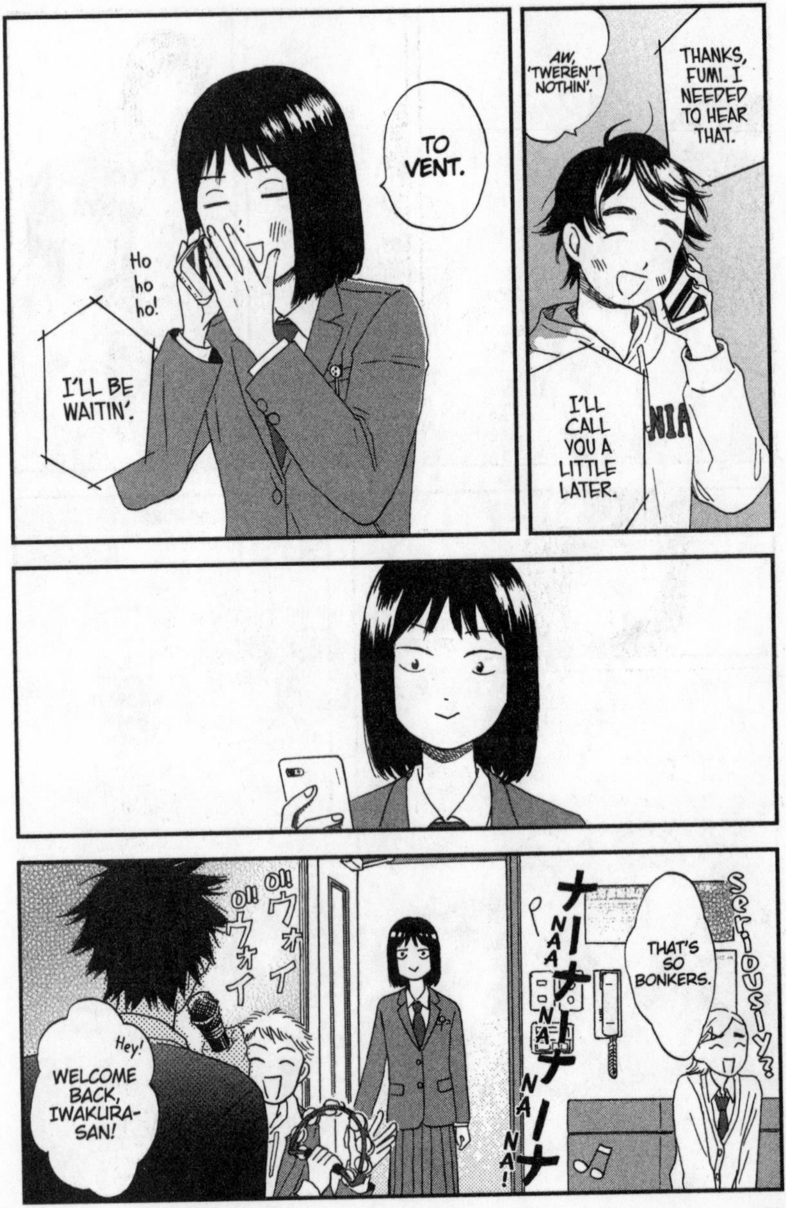
THANKS, FUMI. I NEEDED TO HEAR THAT.
AW, 'TWEREN'T NOTHIN'.
I'LL CALL YOU A LITTLE LATER.
TO VENT.
Ho ho ho!
I'LL BE WAITIN'.
Seriously?
THAT'S SO BONKERS.
NAA NA NA NA NA!
ナーナ ナーナ
OI! OI!
ウォイ ウォイ
Hey!
WELCOME BACK, IWAKURA-SAN!

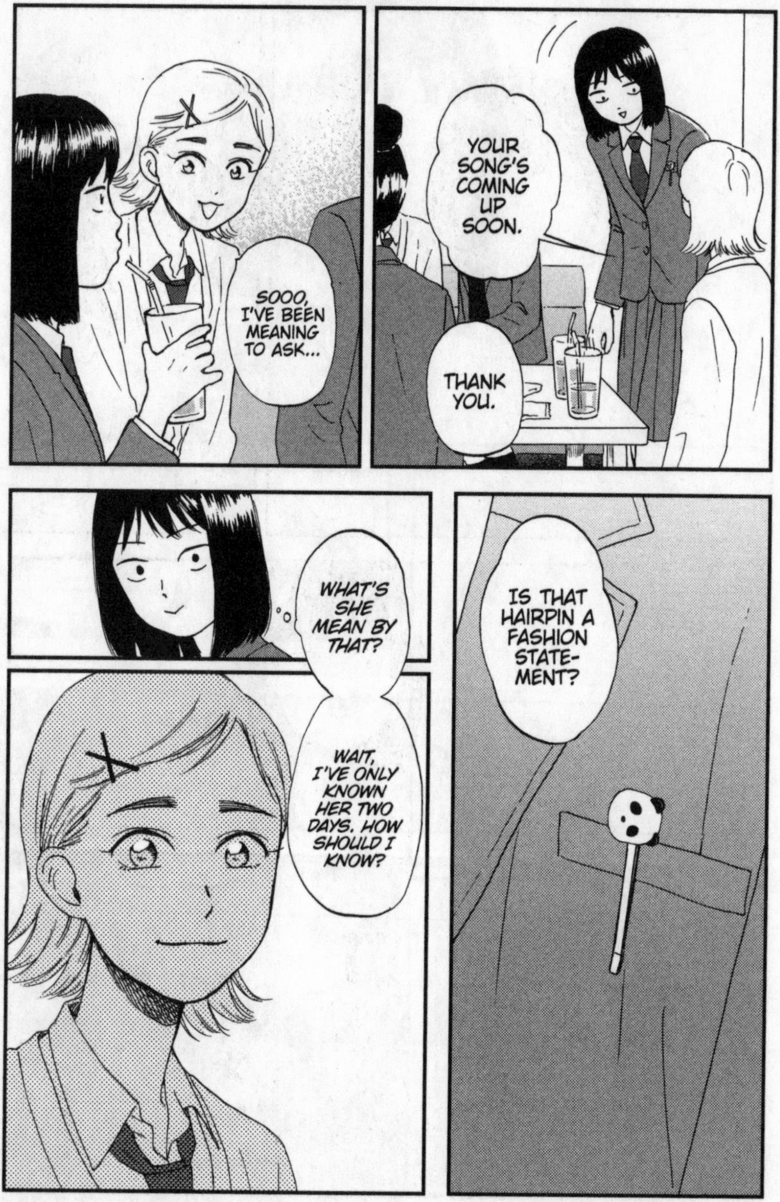
YOUR SONG'S COMING UP SOON.
THANK YOU.
SOOO, I'VE BEEN MEANING TO ASK...
IS THAT HAIRPIN A FASHION STATEMENT?
WHAT'S SHE MEAN BY THAT?
WAIT, I'VE ONLY KNOWN HER TWO DAYS. HOW SHOULD I KNOW?

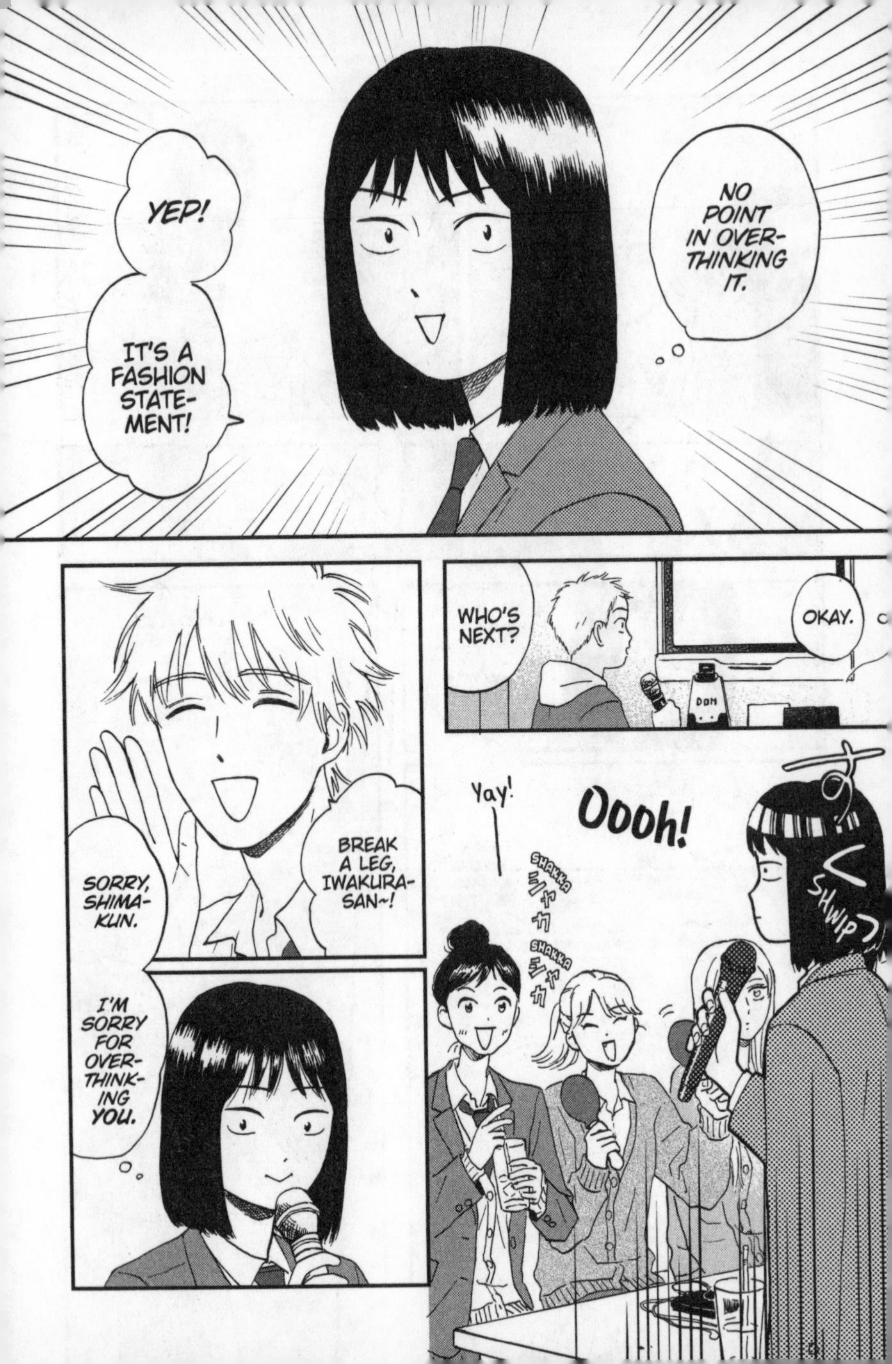
NO POINT IN OVER-THINKING IT.
YEP!
IT'S A FASHION STATEMENT!
WHO'S NEXT?
OKAY.
BREAK A LEG, IWAKURA-SAN~!
SORRY, SHIMA-KUN.
SHWIP
Oooh!
Yay!
SHAKKA
SHAKKA
I'M SORRY FOR OVER-THINK-ING YOU.

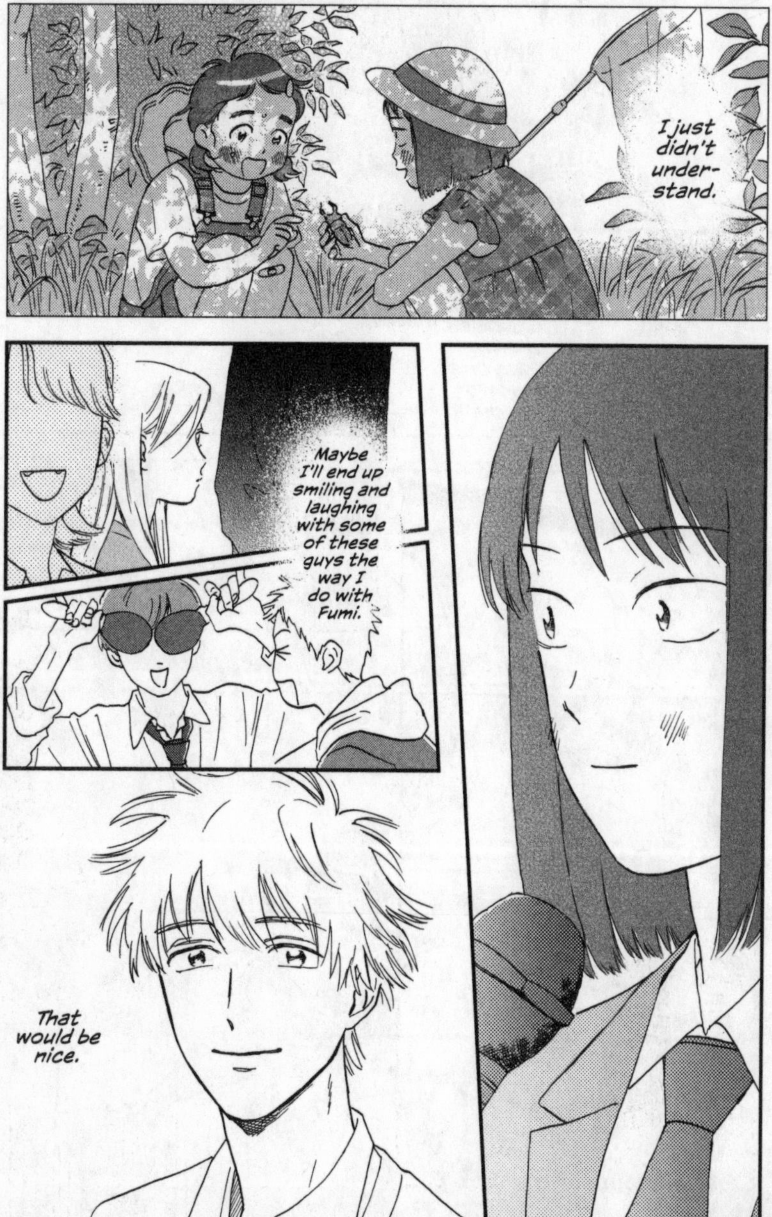
I just didn't under-stand.
Maybe I'll end up smiling and laughing with some of these guys the way I do with Fumi.
That would be nice.

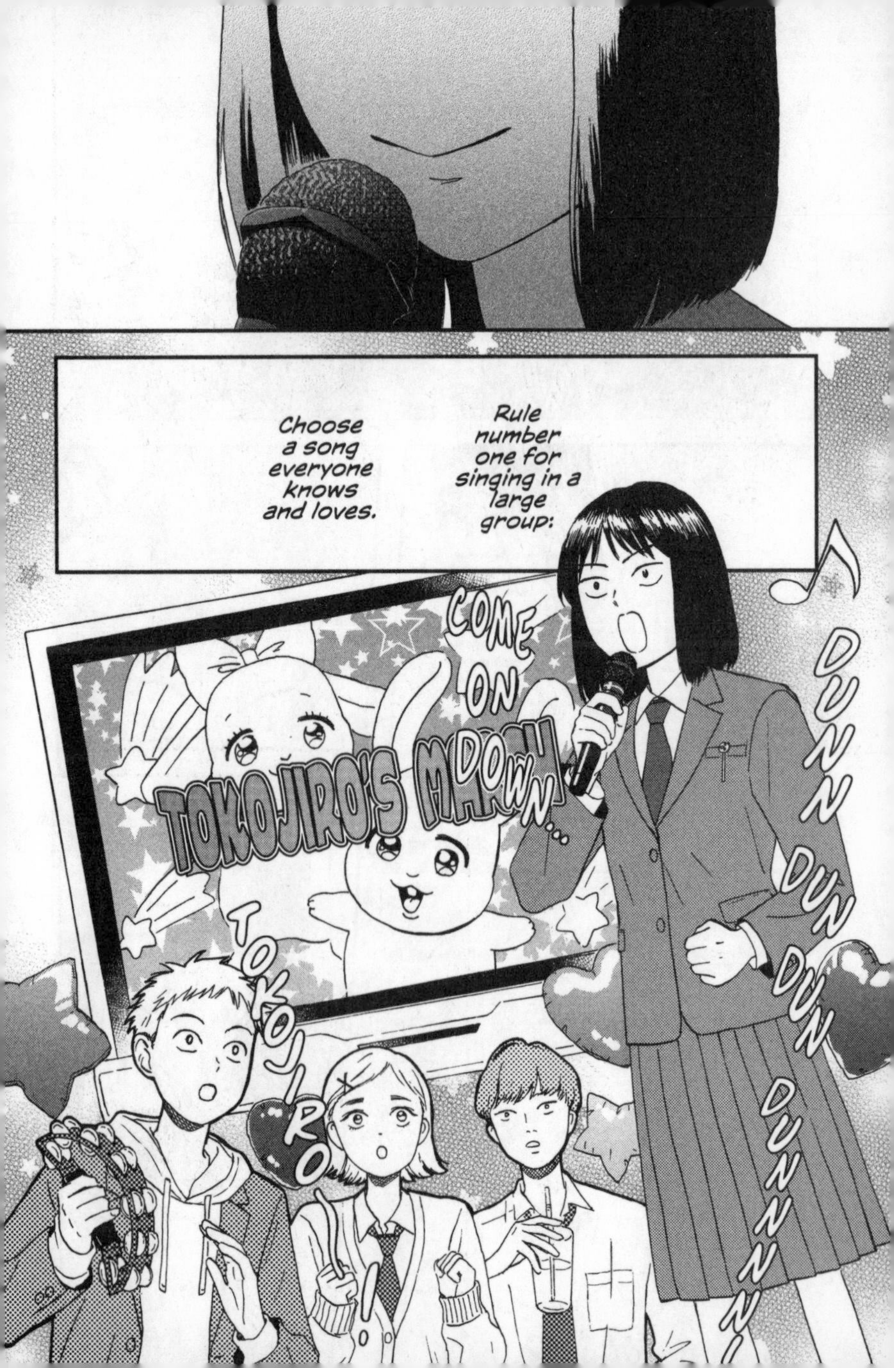
Rule number one for singing in a large group:
Choose a song everyone knows and loves.
COME ON DOWN...
TOKOJIRO'S
DUNN DUN DUN DUNNNNN
TOKOJIRO

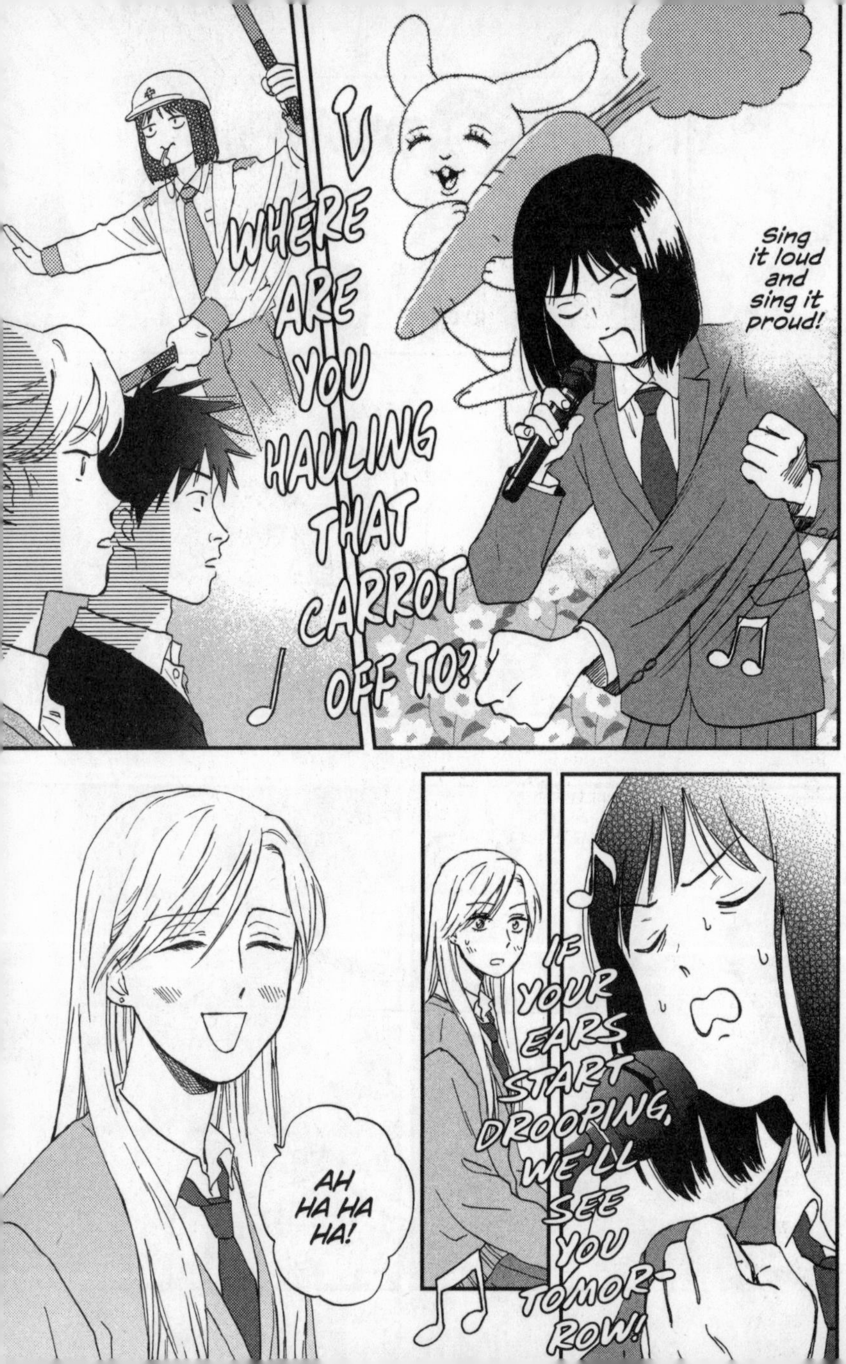
Sing it loud and sing it proud!
WHERE ARE YOU HAULING THAT CARROT OFF TO?
IF YOUR EARS START DROOPING, WE'LL SEE YOU TOMOR-ROW!
AH HA HA HA!

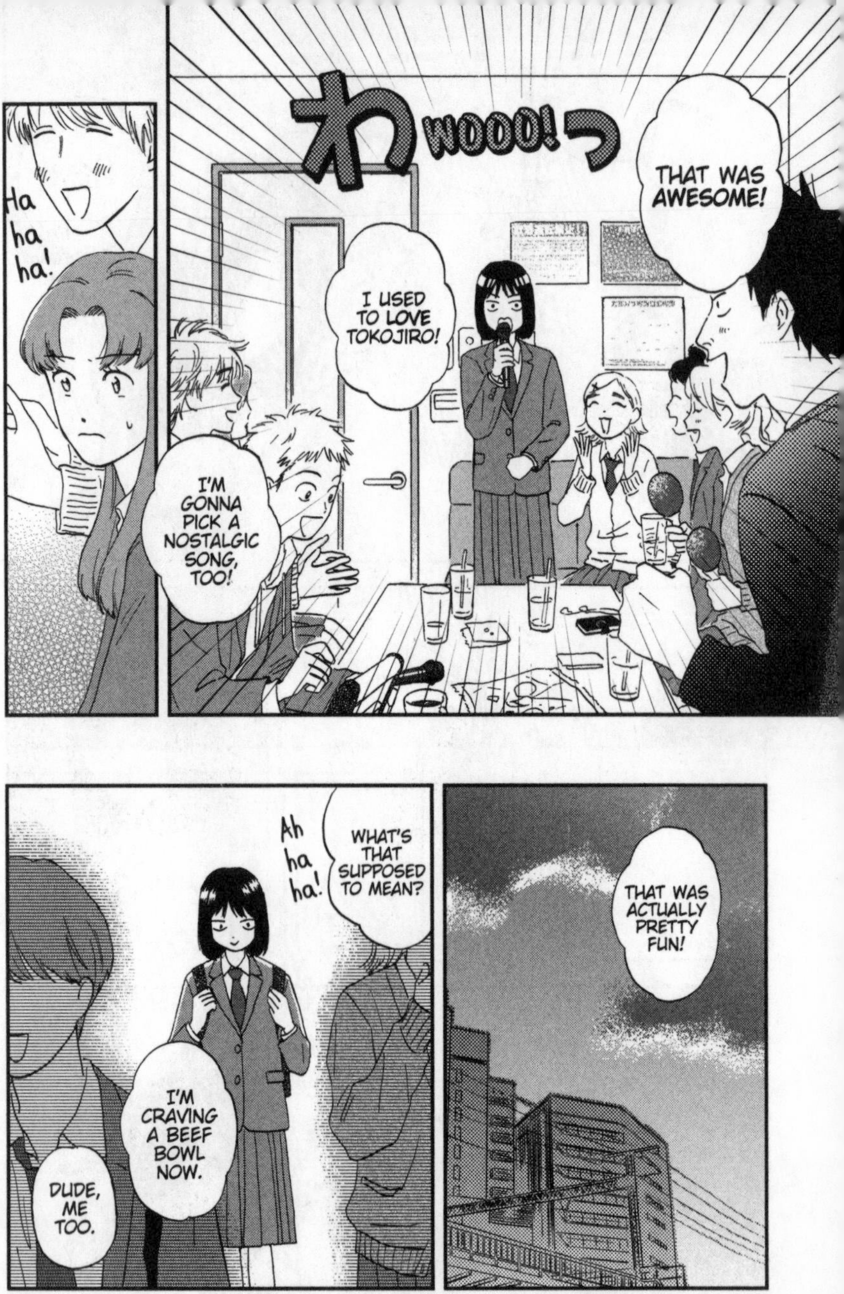
わWOOO!っ
THAT WAS AWESOME!
I USED TO LOVE TOKOJIRO!
I'M GONNA PICK A NOSTALGIC SONG, TOO!
Ha ha ha!
THAT WAS ACTUALLY PRETTY FUN!
WHAT'S THAT SUPPOSED TO MEAN?
Ah ha ha!
I'M CRAVING A BEEF BOWL NOW.
DUDE, ME TOO.

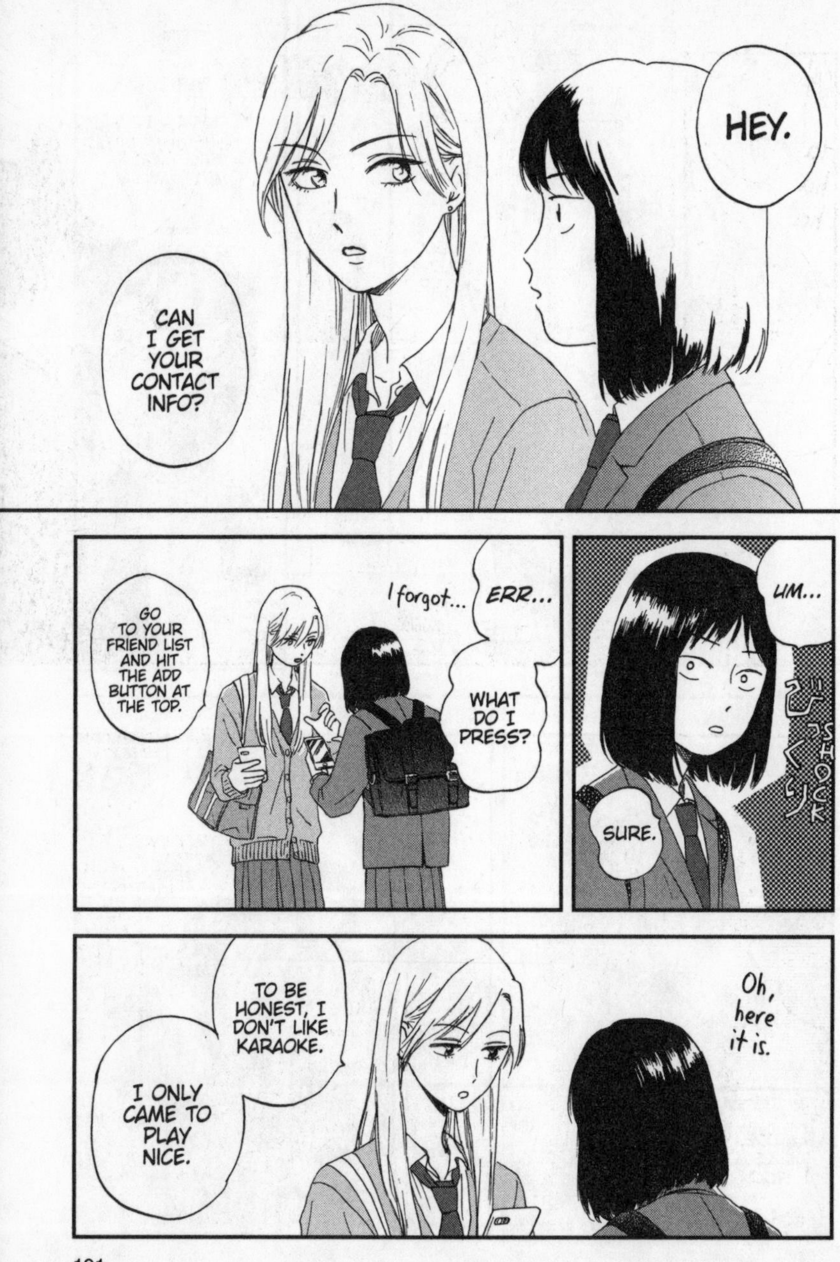
HEY.
CAN I GET YOUR CONTACT INFO?
UM...
SURE.
びっくり
SHOCK
ERR...
I forgot...
WHAT DO I PRESS?
GO TO YOUR FRIEND LIST AND HIT THE ADD BUTTON AT THE TOP.
Oh, here it is.
TO BE HONEST, I DON'T LIKE KARAOKE.
I ONLY CAME TO PLAY NICE.

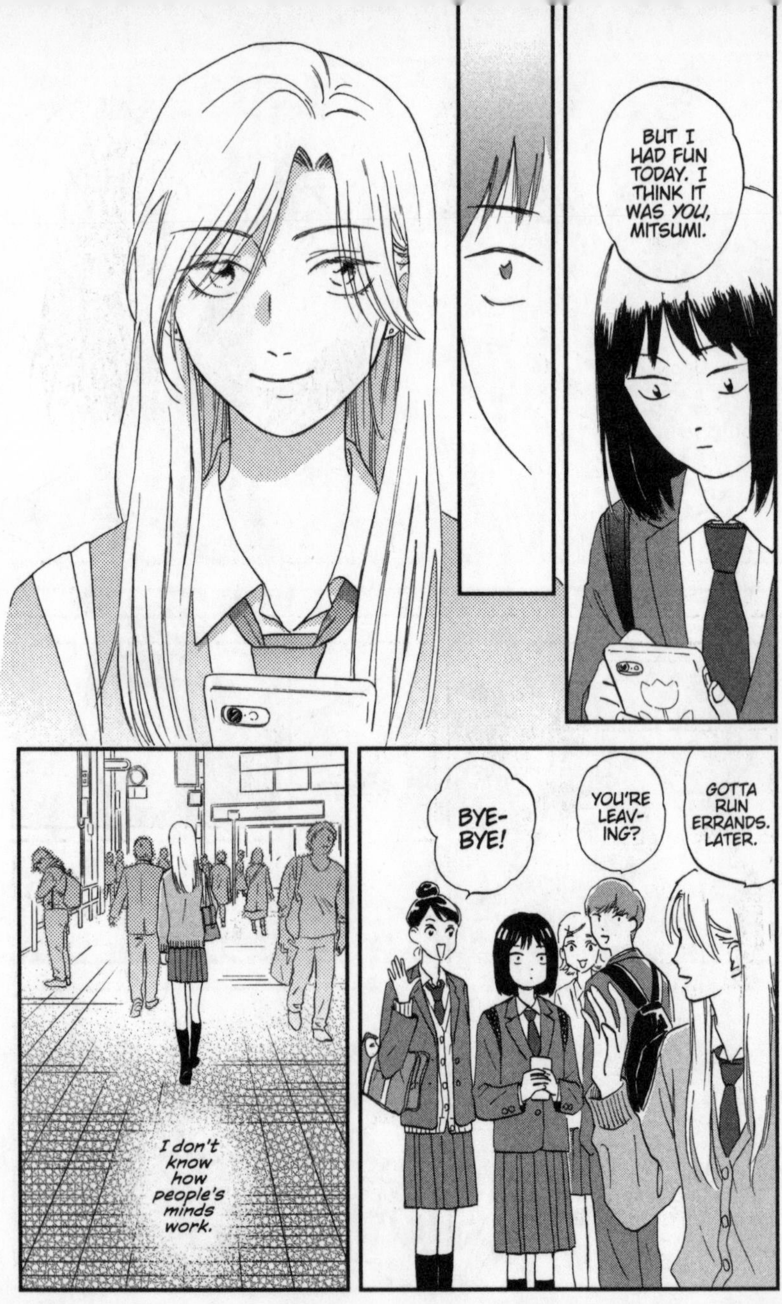
BUT I HAD FUN TODAY. I THINK IT WAS *YOU*, MITSUMI.
GOTTA RUN ERRANDS. LATER.
YOU'RE LEAV-ING?
BYE-BYE!
I don't know how people's minds work.

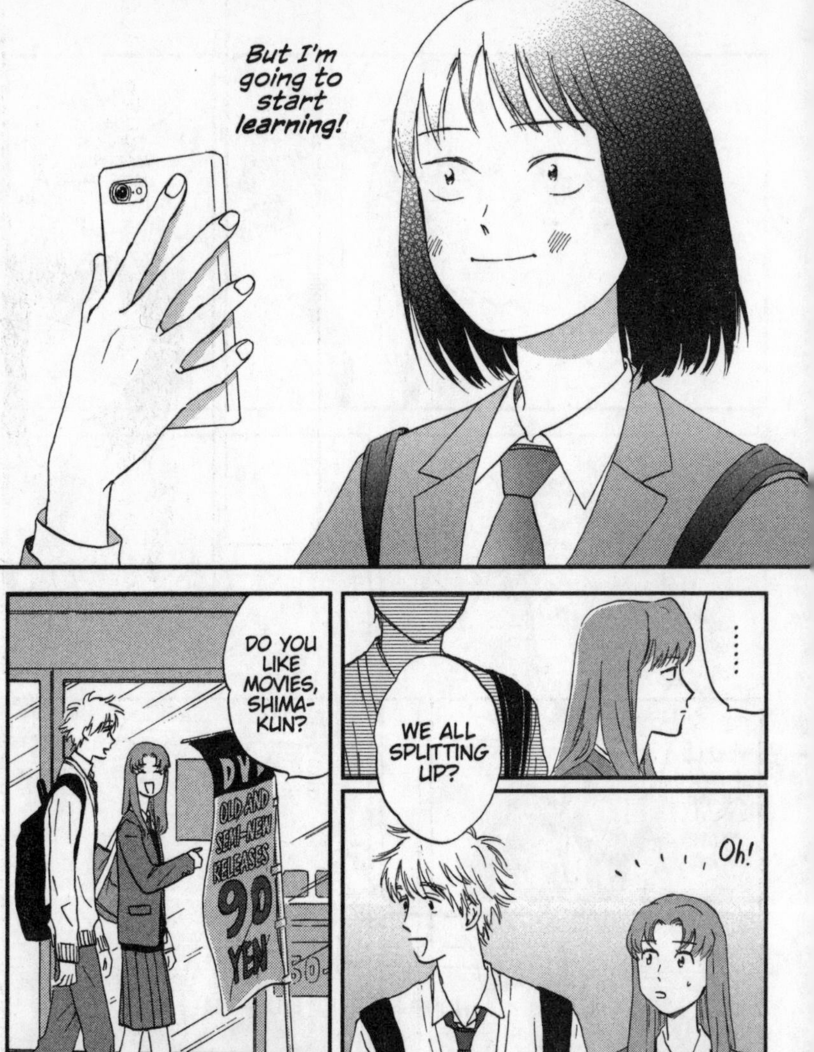
But I'm going to start learning!
......
WE ALL SPLITTING UP?
Oh!
Crud.
I HAVEN'T ASKED IF HE HAS A GIRLFRIEND YET.
GOOD QUESTION.
DO YOU LIKE MOVIES, SHIMA-KUN?
DVD
OLD AND SEMI-NEW RELEASES 90 YEN
SURE, SOMETIMES.

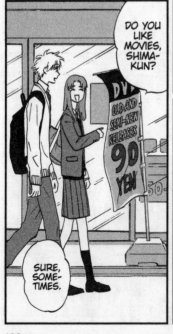

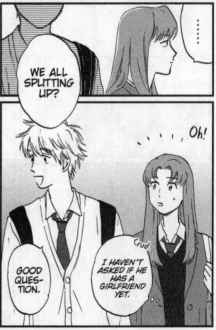

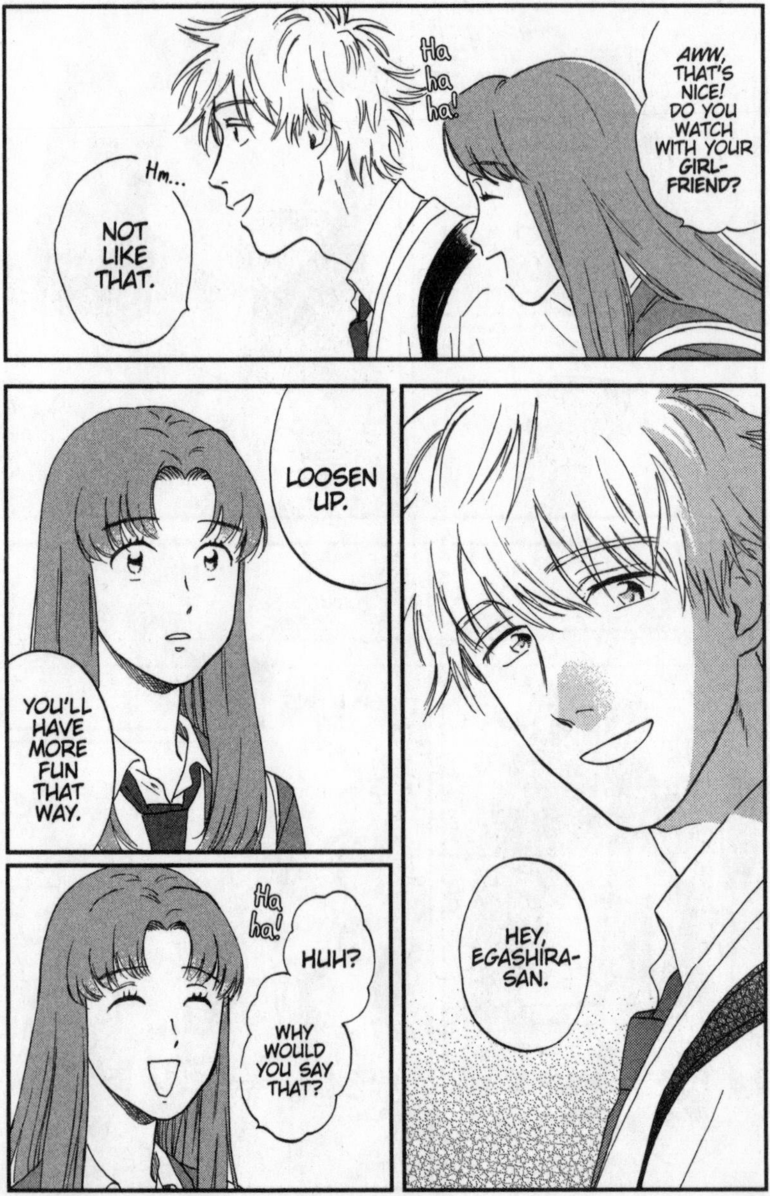
AWW, THAT'S NICE! DO YOU WATCH WITH YOUR GIRL-FRIEND?
Ha ha ha!
Hm...
NOT LIKE THAT.
HEY, EGASHIRA-SAN.
LOOSEN UP.
YOU'LL HAVE MORE FUN THAT WAY.
Ha ha!
HUH?
WHY WOULD YOU SAY THAT?

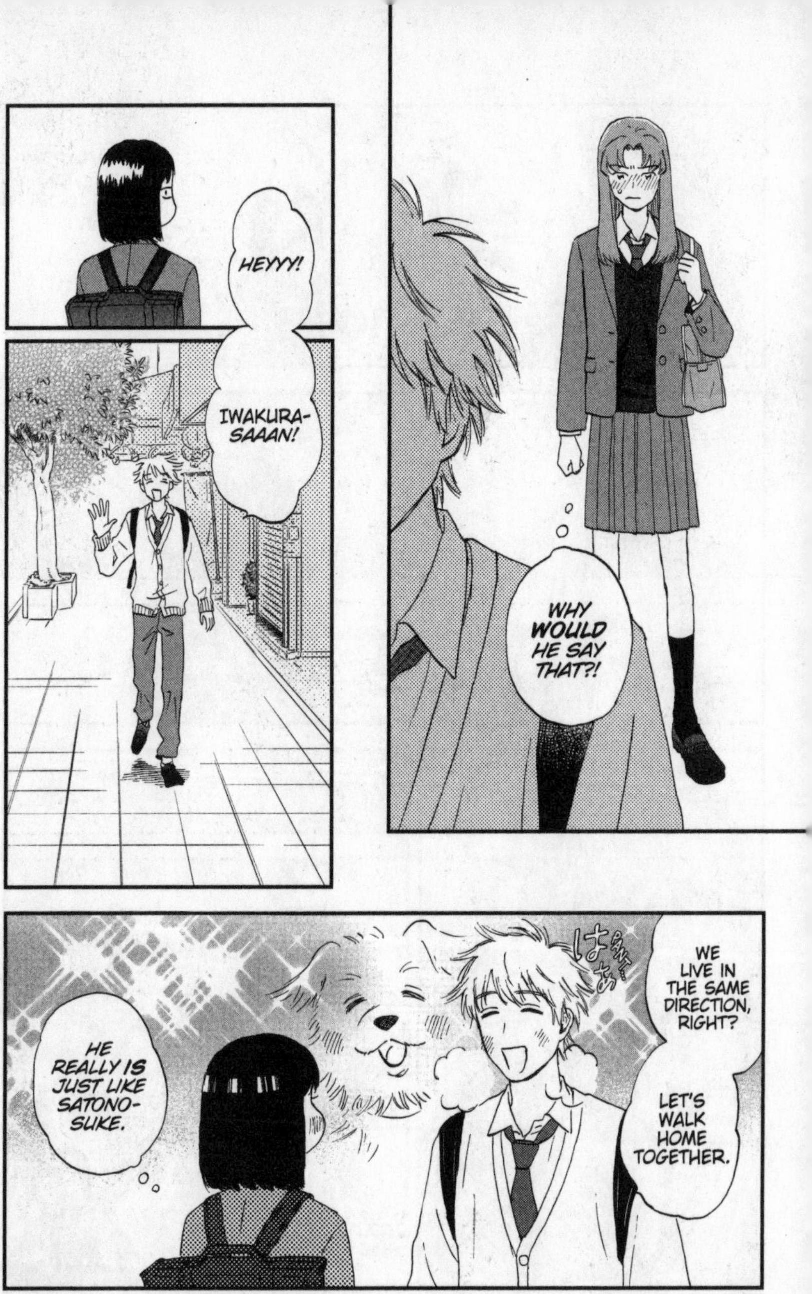
WHY WOULD HE SAY THAT?!
HEYYY!
IWAKURA-SAAAN!
WE LIVE IN THE SAME DIRECTION, RIGHT?
はぁ PANT...
LET'S WALK HOME TOGETHER.
HE REALLY IS JUST LIKE SATONO-SUKE.

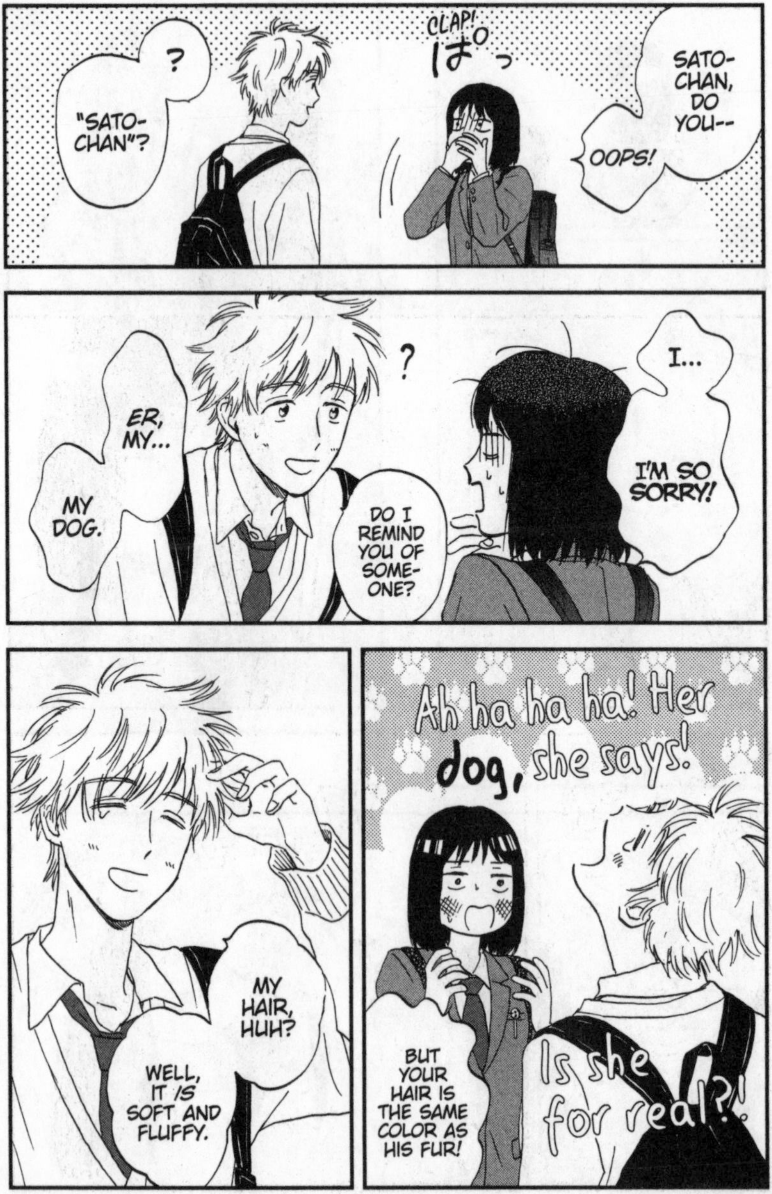
SATO-CHAN, DO YOU--
OOPS!
CLAP! ぱっ
?
"SATO-CHAN"?
I...
I'M SO SORRY!
?
DO I REMIND YOU OF SOME-ONE?
ER, MY...
MY DOG.
Ah ha ha ha! Her dog, she says!
Is she for real?!
BUT YOUR HAIR IS THE SAME COLOR AS HIS FUR!
MY HAIR, HUH?
WELL, IT IS SOFT AND FLUFFY.

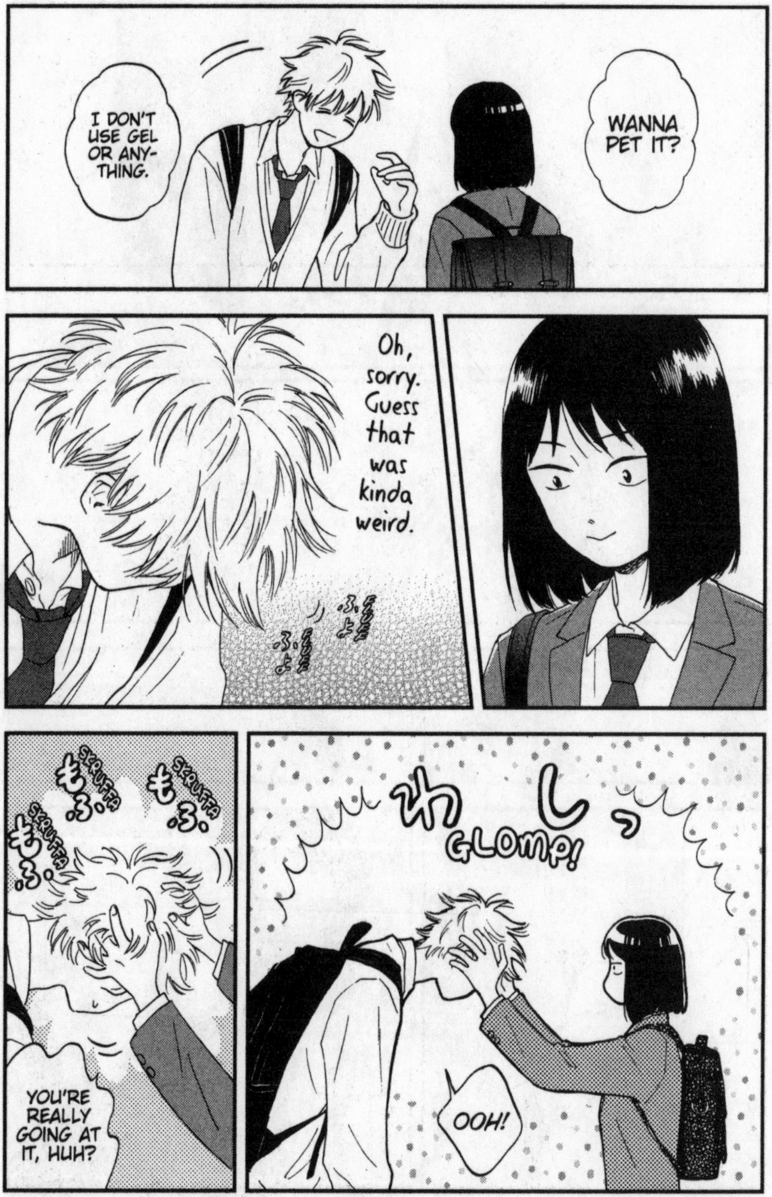
WANNA PET IT?
I DON'T USE GEL OR ANY-THING.
Oh, sorry. Guess that was kinda weird.
ふよ
ふよ
わしっ
GLOMP!
OOH!
もふ SKRUFFA
もふ SKRUFFA
もふ SKRUFFA
YOU'RE REALLY GOING AT IT, HUH?

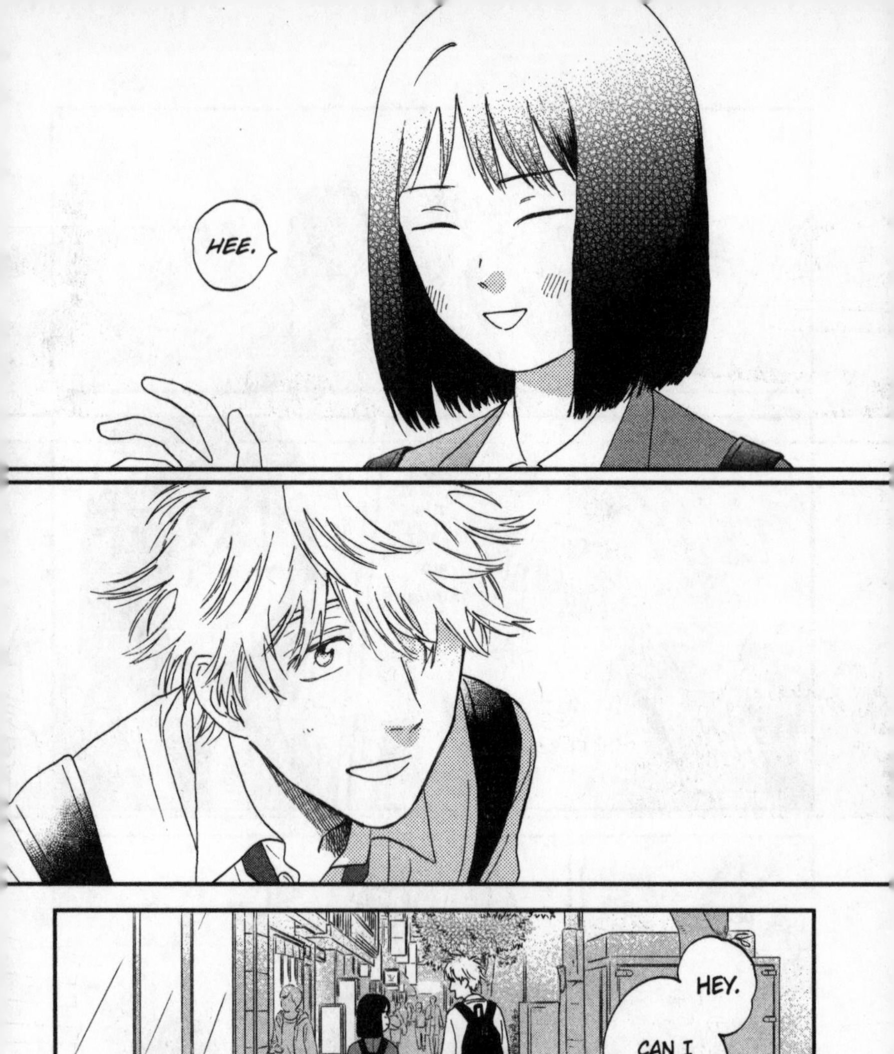
HEE.
HEY.
CAN I CALL YOU MITSUMI-CHAN?
SURE.

Scene② END

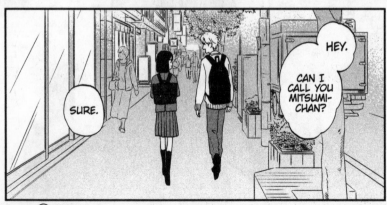

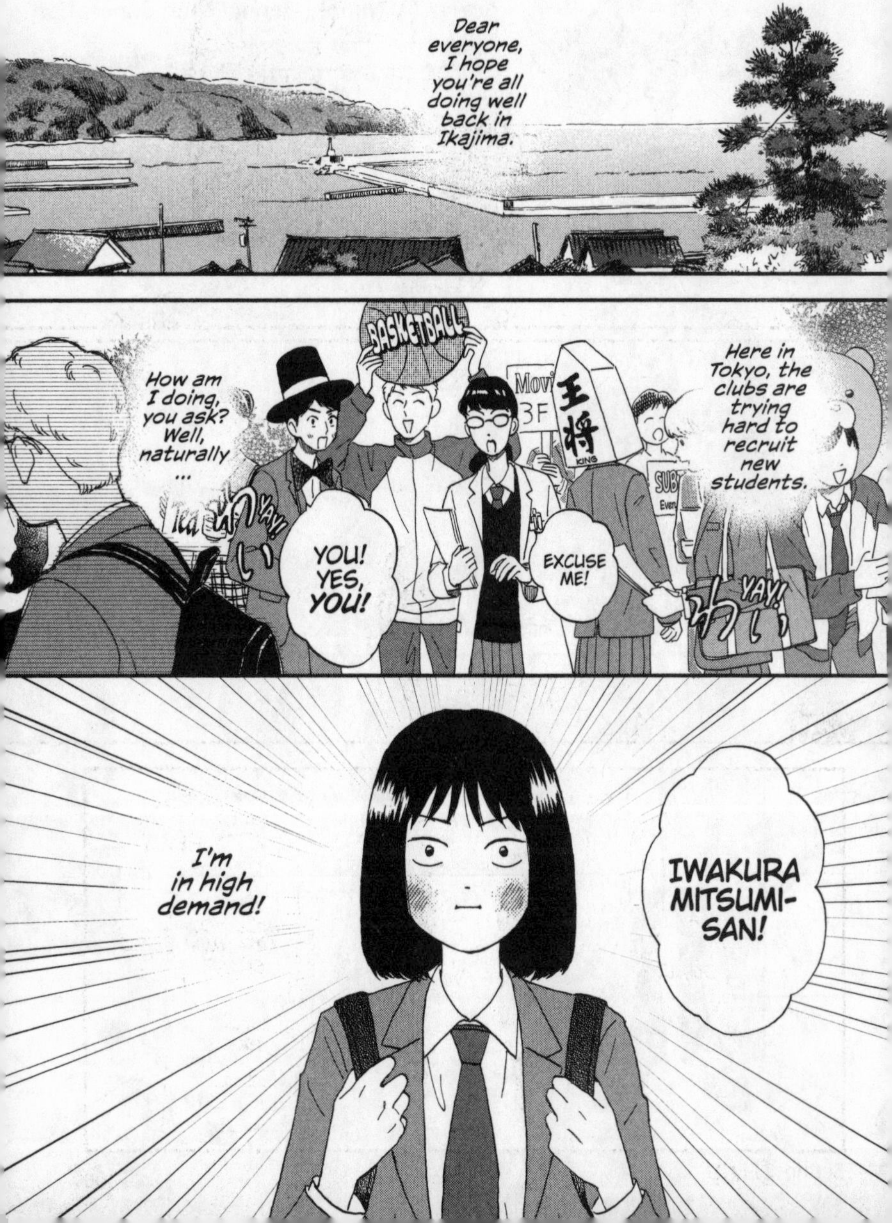
Dear everyone, I hope you're all doing well back in Ikajima.
Here in Tokyo, the clubs are trying hard to recruit new students.
YAY!
EXCUSE ME!
王将
KING
BASKETBALL
YOU! YES, YOU!
YAY!
How am I doing, you ask? Well, naturally ...
IWAKURA MITSUMI-SAN!
I'm in high demand!

Scene ③ *Uhhh...* School Club Contention

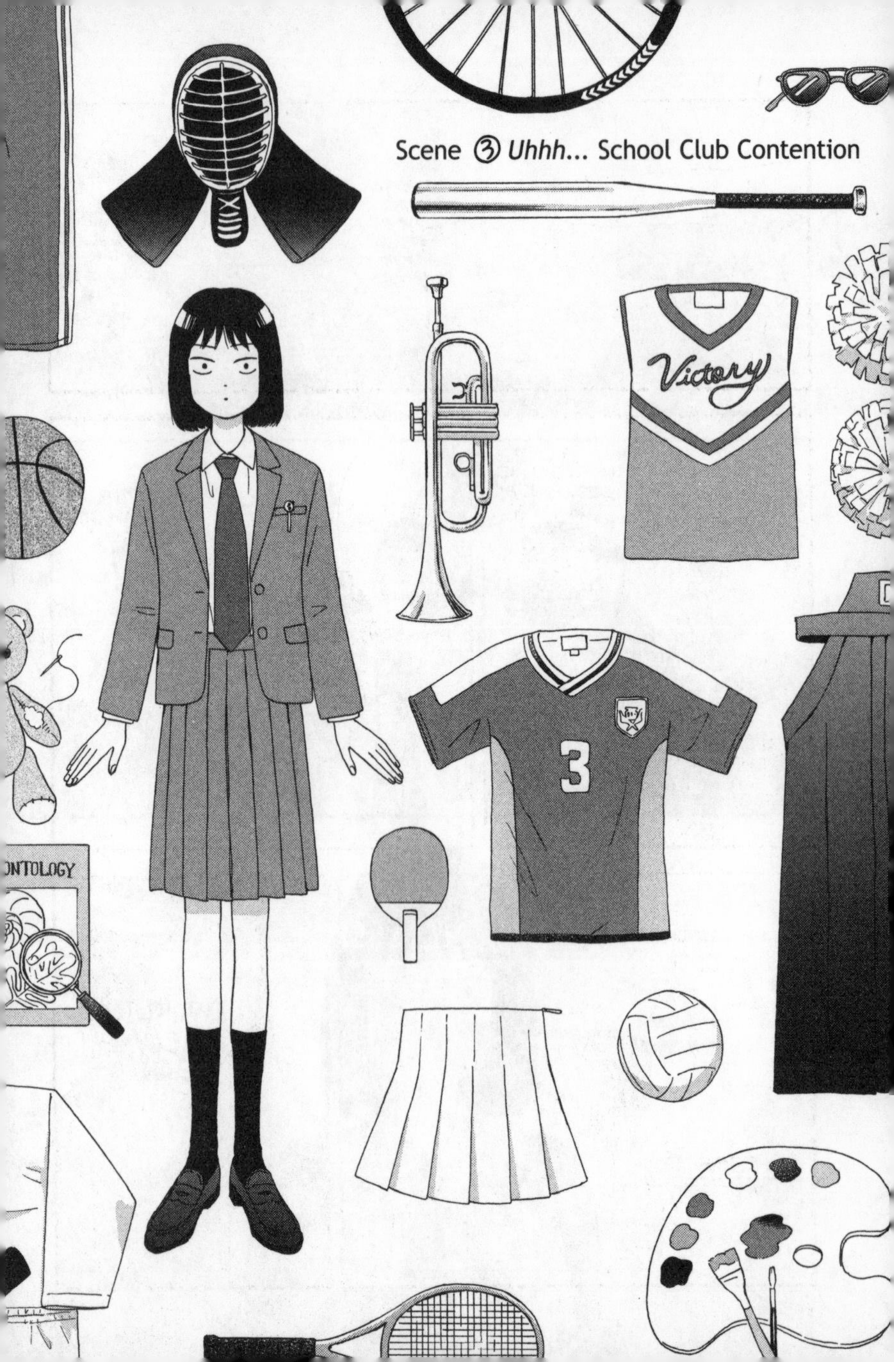
Victory
3
ONTOLOGY

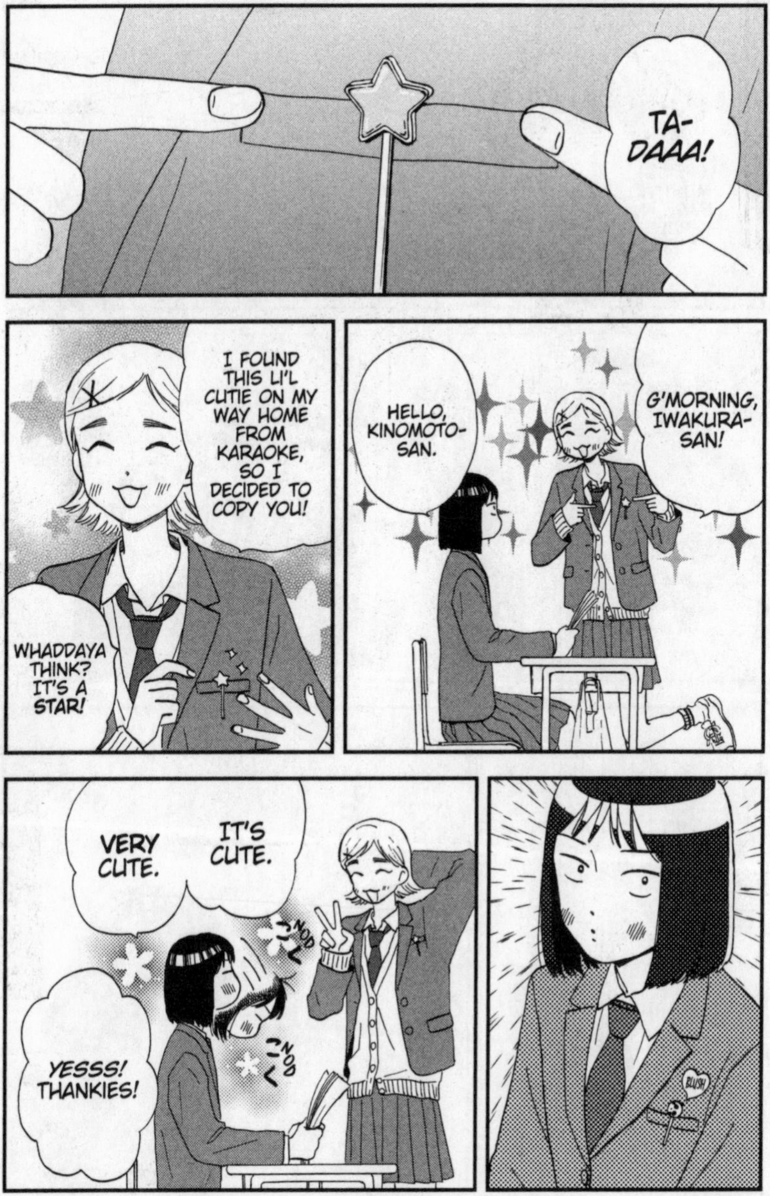
TA-DAAA!
G'MORNING, IWAKURA-SAN!
HELLO, KINOMOTO-SAN.
I FOUND THIS LI'L CUTIE ON MY WAY HOME FROM KARAOKE, SO I DECIDED TO COPY YOU!
WHADDAYA THINK? IT'S A STAR!
BLUSH
IT'S CUTE.
VERY CUTE.
NOD
NOD
YESSS! THANKIES!

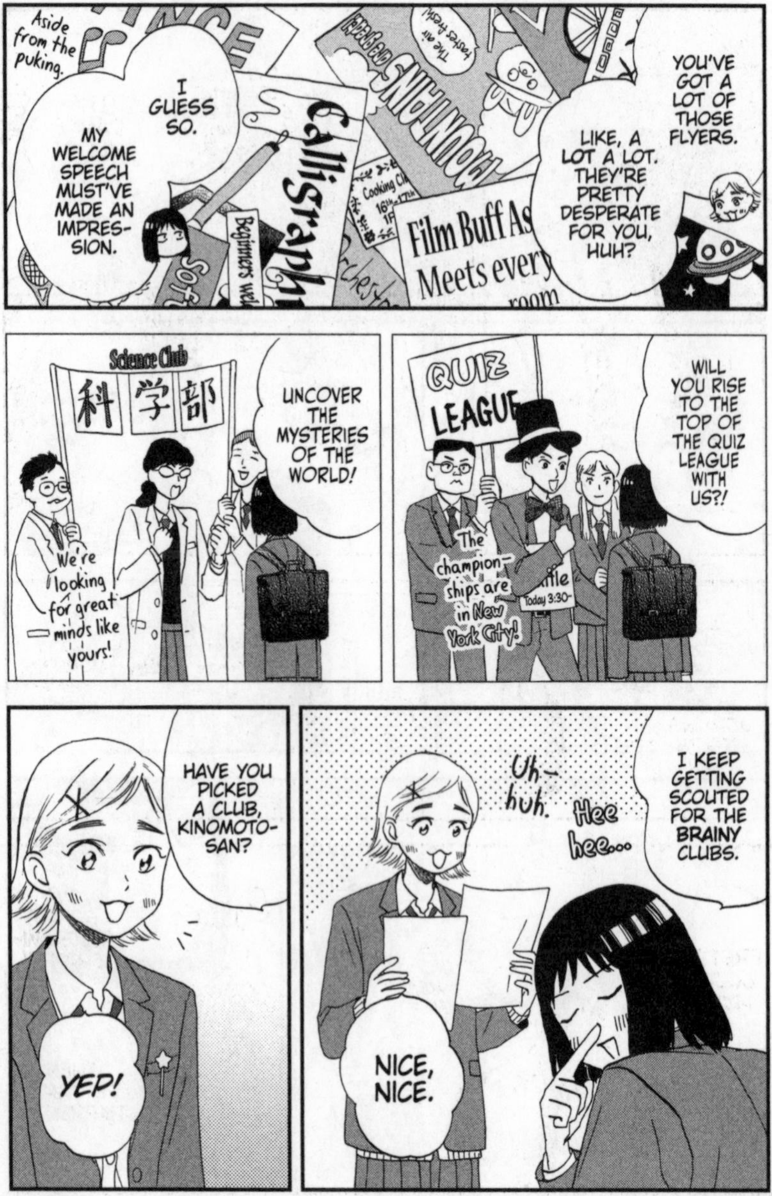

YOU'VE GOT A LOT OF THOSE FLYERS.
LIKE, A LOT A LOT. THEY'RE PRETTY DESPERATE FOR YOU, HUH?
The air tastes fresh!
I GUESS SO.
MY WELCOME SPEECH MUST'VE MADE AN IMPRESSION.
Aside from the puking.
QUIZ LEAGUE
WILL YOU RISE TO THE TOP OF THE QUIZ LEAGUE WITH US?!
The champion-ships are in New York City!
Today 3:30-
Science Club
科学部
UNCOVER THE MYSTERIES OF THE WORLD!
We're looking for great minds like yours!
I KEEP GETTING SCOUTED FOR THE BRAINY CLUBS.
Uh-huh.
Hee hee...
NICE, NICE.
HAVE YOU PICKED A CLUB, KINOMOTO-SAN?
YEP!

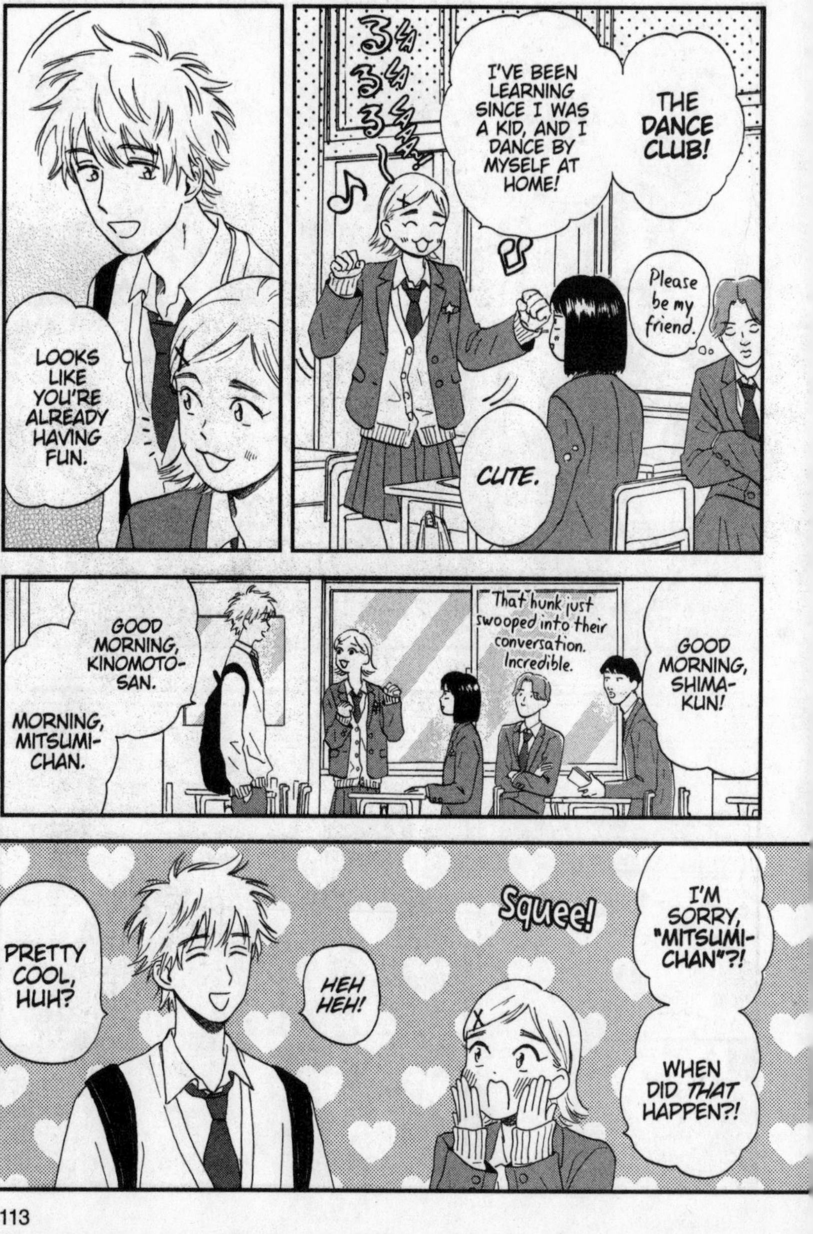
THE DANCE CLUB!
I'VE BEEN LEARNING SINCE I WAS A KID, AND I DANCE BY MYSELF AT HOME!
Please be my friend.
CUTE.
LOOKS LIKE YOU'RE ALREADY HAVING FUN.
GOOD MORNING, SHIMA-KUN!
That hunk just swooped into their conversation. Incredible.
GOOD MORNING, KINOMOTO-SAN.
MORNING, MITSUMI-CHAN.
I'M SORRY, "MITSUMI-CHAN"?!
WHEN DID *THAT* HAPPEN?!
Squee!
HEH HEH!
PRETTY COOL, HUH?

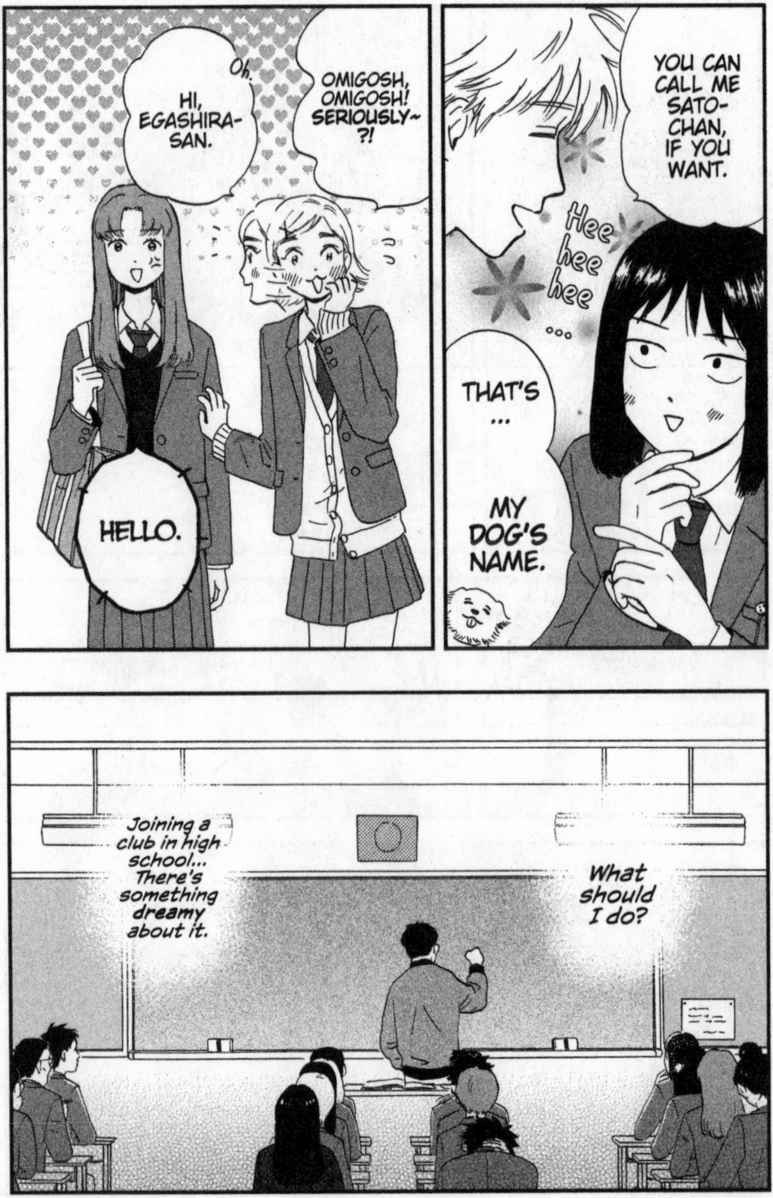
YOU CAN CALL ME SATO-CHAN, IF YOU WANT.
Hee hee hee ...
THAT'S ...
MY DOG'S NAME.
OMIGOSH, OMIGOSH! SERIOUSLY~ ?!
Oh.
HI, EGASHIRA-SAN.
HELLO.
Joining a club in high school... There's something dreamy about it.
What should I do?

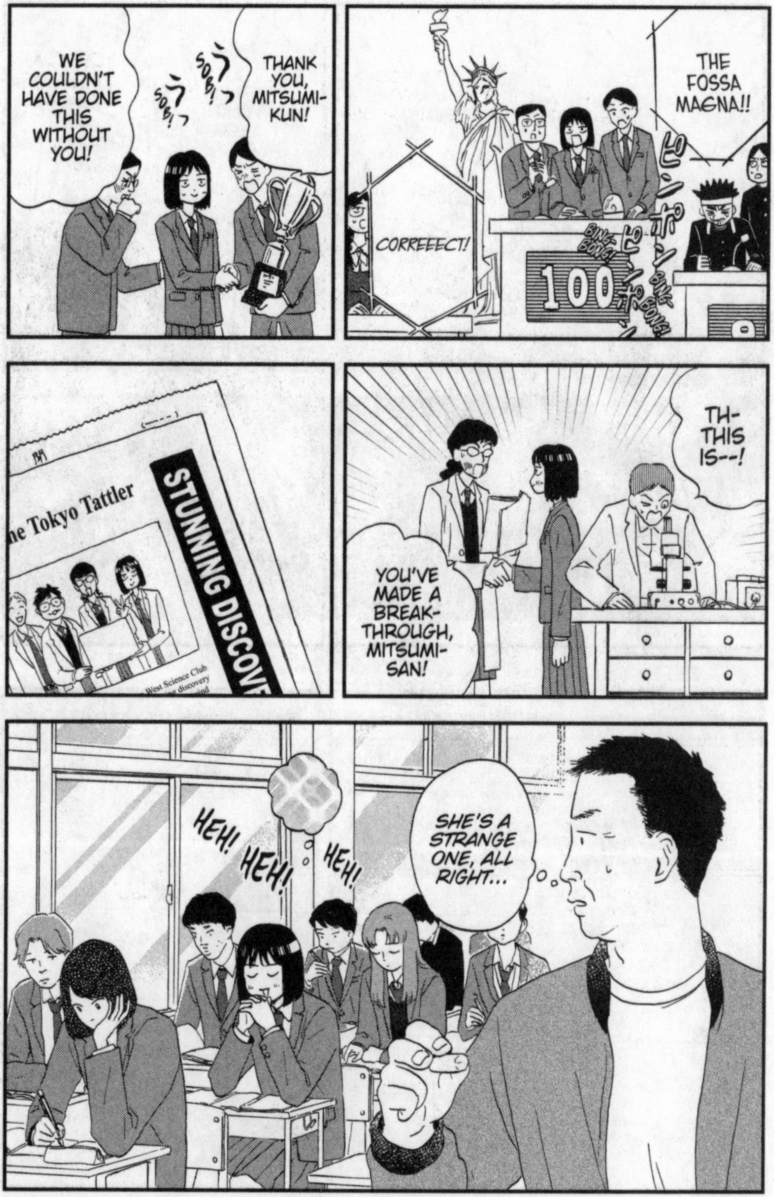
THE FOSSA MAGNA!!
CORREEECT!
BING-BONG!
BING-BONG!
100
0
THANK YOU, MITSUMI-KUN!
SOB!
SOB!
WE COULDN'T HAVE DONE THIS WITHOUT YOU!
TH-THIS IS--!
YOU'VE MADE A BREAK-THROUGH, MITSUMI-SAN!
he Tokyo Tattler
STUNNING DISCOV
West Science Club
SHE'S A STRANGE ONE, ALL RIGHT...
HEH!
HEH!
HEH!

We only covered three subjects this time, though.

	Overall	
English	579	
194	600	
200	12/240	

HERE'S YOUR TEST RESULTS!

YOU'LL SEE YOUR CLASS RANKING IN THE CORNER.

This school prides itself on preparing high schoolers for university.

I need to stop getting lost in feckless daydreams...

and further my education for the greater good.

What's wrong with a little daydreaming...?

HOLY CRAP, WATANABE! YOU GOT THIRD IN THE--

EYES TO YOURSELF.

WHUD

I should have known.

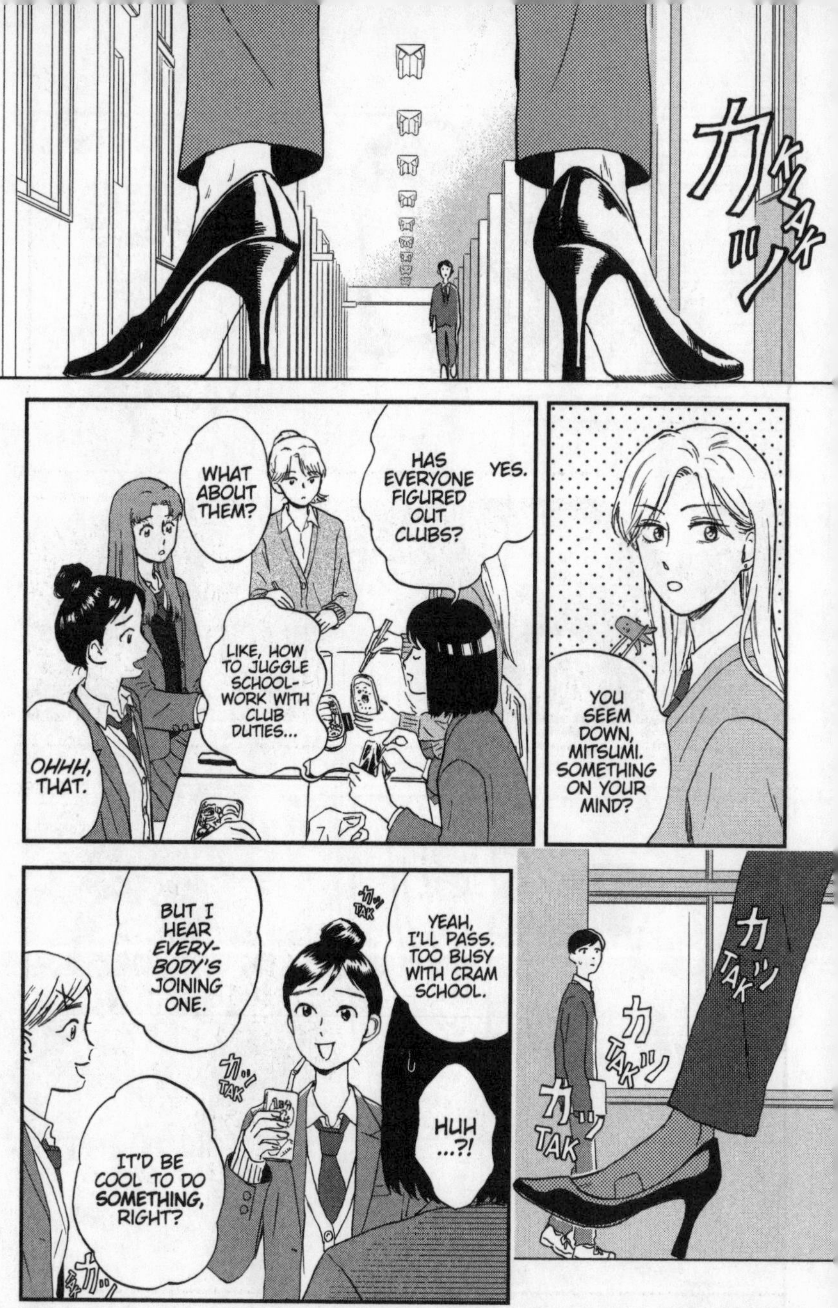
カッ
KLAK
YOU SEEM DOWN, MITSUMI. SOMETHING ON YOUR MIND?
YES.
HAS EVERYONE FIGURED OUT CLUBS?
WHAT ABOUT THEM?
LIKE, HOW TO JUGGLE SCHOOL-WORK WITH CLUB DUTIES...
OHHH, THAT.
カッ TAK
カッ TAK
カッ TAK
YEAH, I'LL PASS. TOO BUSY WITH CRAM SCHOOL.
カッ TAK
BUT I HEAR EVERY-BODY'S JOINING ONE.
カッ TAK
HUH ...?!
IT'D BE COOL TO DO SOMETHING, RIGHT?
カッ TAK

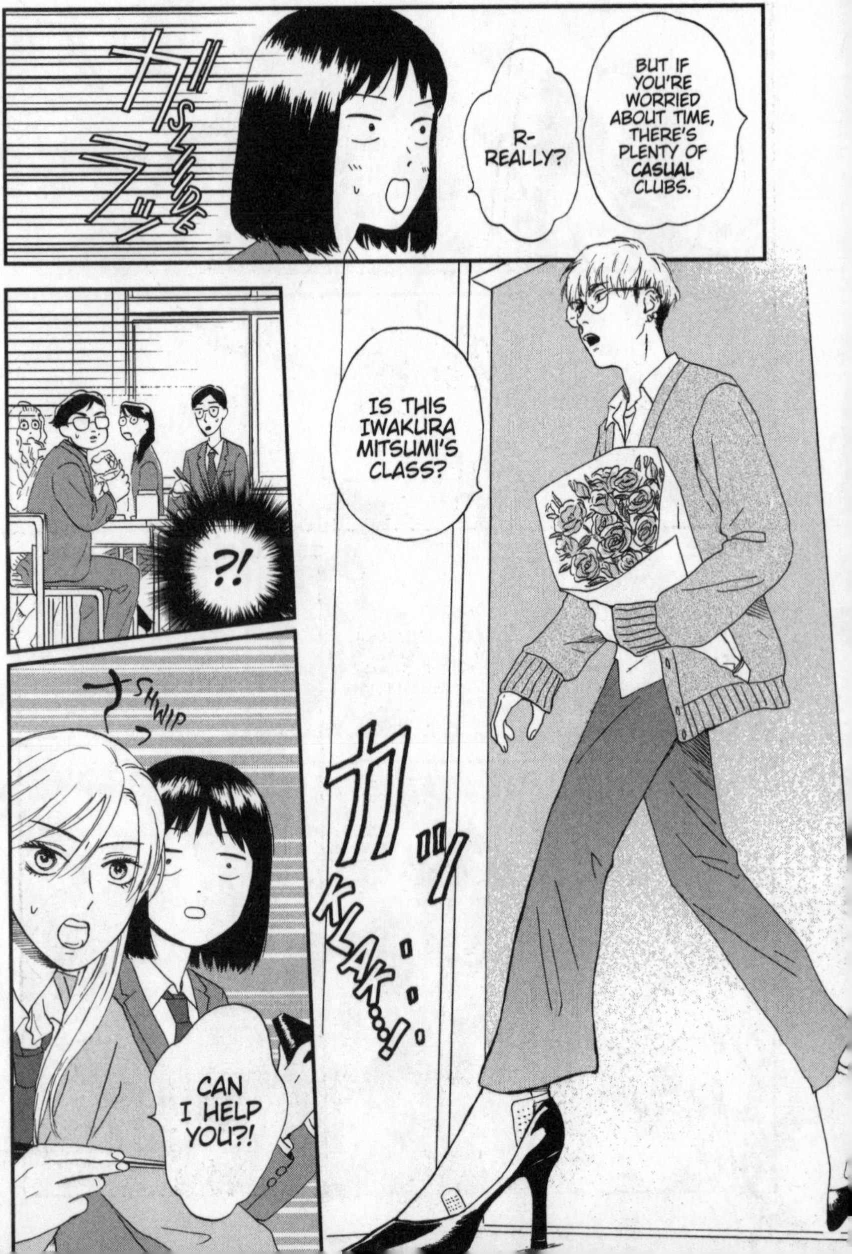
BUT IF YOU'RE WORRIED ABOUT TIME, THERE'S PLENTY OF CASUAL CLUBS.
R-REALLY?
SLIDE
IS THIS IWAKURA MITSUMI'S CLASS?
KLAK...!
?!
SHWIP
CAN I HELP YOU?!

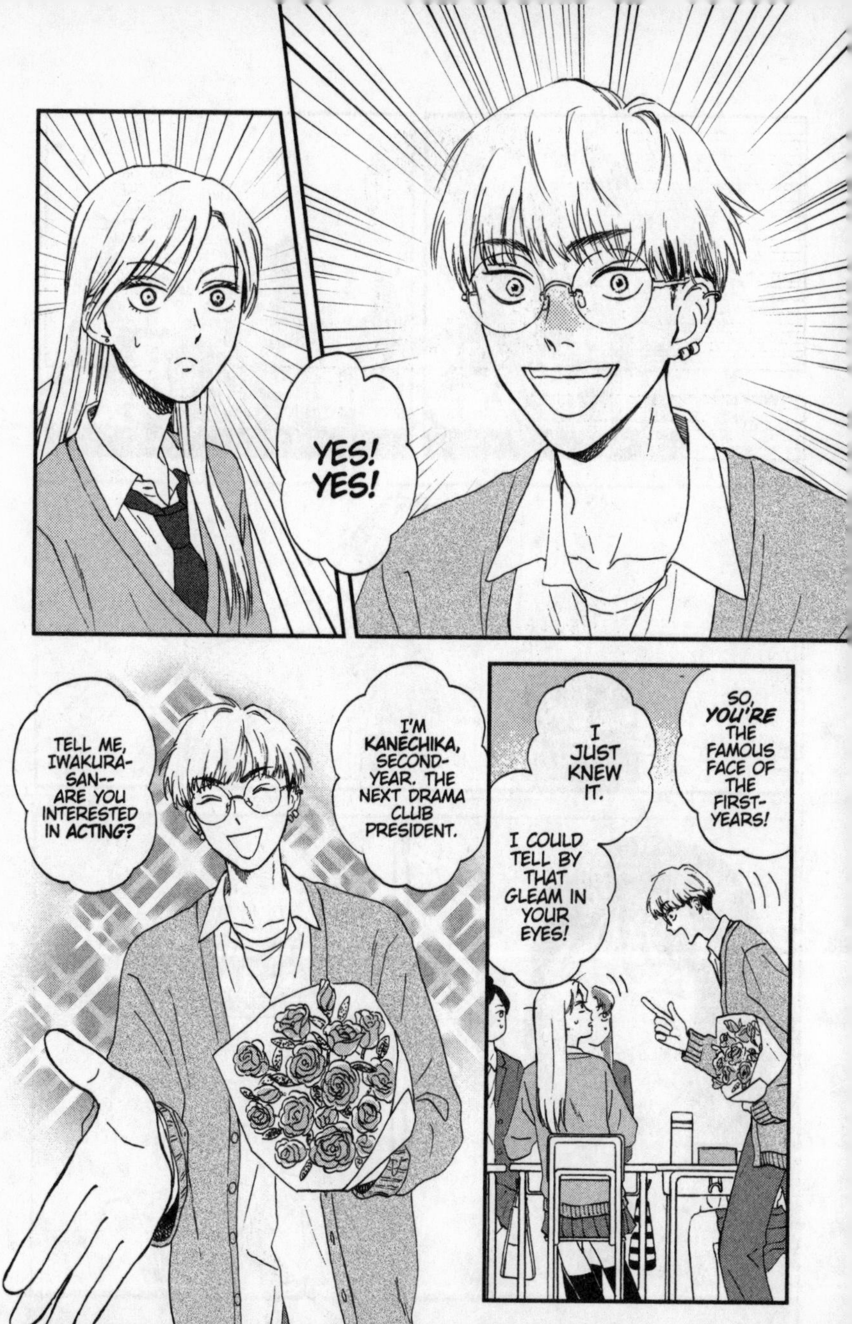
YES! YES!
SO, *YOU'RE* THE FAMOUS FACE OF THE FIRST-YEARS!
I JUST KNEW IT.
I COULD TELL BY THAT GLEAM IN YOUR EYES!
I'M KANECHIKA, SECOND-YEAR. THE NEXT DRAMA CLUB PRESIDENT.
TELL ME, IWAKURA-SAN--ARE YOU INTERESTED IN ACTING?

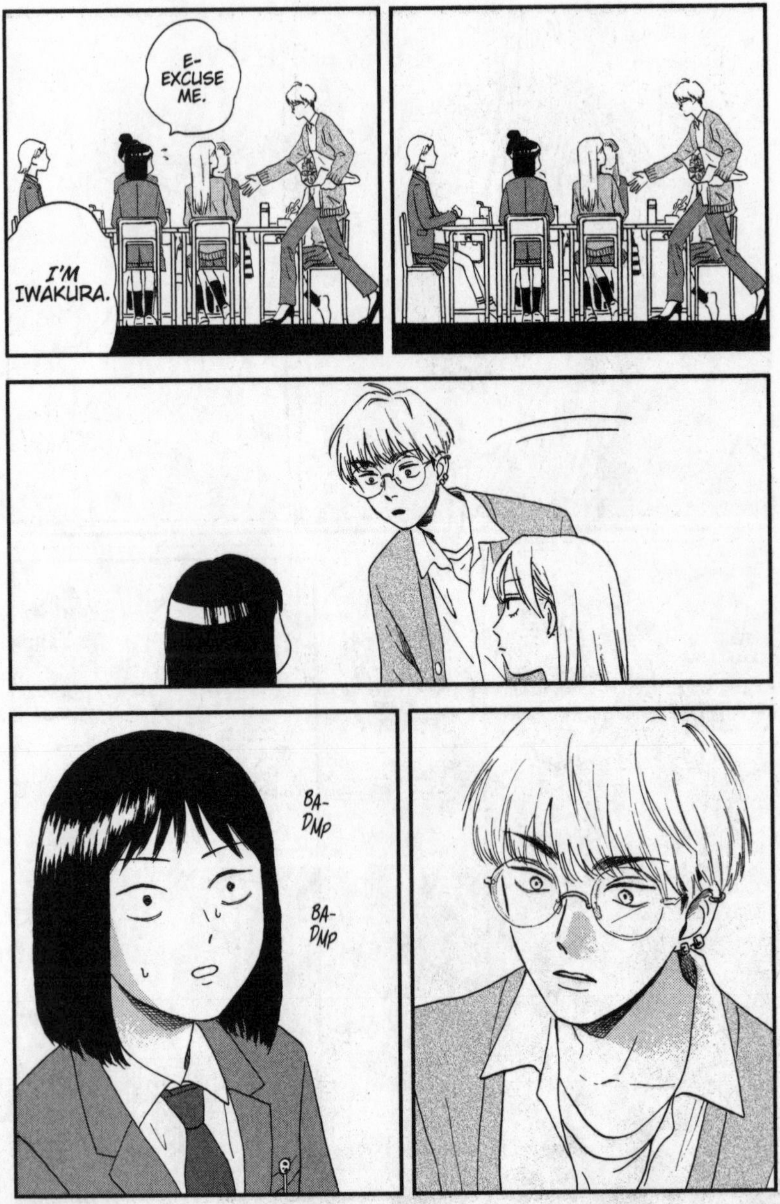
E-EXCUSE ME.
I'M IWAKURA.
BA-DMP
BA-DMP

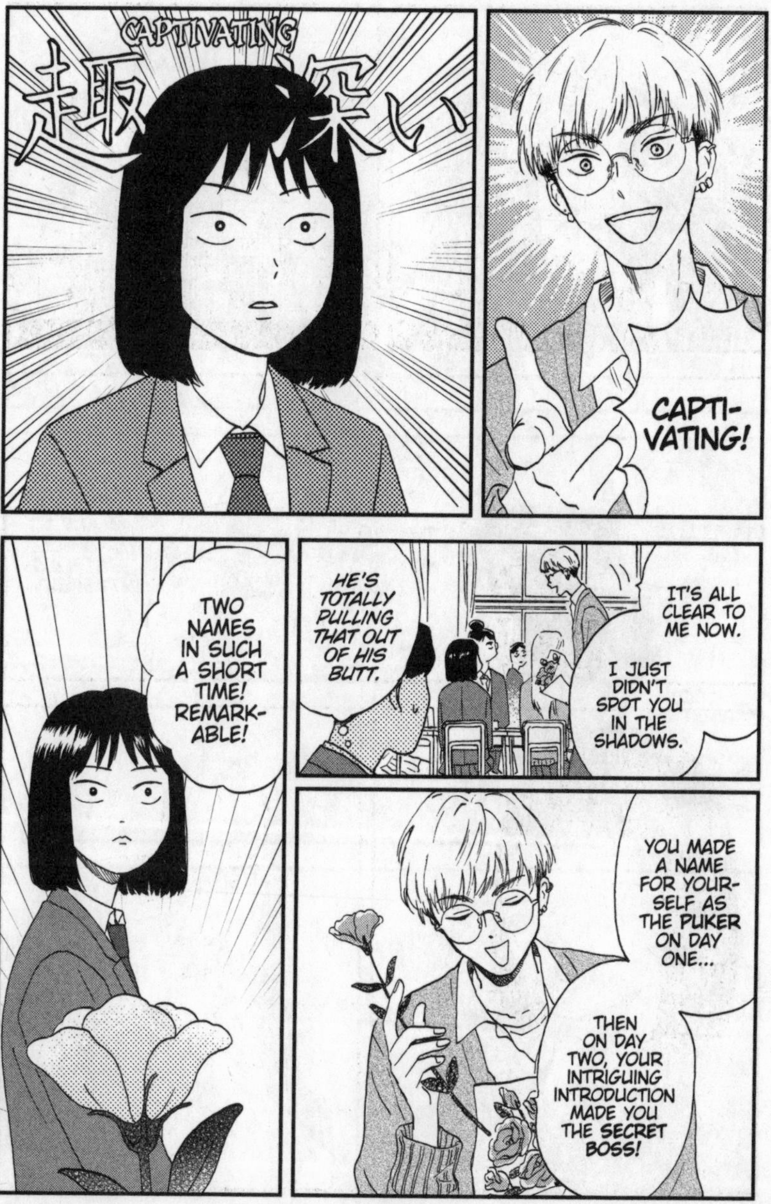
CAPTI-VATING!
CAPTIVATING
趣深い
IT'S ALL CLEAR TO ME NOW.
I JUST DIDN'T SPOT YOU IN THE SHADOWS.
HE'S TOTALLY PULLING THAT OUT OF HIS BUTT.
YOU MADE A NAME FOR YOUR-SELF AS THE PUKER ON DAY ONE...
THEN ON DAY TWO, YOUR INTRIGUING INTRODUCTION MADE YOU THE SECRET BOSS!
TWO NAMES IN SUCH A SHORT TIME! REMARK-ABLE!

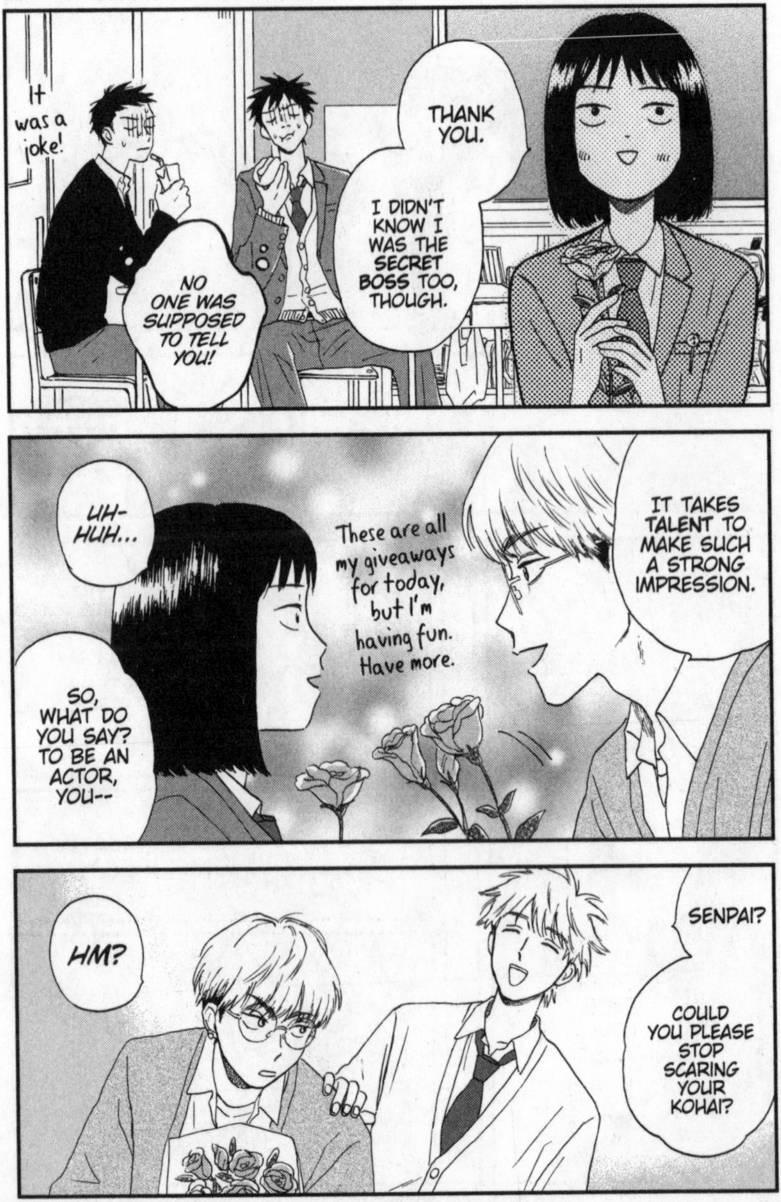
THANK YOU.
I DIDN'T KNOW I WAS THE SECRET BOSS TOO, THOUGH.
NO ONE WAS SUPPOSED TO TELL YOU!
It was a joke!
IT TAKES TALENT TO MAKE SUCH A STRONG IMPRESSION.
These are all my giveaways for today, but I'm having fun. Have more.
UH-HUH...
SO, WHAT DO YOU SAY? TO BE AN ACTOR, YOU--
SENPAI?
COULD YOU PLEASE STOP SCARING YOUR KOHAI?
HM?

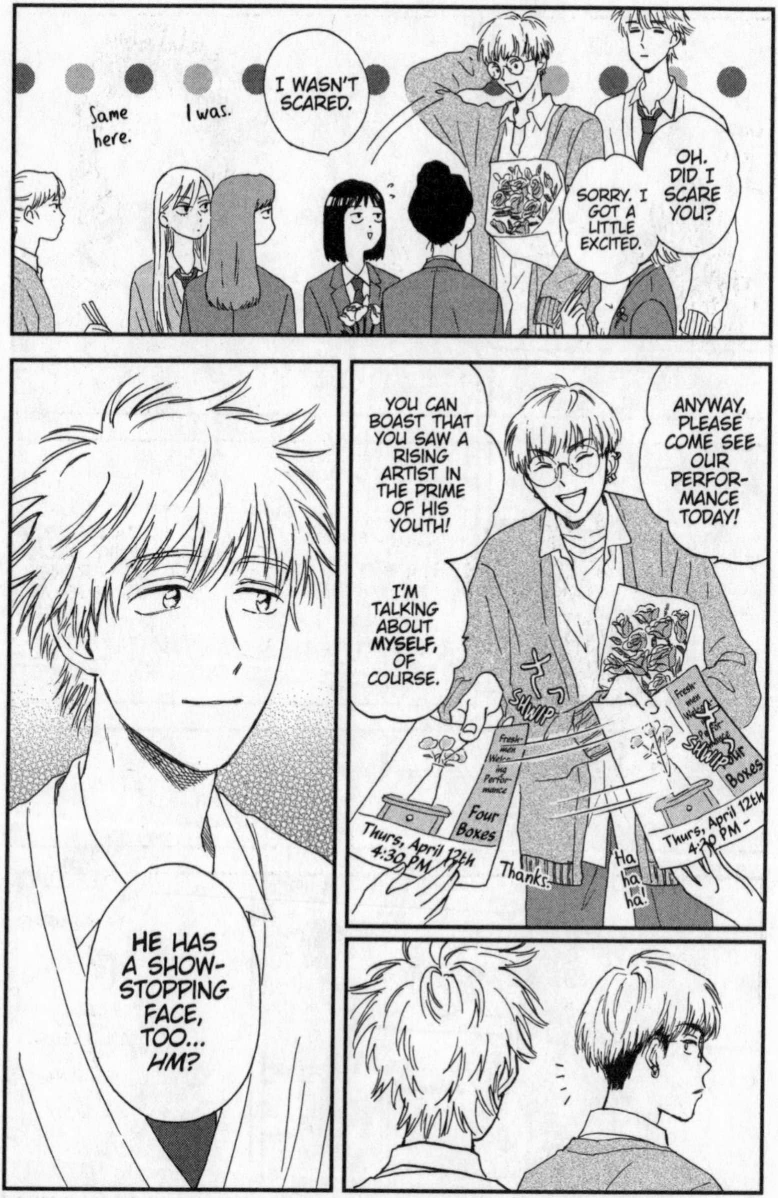
OH. DID I SCARE YOU?
SORRY. I GOT A LITTLE EXCITED.
I WASN'T SCARED.
I was.
Same here.
ANYWAY, PLEASE COME SEE OUR PERFORMANCE TODAY!
YOU CAN BOAST THAT YOU SAW A RISING ARTIST IN THE PRIME OF HIS YOUTH!
I'M TALKING ABOUT MYSELF, OF COURSE.
SHWIP
SHWIP
Boxes
Thurs, April 12th 4:30 PM -
Ha ha ha!
Freshmen Welcoming Performance
Four Boxes
Thurs, April 12th 4:30 PM
Thanks.
HE HAS A SHOW-STOPPING FACE, TOO... HM?

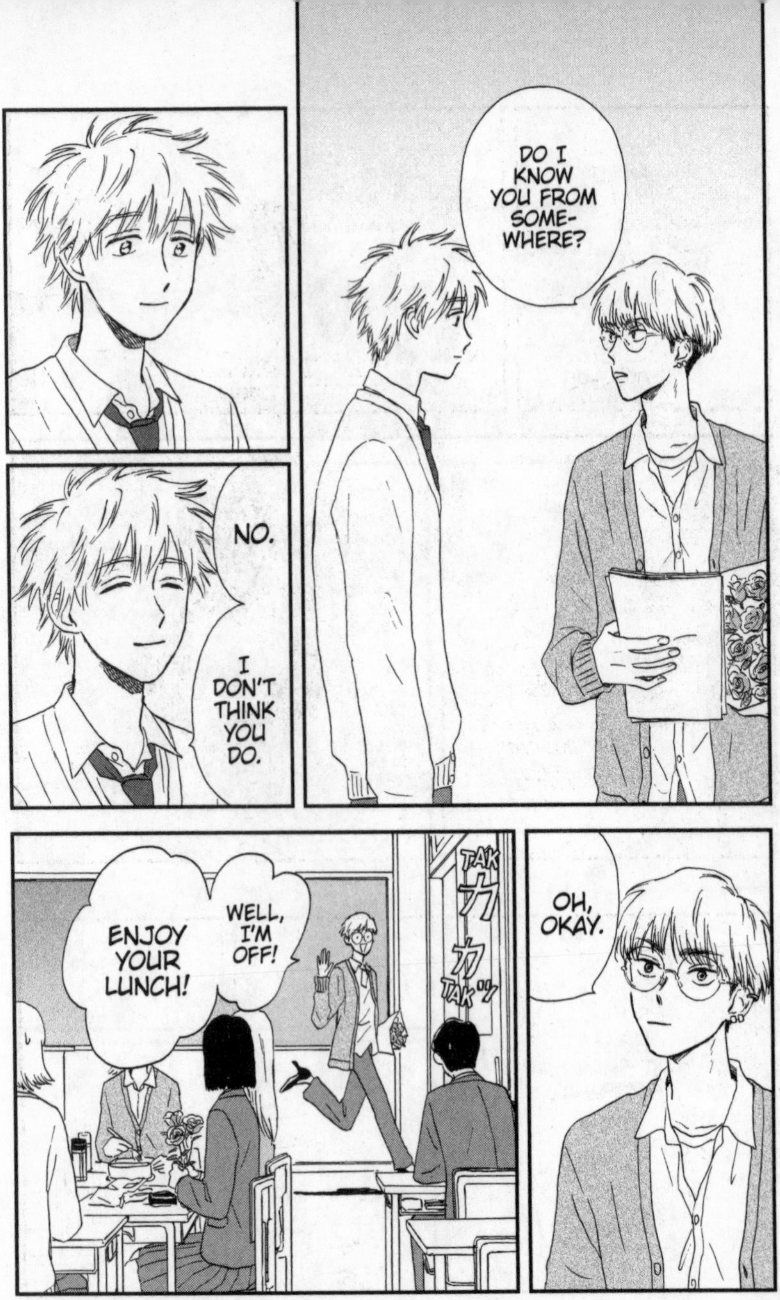
DO I KNOW YOU FROM SOME-WHERE?
NO.
I DON'T THINK YOU DO.
OH, OKAY.
TAK カ
カ TAK ッ
WELL, I'M OFF!
ENJOY YOUR LUNCH!

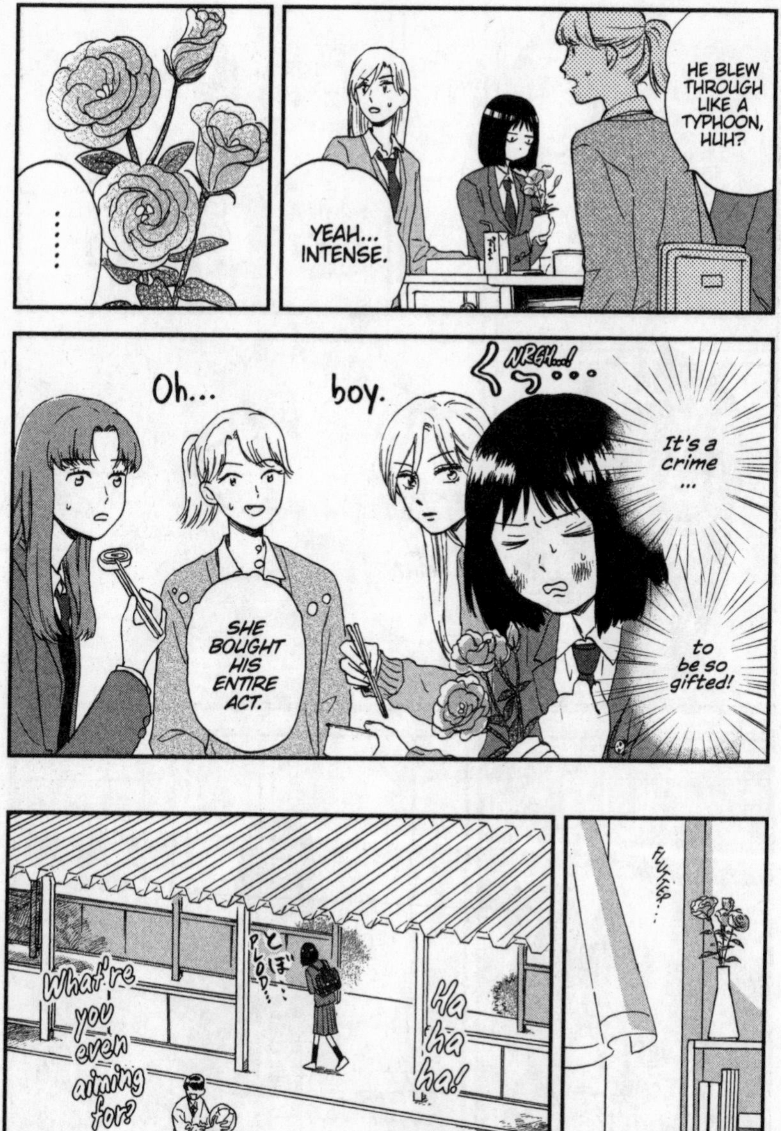
HE BLEW THROUGH LIKE A TYPHOON, HUH?
YEAH... INTENSE.
......
NRGH...!
...
It's a crime ...
to be so gifted!
Oh...
boy.
SHE BOUGHT HIS ENTIRE ACT.
FLUTTER...
Ha ha ha!
とぼ PLOD...
What're you even aiming for?

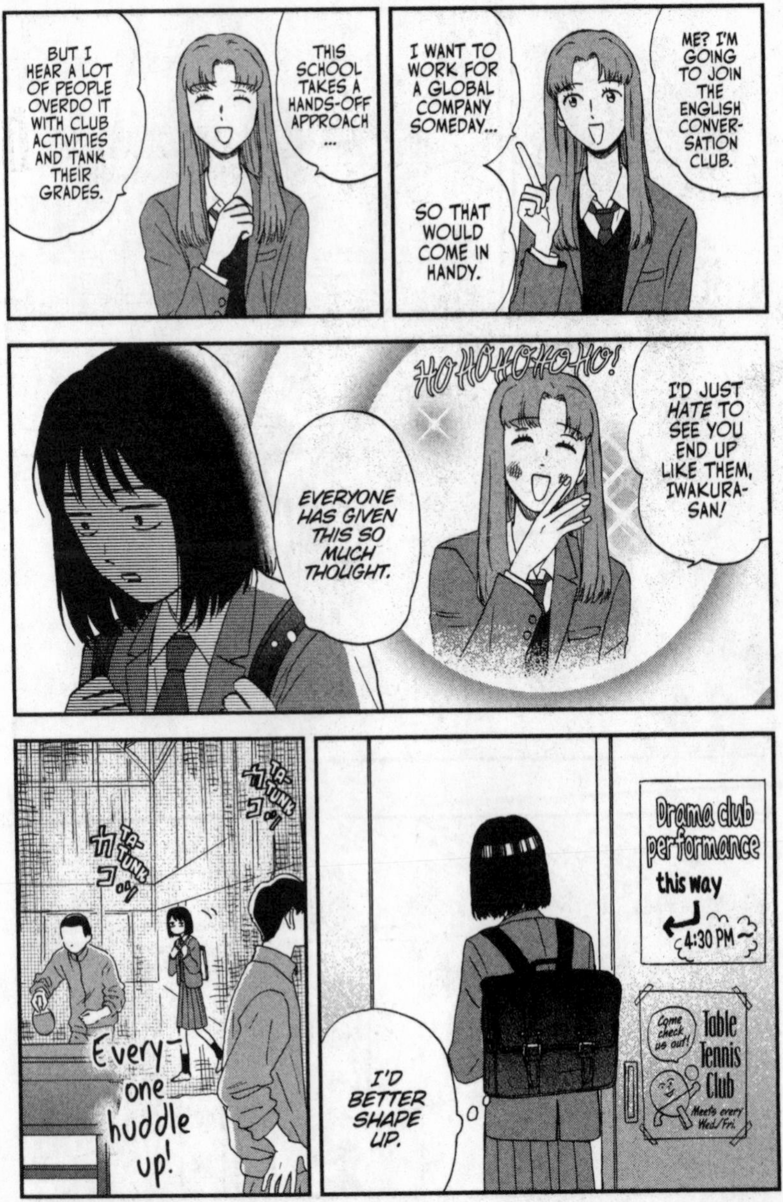

ME? I'M GOING TO JOIN THE ENGLISH CONVER-SATION CLUB.
I WANT TO WORK FOR A GLOBAL COMPANY SOMEDAY...
SO THAT WOULD COME IN HANDY.
THIS SCHOOL TAKES A HANDS-OFF APPROACH ...
BUT I HEAR A LOT OF PEOPLE OVERDO IT WITH CLUB ACTIVITIES AND TANK THEIR GRADES.
HOHOHOHOHOHO!
I'D JUST HATE TO SEE YOU END UP LIKE THEM, IWAKURA-SAN!
EVERYONE HAS GIVEN THIS SO MUCH THOUGHT.
Drama club performance
this way
4:30 PM
Come check us out!
Table Tennis Club
Meets every Wed/Fri.
I'D BETTER SHAPE UP.
TA-TUNK
TA-TUNK
Every-one huddle up!

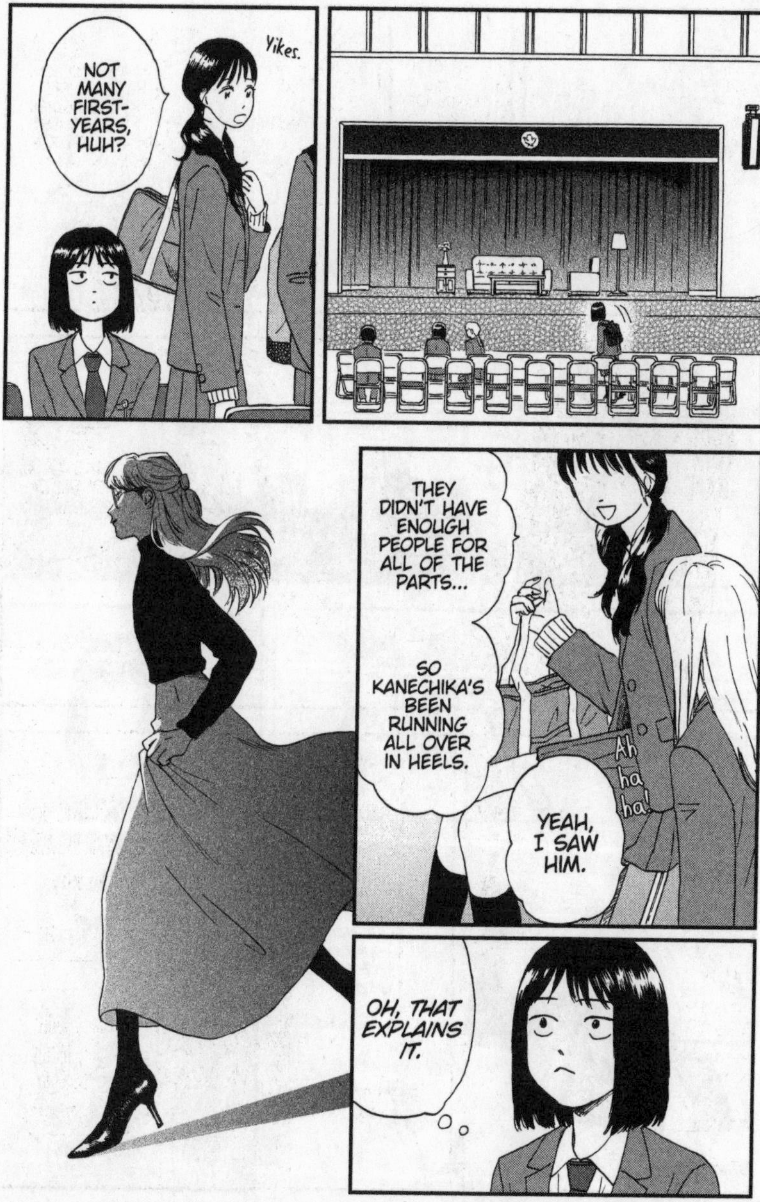
Yikes.
NOT MANY FIRST-YEARS, HUH?
THEY DIDN'T HAVE ENOUGH PEOPLE FOR ALL OF THE PARTS...
SO KANECHIKA'S BEEN RUNNING ALL OVER IN HEELS.
Ah ha ha!
YEAH, I SAW HIM.
OH, THAT EXPLAINS IT.

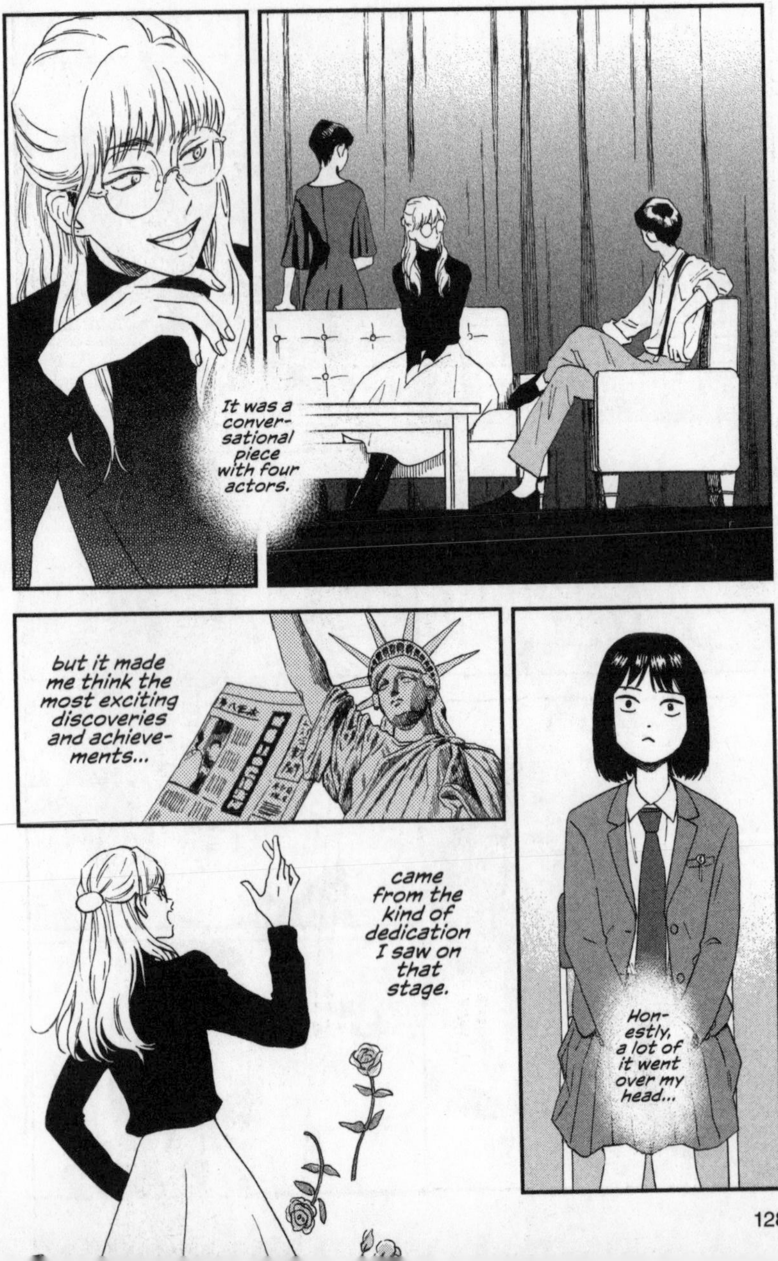
It was a conversational piece with four actors.
Honestly, a lot of it went over my head...
but it made me think the most exciting discoveries and achievements...
came from the kind of dedication I saw on that stage.

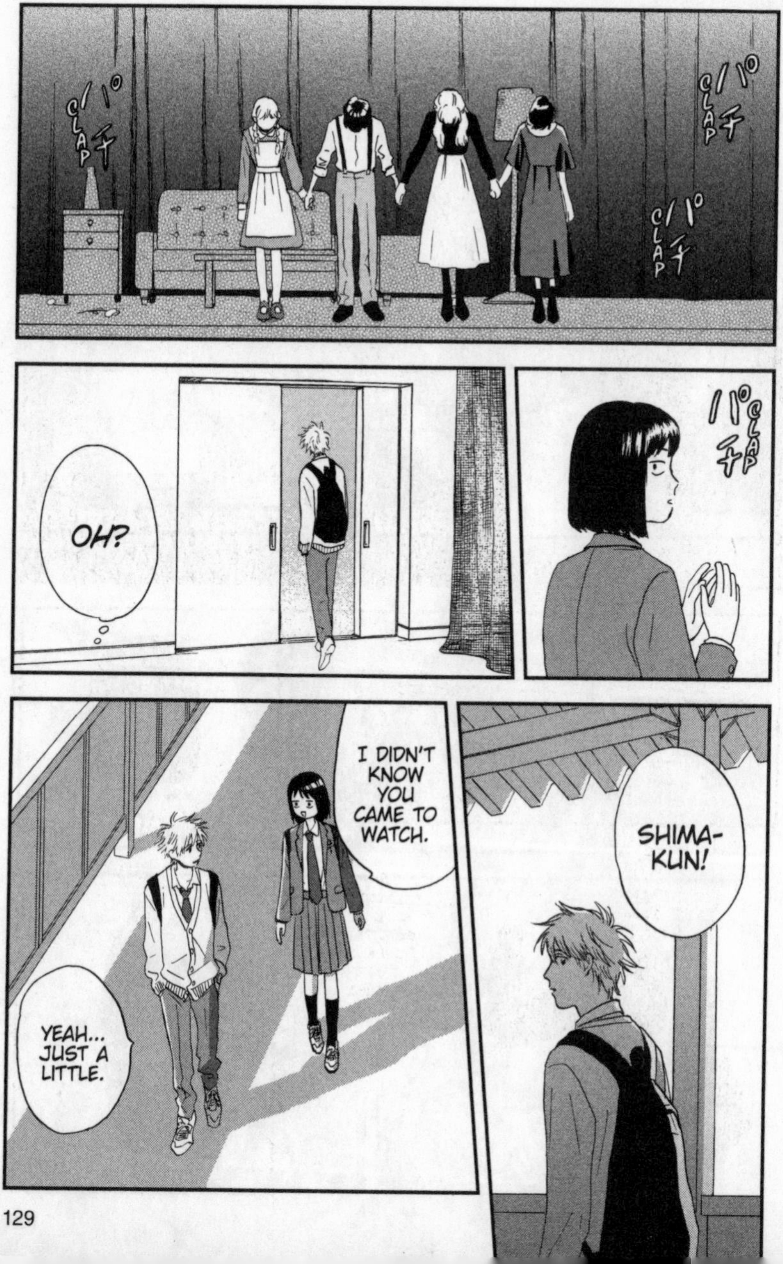
パチ CLAP
パチ CLAP
パチ CLAP
パチ CLAP
OH?
SHIMA-KUN!
I DIDN'T KNOW YOU CAME TO WATCH.
YEAH... JUST A LITTLE.

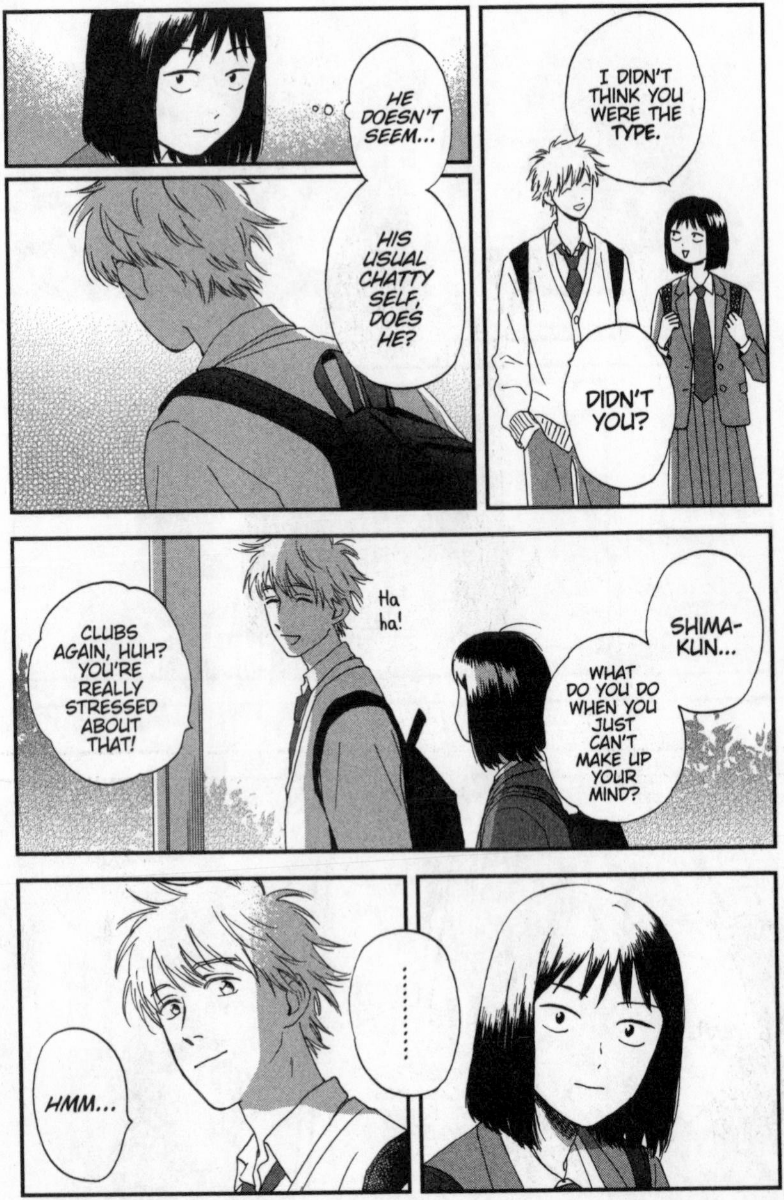
I DIDN'T THINK YOU WERE THE TYPE.
DIDN'T YOU?
HE DOESN'T SEEM...
HIS USUAL CHATTY SELF, DOES HE?
SHIMA-KUN...
WHAT DO YOU DO WHEN YOU JUST CAN'T MAKE UP YOUR MIND?
Ha ha!
CLUBS AGAIN, HUH? YOU'RE REALLY STRESSED ABOUT THAT!
......
HMM...

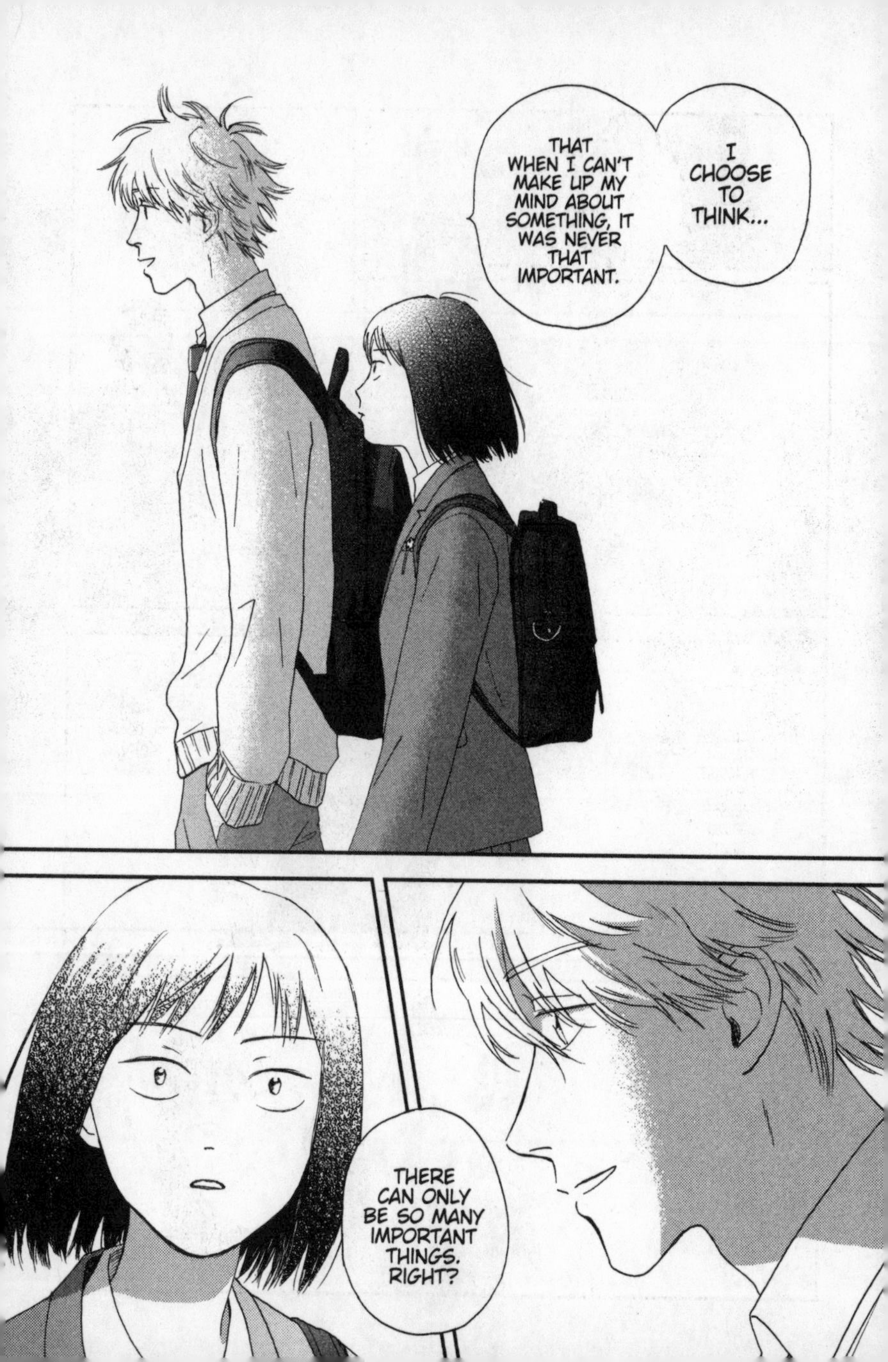
I CHOOSE TO THINK...
THAT WHEN I CAN'T MAKE UP MY MIND ABOUT SOMETHING, IT WAS NEVER THAT IMPORTANT.
THERE CAN ONLY BE SO MANY IMPORTANT THINGS. RIGHT?

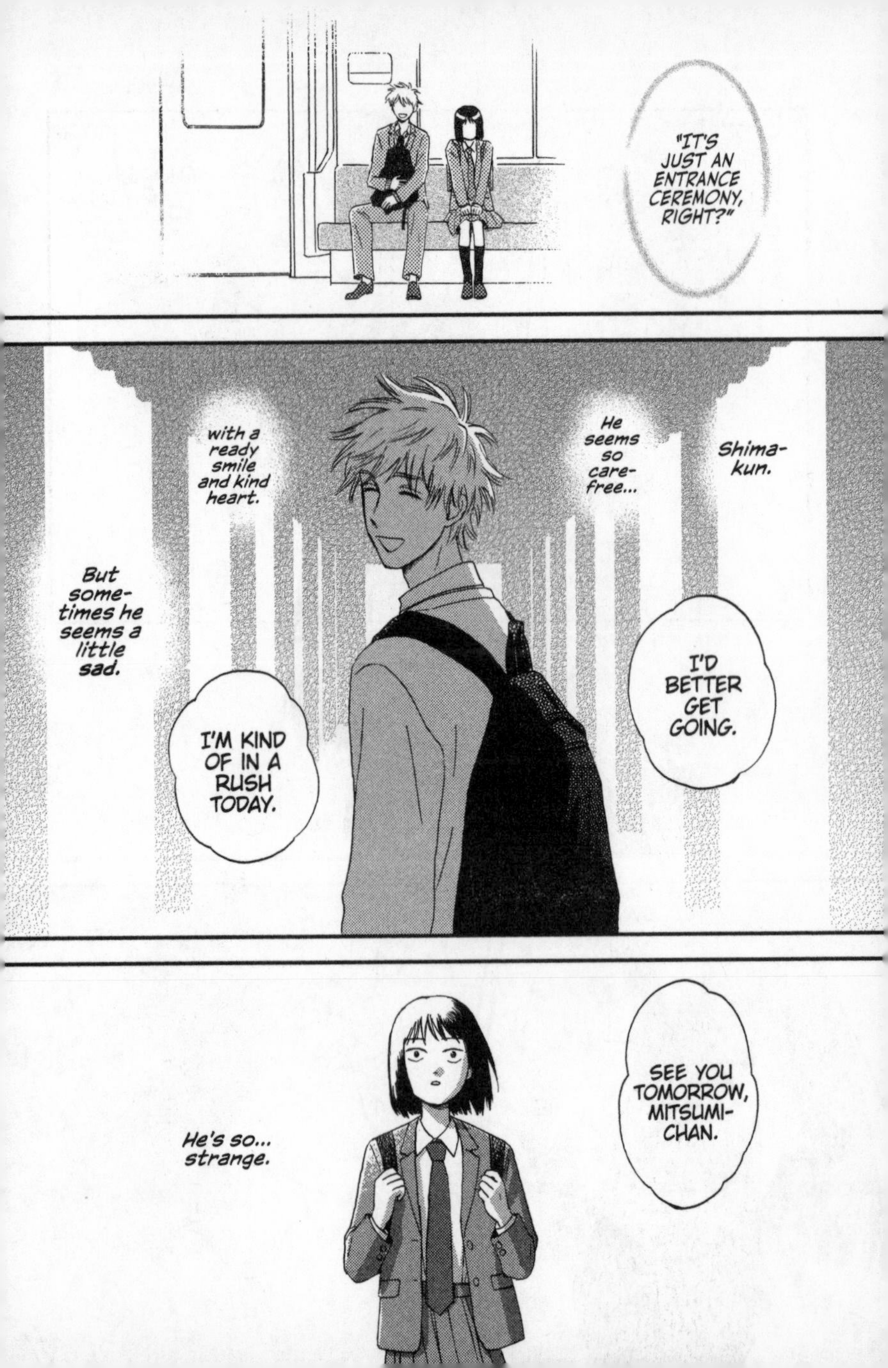
"IT'S JUST AN ENTRANCE CEREMONY, RIGHT?"
Shima-kun.
He seems so care-free...
with a ready smile and kind heart.
I'D BETTER GET GOING.
But some-times he seems a little sad.
I'M KIND OF IN A RUSH TODAY.
SEE YOU TOMORROW, MITSUMI-CHAN.
He's so... strange.

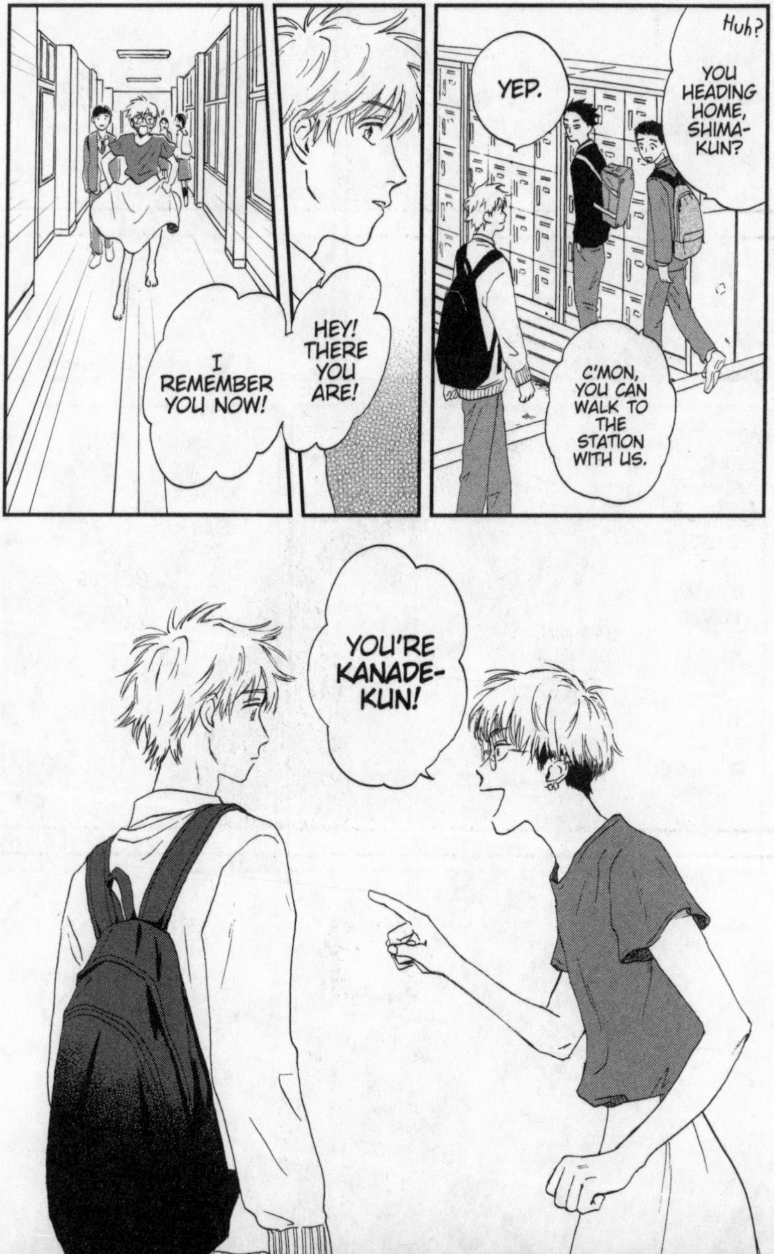
Huh?
YOU HEADING HOME, SHIMA-KUN?
YEP.
C'MON, YOU CAN WALK TO THE STATION WITH US.
HEY! THERE YOU ARE!
I REMEMBER YOU NOW!
YOU'RE KANADE-KUN!

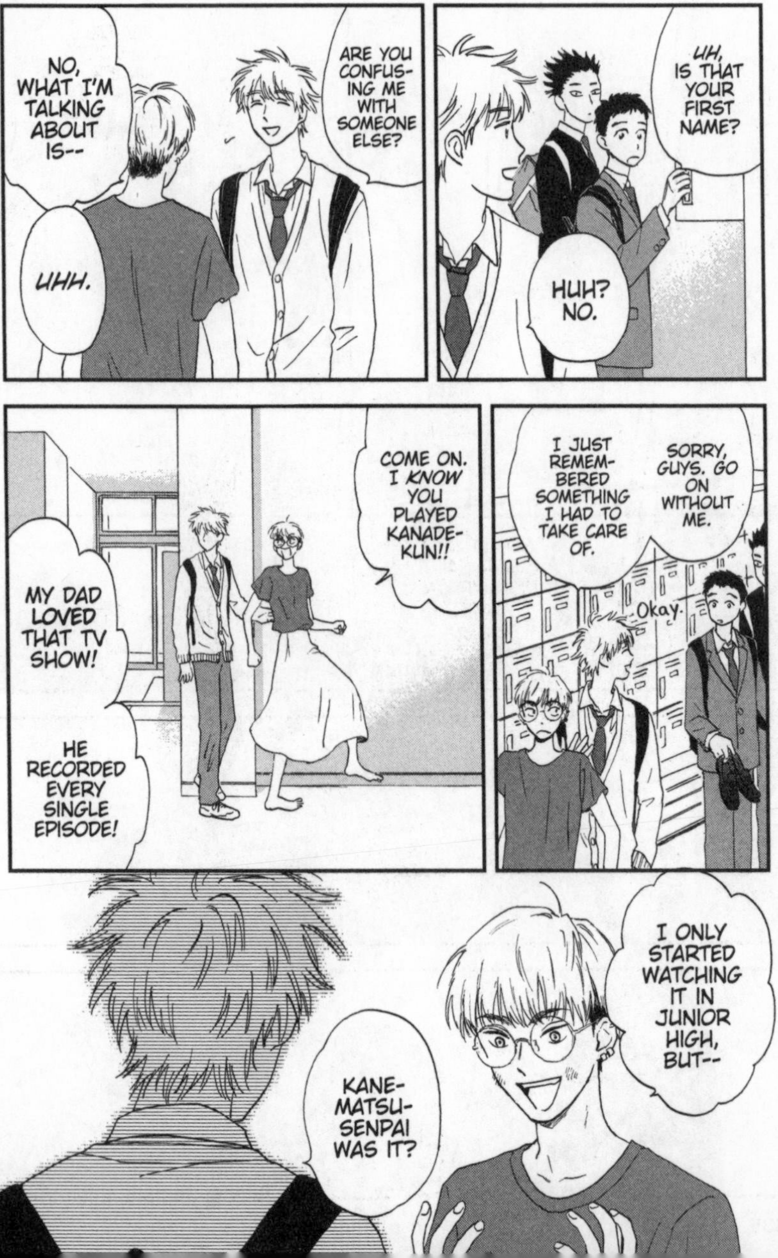
UH, IS THAT YOUR FIRST NAME?
HUH? NO.
ARE YOU CONFUSING ME WITH SOMEONE ELSE?
NO, WHAT I'M TALKING ABOUT IS--
UHH.
SORRY, GUYS. GO ON WITHOUT ME.
I JUST REMEMBERED SOMETHING I HAD TO TAKE CARE OF.
Okay.
COME ON. I *KNOW* YOU PLAYED KANADE-KUN!!
MY DAD LOVED THAT TV SHOW!
HE RECORDED EVERY SINGLE EPISODE!
I ONLY STARTED WATCHING IT IN JUNIOR HIGH, BUT--
KANEMATSU-SENPAI WAS IT?

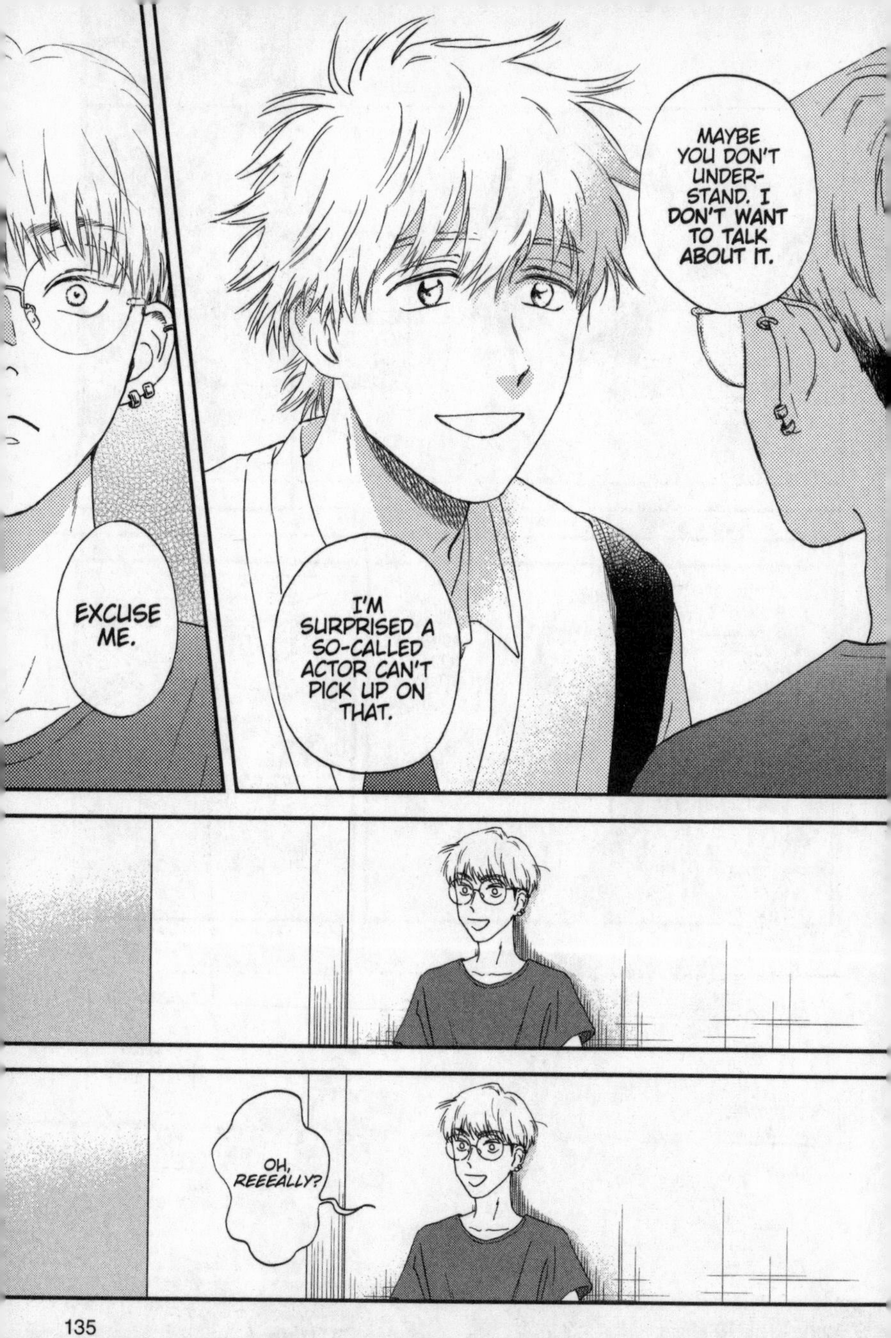
MAYBE YOU DON'T UNDER-STAND. I DON'T WANT TO TALK ABOUT IT.
I'M SURPRISED A SO-CALLED ACTOR CAN'T PICK UP ON THAT.
EXCUSE ME.
OH, REEEALLY?

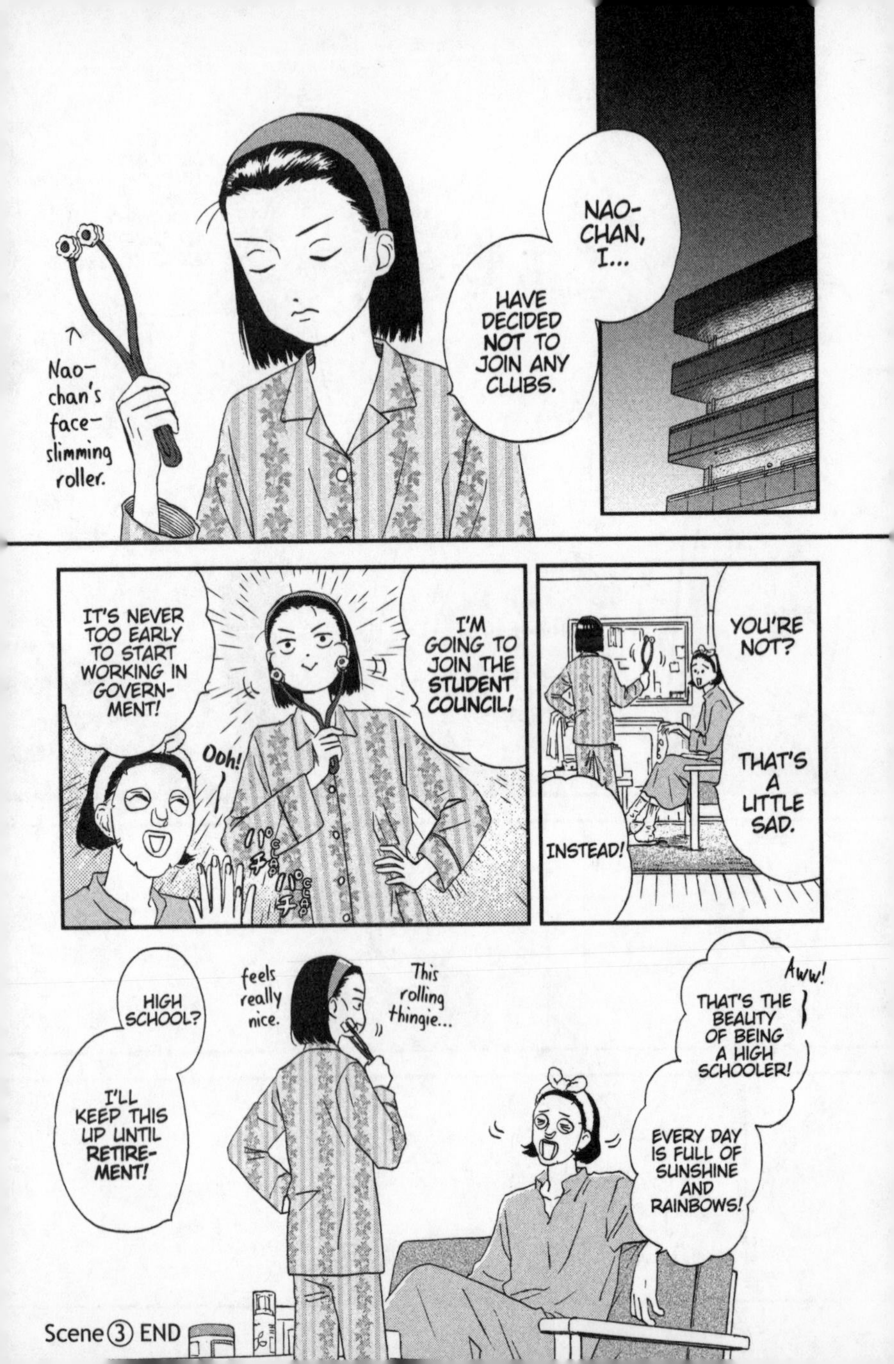
NAO-CHAN, I...
HAVE DECIDED NOT TO JOIN ANY CLUBS.
Nao-chan's face-slimming roller.
YOU'RE NOT?
THAT'S A LITTLE SAD.
INSTEAD!
I'M GOING TO JOIN THE STUDENT COUNCIL!
IT'S NEVER TOO EARLY TO START WORKING IN GOVERNMENT!
Ooh!
CLAP
CLAP
Aww!
THAT'S THE BEAUTY OF BEING A HIGH SCHOOLER!
EVERY DAY IS FULL OF SUNSHINE AND RAINBOWS!
This rolling thingie...
feels really nice.
HIGH SCHOOL?
I'LL KEEP THIS UP UNTIL RETIREMENT!
Scene 3 END

Skip
and
Loafer

Skip and Loafer

Scene ④ *Mmm...* A Dreamy Student Council

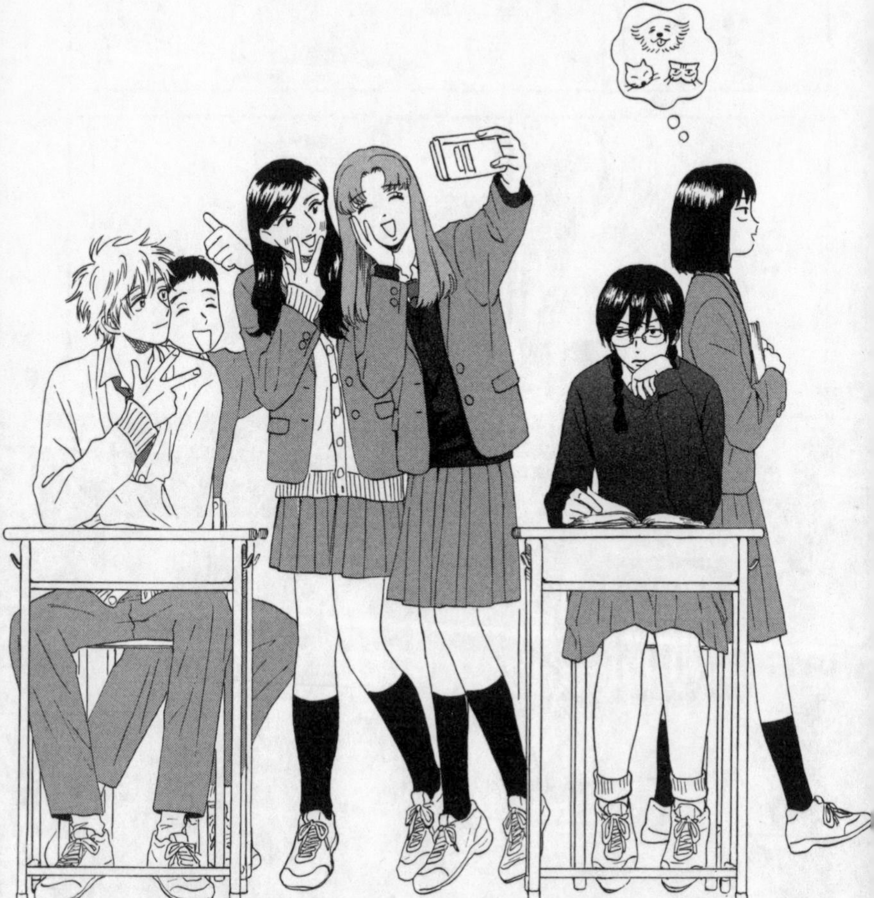

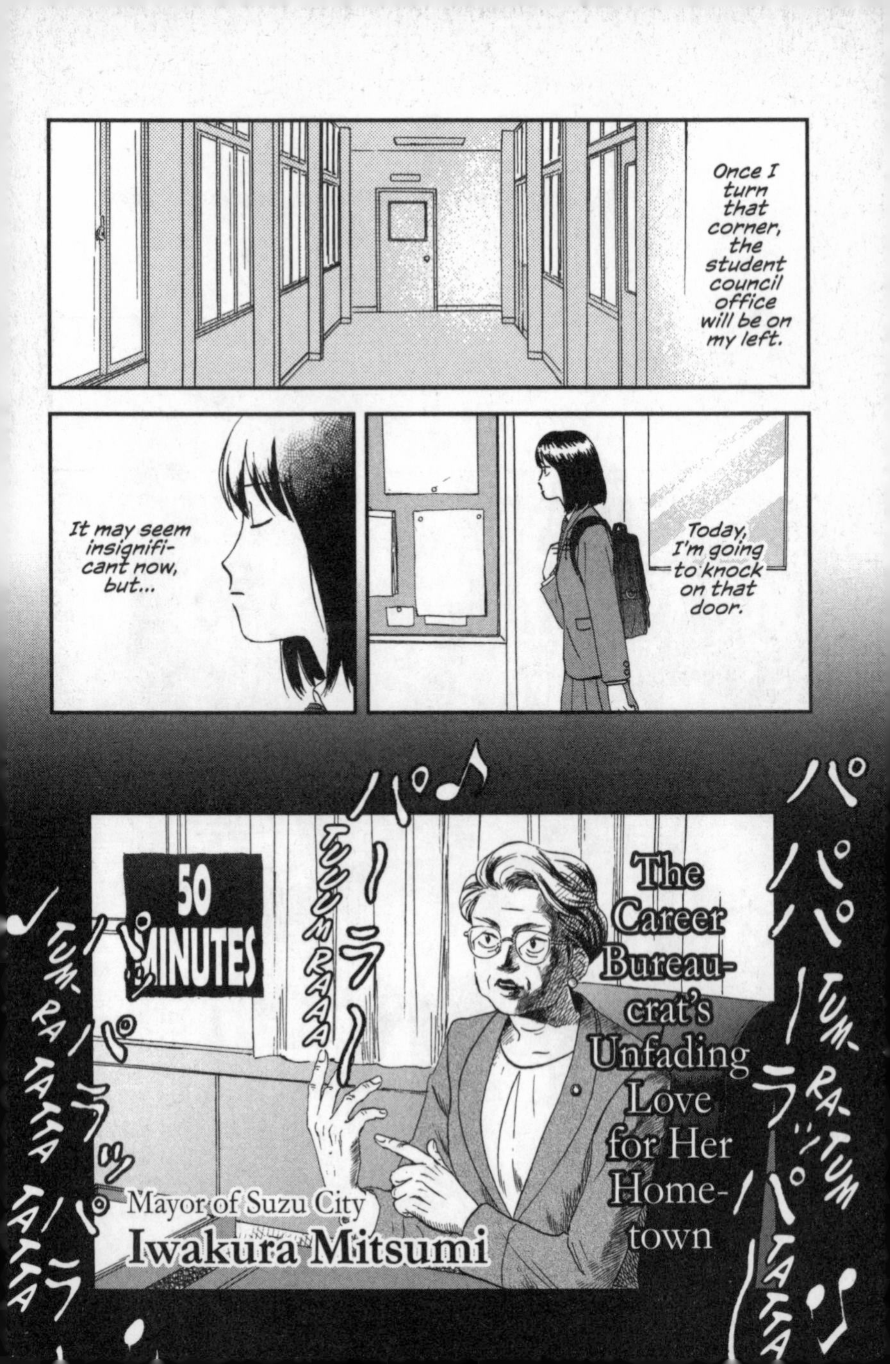
Once I turn that corner, the student council office will be on my left.
Today, I'm going to knock on that door.
It may seem insignificant now, but...
TUM-RA-TUM TATTA
TUM RAAAA
TUM-RA TATTA TATTA
50 MINUTES
The Career Bureaucrat's Unfading Love for Her Hometown
Mayor of Suzu City
Iwakura Mitsumi

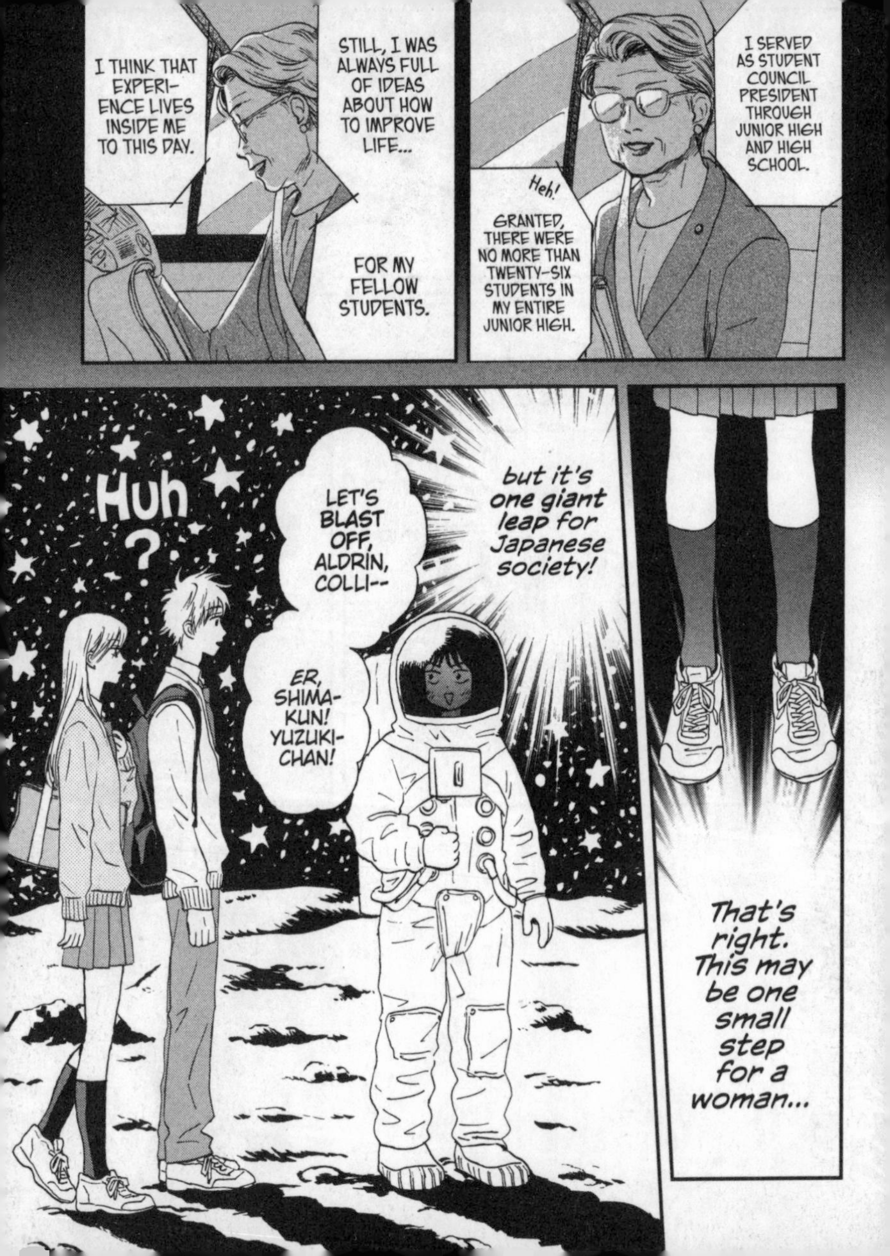
I SERVED AS STUDENT COUNCIL PRESIDENT THROUGH JUNIOR HIGH AND HIGH SCHOOL.
Heh!
GRANTED, THERE WERE NO MORE THAN TWENTY-SIX STUDENTS IN MY ENTIRE JUNIOR HIGH.
STILL, I WAS ALWAYS FULL OF IDEAS ABOUT HOW TO IMPROVE LIFE...
FOR MY FELLOW STUDENTS.
I THINK THAT EXPERI-ENCE LIVES INSIDE ME TO THIS DAY.
That's right. This may be one small step for a woman...
but it's one giant leap for Japanese society!
LET'S BLAST OFF, ALDRIN, COLLI--
ER, SHIMA-KUN! YUZUKI-CHAN!
Huh?

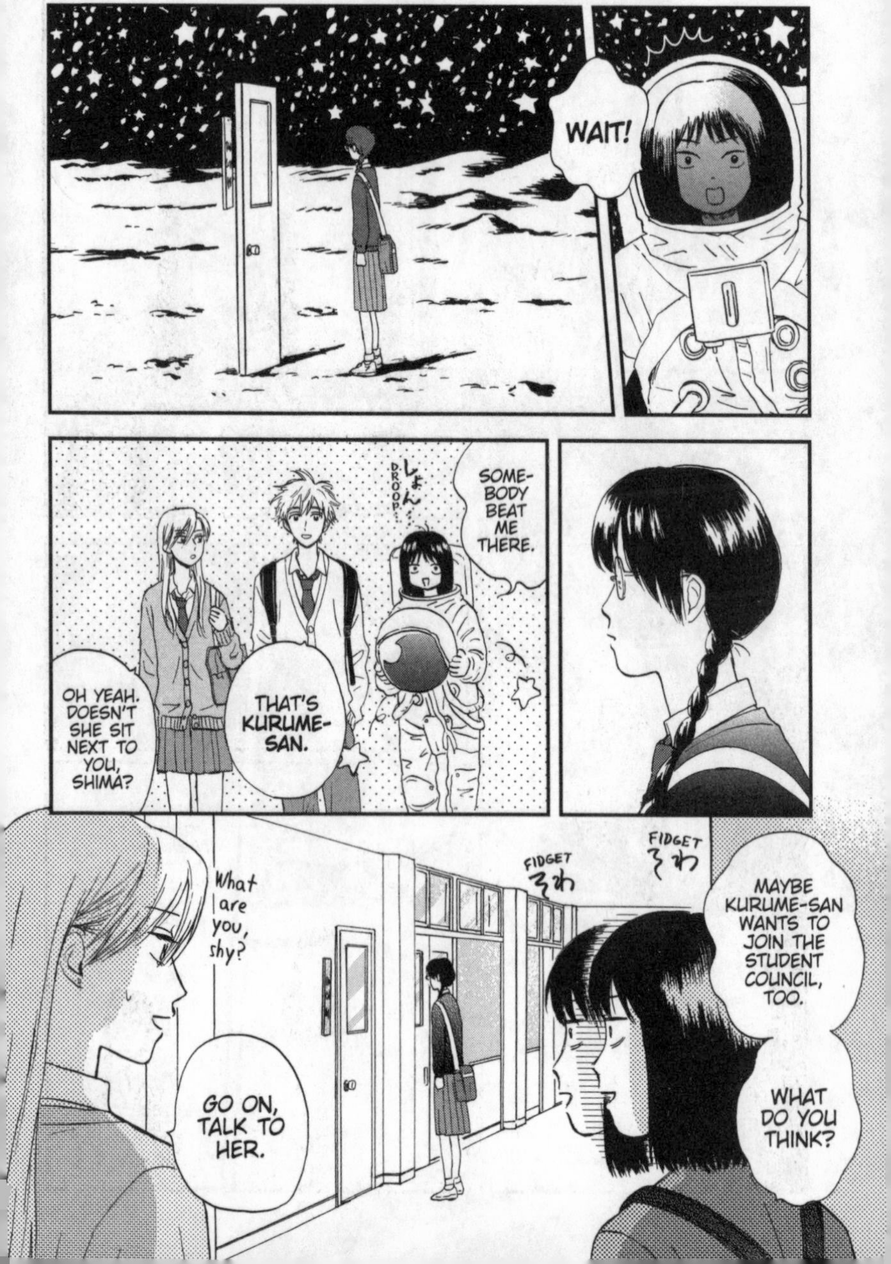
WAIT!
SOME-BODY BEAT ME THERE.
しょん… DROOP…
THAT'S KURUME-SAN.
OH YEAH. DOESN'T SHE SIT NEXT TO YOU, SHIMA?
MAYBE KURUME-SAN WANTS TO JOIN THE STUDENT COUNCIL, TOO.
FIDGET そわ
FIDGET そわ
WHAT DO YOU THINK?
What are you, shy?
GO ON, TALK TO HER.

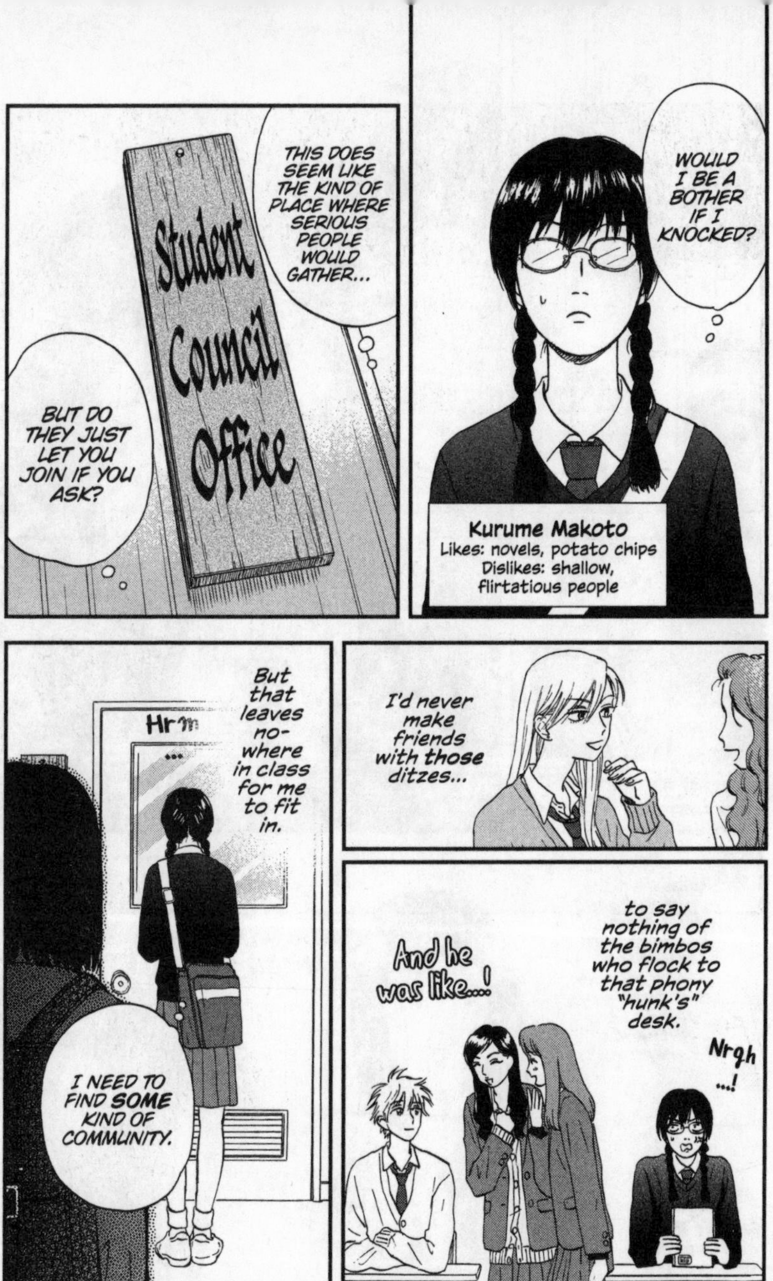
WOULD I BE A BOTHER IF I KNOCKED?
Kurume Makoto
Likes: novels, potato chips
Dislikes: shallow, flirtatious people
THIS DOES SEEM LIKE THE KIND OF PLACE WHERE SERIOUS PEOPLE WOULD GATHER...
Student Council Office
BUT DO THEY JUST LET YOU JOIN IF YOU ASK?
I'd never make friends with those ditzes...
to say nothing of the bimbos who flock to that phony "hunk's" desk.
And he was like...!
Nrgh ...!
But that leaves no-where in class for me to fit in.
Hrm ...
I NEED TO FIND SOME KIND OF COMMUNITY.

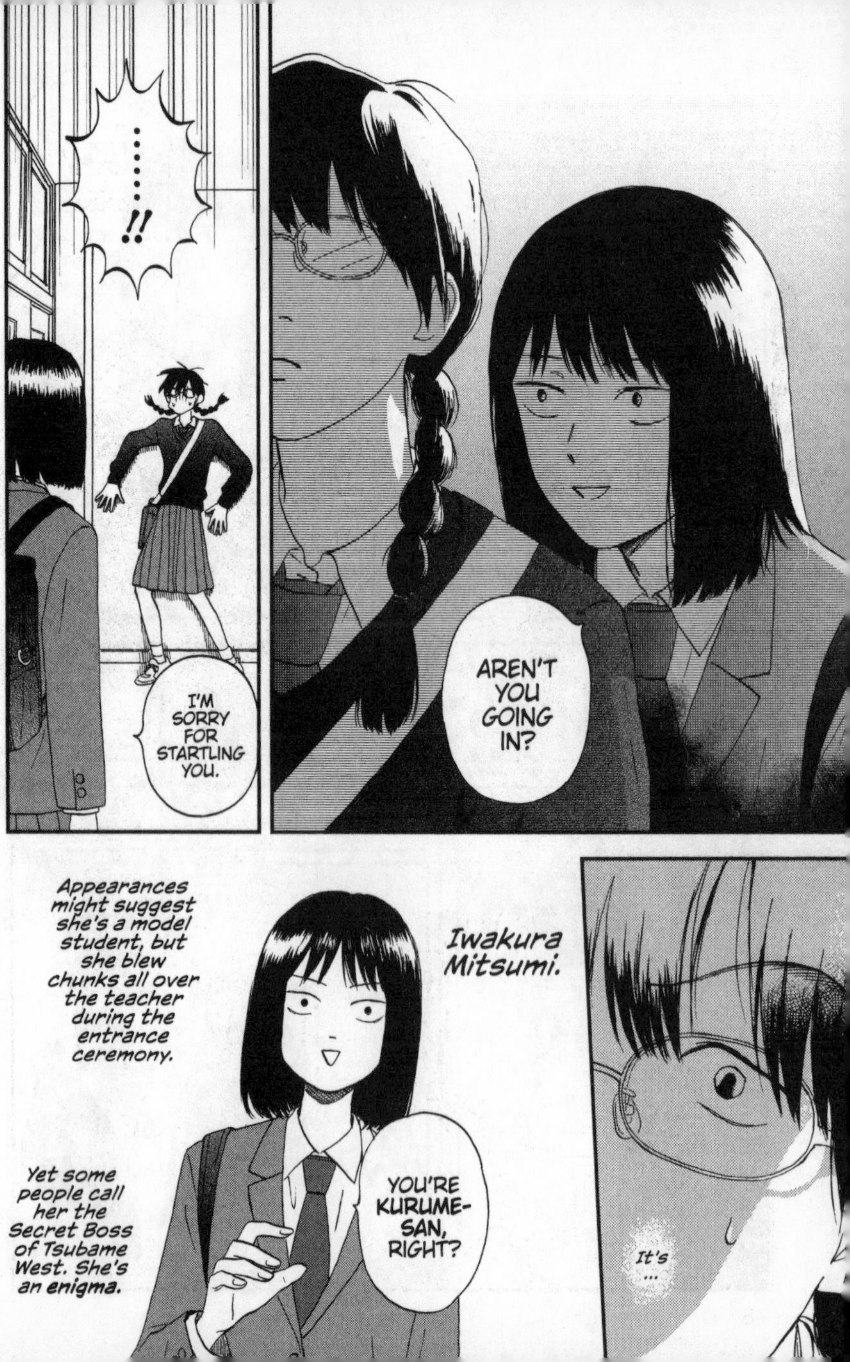
AREN'T YOU GOING IN?
......!!
I'M SORRY FOR STARTLING YOU.
It's ...
Iwakura Mitsumi.
Appearances might suggest she's a model student, but she blew chunks all over the teacher during the entrance ceremony.
YOU'RE KURUME-SAN, RIGHT?
Yet some people call her the Secret Boss of Tsubame West. She's an enigma.

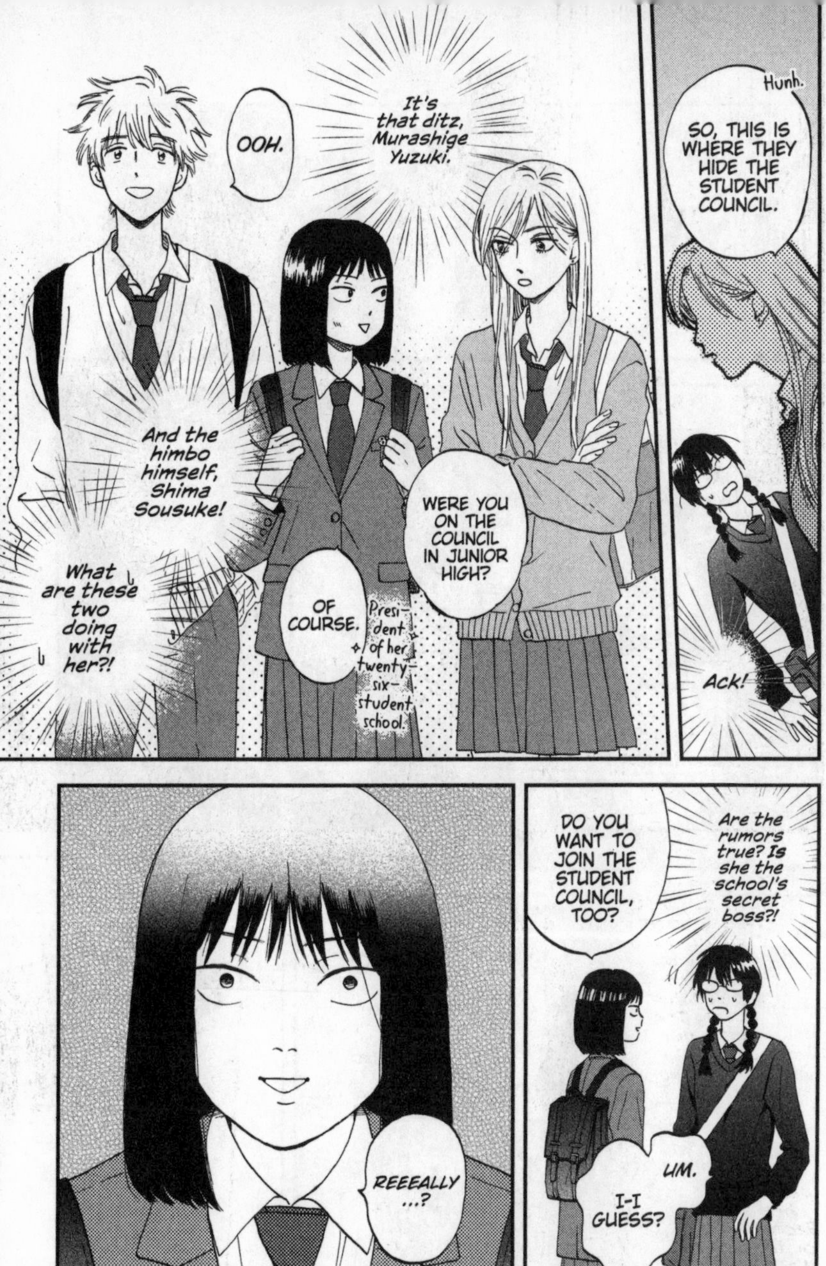
Hunh.
SO, THIS IS WHERE THEY HIDE THE STUDENT COUNCIL.
Ack!
It's that ditz, Murashige Yuzuki.
OOH.
WERE YOU ON THE COUNCIL IN JUNIOR HIGH?
And the himbo himself, Shima Sousuke!
OF COURSE.
President of her twenty-six-student school.
What are these two doing with her?!
Are the rumors true? Is she the school's secret boss?!
DO YOU WANT TO JOIN THE STUDENT COUNCIL, TOO?
UM.
I-I GUESS?
REEEALLY ...?

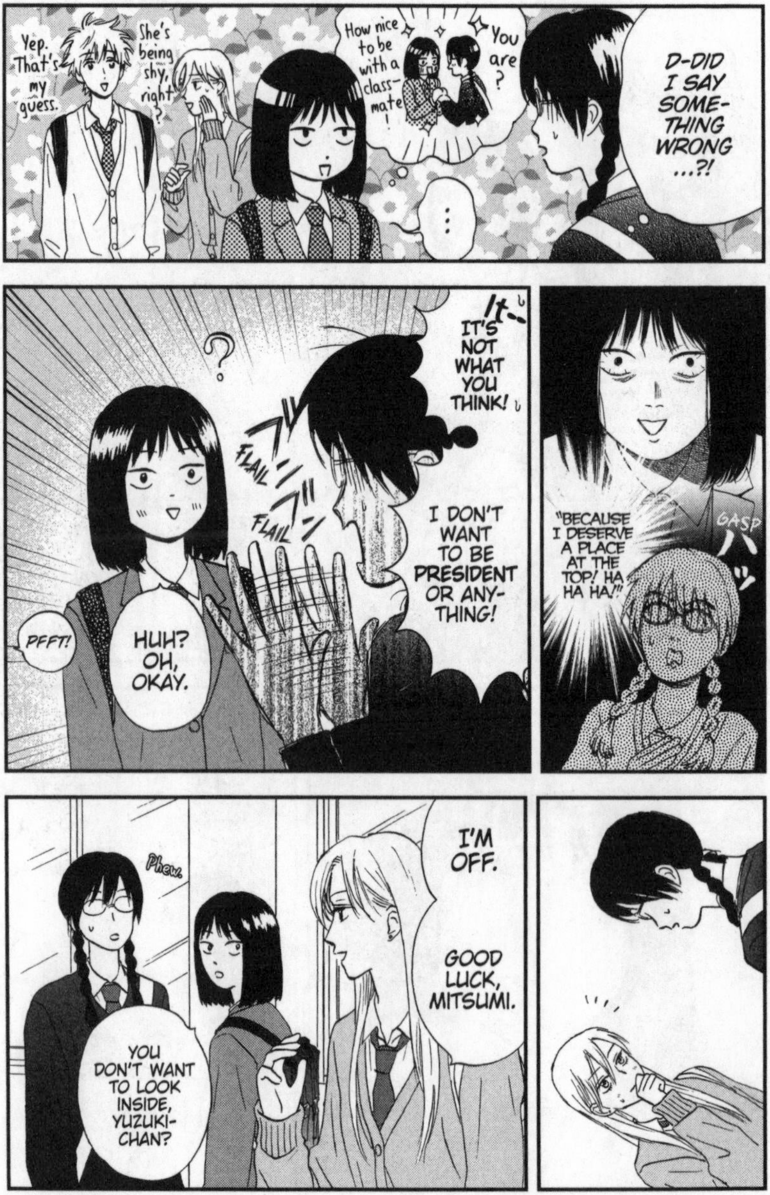
D-DID I SAY SOMETHING WRONG ...?!
You are?
How nice to be with a classmate!
...
She's being shy, right?
Yep. That's my guess.
GASP
"BECAUSE I DESERVE A PLACE AT THE TOP! HA HA HA!"
It--
IT'S NOT WHAT YOU THINK!
I DON'T WANT TO BE PRESIDENT OR ANYTHING!
FLAIL
FLAIL
?
HUH? OH, OKAY.
PFFT!
I'M OFF.
GOOD LUCK, MITSUMI.
Phew.
YOU DON'T WANT TO LOOK INSIDE, YUZUKI-CHAN?

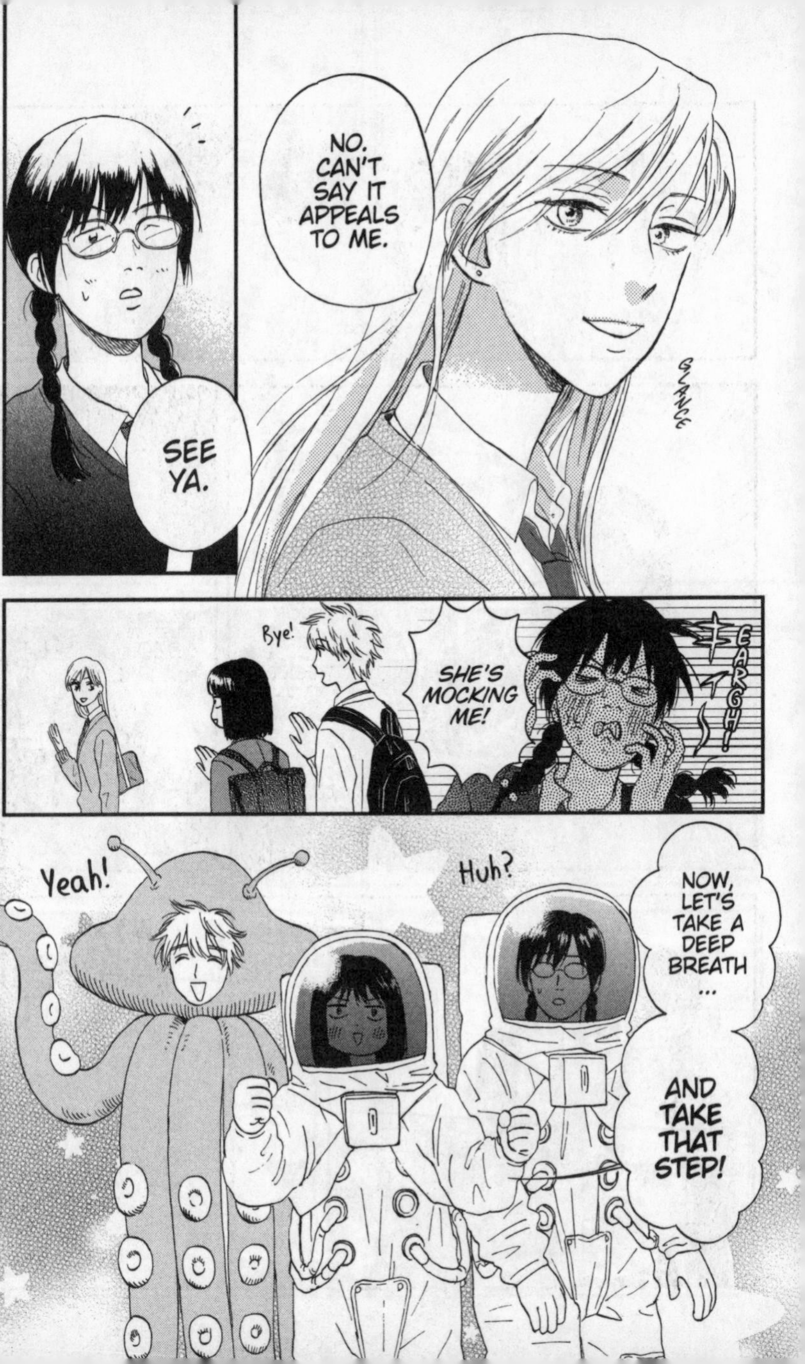
NO. CAN'T SAY IT APPEALS TO ME.
GLANCE
SEE YA.
EARGH!
SHE'S MOCKING ME!
Bye!
NOW, LET'S TAKE A DEEP BREATH ...
AND TAKE THAT STEP!
Huh?
Yeah!

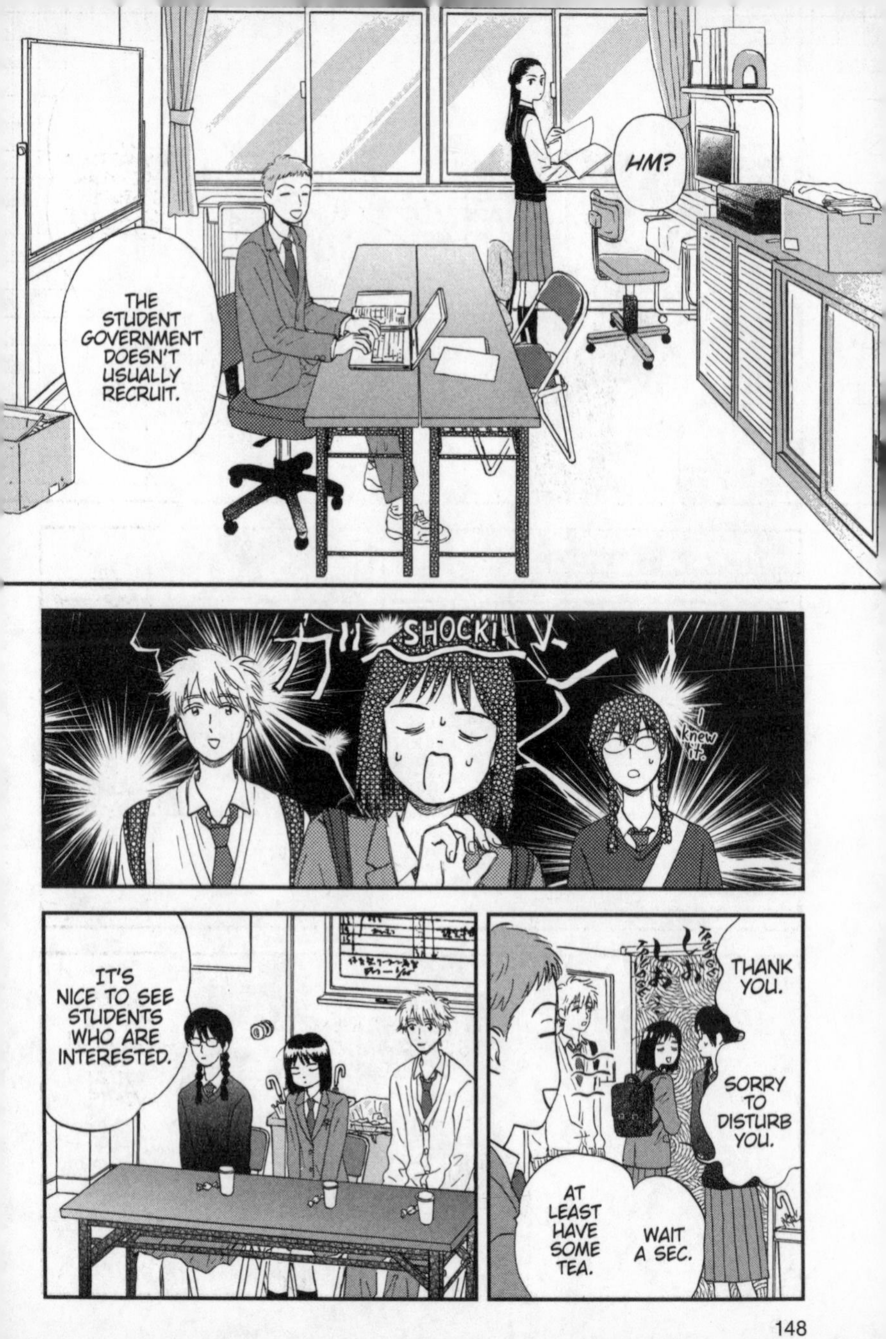
HM?
THE STUDENT GOVERNMENT DOESN'T USUALLY RECRUIT.
SHOCK!
I knew it.
THANK YOU.
SORRY TO DISTURB YOU.
WAIT A SEC.
AT LEAST HAVE SOME TEA.
IT'S NICE TO SEE STUDENTS WHO ARE INTERESTED.

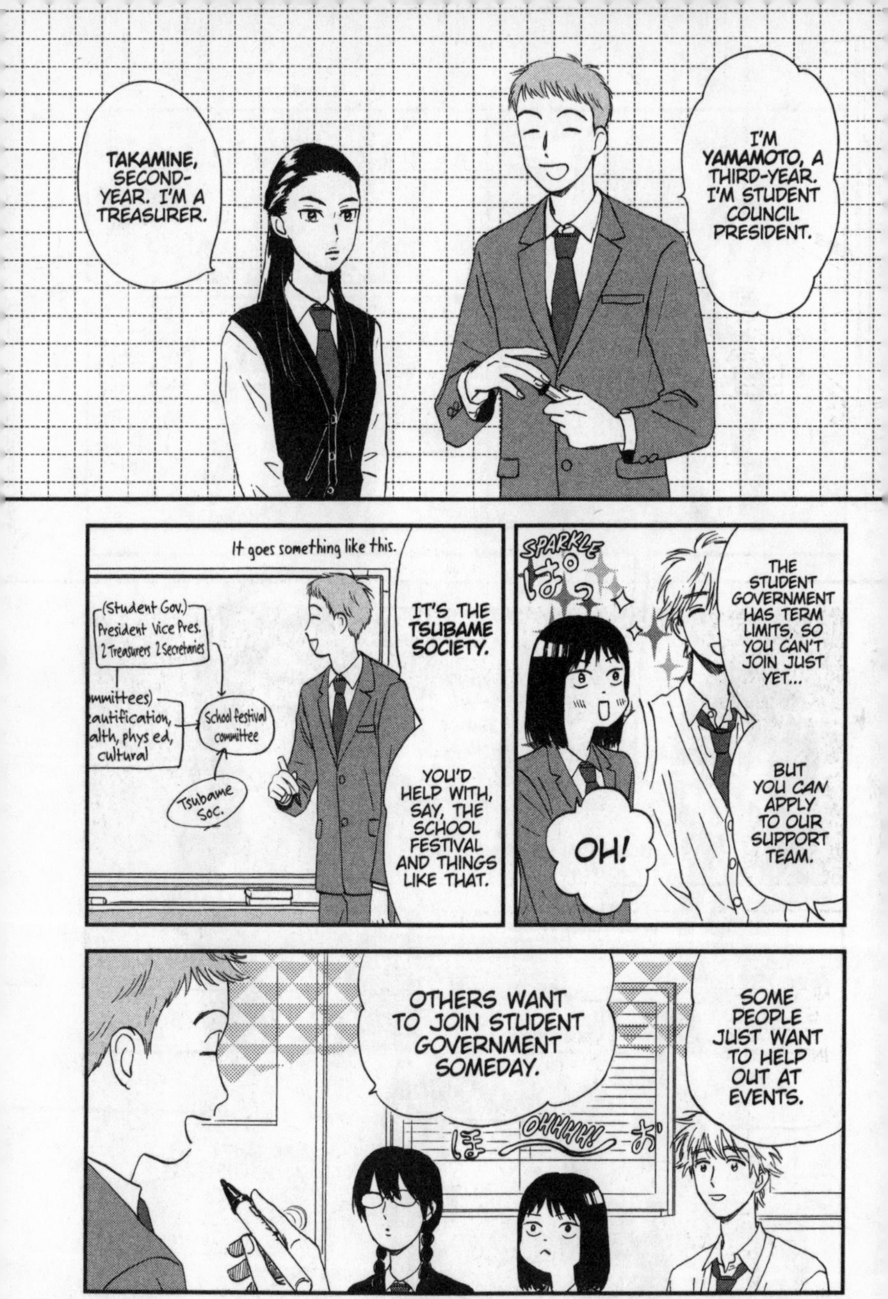
I'M YAMAMOTO, A THIRD-YEAR. I'M STUDENT COUNCIL PRESIDENT.
TAKAMINE, SECOND-YEAR. I'M A TREASURER.
SPARKLE
ぱっ
THE STUDENT GOVERNMENT HAS TERM LIMITS, SO YOU CAN'T JOIN JUST YET...
BUT YOU CAN APPLY TO OUR SUPPORT TEAM.
OH!
It goes something like this.
IT'S THE TSUBAME SOCIETY.
YOU'D HELP WITH, SAY, THE SCHOOL FESTIVAL AND THINGS LIKE THAT.
(Student Gov.) President Vice Pres. 2 Treasurers 2 Secretaries
mmittees) eautification, alth, phys ed, cultural
School festival committee
Tsubame Soc.
SOME PEOPLE JUST WANT TO HELP OUT AT EVENTS.
OTHERS WANT TO JOIN STUDENT GOVERNMENT SOMEDAY.
ほ OHHHH! お

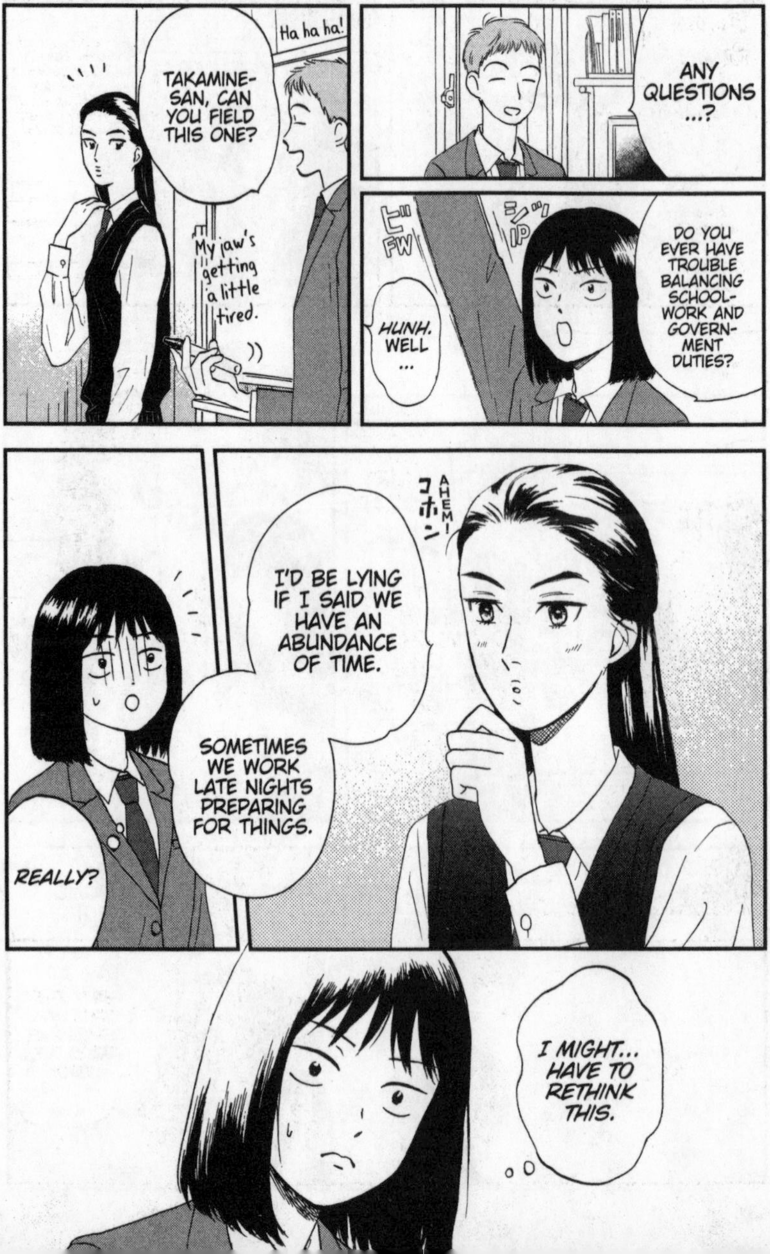
ANY QUESTIONS ...?
DO YOU EVER HAVE TROUBLE BALANCING SCHOOL-WORK AND GOVERNMENT DUTIES?
ZIP
FW
HUNH. WELL ...
Ha ha ha!
TAKAMINE-SAN, CAN YOU FIELD THIS ONE?
My jaw's getting a little tired.
AHEM!
I'D BE LYING IF I SAID WE HAVE AN ABUNDANCE OF TIME.
SOMETIMES WE WORK LATE NIGHTS PREPARING FOR THINGS.
REALLY?
I MIGHT... HAVE TO RETHINK THIS.

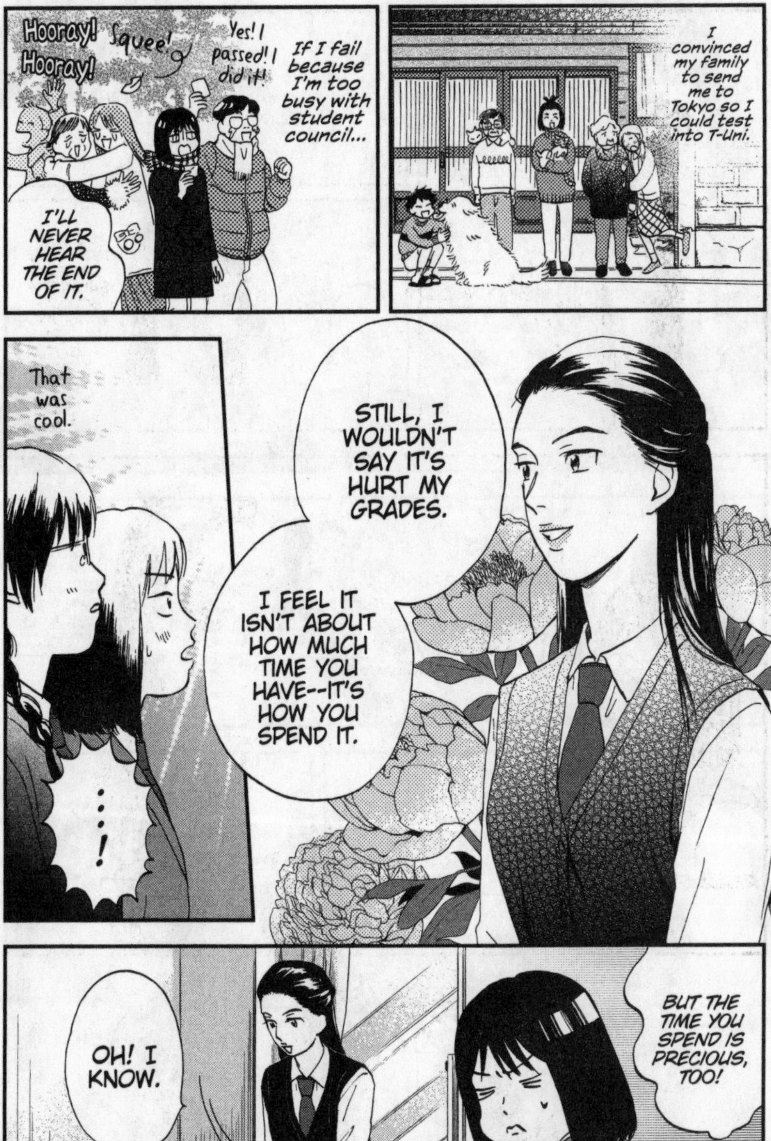
I convinced my family to send me to Tokyo so I could test into T-Uni.
If I fail because I'm too busy with student council...
Yes! I passed! I did it!
Squee!
Hooray! Hooray!
I'LL NEVER HEAR THE END OF IT.
STILL, I WOULDN'T SAY IT'S HURT MY GRADES.
I FEEL IT ISN'T ABOUT HOW MUCH TIME YOU HAVE--IT'S HOW YOU SPEND IT.
That was cool.
...!
BUT THE TIME YOU SPEND IS PRECIOUS, TOO!
OH! I KNOW.

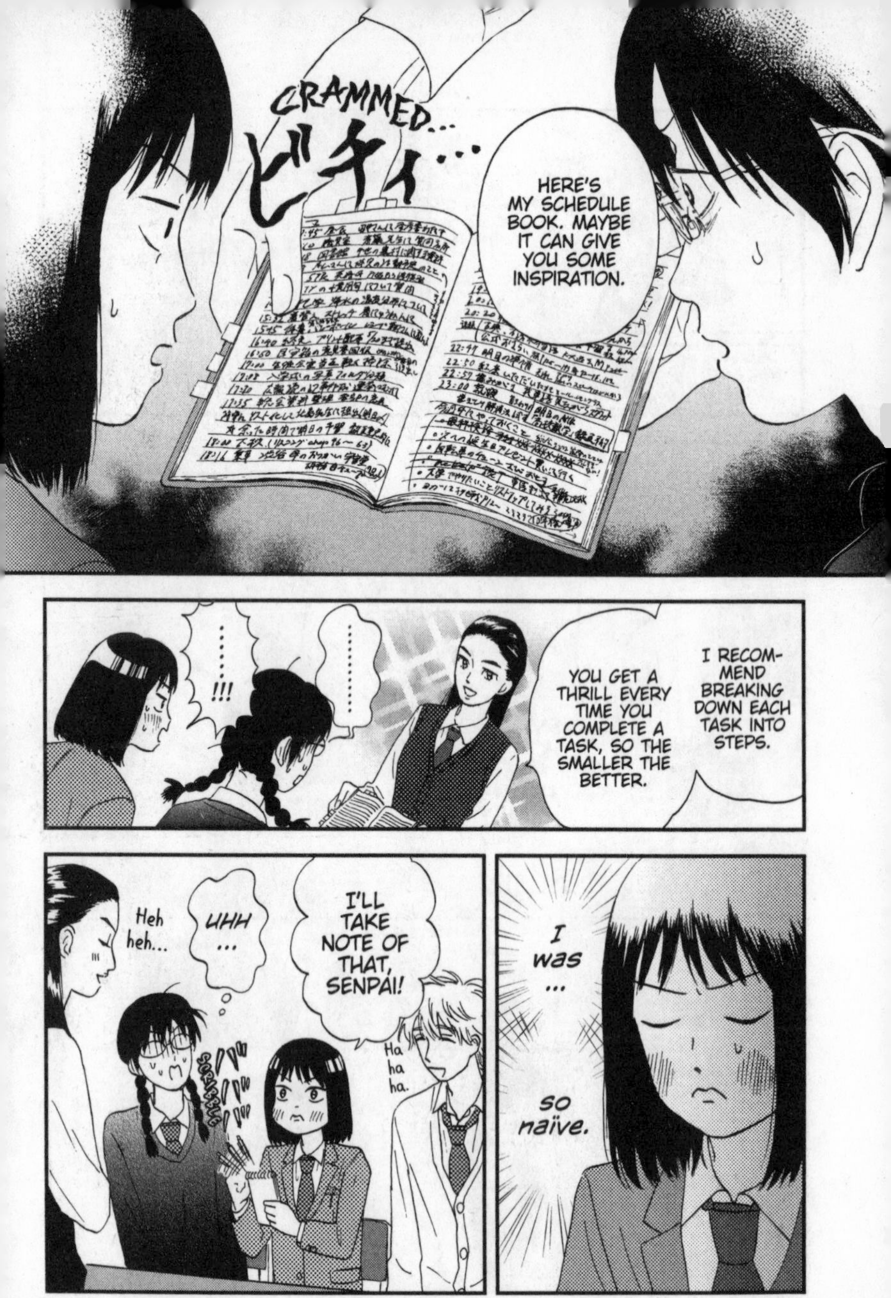
HERE'S MY SCHEDULE BOOK. MAYBE IT CAN GIVE YOU SOME INSPIRATION.
CRAMMED...
ビチィ…
I RECOMMEND BREAKING DOWN EACH TASK INTO STEPS.
YOU GET A THRILL EVERY TIME YOU COMPLETE A TASK, SO THE SMALLER THE BETTER.
......
......!!!
I was ...
so naïve.
I'LL TAKE NOTE OF THAT, SENPAI!
Ha ha ha.
UHH ...
Heh heh...
SCRIBBLE

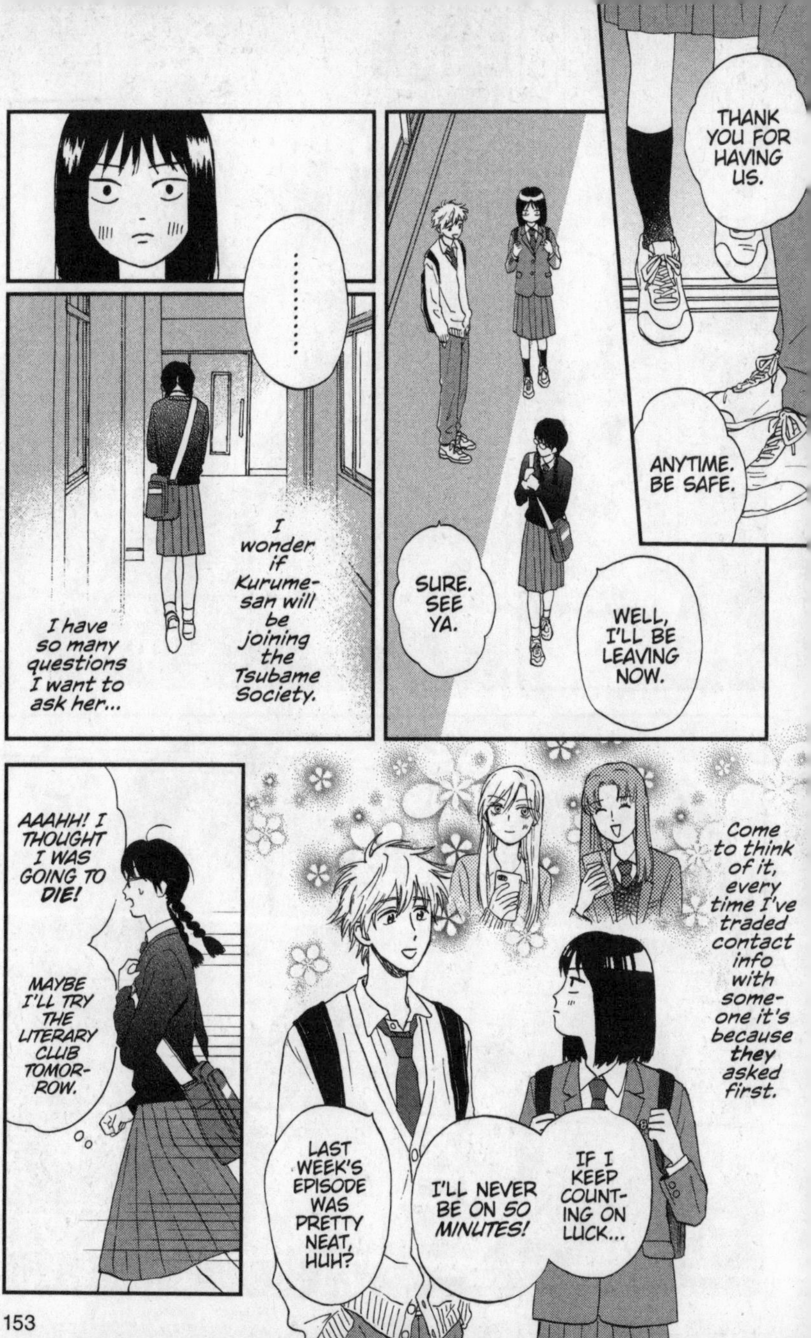
THANK YOU FOR HAVING US.
ANYTIME. BE SAFE.
WELL, I'LL BE LEAVING NOW.
SURE. SEE YA.
......
I wonder if Kurume-san will be joining the Tsubame Society.
I have so many questions I want to ask her...
Come to think of it, every time I've traded contact info with someone it's because they asked first.
IF I KEEP COUNTING ON LUCK...
I'LL NEVER BE ON 50 MINUTES!
LAST WEEK'S EPISODE WAS PRETTY NEAT, HUH?
AAAHH! I THOUGHT I WAS GOING TO DIE!
MAYBE I'LL TRY THE LITERARY CLUB TOMORROW.

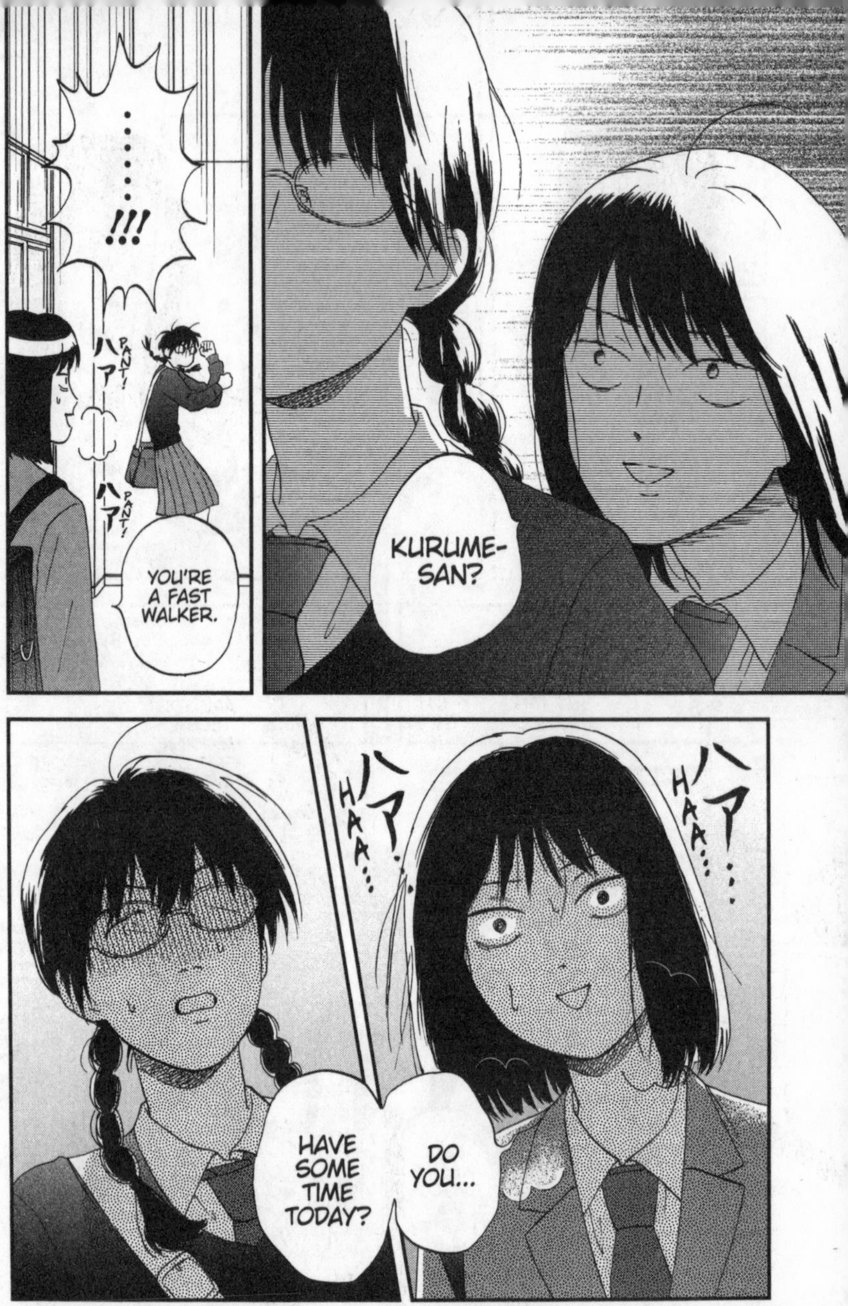
KURUME-SAN?
......!!!
ハア PANT!
ハア PANT!
YOU'RE A FAST WALKER.
ハア HAA...
ハア HAA...
DO YOU...
HAVE SOME TIME TODAY?

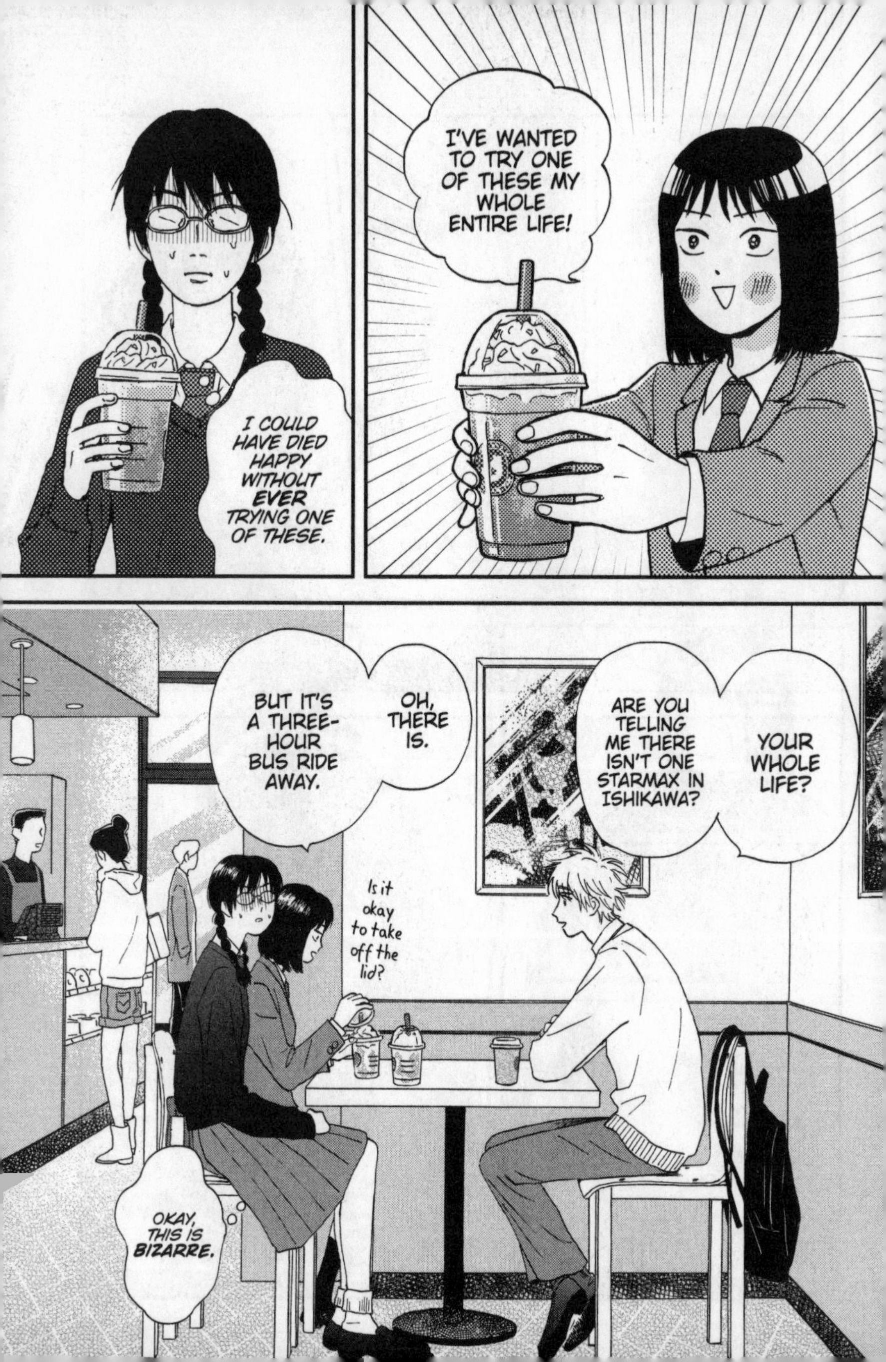
I'VE WANTED TO TRY ONE OF THESE MY WHOLE ENTIRE LIFE!
I COULD HAVE DIED HAPPY WITHOUT EVER TRYING ONE OF THESE.
YOUR WHOLE LIFE?
ARE YOU TELLING ME THERE ISN'T ONE STARMAX IN ISHIKAWA?
OH, THERE IS.
BUT IT'S A THREE-HOUR BUS RIDE AWAY.
Is it okay to take off the lid?
OKAY, THIS IS BIZARRE.

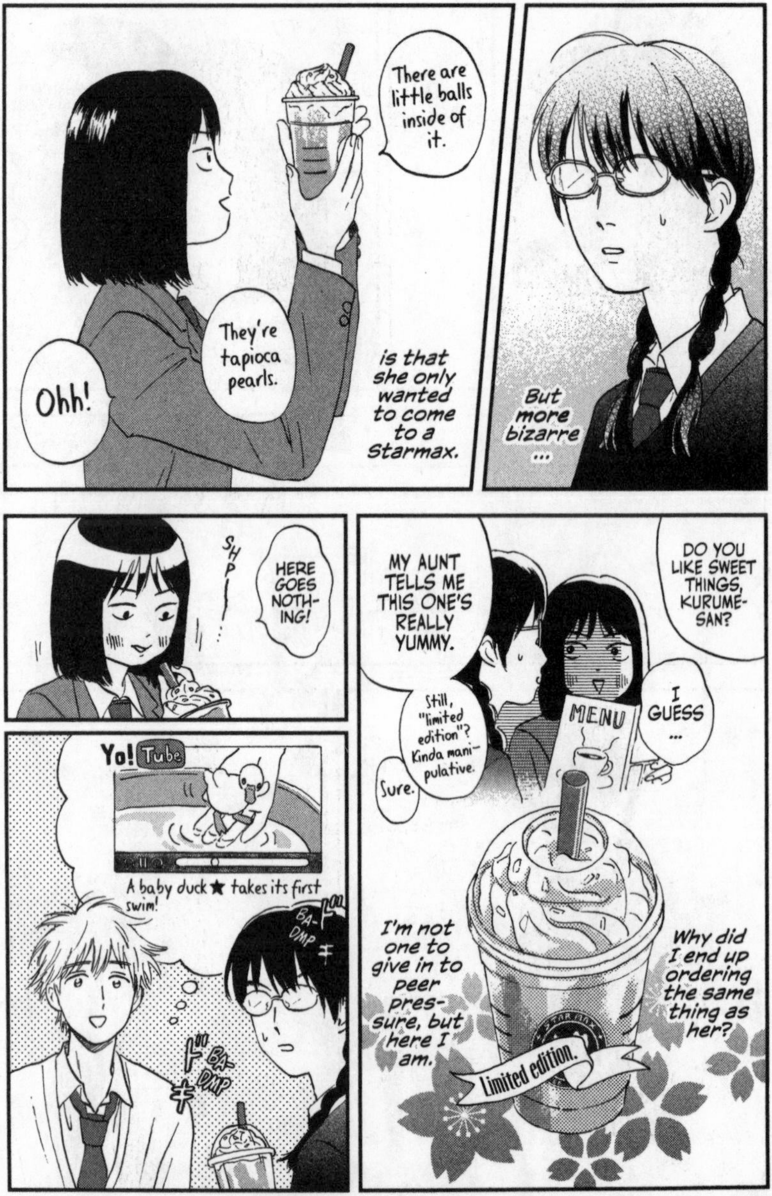
But more bizarre ...
is that she only wanted to come to a Starmax.
There are little balls inside of it.
They're tapioca pearls.
Ohh!
DO YOU LIKE SWEET THINGS, KURUME-SAN?
MY AUNT TELLS ME THIS ONE'S REALLY YUMMY.
I GUESS ...
Still, "limited edition"? Kinda manipulative.
Sure.
MENU
Why did I end up ordering the same thing as her?
I'm not one to give in to peer pressure, but here I am.
Limited edition.
HERE GOES NOTHING!
SHP...
Yo! Tube
A baby duck★ takes its first swim!
BA-DMP
BA-DMP

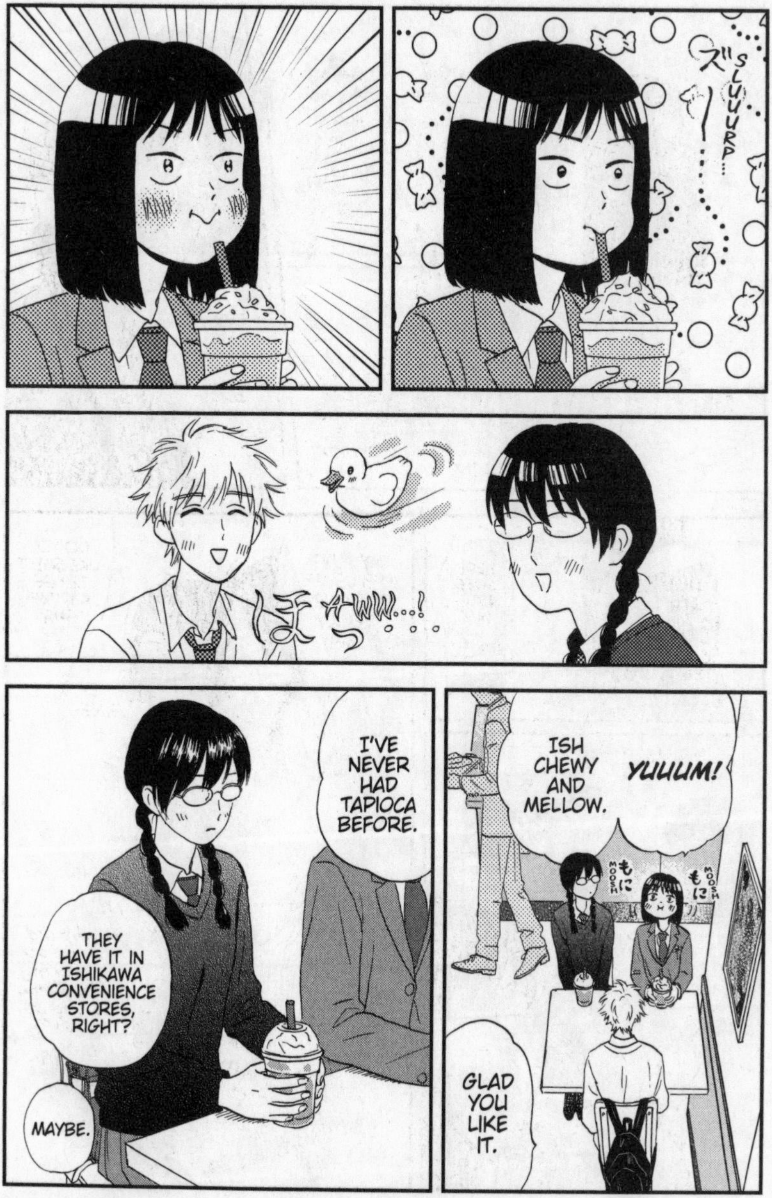
ズー
SLUUURP...
ほっ
AWW...!
ISH CHEWY AND MELLOW.
YUUUM!
もに MOOSH
もに MOOSH
GLAD YOU LIKE IT.
I'VE NEVER HAD TAPIOCA BEFORE.
THEY HAVE IT IN ISHIKAWA CONVENIENCE STORES, RIGHT?
MAYBE.

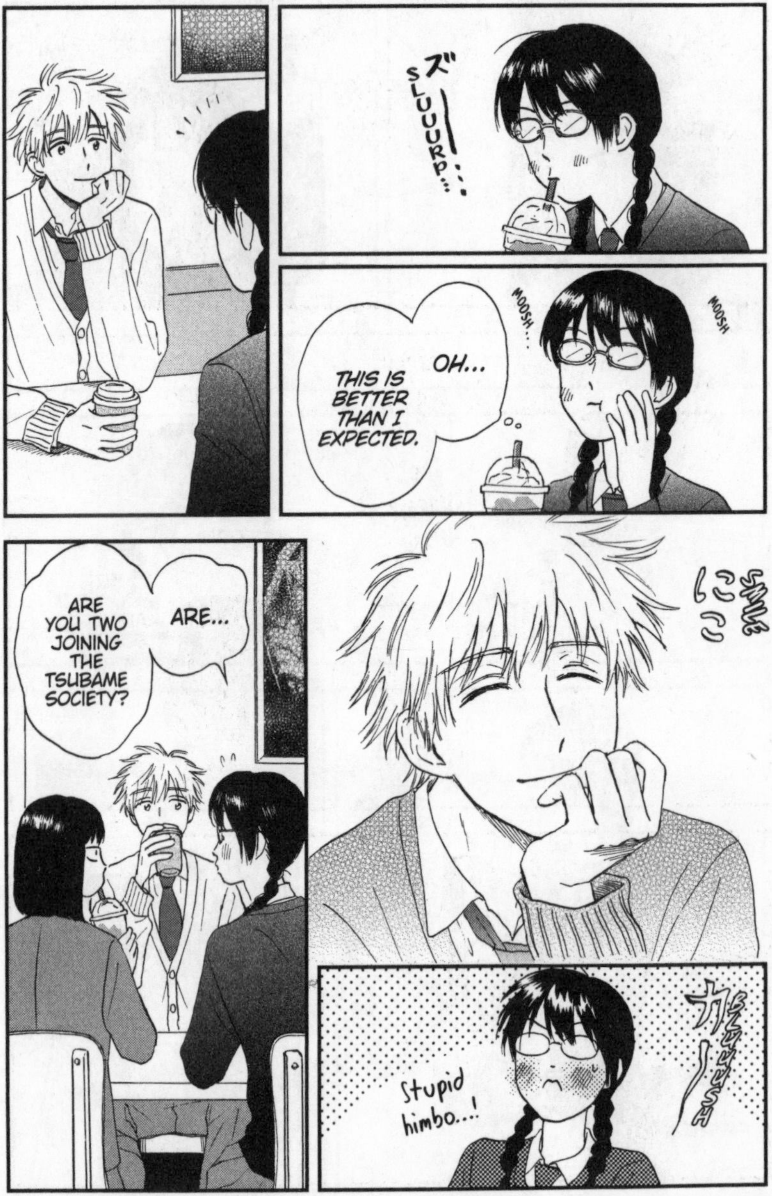
ズ
SLUUUURP...
MOOSH...
MOOSH
OH...
THIS IS BETTER THAN I EXPECTED.
にこ
SMILE
カー
BLUUUSH
Stupid himbo...!
ARE...
ARE YOU TWO JOINING THE TSUBAME SOCIETY?

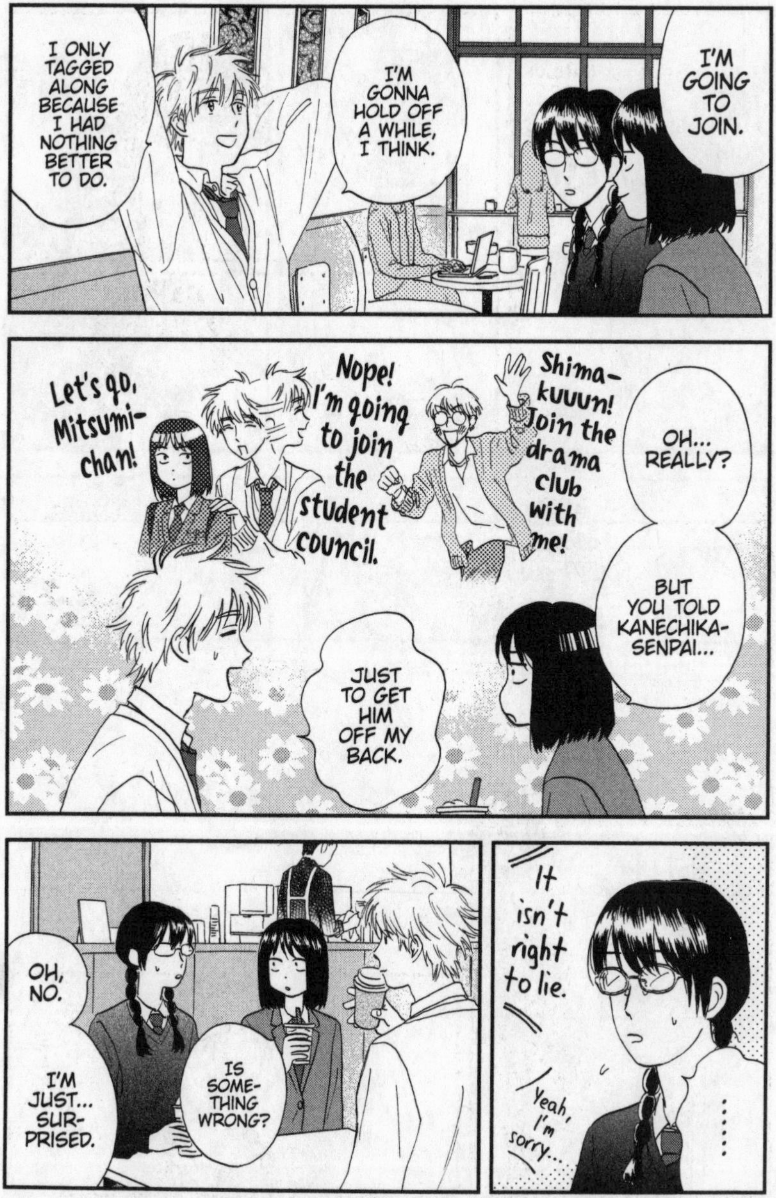
I'M GOING TO JOIN.
I'M GONNA HOLD OFF A WHILE, I THINK.
I ONLY TAGGED ALONG BECAUSE I HAD NOTHING BETTER TO DO.
OH... REALLY?
Shima-kuuun! Join the drama club with me!
Nope! I'm going to join the student council.
Let's go, Mitsumi-chan!
BUT YOU TOLD KANECHIKA-SENPAI...
JUST TO GET HIM OFF MY BACK.
It isn't right to lie.
......
Yeah, I'm sorry...
IS SOMETHING WRONG?
OH, NO.
I'M JUST... SURPRISED.

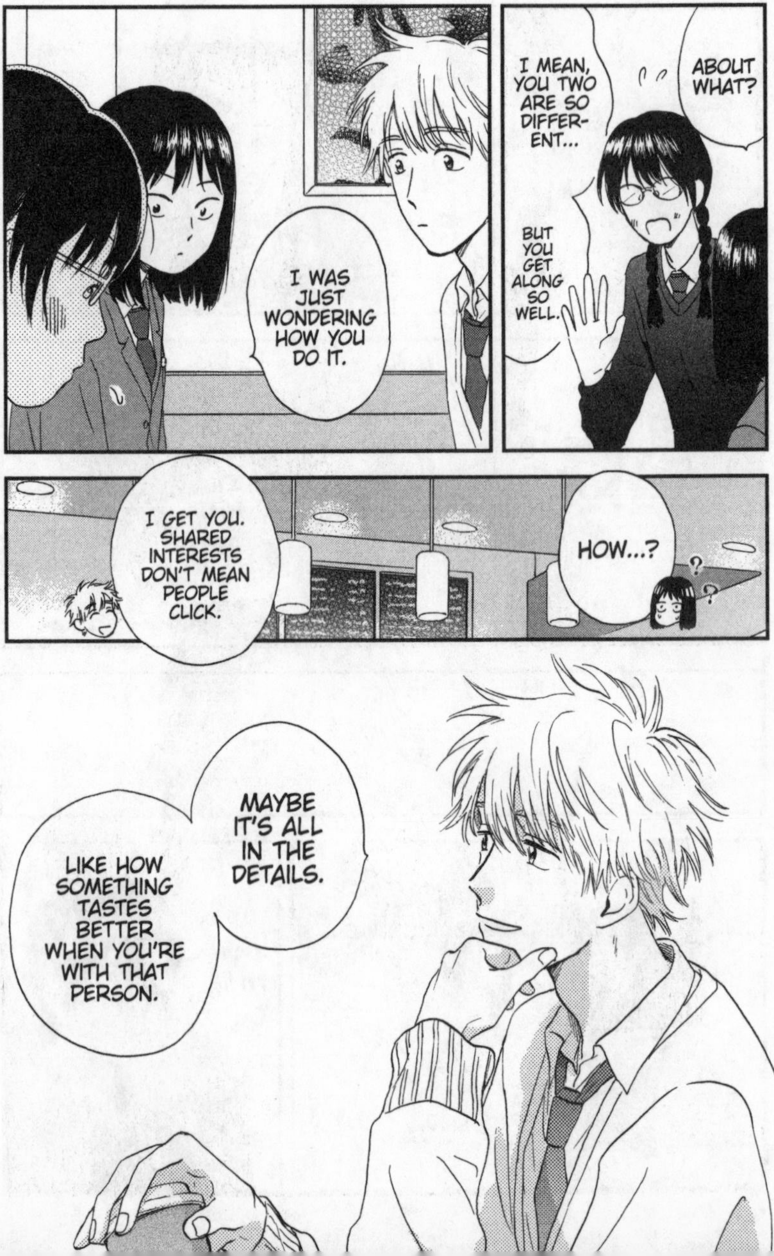
ABOUT WHAT?
I MEAN, YOU TWO ARE SO DIFFER- ENT...
BUT YOU GET ALONG SO WELL.
I WAS JUST WONDERING HOW YOU DO IT.
HOW...?
I GET YOU. SHARED INTERESTS DON'T MEAN PEOPLE CLICK.
MAYBE IT'S ALL IN THE DETAILS.
LIKE HOW SOMETHING TASTES BETTER WHEN YOU'RE WITH THAT PERSON.

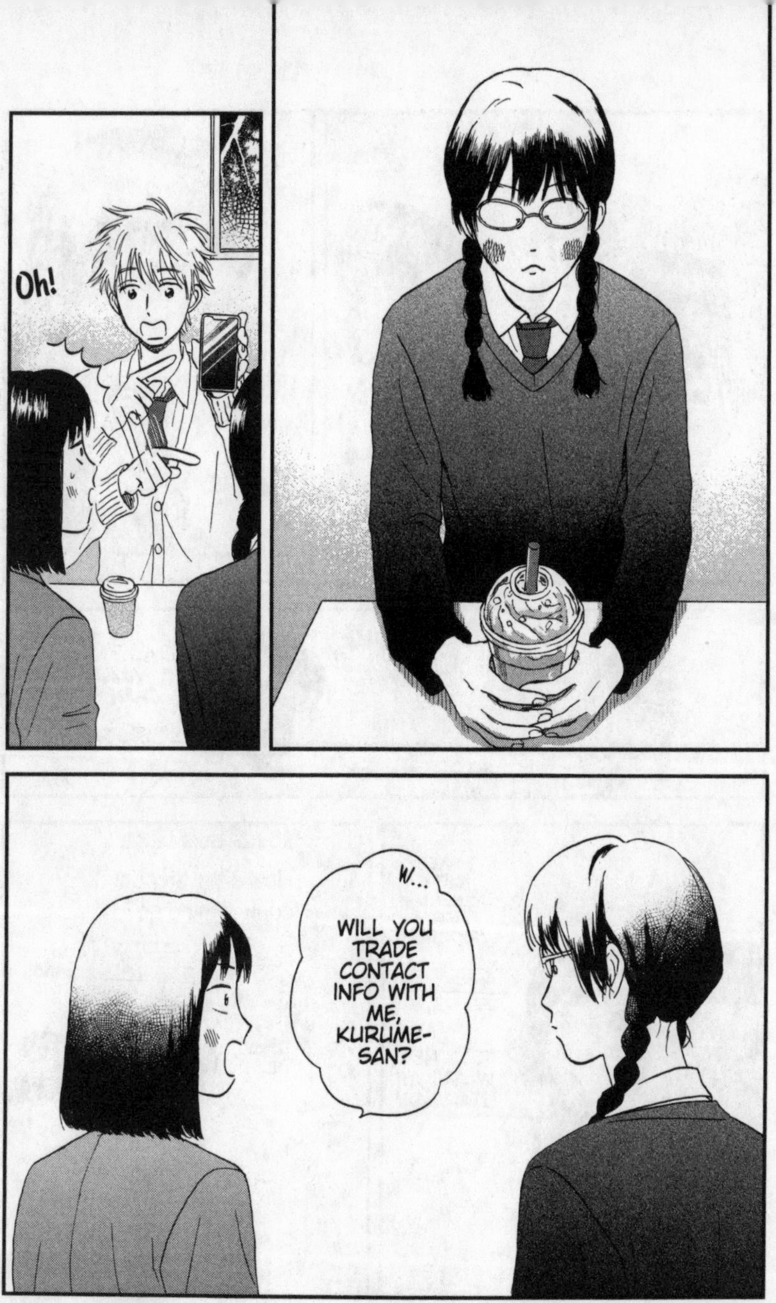
Oh!
W...
WILL YOU TRADE CONTACT INFO WITH ME, KURUME-SAN?

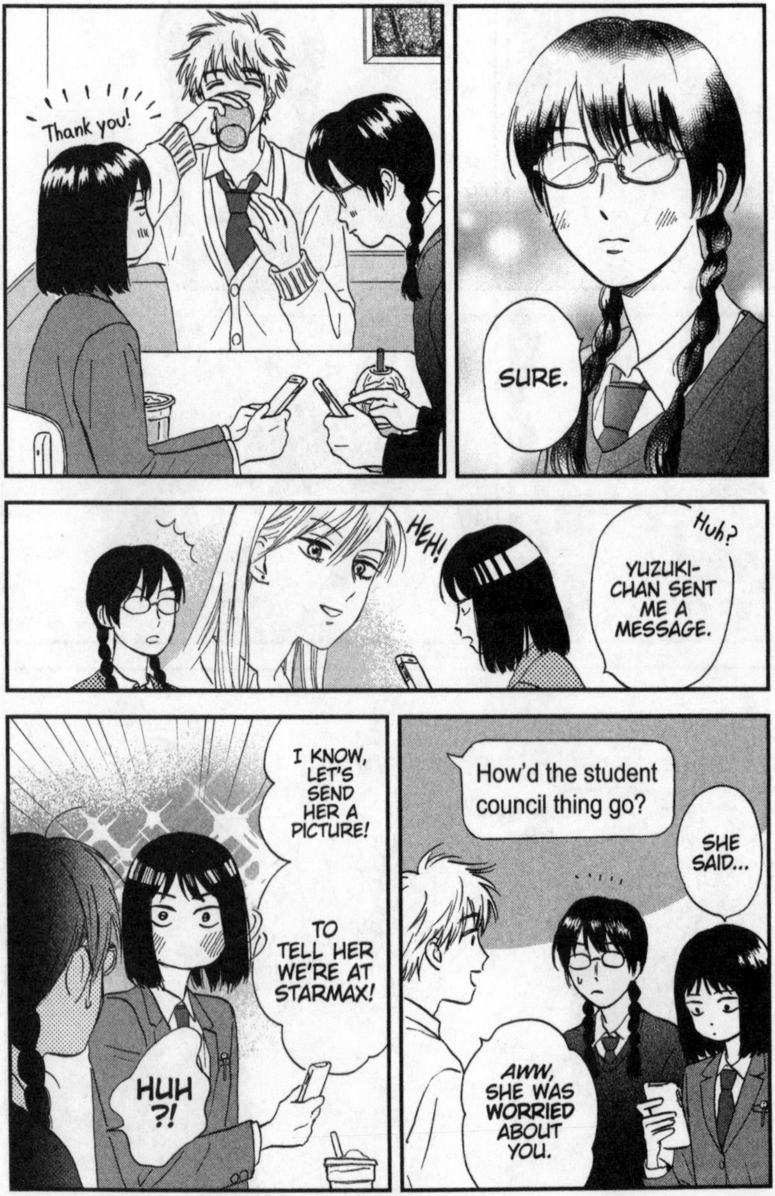
SURE.
Thank you!
Huh?
YUZUKI-CHAN SENT ME A MESSAGE.
HEH!
How'd the student council thing go?
SHE SAID...
AWW, SHE WAS WORRIED ABOUT YOU.
I KNOW, LET'S SEND HER A PICTURE!
TO TELL HER WE'RE AT STARMAX!
HUH?!

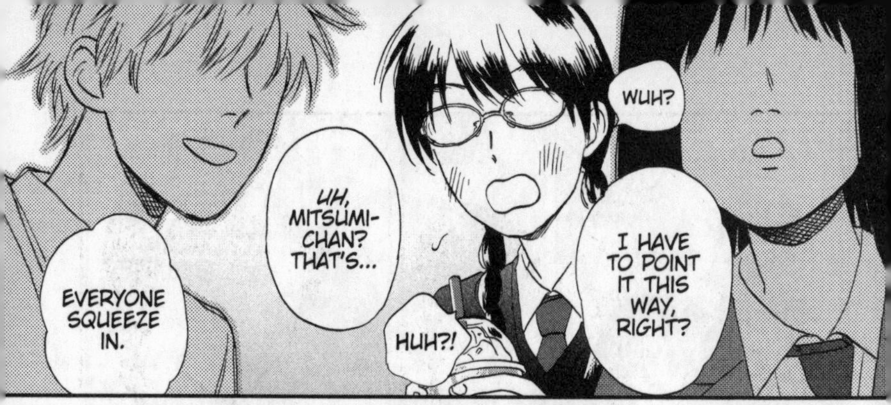
WUH?
I HAVE TO POINT IT THIS WAY, RIGHT?
UH, MITSUMI-CHAN? THAT'S...
HUH?!
EVERYONE SQUEEZE IN.
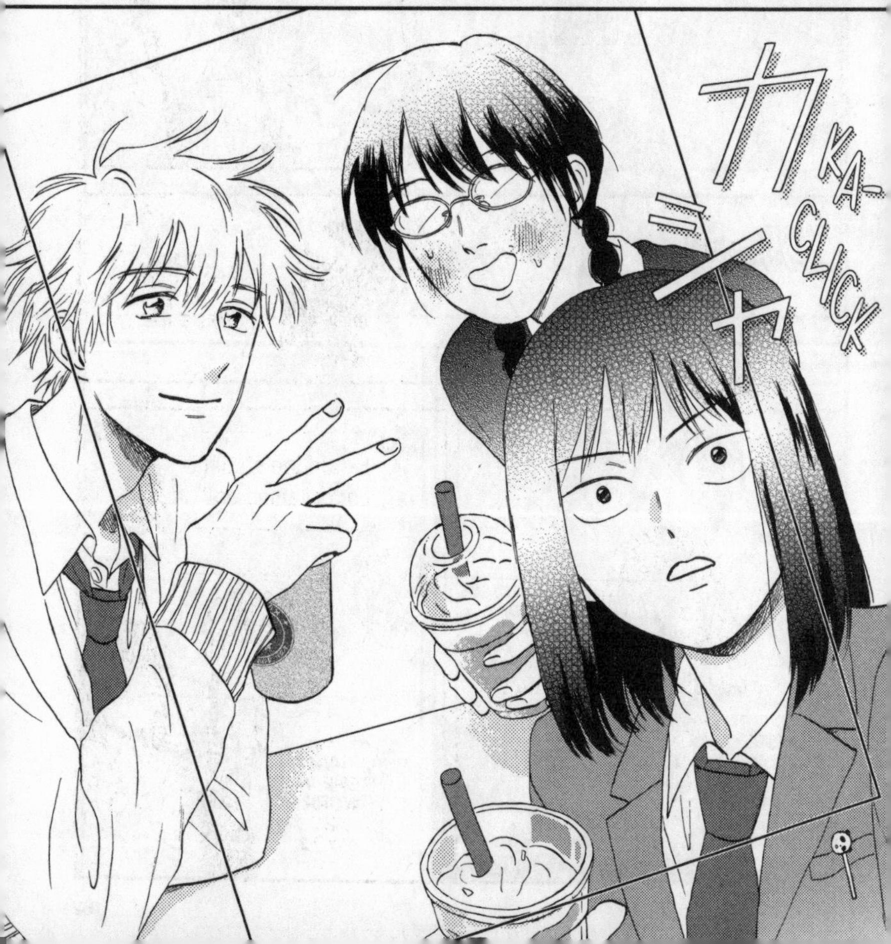
KA-CLICK

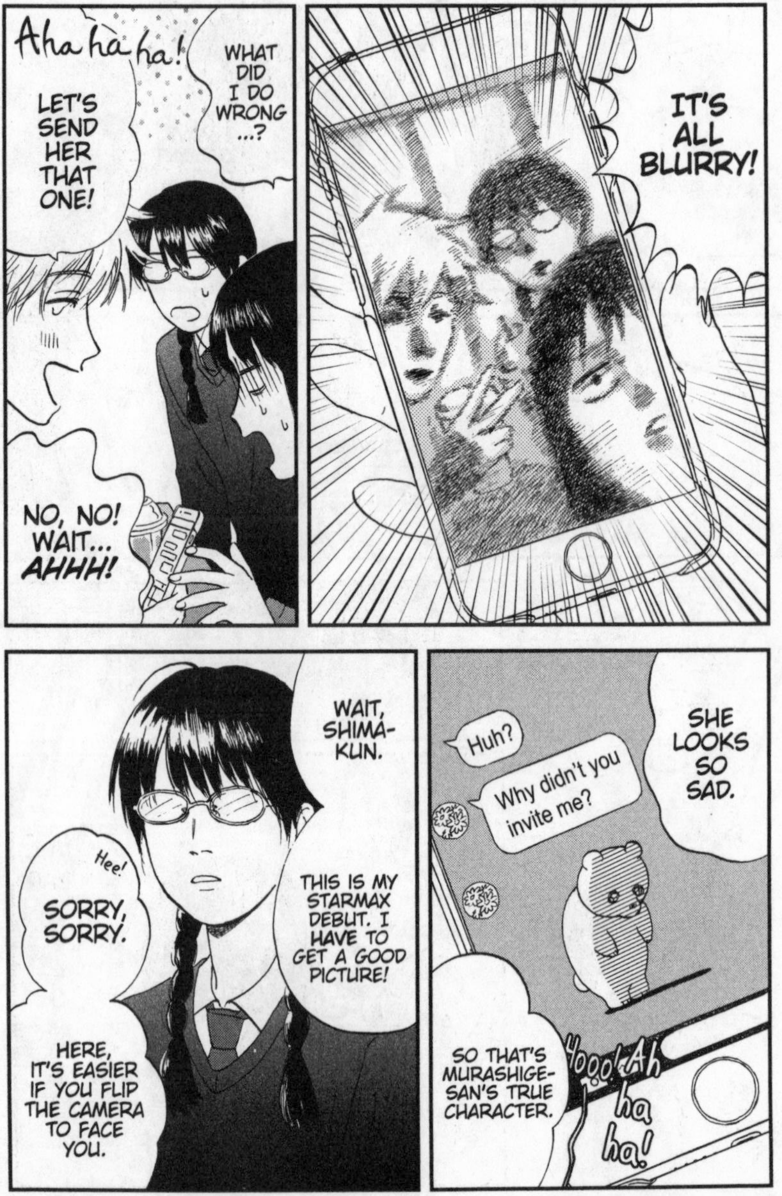
IT'S ALL BLURRY!
WHAT DID I DO WRONG ...?
Ahahaha!
LET'S SEND HER THAT ONE!
NO, NO! WAIT... AHHH!
SHE LOOKS SO SAD.
Huh?
Why didn't you invite me?
SO THAT'S MURASHIGE-SAN'S TRUE CHARACTER.
Yooo! Ah ha ha!
WAIT, SHIMA-KUN.
THIS IS MY STARMAX DEBUT. I HAVE TO GET A GOOD PICTURE!
Hee!
SORRY, SORRY.
HERE, IT'S EASIER IF YOU FLIP THE CAMERA TO FACE YOU.

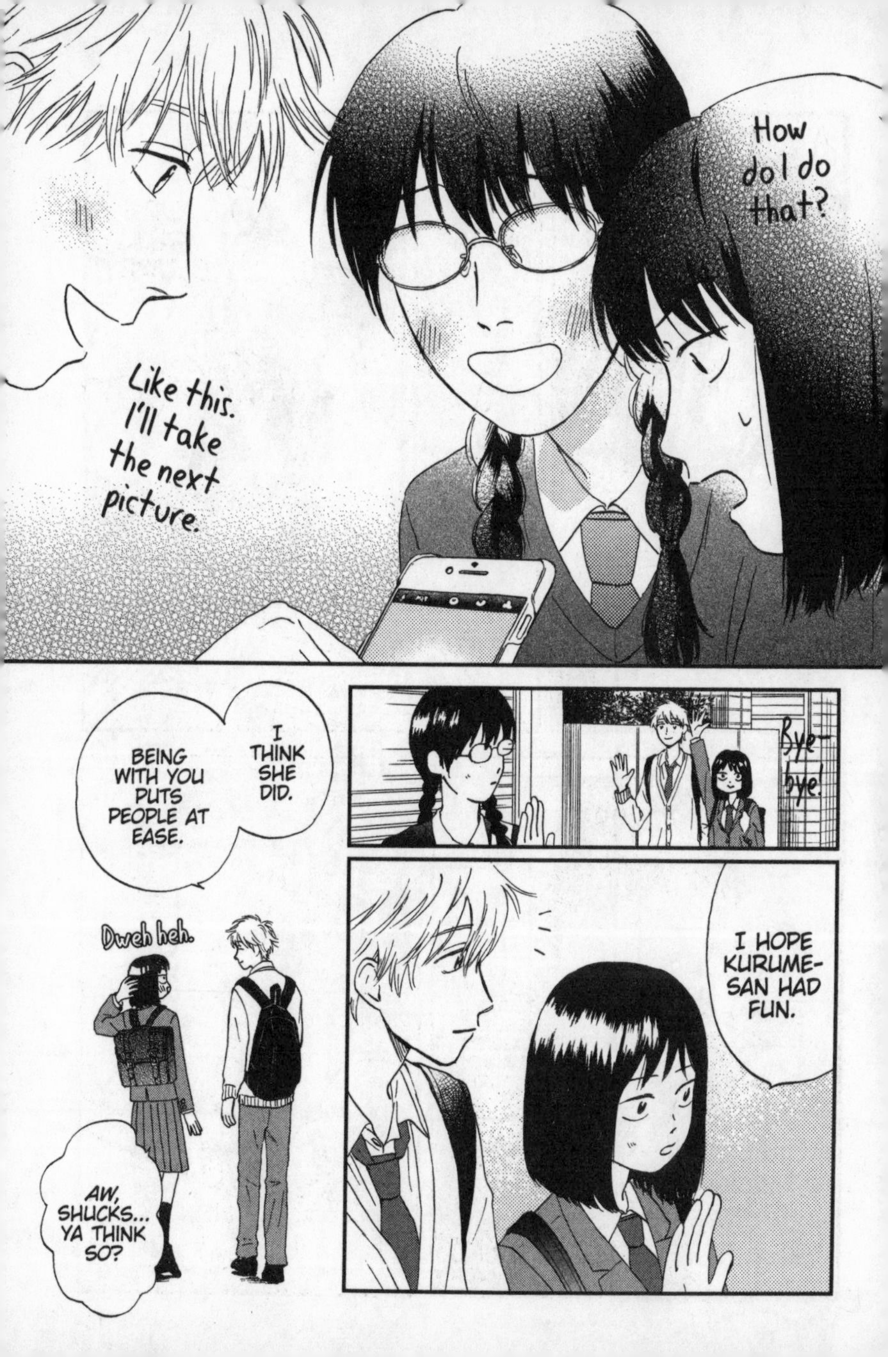
How do I do that?
Like this. I'll take the next picture.
Bye-bye!
I HOPE KURUME-SAN HAD FUN.
I THINK SHE DID.
BEING WITH YOU PUTS PEOPLE AT EASE.
Dweh heh.
AW, SHUCKS... YA THINK SO?

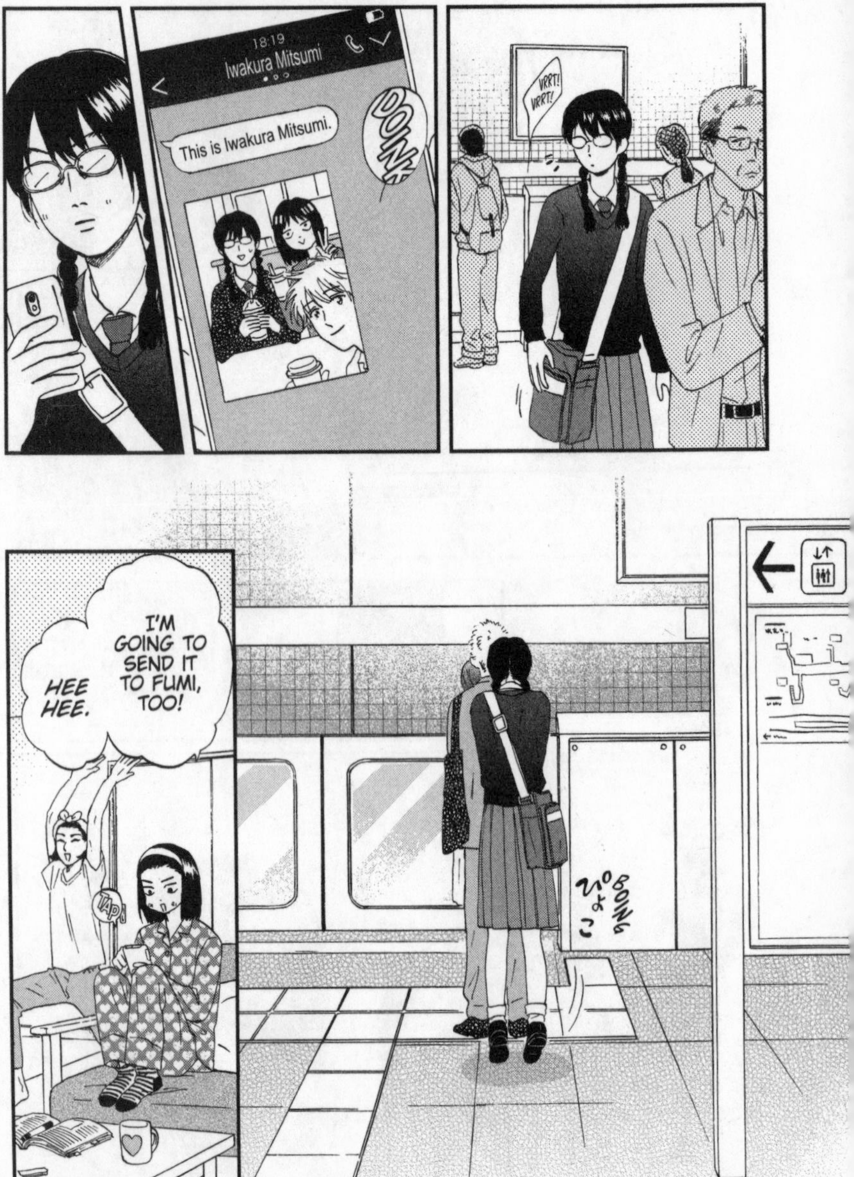
VRRT!
VRRT!
18:19
Iwakura Mitsumi
This is Iwakura Mitsumi.
DOINK
BOING
ぴょこ
I'M GOING TO SEND IT TO FUMI, TOO!
HEE HEE.
TAP

Scene ④ END

Skip
and
Loafer

Skip
and
Loafer

Scene ⑤ *Brzap!* Electric Movie Theater

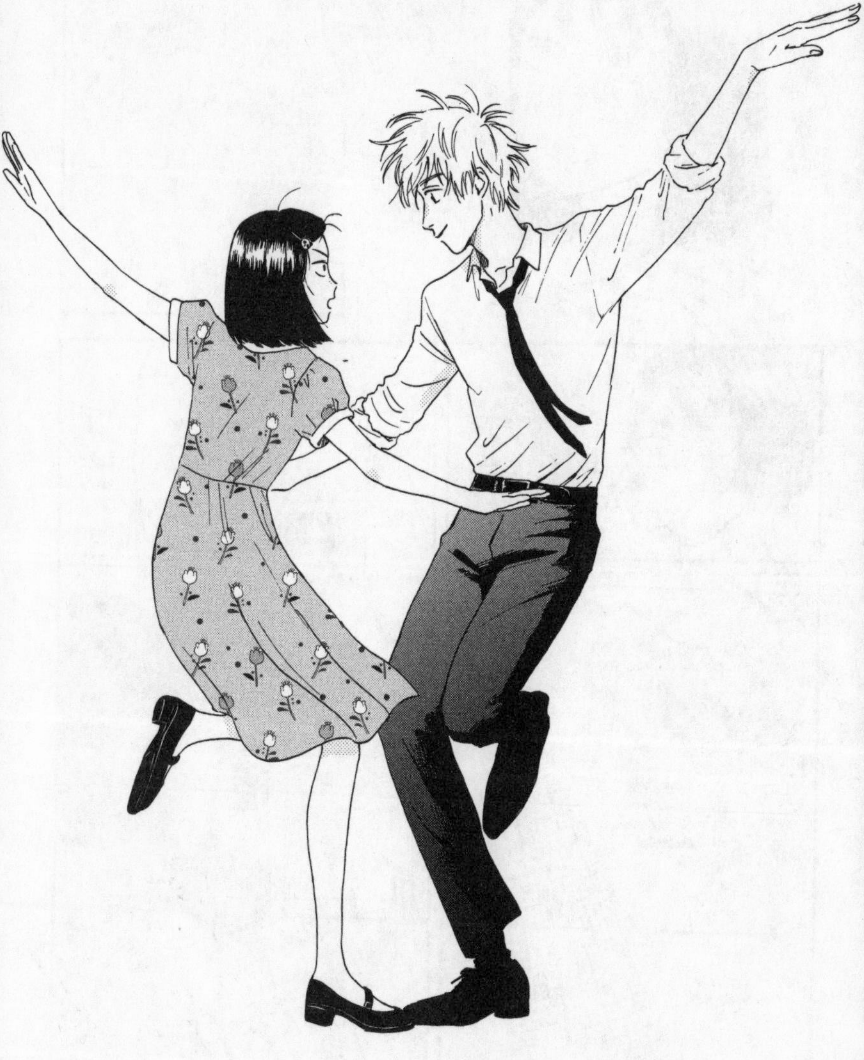

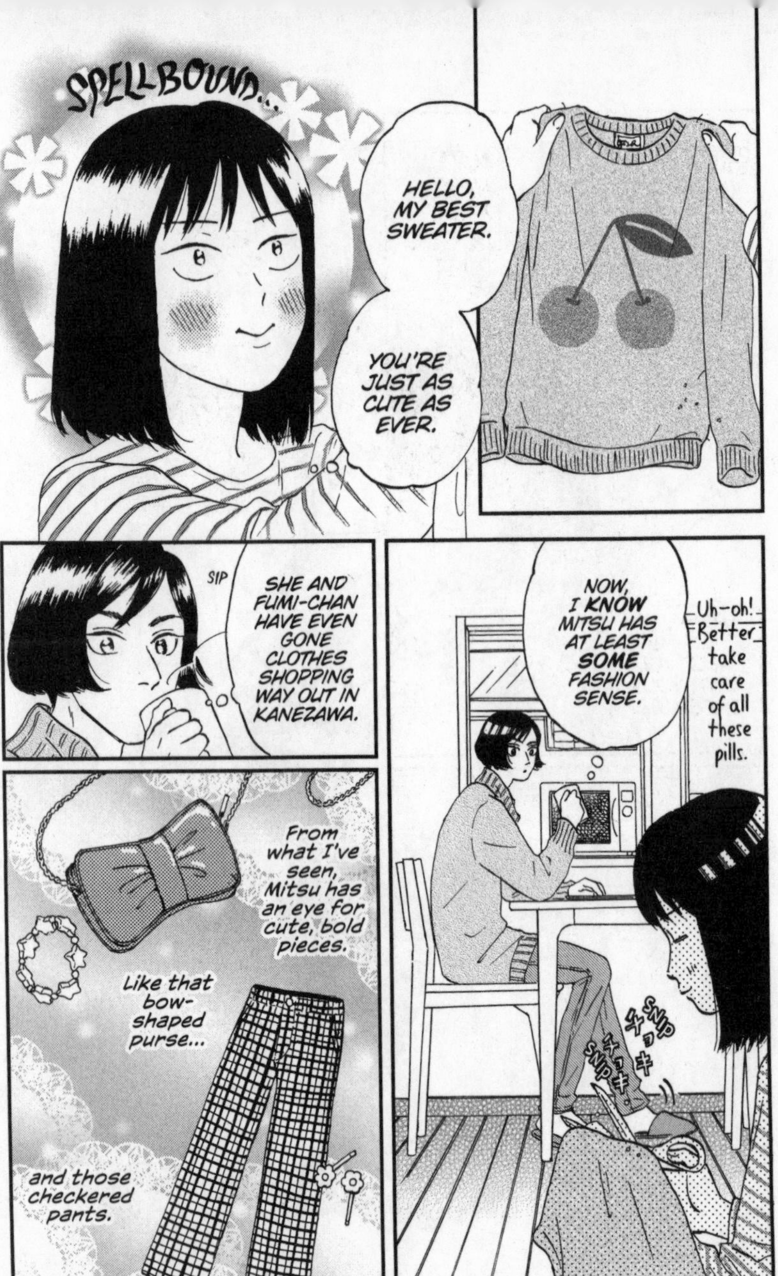
HELLO, MY BEST SWEATER.
YOU'RE JUST AS CUTE AS EVER.
SPELLBOUND...
Uh-oh! Better take care of all these pills.
NOW, I KNOW MITSU HAS AT LEAST SOME FASHION SENSE.
SNIP
SNIP
SIP
SHE AND FUMI-CHAN HAVE EVEN GONE CLOTHES SHOPPING WAY OUT IN KANEZAWA.
From what I've seen, Mitsu has an eye for cute, bold pieces.
Like that bow-shaped purse...
and those checkered pants.

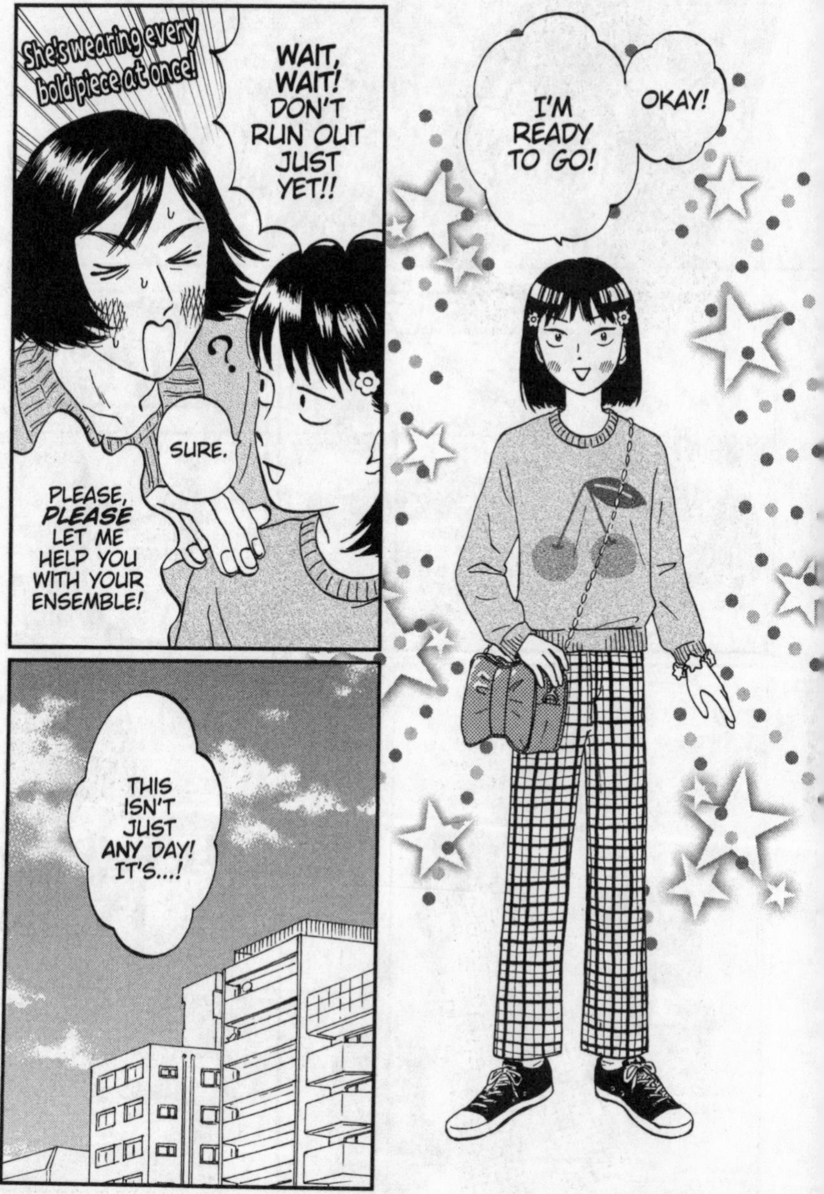
OKAY!
I'M READY TO GO!
WAIT, WAIT! DON'T RUN OUT JUST YET!!
She's wearing every bold piece at once!
SURE.
PLEASE, PLEASE LET ME HELP YOU WITH YOUR ENSEMBLE!
THIS ISN'T JUST ANY DAY! IT'S...!

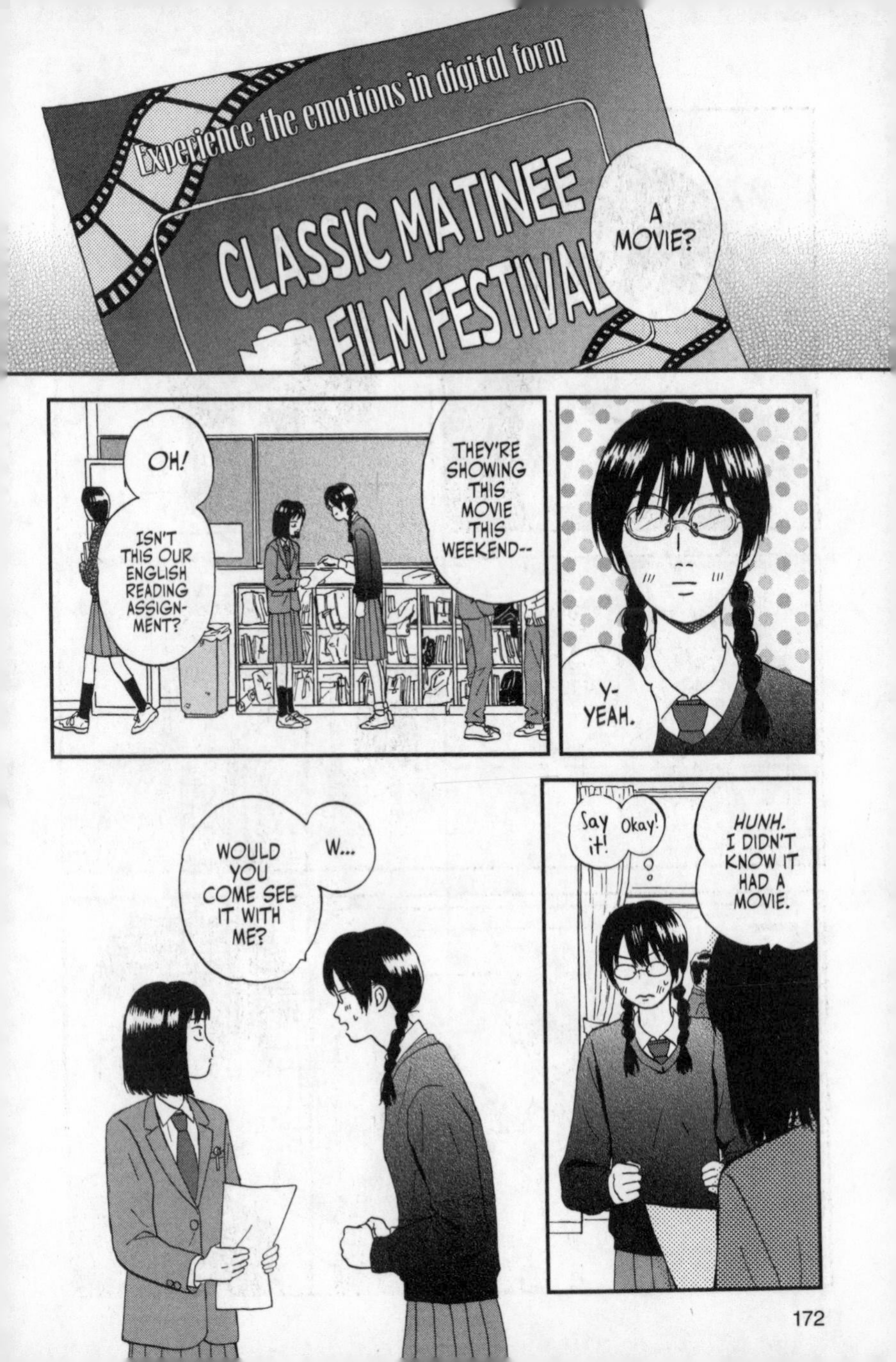
Experience the emotions in digital form
CLASSIC MATINEE FILM FESTIVAL
A MOVIE?
Y- YEAH.
THEY'RE SHOWING THIS MOVIE THIS WEEKEND--
OH!
ISN'T THIS OUR ENGLISH READING ASSIGNMENT?
HUNH. I DIDN'T KNOW IT HAD A MOVIE.
Okay!
Say it!
W...
WOULD YOU COME SEE IT WITH ME?

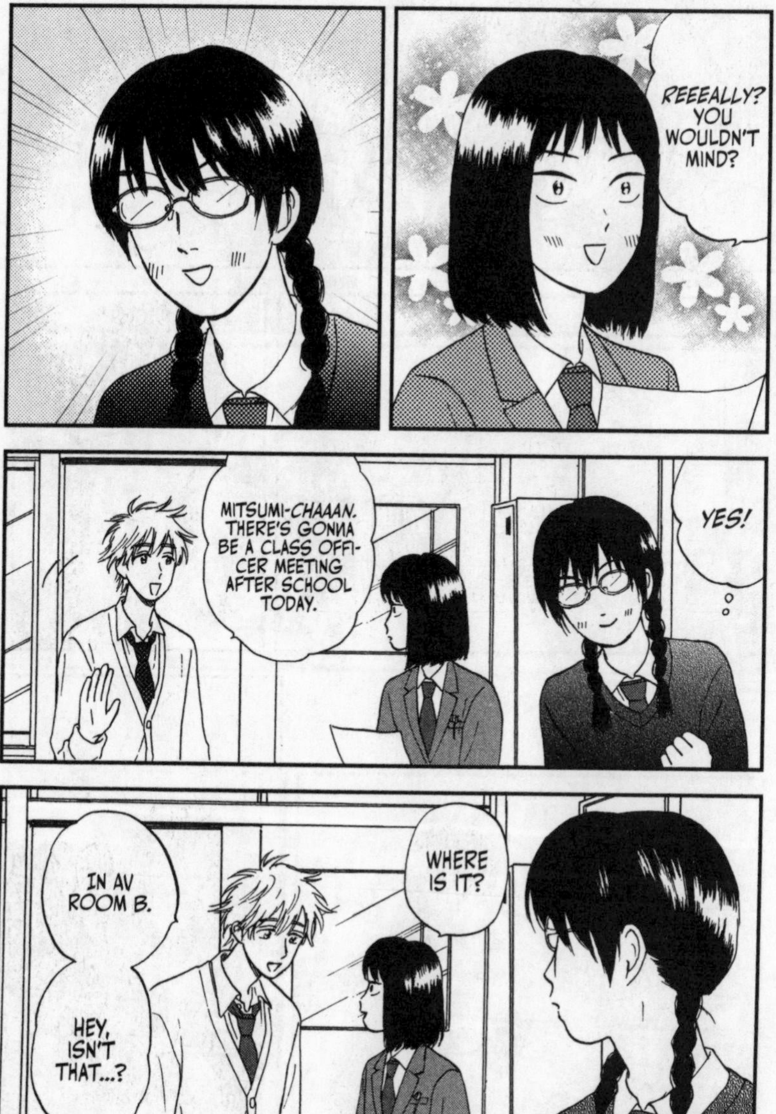
REEEALLY? YOU WOULDN'T MIND?
YES!
MITSUMI-CHAAAN. THERE'S GONNA BE A CLASS OFFICER MEETING AFTER SCHOOL TODAY.
WHERE IS IT?
IN AV ROOM B.
HEY, ISN'T THAT...?

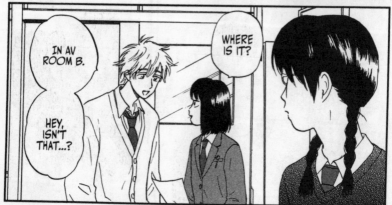

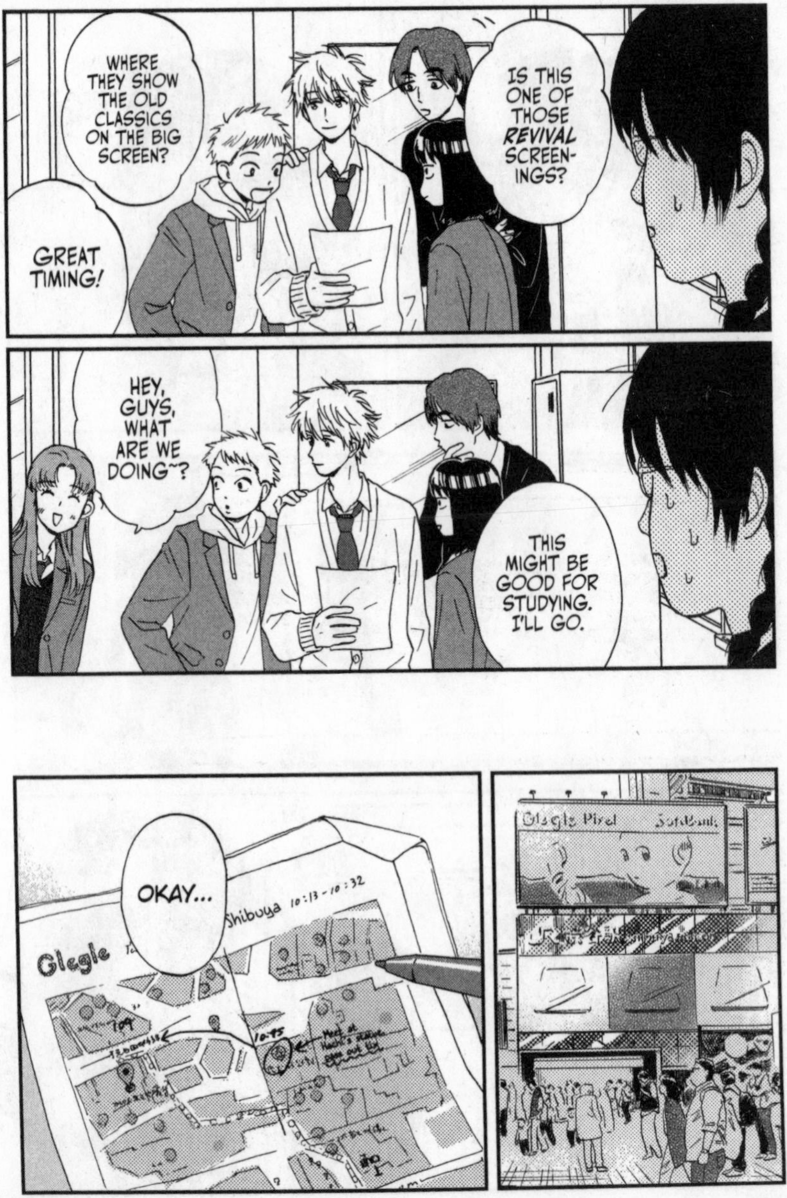
IS THIS ONE OF THOSE *REVIVAL* SCREEN-INGS?
WHERE THEY SHOW THE OLD CLASSICS ON THE BIG SCREEN?
GREAT TIMING!
THIS MIGHT BE GOOD FOR STUDYING. I'LL GO.
HEY, GUYS, WHAT ARE WE DOING~?
OKAY...
Glegle
Shibuya 10:13-10:32

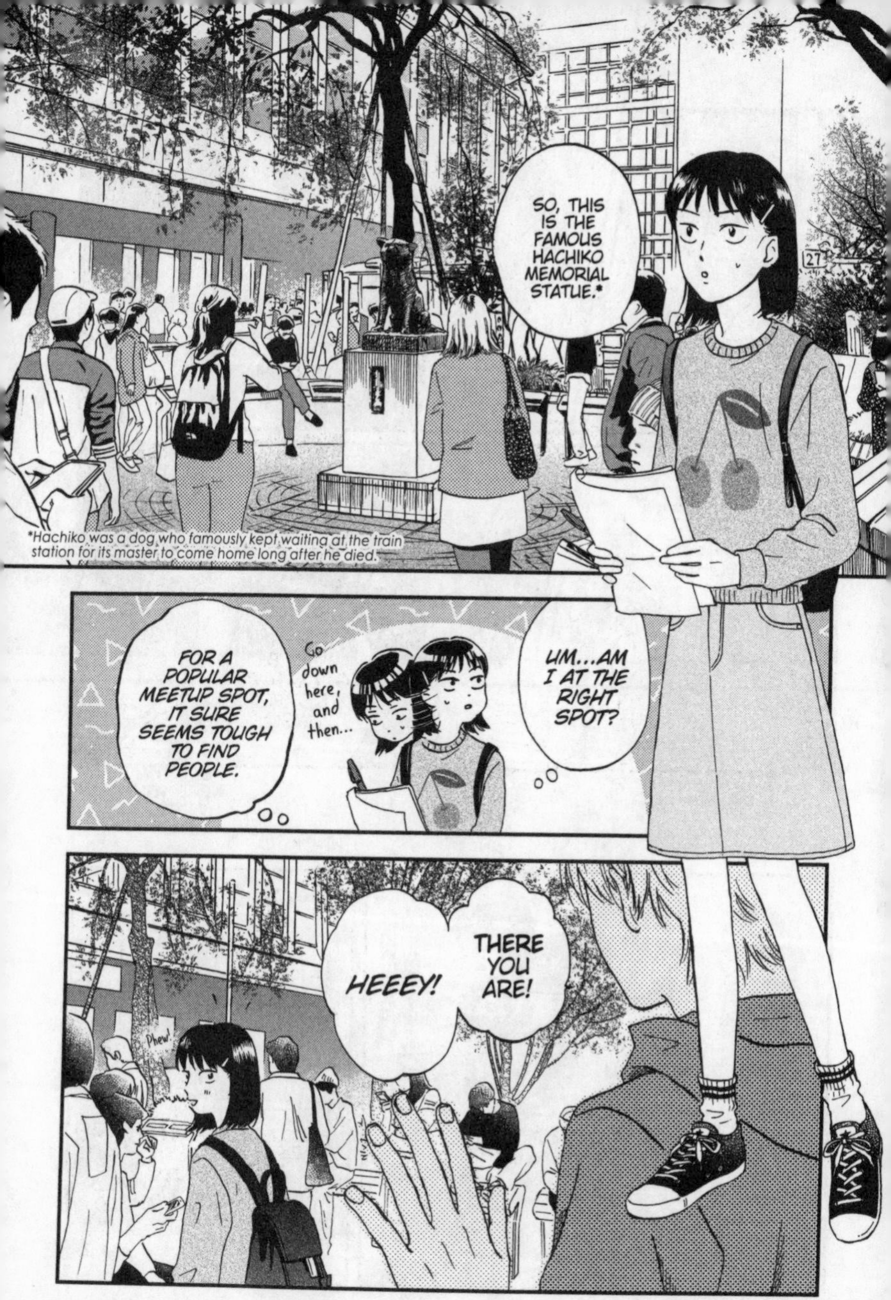
SO, THIS IS THE FAMOUS HACHIKO MEMORIAL STATUE.*
27
UM...AM I AT THE RIGHT SPOT?
Go down here, and then...
FOR A POPULAR MEETUP SPOT, IT SURE SEEMS TOUGH TO FIND PEOPLE.
THERE YOU ARE!
HEEEY!
Phew!
*Hachiko was a dog who famously kept waiting at the train station for its master to come home long after he died.

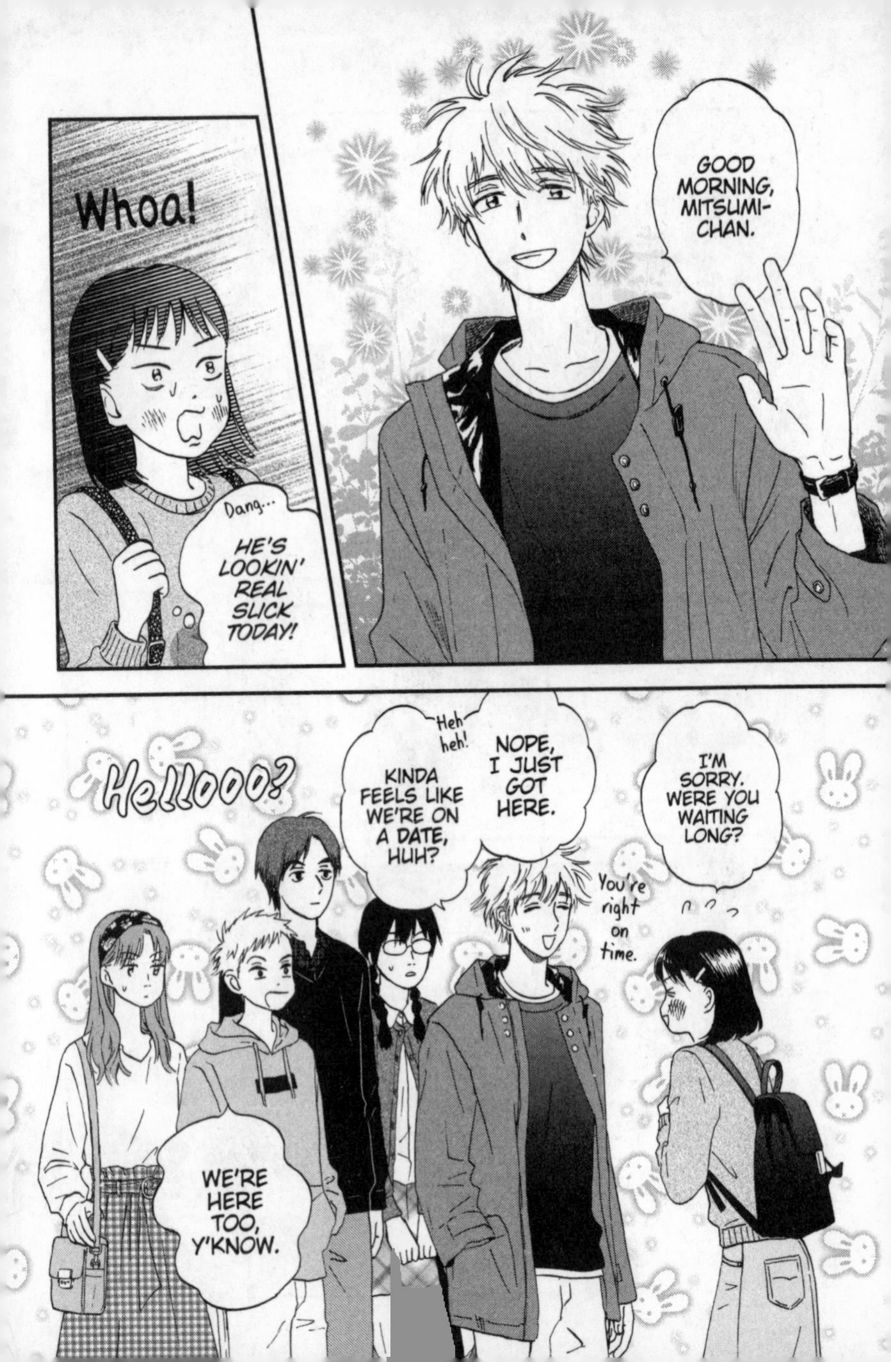
GOOD MORNING, MITSUMI-CHAN.
Whoa!
Dang...
HE'S LOOKIN' REAL SLICK TODAY!
I'M SORRY. WERE YOU WAITING LONG?
You're right on time.
NOPE, I JUST GOT HERE.
Heh heh!
KINDA FEELS LIKE WE'RE ON A DATE, HUH?
Hellooo?
WE'RE HERE TOO, Y'KNOW.

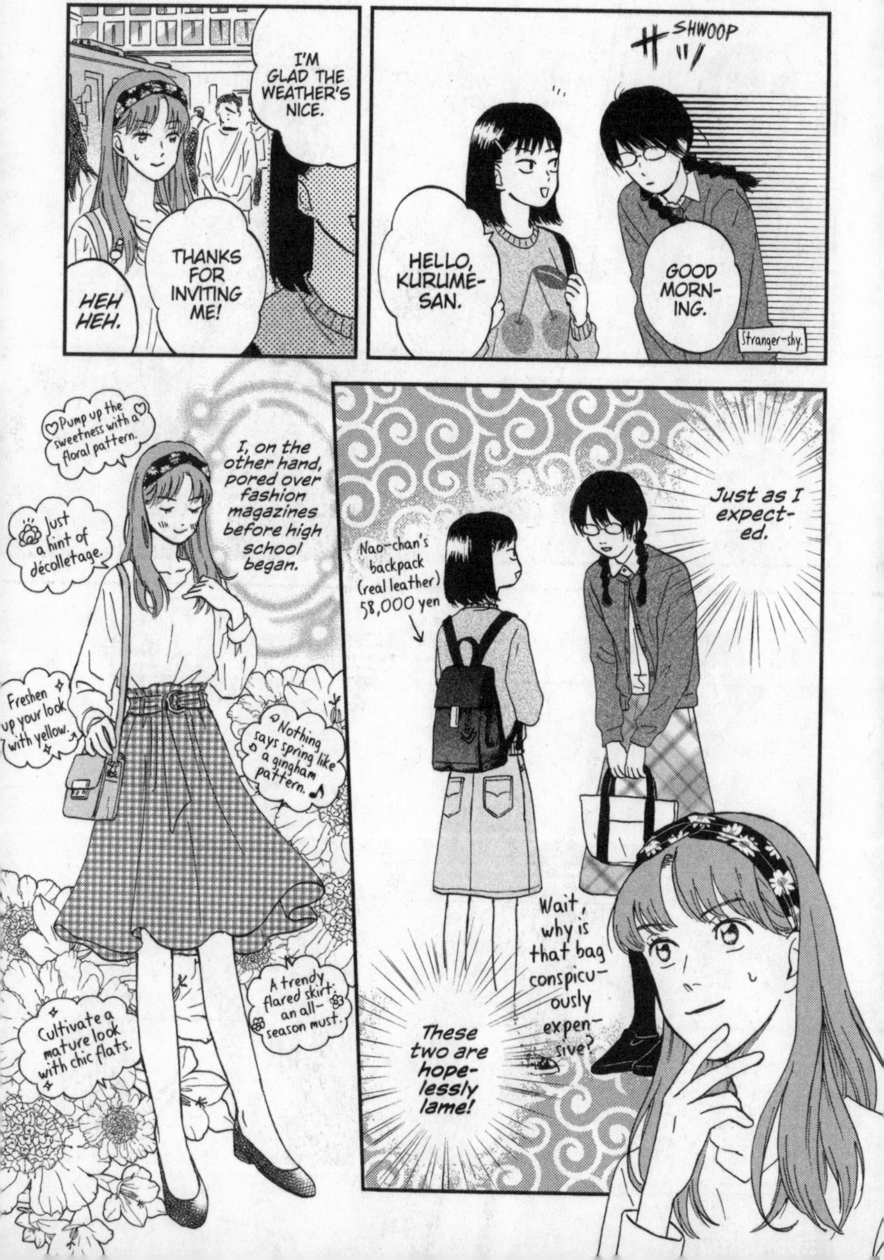
SHWOOP
...
GOOD MORNING.
Stranger-shy.
HELLO, KURUME-SAN.
I'M GLAD THE WEATHER'S NICE.
THANKS FOR INVITING ME!
HEH HEH.
Just as I expected.
Nao-chan's backpack (real leather) 58,000 yen
Wait, why is that bag conspicuously expensive?
These two are hopelessly lame!
I, on the other hand, pored over fashion magazines before high school began.
Pump up the sweetness with a floral pattern.
Just a hint of décolletage.
Nothing says spring like a gingham pattern.
Freshen up your look with yellow.
A trendy flared skirt: an all-season must.
Cultivate a mature look with chic flats.

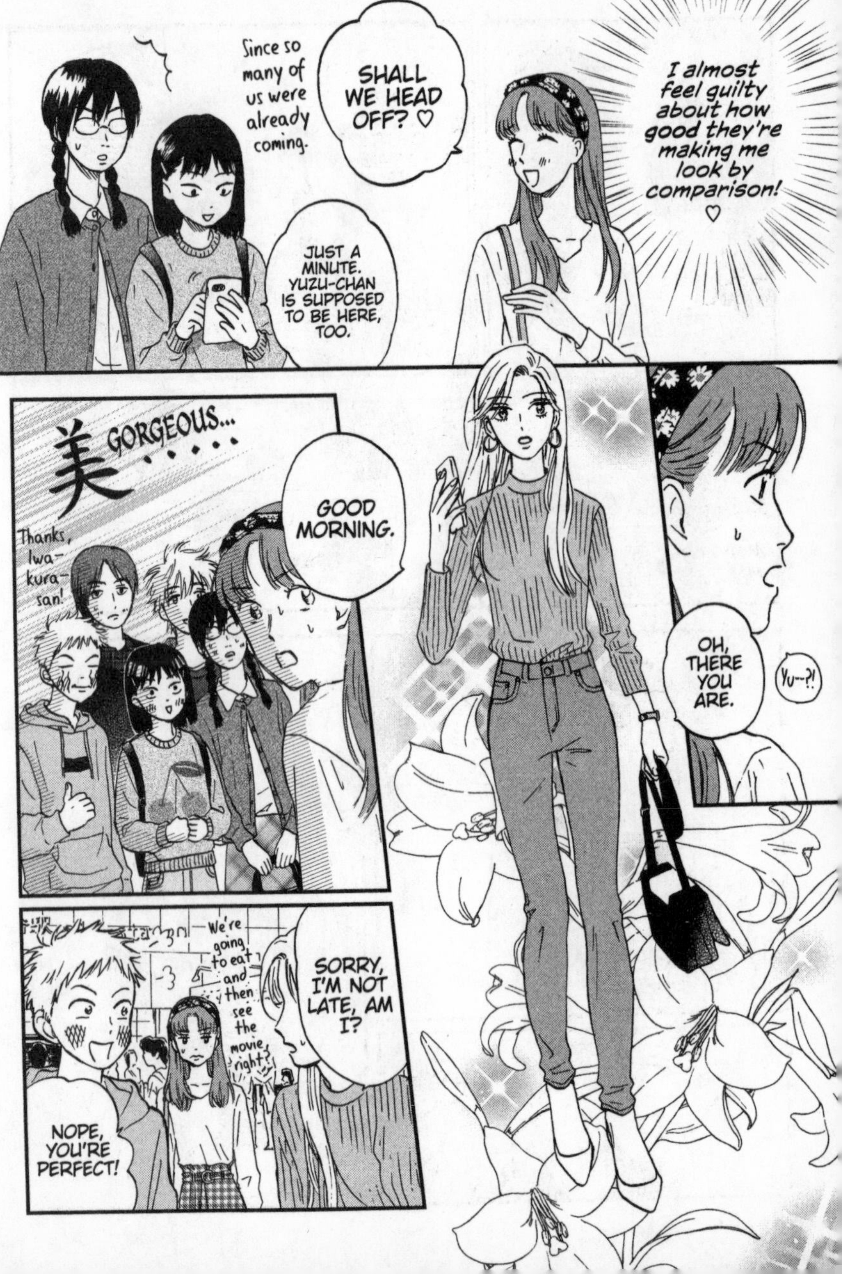
I almost feel guilty about how good they're making me look by comparison! ♡
SHALL WE HEAD OFF? ♡
Since so many of us were already coming.
JUST A MINUTE. YUZU-CHAN IS SUPPOSED TO BE HERE, TOO.
OH, THERE YOU ARE.
Yu--?!
GOOD MORNING.
美 GORGEOUS.......
Thanks, Iwa-kura-san!
SORRY, I'M NOT LATE, AM I?
We're going to eat and then see the movie, right?
NOPE, YOU'RE PERFECT!

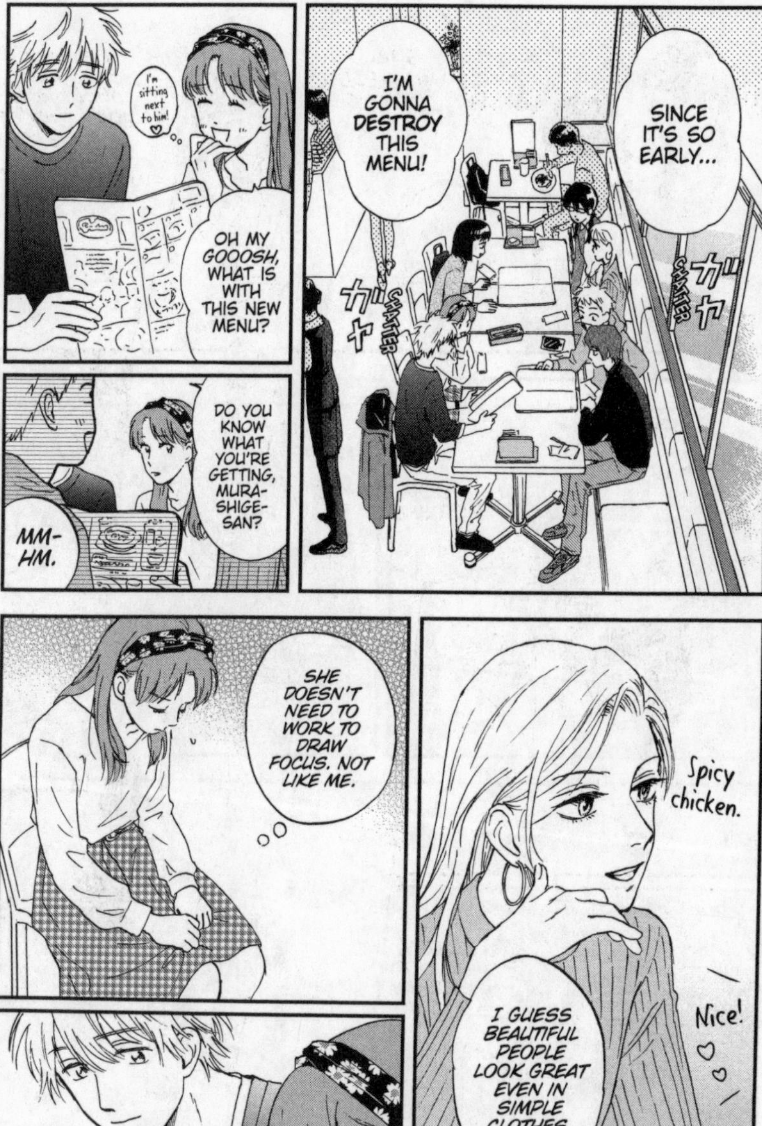
SINCE IT'S SO EARLY...
ガヤ
SHATTER
I'M GONNA DESTROY THIS MENU!
ガヤ
SHATTER
OH MY GOOOSH, WHAT IS WITH THIS NEW MENU?
I'm sitting next to him! ♡
DO YOU KNOW WHAT YOU'RE GETTING, MURA-SHIGE-SAN?
MM-HM.
Spicy chicken.
Nice! ♡ ♡
I GUESS BEAUTIFUL PEOPLE LOOK GREAT EVEN IN SIMPLE CLOTHES.
SHE DOESN'T NEED TO WORK TO DRAW FOCUS. NOT LIKE ME.

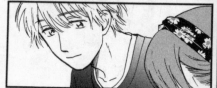

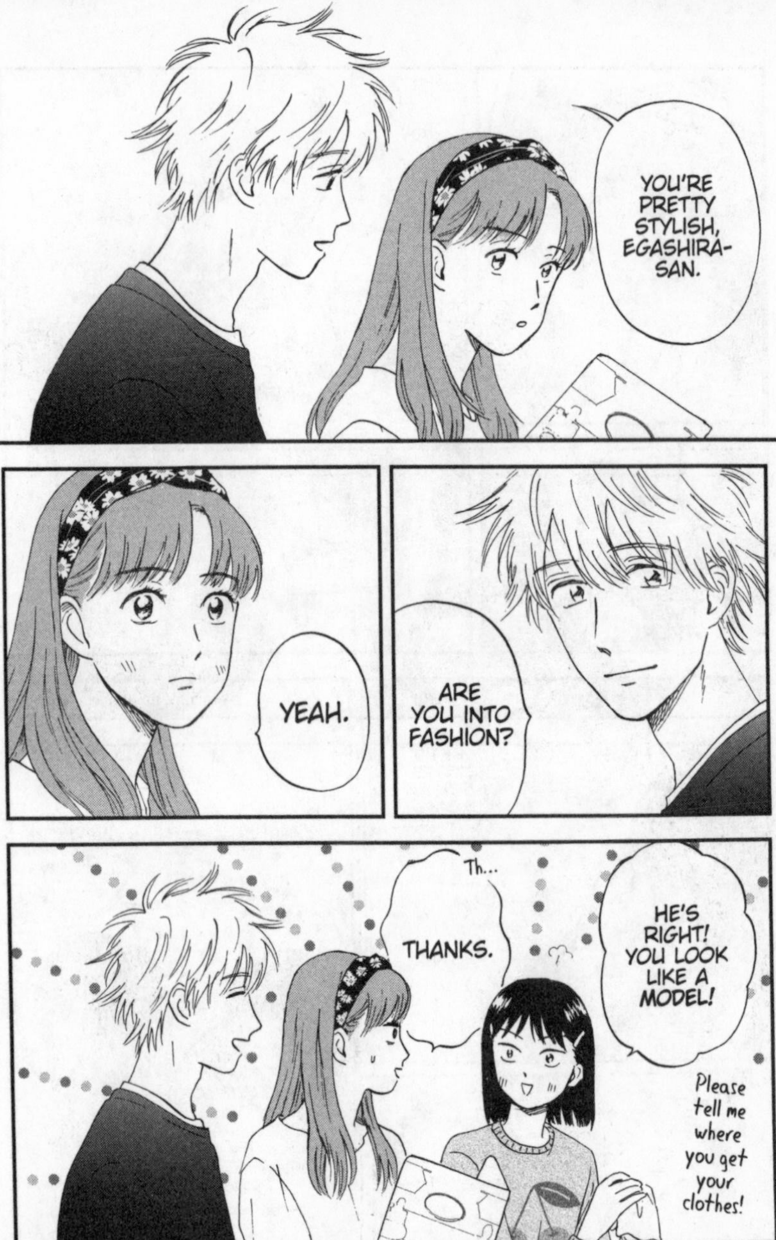
YOU'RE PRETTY STYLISH, EGASHIRA-SAN.
ARE YOU INTO FASHION?
YEAH.
HE'S RIGHT! YOU LOOK LIKE A MODEL!
Please tell me where you get your clothes!
Th...
THANKS.

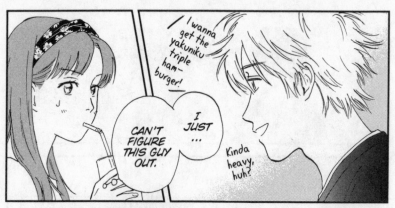

I wanna get the yakuniku triple ham-burger!
Kinda heavy, huh?
I JUST ... CAN'T FIGURE THIS GUY OUT.
OH, THAT QUIZ WE HAD THE OTHER DAY?
MAN, THAT QUESTION WAS TRICKY.
YOU SHOULD TRY THIS APP. IT'S GREAT FOR LEARNING VOCAB.
OOH.
It's so easy!
I USE THAT APP, TOO!
IT'S PRETTY GREAT, HUH?

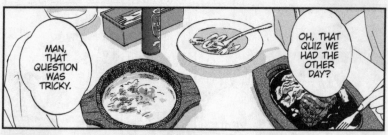

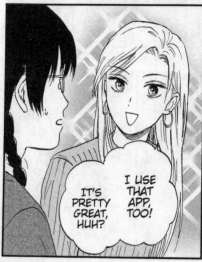

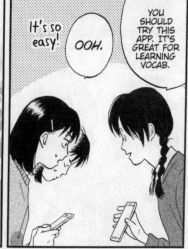

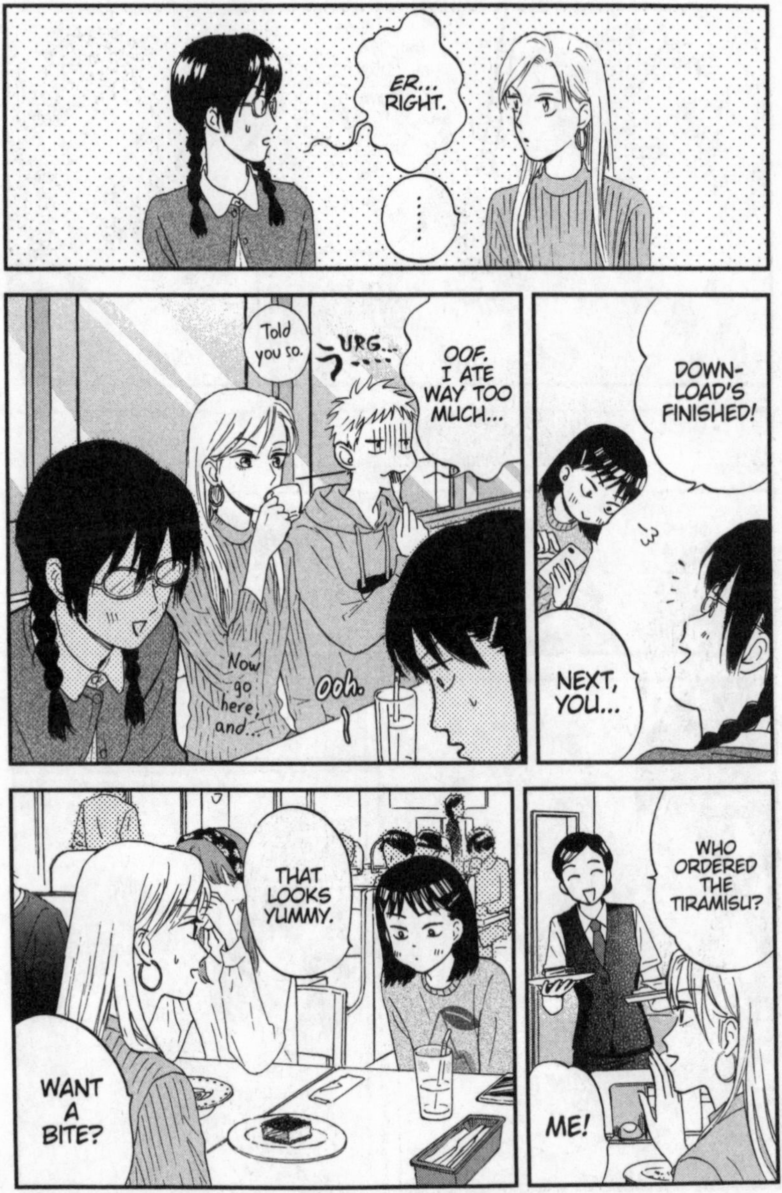
ER... RIGHT.
......
DOWN-LOAD'S FINISHED!
NEXT, YOU...
OOF. I ATE WAY TOO MUCH...
URG...
Told you so.
Ooh.
Now go here, and...
WHO ORDERED THE TIRAMISU?
ME!
THAT LOOKS YUMMY.
WANT A BITE?

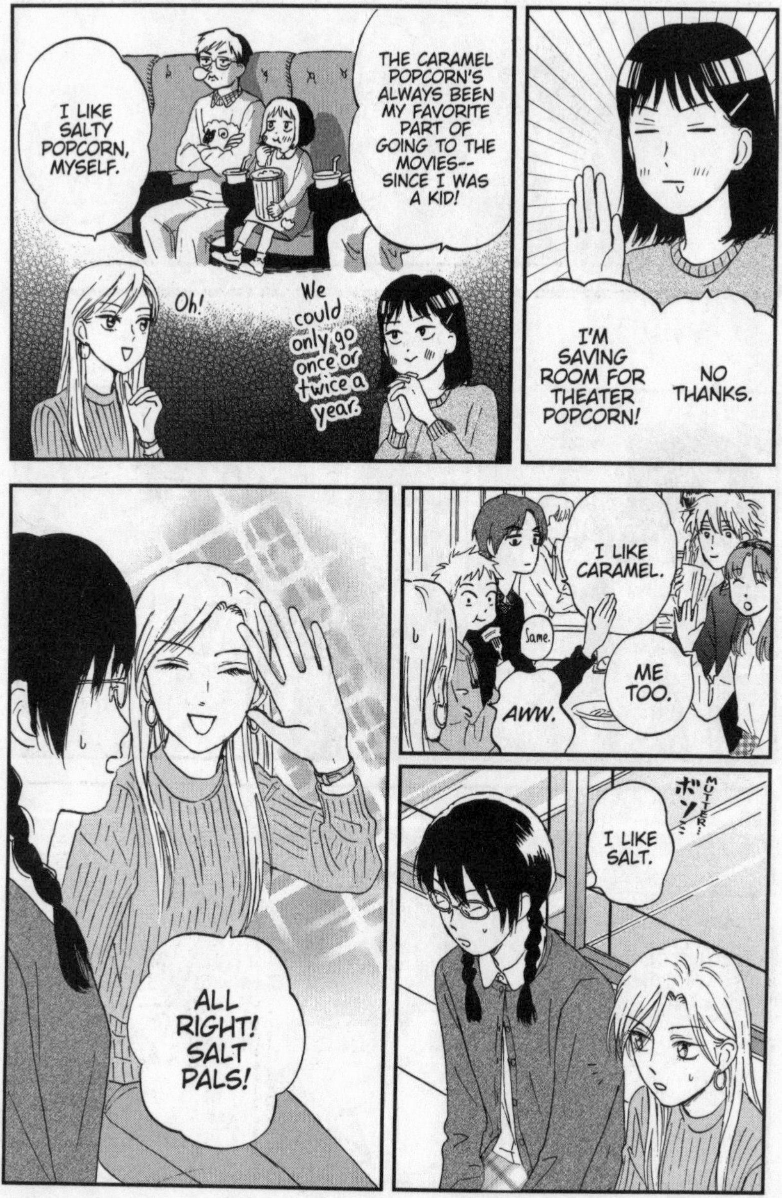
NO THANKS.
I'M SAVING ROOM FOR THEATER POPCORN!
THE CARAMEL POPCORN'S ALWAYS BEEN MY FAVORITE PART OF GOING TO THE MOVIES-- SINCE I WAS A KID!
I LIKE SALTY POPCORN, MYSELF.
We could only go once or twice a year.
Oh!
I LIKE CARAMEL.
Same.
ME TOO.
AWW.
ボソッ
MUTTER...
I LIKE SALT.
ALL RIGHT! SALT PALS!

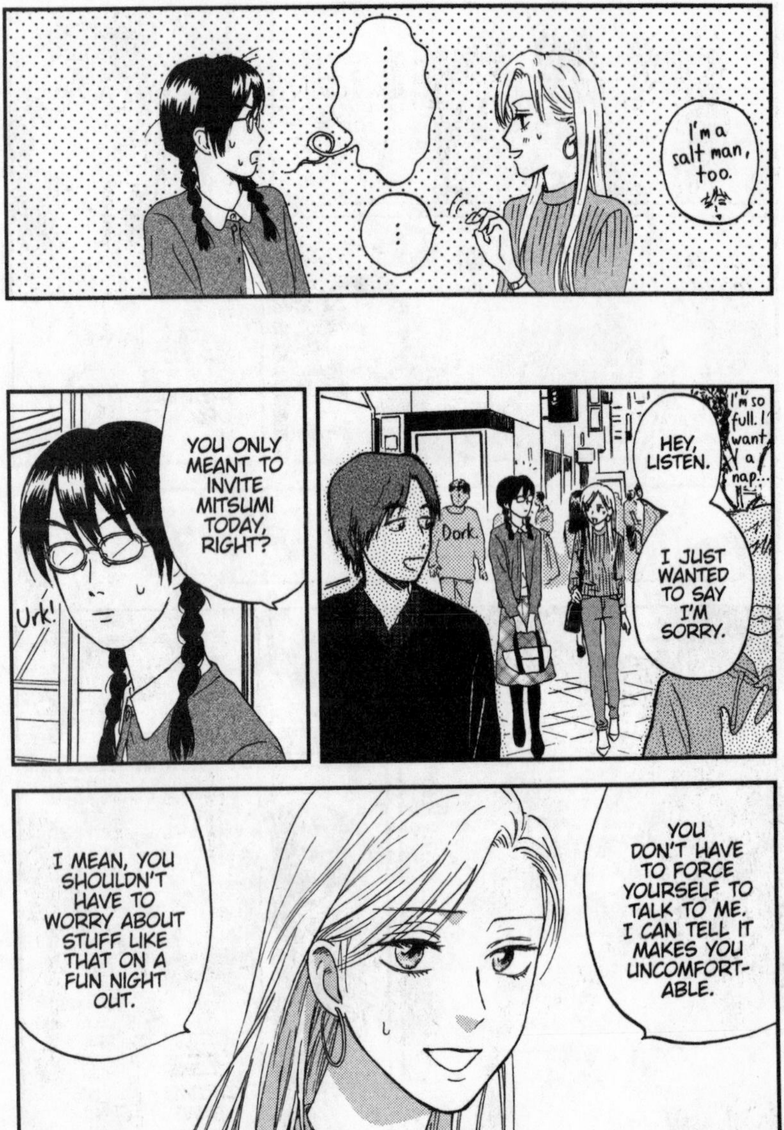
I'm a salt man, too.
......
...
I'm so full. I want a nap...
HEY, LISTEN.
I JUST WANTED TO SAY I'M SORRY.
Dork.
YOU ONLY MEANT TO INVITE MITSUMI TODAY, RIGHT?
Urk!
YOU DON'T HAVE TO FORCE YOURSELF TO TALK TO ME. I CAN TELL IT MAKES YOU UNCOMFORT-ABLE.
I MEAN, YOU SHOULDN'T HAVE TO WORRY ABOUT STUFF LIKE THAT ON A FUN NIGHT OUT.

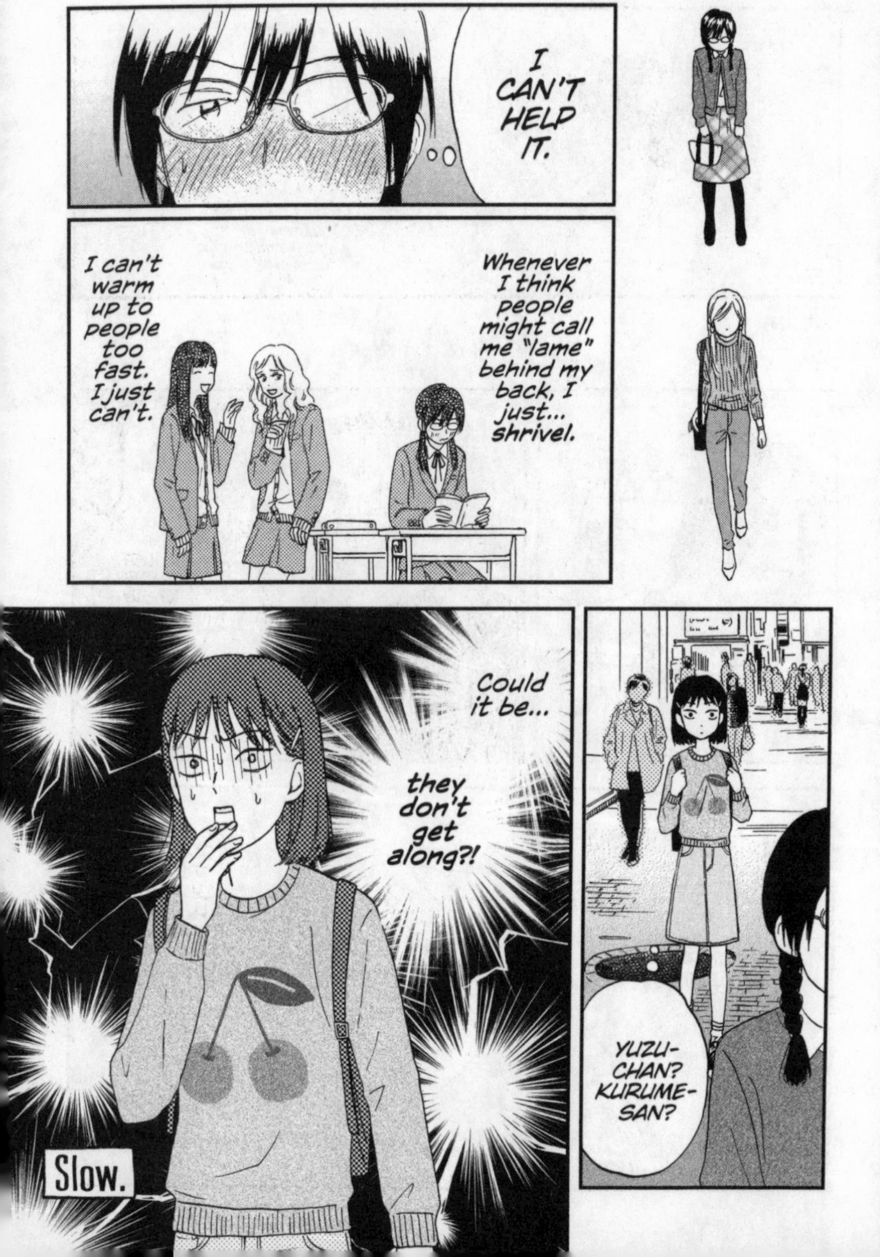
I CAN'T HELP IT.
Whenever I think people might call me "lame" behind my back, I just... shrivel.
I can't warm up to people too fast. I just can't.
YUZU-CHAN? KURUME-SAN?
Could it be...
they don't get along?!
Slow.

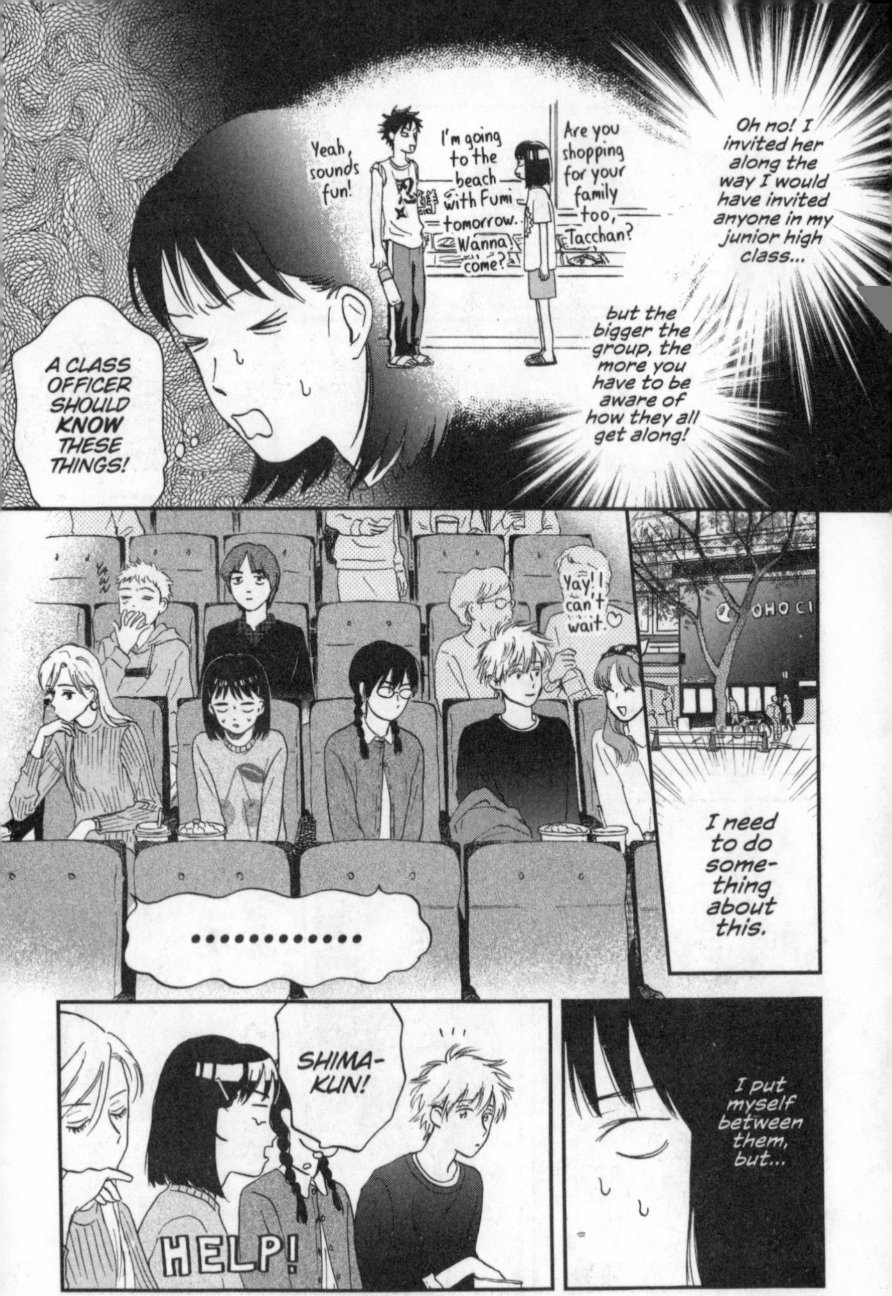
Oh no! I invited her along the way I would have invited anyone in my junior high class...
but the bigger the group, the more you have to be aware of how they all get along!
Are you shopping for your family too, Tacchan?
I'm going to the beach with Fumi tomorrow. Wanna come?
Yeah, sounds fun!
A CLASS OFFICER SHOULD KNOW THESE THINGS!
I need to do something about this.
Yay! I can't wait.
YAWN
....
I put myself between them, but...
SHIMA-KUN!
HELP!

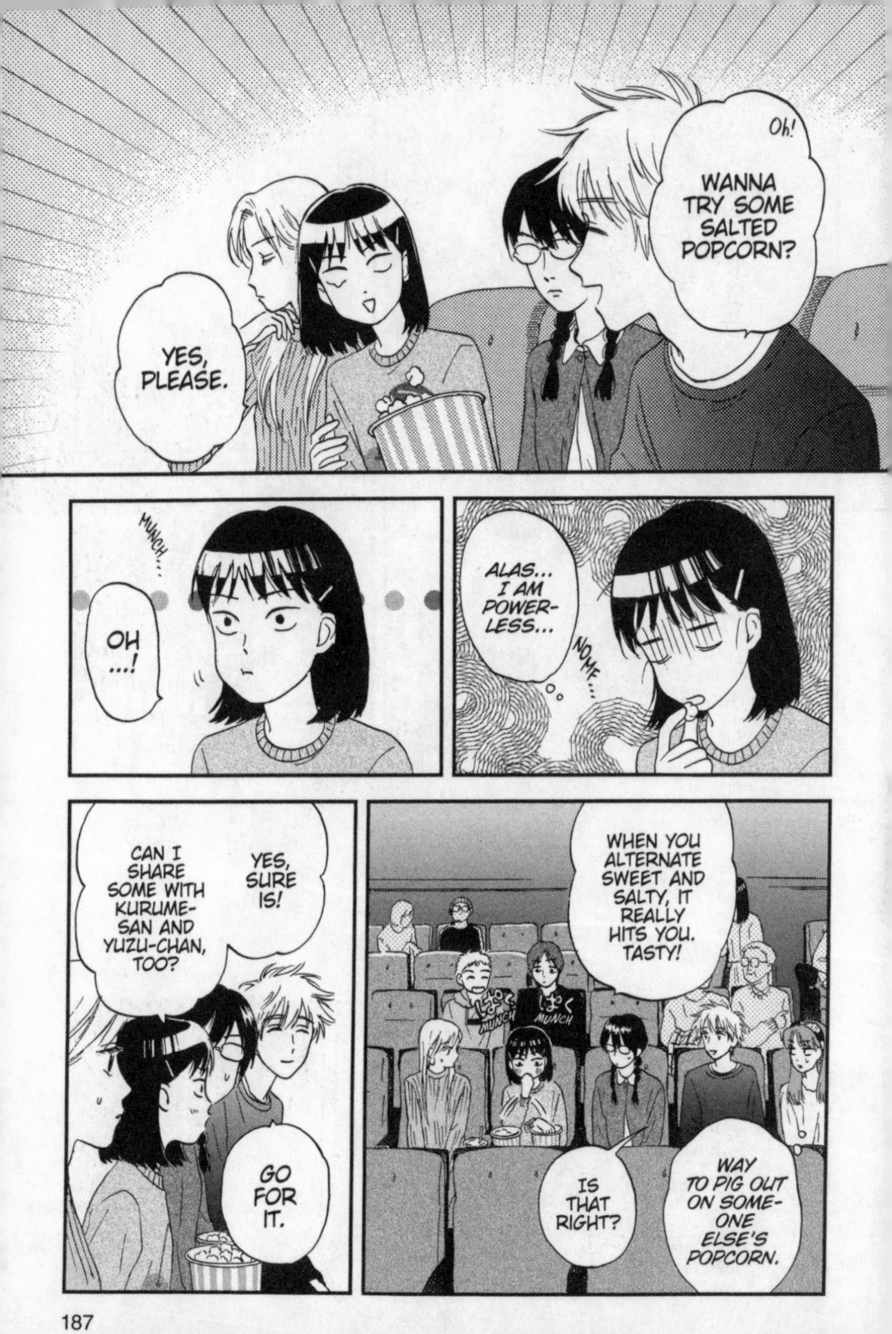
Oh!
WANNA TRY SOME SALTED POPCORN?
YES, PLEASE.
ALAS... I AM POWERLESS...
NOMF...
MUNCH...
OH ...!
WHEN YOU ALTERNATE SWEET AND SALTY, IT REALLY HITS YOU. TASTY!
ぱく MUNCH
ぱく MUNCH
WAY TO PIG OUT ON SOME-ONE ELSE'S POPCORN.
IS THAT RIGHT?
YES, SURE IS!
CAN I SHARE SOME WITH KURUME-SAN AND YUZU-CHAN, TOO?
GO FOR IT.

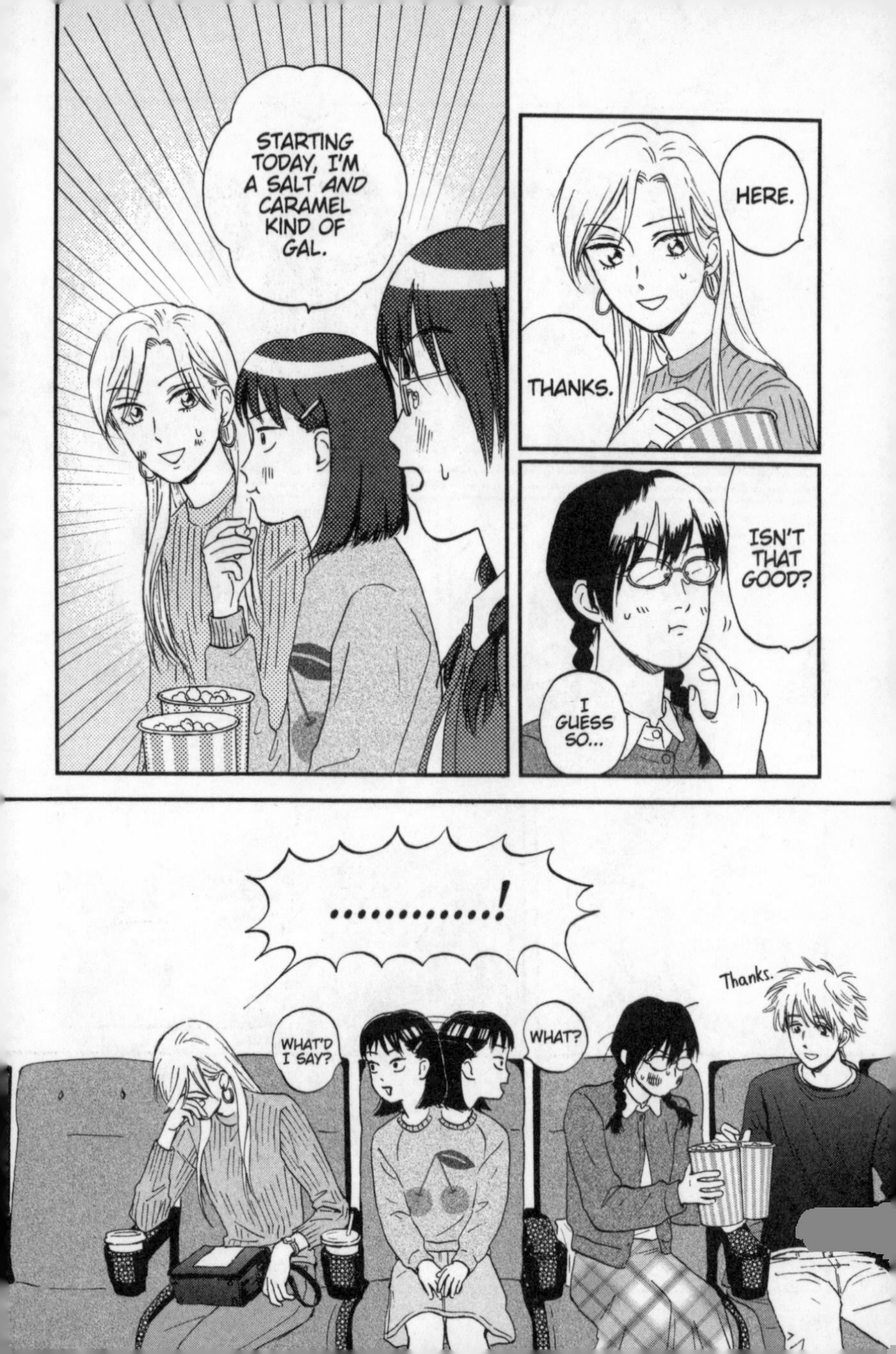
HERE.
THANKS.
ISN'T THAT GOOD?
I GUESS SO...
STARTING TODAY, I'M A SALT AND CARAMEL KIND OF GAL.
............!
Thanks.
WHAT?
WHAT'D I SAY?

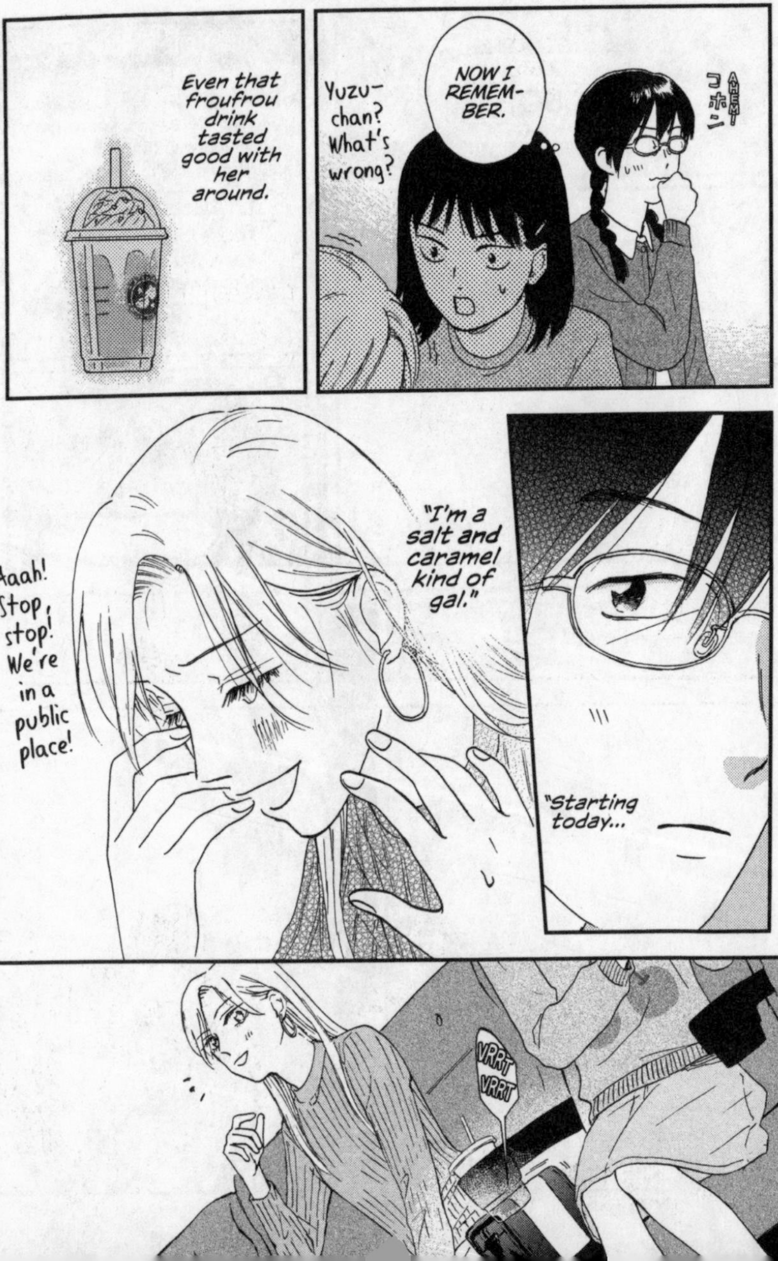
AHEM!
コホン
NOW I REMEMBER.
Yuzu-chan? What's wrong?
Even that froufrou drink tasted good with her around.
"Starting today...
"I'm a salt and caramel kind of gal."
Aaah! Stop, stop! We're in a public place!
VRRT VRRT

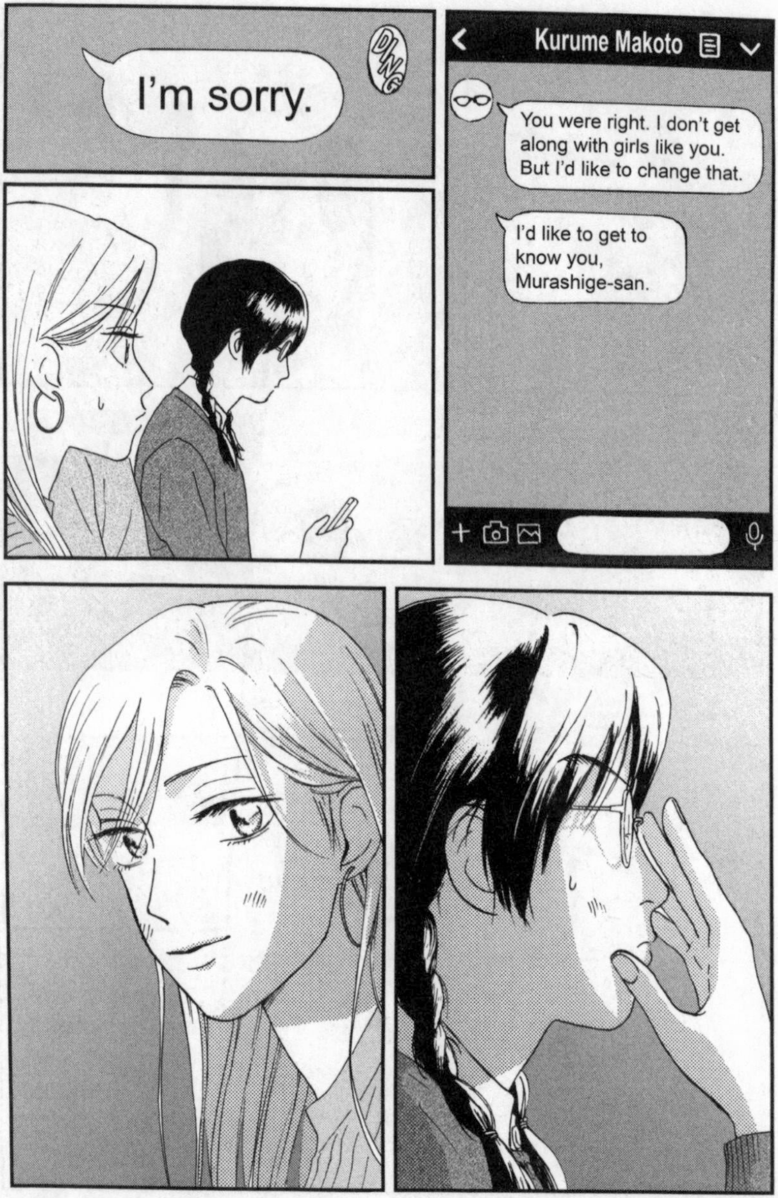
Kurume Makoto
You were right. I don't get along with girls like you. But I'd like to change that.
I'd like to get to know you, Murashige-san.
DING
I'm sorry.

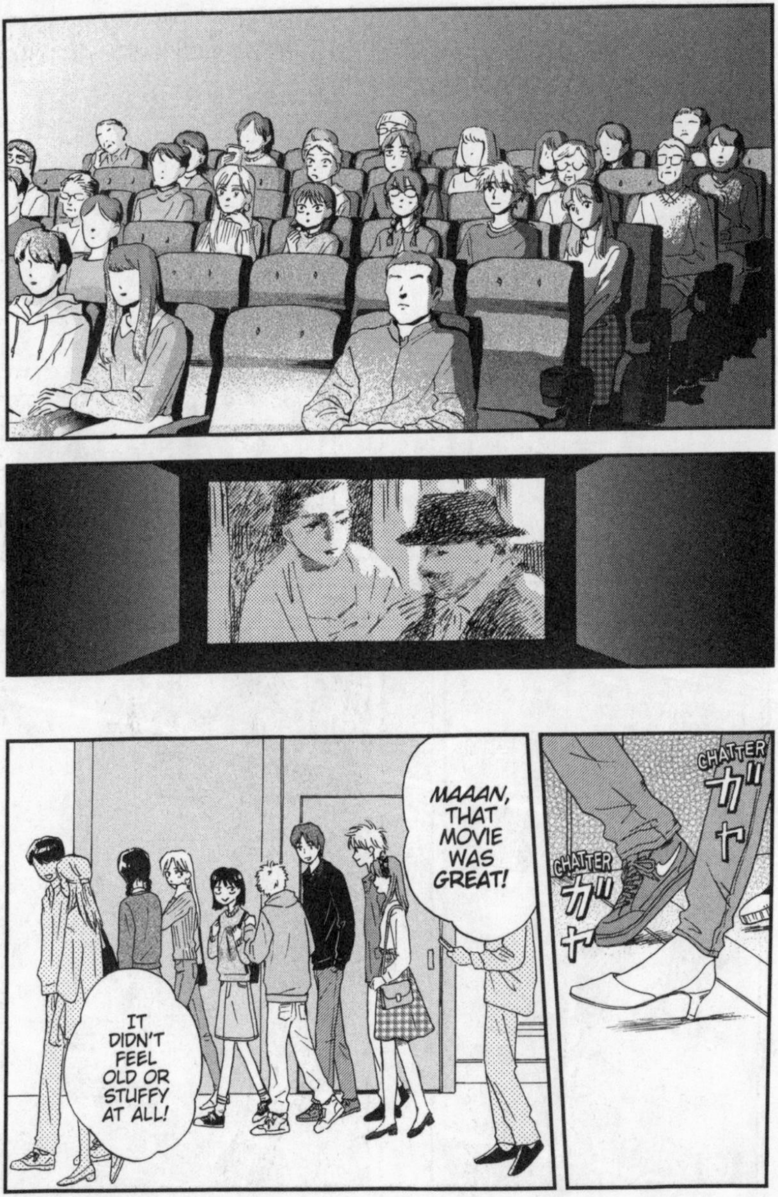
CHATTER ガヤ
CHATTER ガヤ
MAAAN, THAT MOVIE WAS GREAT!
IT DIDN'T FEEL OLD OR STUFFY AT ALL!

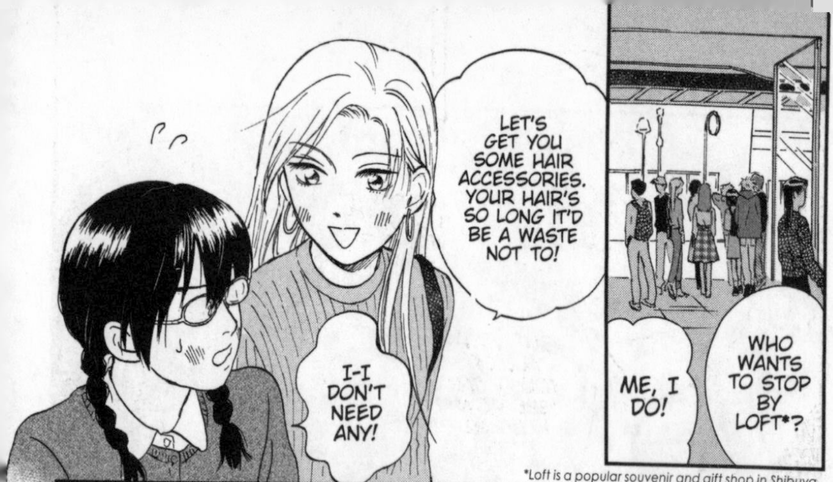
WHO WANTS TO STOP BY LOFT*?
ME, I DO!
LET'S GET YOU SOME HAIR ACCESSORIES. YOUR HAIR'S SO LONG IT'D BE A WASTE NOT TO!
I-I DON'T NEED ANY!

*Loft is a popular souvenir and gift shop in Shibuya.

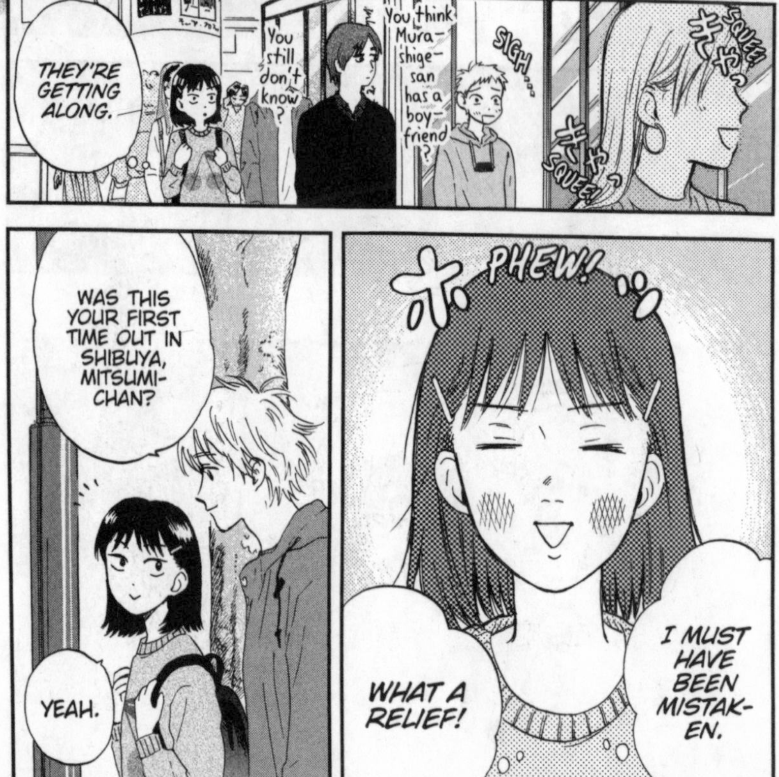
SQUEE!
SQUEE!
SIGH...
You think Mura-shige-san has a boy-friend?
You still don't know?
THEY'RE GETTING ALONG.
PHEW!
I MUST HAVE BEEN MISTAK-EN.
WHAT A RELIEF!
WAS THIS YOUR FIRST TIME OUT IN SHIBUYA, MITSUMI-CHAN?
YEAH.

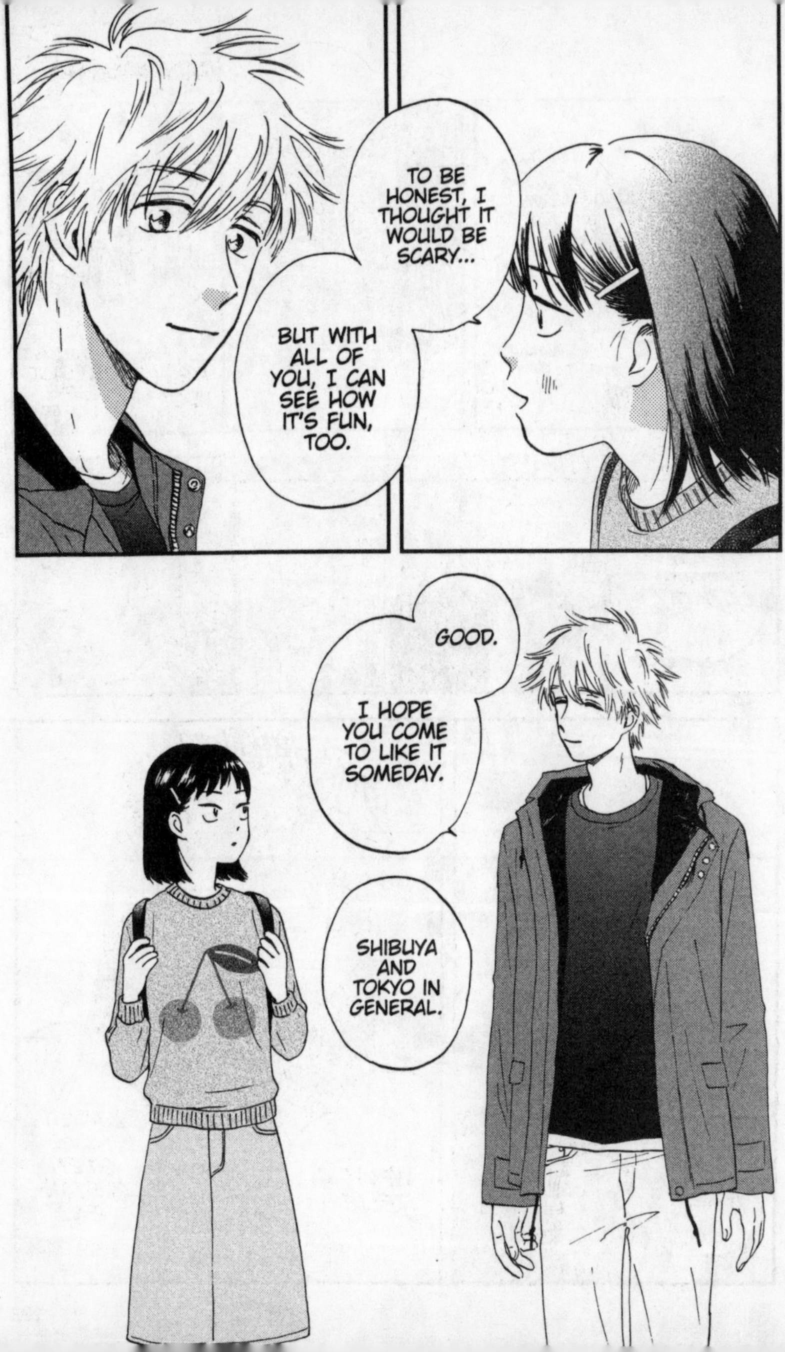
TO BE HONEST, I THOUGHT IT WOULD BE SCARY...
BUT WITH ALL OF YOU, I CAN SEE HOW IT'S FUN, TOO.
GOOD.
I HOPE YOU COME TO LIKE IT SOMEDAY.
SHIBUYA AND TOKYO IN GENERAL.

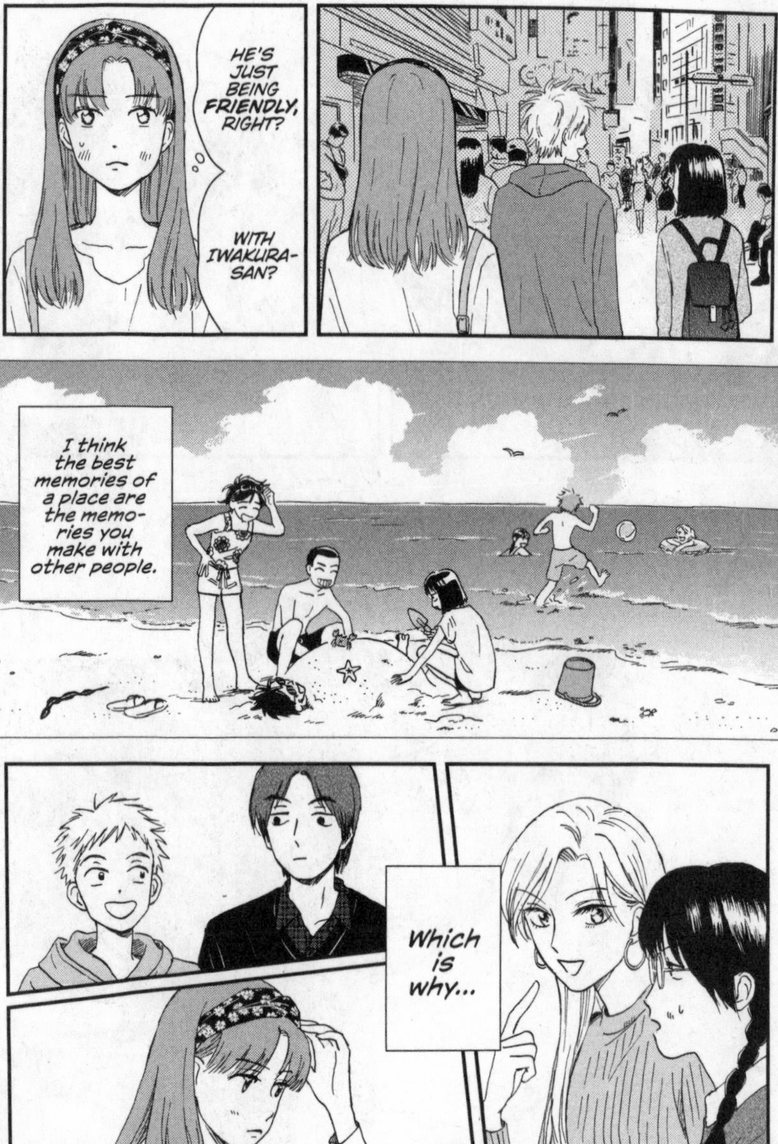
HE'S JUST BEING FRIENDLY, RIGHT?
WITH IWAKURA-SAN?
I think the best memories of a place are the memories you make with other people.
Which is why...

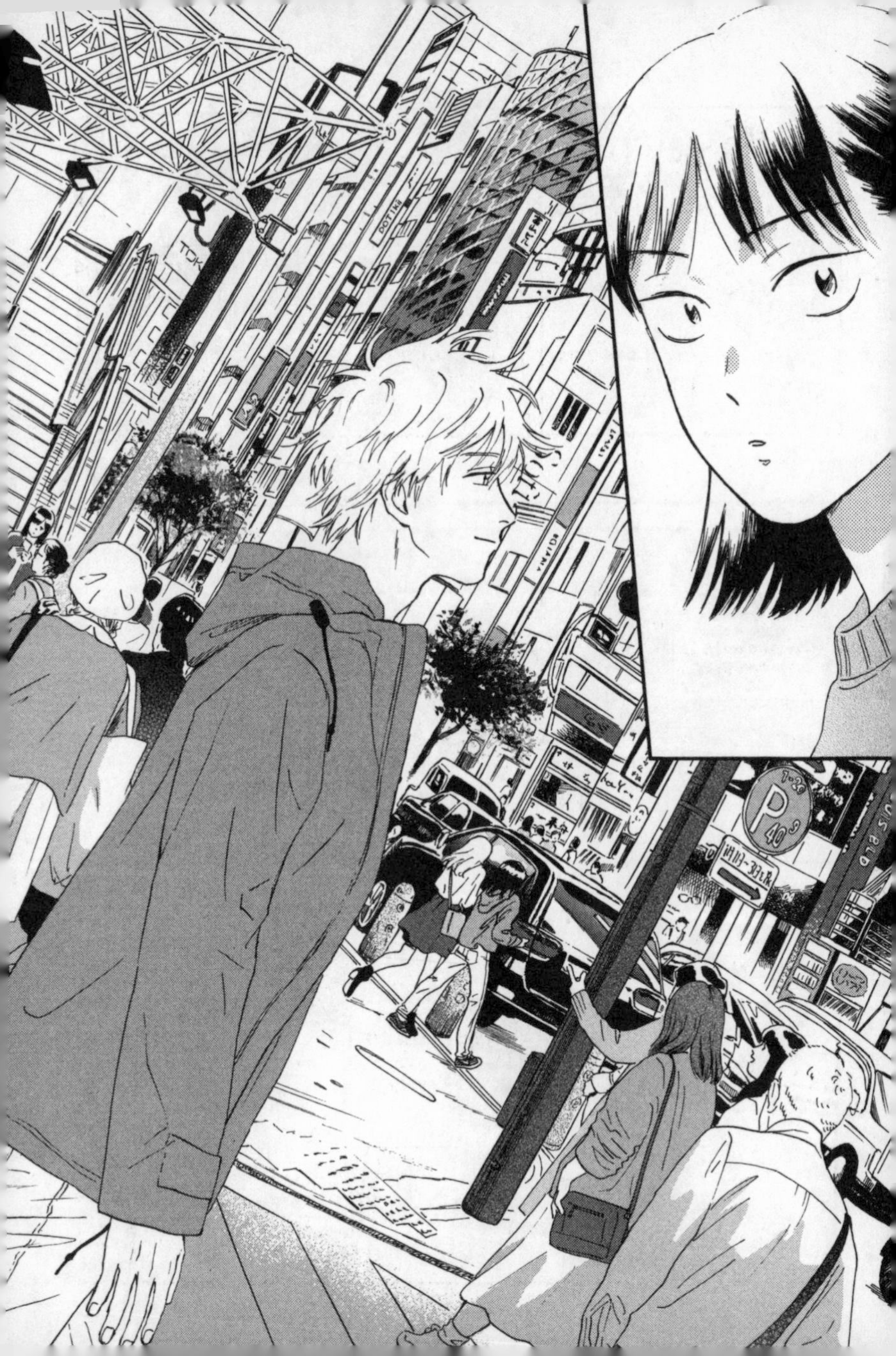

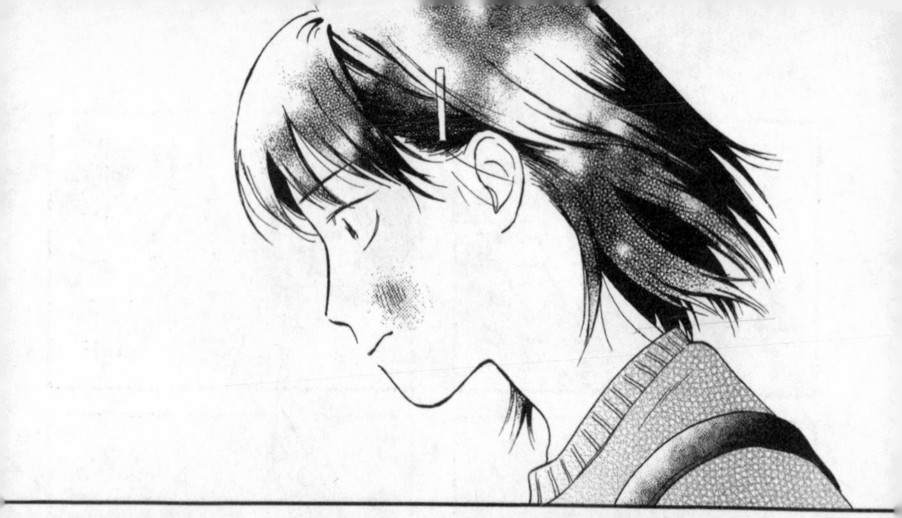

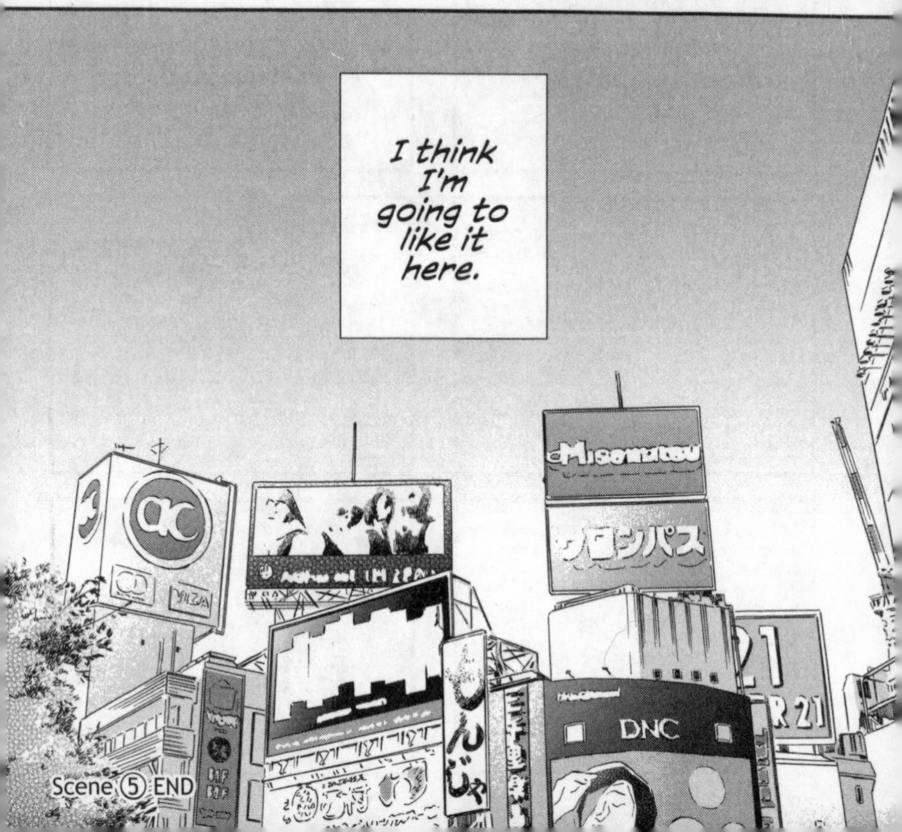
I think I'm going to like it here.
DNC
R 21
Scene 5 END

Twinsies

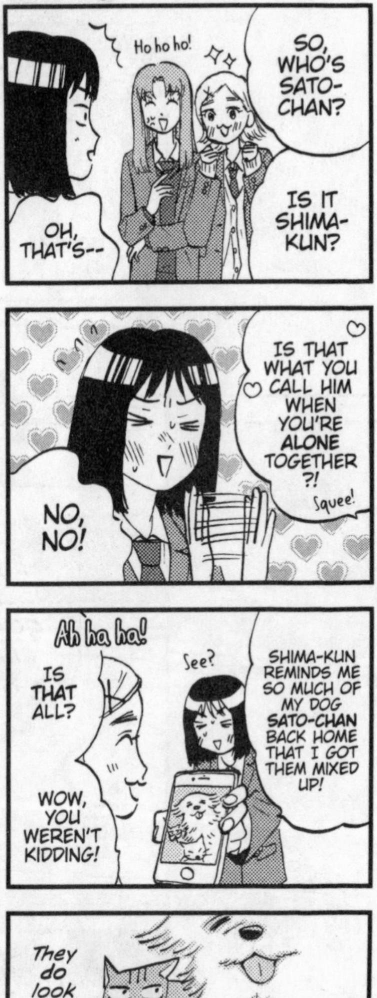
SO, WHO'S SATO-CHAN?
IS IT SHIMA-KUN?
Ho ho ho!
OH, THAT'S--
IS THAT WHAT YOU CALL HIM WHEN YOU'RE ALONE TOGETHER?!
Squee!
NO, NO!
SHIMA-KUN REMINDS ME SO MUCH OF MY DOG SATO-CHAN BACK HOME THAT I GOT THEM MIXED UP!
See?
Ah ha ha!
IS THAT ALL?
WOW, YOU WEREN'T KIDDING!
They do look alike.

The Taste of Home

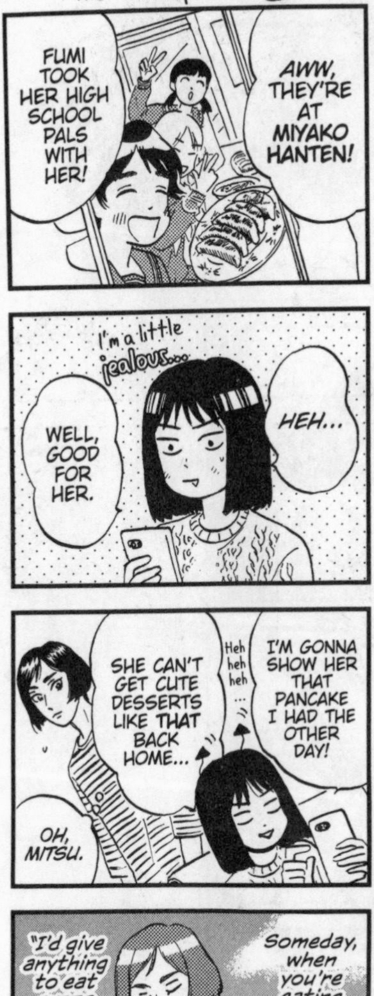
AWW, THEY'RE AT MIYAKO HANTEN!
FUMI TOOK HER HIGH SCHOOL PALS WITH HER!
HEH...
I'm a little jealous...
WELL, GOOD FOR HER.
I'M GONNA SHOW HER THAT PANCAKE I HAD THE OTHER DAY!
Heh heh heh...
SHE CAN'T GET CUTE DESSERTS LIKE THAT BACK HOME...
OH, MITSU.
Someday, when you're eating your fancy lunch, you'll think to yourself...
"I'd give anything to eat gyoza from Miyako Hanten again..."

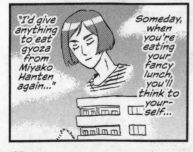

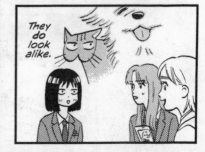

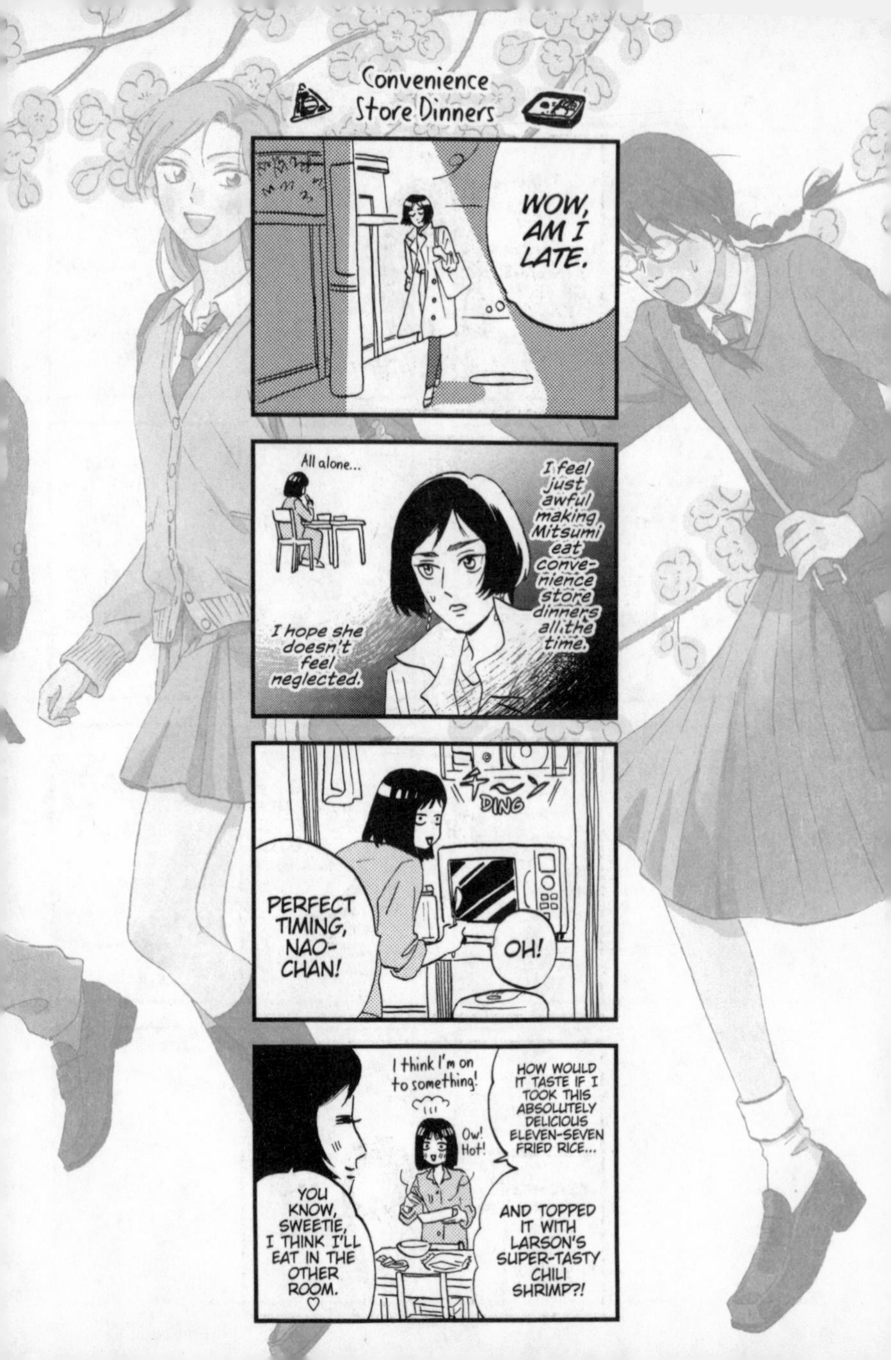
Convenience Store Dinners
WOW, AM I LATE.
I feel just awful making Mitsumi eat convenience store dinners all the time.
All alone...
I hope she doesn't feel neglected.
DING
OH!
PERFECT TIMING, NAO-CHAN!
HOW WOULD IT TASTE IF I TOOK THIS ABSOLUTELY DELICIOUS ELEVEN-SEVEN FRIED RICE...
AND TOPPED IT WITH LARSON'S SUPER-TASTY CHILI SHRIMP?!
I think I'm on to something!
Ow! Hot!
YOU KNOW, SWEETIE, I THINK I'LL EAT IN THE OTHER ROOM. ♡

The Digital World

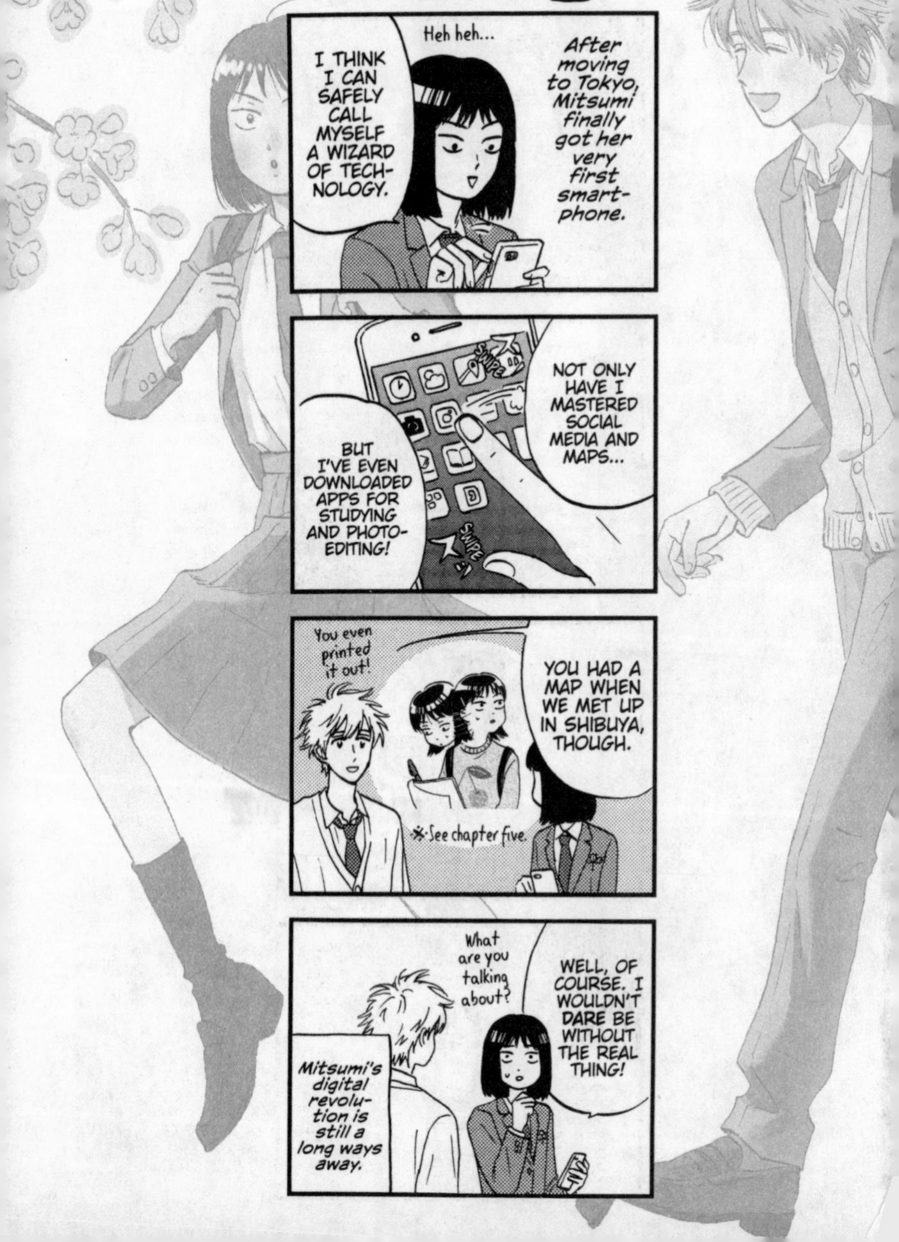
After moving to Tokyo, Mitsumi finally got her very first smartphone.
Heh heh...
I THINK I CAN SAFELY CALL MYSELF A WIZARD OF TECHNOLOGY.
SWIPE
NOT ONLY HAVE I MASTERED SOCIAL MEDIA AND MAPS...
BUT I'VE EVEN DOWNLOADED APPS FOR STUDYING AND PHOTO-EDITING!
SWIPE
YOU HAD A MAP WHEN WE MET UP IN SHIBUYA, THOUGH.
You even printed it out!
※See chapter five.
What are you talking about?
WELL, OF COURSE. I WOULDN'T DARE BE WITHOUT THE REAL THING!
Mitsumi's digital revolution is still a long ways away.

SEVEN SEAS ENTERTAINMENT PRESENTS

Skip and Loafer

Vol. 1

story and art by Misaki Takamatsu

TRANSLATION
Nicole Frasik

ADAPTATION
T. Campbell

LETTERING
Vanessa Satone

COVER & LOGO DESIGN
Hanase Qi

PROOFREADER
Kurestin Armada

EDITOR
Shanti Whitesides

PREPRESS TECHNICIAN
Rhiannon Rasmussen-Silverstein

PRODUCTION ASSOCIATE
Christa Miesner

PRODUCTION MANAGER
Lissa Pattillo

MANAGING EDITOR
Julie Davis

ASSOCIATE PUBLISHER
Adam Arnold

PUBLISHER
Jason DeAngelis

Skip To Loafers Vol. 1

First published in Japan in 2019 by Kodansha Ltd., Tokyo.
Publication rights for this English edition arranged through Kodansha Ltd., Tokyo.

Seven Seas press and purchase enquiries can be sent to Marketing Manager Lianne Sentar at press@gomanga.com. Information regarding the distribution and purchase of digital editions is available from Digital Manager CK Russell at digital@gomanga.com.

ISBN: 978-1-64827-588-3
Printed in Canada
First Printing: August 2021
10 9 8 7 6 5 4 3 2 1

READING DIRECTIONS

This book reads from ***right to left***, Japanese style. If this is your first time reading manga, you start reading from the top right panel on each page and take it from there. If you get lost, just follow the numbered diagram here. It may seem backwards at first, but you'll get the hang of it! Have fun!!

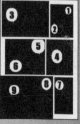

1
2
3
4
5
6
7
8
9